MEDIUM ÆVUM MONOGRAPHS
NEW SERIES

MEDIUM ÆVUM MONOGRAPHS
NEW SERIES XXI

THREE RECEPTARIA FROM MEDIEVAL ENGLAND

THE LANGUAGES OF MEDICINE IN THE FOURTEENTH CENTURY

Edited by
TONY HUNT
University of Oxford

with the collaboration of
MICHAEL BENSKIN
University of Oslo

The Society for the Study of
Medieval Languages and Literature
Oxford
2001

THE SOCIETY FOR THE STUDY OF
MEDIEVAL LANGUAGES AND LITERATURE

ISBN-13: 978-0-907570-14-1 (pb)

British Library Cataloguing in Publication Data

A catalogue record for this book
is available from the British Library

First published 2001
This reprint first issued 2015

Typeset by Oxbow Books

CONTENTS

ACKNOWLEDGEMENTS

This edition would need no preface were it not for the beneficence of Professor Michael Benskin. When I first showed him examples of the Middle English texts he at once volunteered to examine them and check my transcription. Further, he offered to write an account of the language at a level which I was quite incapable of achieving. The combination of his generosity and meticulousness deserves the gratitude of the reader as well as my own heartfelt thanks.

The present study represents an edition of just over 1500 medical receipts transmitted in three fourteenth-century compendia. I have included, as part of the fuller medical context, the introductory treatises in the First Corpus Compendium. The edition of the receipts marks the first stage of a project devoted to establishing a taxonomy of the receipt-collections (*receptaria*) of medieval England. The present compendia have been chosen for three reasons. First, they offer a wide variety of medical treatments topically arranged. Second, they reflect a period in the history of medical texts which has been inadequately studied, most published medical receipts in Middle English having been printed from fifteenth-century sources. Third, as a corollary of the previous point, the compendia chosen illustrate the linguistic phenomenon of code-switching and code-mixing.[1] In the Rawlinson compilation 34% of the receipts are in Latin, the rest in Anglo-Norman; in the First Corpus Compendium 36% are in Anglo-Norman and the rest evenly divided between English and Latin; the Second Compendium, offers 186 receipts, all in English save one in French. They thus offer a fascinating glimpse into the use of three languages in fourteenth-century England.

1 See T. Hunt, "Codeswitching in Medical Texts" in D. A. Trotter (ed.), *Multilingualism in Later Medieval Britain* (Cambridge, 1999), pp. 131–47.

Eventually a scientifically based taxonomy of receipt collections will confirm the status of the languages and shed more light on the formation of a vernacular medical terminology. Further work will also facilitate the identification of sources and patterns of transmission. A taxonomy will be based on a wide range of variables: arrangement of receipts (topical or not), length of receipts, provision and nature of rubrics, presence of multilingualism, existence of glosses or annotation, provision of an index, indication of dosages, inclusion of charms, prognostications and other pseudo-medical material, use of quotations and names of authorities (including use of the first person singular), admission of anecdotal material, familiarity with the more advanced pharmaceutical preparations of the *Antidotarium Nicolai* and more.

I am grateful to the staff of Duke Humfrey's Library, the Bodleian Library, for their unfailing helpfulness as also to Mrs Gill Cannell of the Parker Library, Corpus Christi College, Cambridge. I am further indebted to the Master and Fellows of Corpus for permission to publish.

ABBREVIATIONS USED IN THE NOTES

The notes to each of the three receipt-collections are designed to elucidate the textual transmission of the receipts by adducing parallels and drawing attention to variant readings. The following abbreviations are used:

D W.R. Dawson, *A Leechbook or Collection of Medical Receipts of the Fifteenth Century* (London, 1934) (ref. by receipt number)

H F. Heinrich, *Ein mittelenglisches Medizinbuch* (Halle a. S., 1896) (ref. by page number)

HE G. Henslow, *Medical Works of the Fourteenth Century* (London, 1899) (ref. by page and line number)

Hunt T. Hunt, *Popular Medicine in Thirteenth-Century England* (Cambridge, 1991) (ref. by page and receipt number)

Jör. J. Jörimann, *Frühmittelalterliche Rezeptarien*, Beiträge zur Geschichte der Medizin 1 (Zürich / Leipzig, 1925) (ref. by page and section number)

LH 'Lettre d'Hippocrate' in T. Hunt, *Popular Medicine* ... pp.100–41 (ref. by receipt number)

M G. Müller, *Aus mittelenglischen Medizintexten. Die Prosa-rezepte des Stockholmer*

Miszellankodex X.90, Kölner Anglistische Arbeiten 10 (Leipzig, 1929) (ref. by page and line number)

O M.S. Ogden (ed.), *The 'Liber de diversis medicinis' in the Thornton Manuscript (MS Lincoln Cathedral A.5.32)* EETS OS 207 (London, 1938) (ref. by page and line number)

R MS Oxford, Bodleian Library, Rawlinson C 814, present vol. pp. 7–78

Rel.ant. *Reliquae antiquae* ed. Th. Wright & J.O. Halliwell, vol.1 (1841), pp.51–55 (ref. by page number)

S H. Schöffler, *Beiträge zur mittelenglischen Medizin-literatur* II. *Practica phisicalia Magistri Johannis de Burgundia*, Sächs. Forschungsinstitute in Leipzig, Forschungsinstitut für neuere Philologie III Anglistische Abt. Heft 1 (Halle a.S., 1919), pp.145–260 (ref. by page and line number)

Sig. H.E. Sigerist, *Studien und Texte zur frühmittelalterlichen Rezeptliteratur*, Studien zur Geschichte der Medizin 13 (Leipzig, 1923), pp.160–67 [MS Cambr. U.L. Gg.v.35 (s.xi)] (ref. by page number)

T 'Trinity Practica' in T. Hunt, *Anglo-Norman Medicine* 2 (Cambridge, 1997), pp.190–275 (ref. by paragraph number)

Thes. Peter of Spain, *Thesaurus pauperum* in *Obras Médicas de Pedro Hispano* ed. M.H. da Rocha Pereira (Coimbra, 1973), pp.77–301 (ref. by page and receipt number)

CHAPTER ONE
THE RAWLINSON COMPENDIUM

MS Oxford, Bodleian Library, Rawlinson C 814 (S.C.12654), of the first half of the fourteenth century, is largely composed of an Anglo-Norman medical compendium which, though recorded by Macray's catalogue,[1] has never been described or edited. Exceptionally for this type of work[2] a serious attempt was made to provide a comprehensive index of its contents, which is reproduced below as part of the edition. The MS consists of 87 folios, written in a variety of hands of the first half of the fourteenth century. The folios measure approx. 207 × 144mm, the writing block for the medical compendium being 146 × 90mm. Folios 1–6 have sustained damage to the lower edge and the top corners of folios 53–55 have been badly gnawed, with a modest loss of text. The contents of the MS may be summarized as follows:

f.1v (first hand) A list in Anglo-Norman of nine Archangels and the advantages which thinking of them will bring:[3]

> Eyetz en memorie seint Michel quant matyn leveretz, et tout le jour joyus serrez.
> Seint Gabriel en toneyre, et saunz peril passerez.
> Seint Raphael quant tu mangeras ou beverez, et toutes choses toi abounderount.
> Seint Uriel com toun adversarie toi acountera, et tu le venqeras.
> Seint Barachiel quant tu vendras au jugement, et tous obeierount a ta volenté.
> Seint Raguel quant tu comenceras grant chemyn, et seynement le frez et ové joye revendrez.

[1] G.D. Macray, *Catalogi codicum manuscriptorum Bibliothecae Bodleianae, partis quintae, fasciculus secundus, viri munificentissimi Ricardi Rawlinson, J.C.D. codicem classem tertiam* (Oxonii, 1878), cols. 421–2.

[2] A comparable case is MS London B.L. Add.15236 in Hunt, *Popular Medicine*, pp.217ff.

[3] There is a similar text in MS London, British Library, Harley 1260 f.234ra–b and in Harley 2253 f.134r.

Seint Panthassaron quant tu vendras sur les mau janz, et toux s'enjoyerount. Seint Molencioun quant tu averas perdu amour de seignur, et a grant joye recoverez.
Seint Tobiel [sic], seint Barachiel et seint Molencioun quant vous vendrez ou irrez au prince ou a vostre seignurage, et bien te avendra. Seint Uriel et seint Thobies quant vous entrés en mier ou en nief ou en bat, et saunz peril serrez.

ff.1v–3r Miscellaneous receipts in French and Latin.

ff.3r–6r (a second hand in black ink) A charm and prayers against thieves:[4]

'Disparibus dampnis pendent tria corpora ramis (Walther, *Initia* 4582/8774)
Dismas et Gesmas medio divina potestas
Summa petit Dismas descendit ad infima Gesmas
Hos versus dicas ne furto tu tua perdas. Pater Noster et Ave Maria. Domine Deus virtutum converte nos et ostende faciem tuam et salvi erimus. Nichil proficiet inimicus in nobis. Et filius iniquitatis non apponet nocere nobis. Domine, exaudi orationem meam et clamor meus ad te veniat. *Oratio* ...'

followed (f.3r/v) by a list of perilous days: 'Ces soun les perilous jours de l'an ...';[5] (f.3v) 'Charme pur suryz et ratouns ...'(in Latin); (f.3v) 'Qui porte verveyne et arthemesie chien ne serpent [ne] luy mordera ne ne serra les [for *las*] en voie'; (f.3v) 'Anasateon est un herbe q'est appellé solmaria e les uns l'apellent solsecle' (incl. magical properties and use as a charm); (f.4r/v) Elitropia (properties and use as a charm); (f.4v) 'Pernez petroile e moilliez de ce un lumynoun devant que le cire ou seu soit mys et celle chandoille veet ardoir desouth eawe'; (f.4v) the badger ('bauseyn'; its magical properties); (f.4v) Mortagon ('portulaca agrestis' and its properties). There then follows a sequence of 'experimenta', namely, (f.5r) treatment for deterring rats and mice, receipt for invisible writing, treatment for putrid teeth, (f.5v) experiment for rendering someone near-naked, receipts for preventing whitening of the hair and for making hair grow. Next come miscellaneous medical receipts: for bloodshot eyes, (f.6r) treatment of haemorrhoids, treatment for 'amor hereos', mostly in Anglo-Norman, but a few in Latin.

f.6v [change of ink] 'Virtutes speciales aque vite et qualiter conjunguntur cum medicinibus. Valet contra infirmitates et passiones et langores et dolores que perveniunt ex causa frigida ...', all in Latin.

[4] See T. Hunt, *Popular Medicine*, pp.82 & 94.

[5] Such lists are frequent in medical and scientific MSS, see T.Hunt, *Anglo-Norman Medicine* 2, pp.236–7, 258 and *id.*, *A History of the Future: Popular Prognostication in Medieval England*, forthcoming.

f.7r [a third hand] Charm inc.'Seynt Lyoun þe pope wrot this letter to kyng Charles and seide ...', ending 'Thes beth þe names of oure lord Jesu Crist ...', to which is added a list in Latin of the names of the Apostles.

ff.7v–8r [a fourth hand] Once more a charm against theft inc. 'Disperibus membris pendent tria corpora ramis' plus various prayers, ending (in red) 'Hoc breve invenit Joseph ab Aramathia super plagam lateris Domini dum tolleret corpus eius de cruce litteris aureis scriptis et nomina filii Dei assignavit, et quicumque christianus illud portaverit, in igne non comburetur nec in aqua peribit nec iudicio nec peste nec passione nec malicia alicuius nec febre nec fulgura nec victus permanebit, et in iudicio non male iudicabitur nec de iure suo aliquid amittet, et omnes inimicos superabit, et eorum insidias non timebit, set si mulier pregnans super se habuerit, non peribit mater neque infans'.

f.8v blank

ff.9ra–11rb [a fifth hand] An index ('Incipiunt capitula') to the compendium on ff.28 *et seq.*, written in double columns, and comprising three series: A–Z; 1–100; i–xlix. Twenty-nine chapter headings are provided for the *Flores thesauri pauperum*, which follows the compendium, and one for the *Practica puerorum*. At the end of the index two plant names are written on f.11ra: 'Fimus terre anglice scabwort', 'Rosa passa anglice harewort'. A list of weights follows (f.11ra/b).

f.11v [a sixth hand] Medical properties of the juniper '*Nota* grana juniperi mane sumpta confortant cerebrum ...'

ff.12r–16v [a seventh hand] A Latin medical treatise inc. 'Morbus est res inferens sensibile nocumentum cum naturali actione membrorum nullo medio ...' (ThK 881),[6] beginning with fevers, leprosy, tetanus etc. 'Explicit iste tractatus'.

ff.16va–24rb [an eighth hand] red rubr. *Incipit liber de conferentibus et nocentibus et primo de cerebro* ... (ThK 246), incomplete.[7]

f.24v [a ninth hand] A charm 'Pur clowere dé chivaux' as follows:

> 'Ditez cestes paroles .iii. foitz quant vous averetz tret hors la clowe ovesque in nomine Patris, e estopez ben le pertuz e alez de par Dieux. Noste Sire fu

[6] L. Thorndike and P. Kibre, *A Catalogue of Incipits of Mediaeval Scientific Writings in Latin*, rev. & augm. ed. (London, 1963), refs. by cols.

[7] See also MSS Oxford, Bodl. Libr. Rawlinson D 251 (s.xiii) ff.43v–45v; London, BL Sloane 3550 (s.xiii) ff.225v–229v.

pris e lyé e clowé e poynte e oynte. Auxi veraiment garrie ceste chival de ceste poynture, in nomine Patris et Filii et Spiritus Sancti. Amen'. This is followed by a Latin receipt for 'Collirium magistri Mauricii ad omnia vicia oculorum' containing many vernacular plant names and concluding 'Et sic predictus M. in Cisilia omnes passiones oculorum curavit'.

ff.25r–27r [a tenth hand] Excerpts from Ps-Arist. *Secreta secretorum*, *De quatuor temporibus anni*[8] ..., (f.27r) *De cura medicorum* ...

f.27v blank

ff.28r–33v [first hand] 'Incipit epistula Aristotilis ad magnum regem Alexandrum Macedonium de sanitate corporis conservanda'.[9] An excerpt from the medical section of the *Secreta secretorum*, without John of Seville's introductory letter to the Queen of Spain. On ff.29r–30r there is much material not found in Suchier's edition (p.478 l.195) and some of the material is rearranged. The first part of the excerpt ends on f.32r with Suchier p.479 l.144, to which is added 'valete'. The second section begins on f.32r 'Oportet quod conservator sanitatis studeat ne substancia cibi ipsius sit aliquid nutrientium medicinali ut cuiusmodi sunt olera et fructus ...' The section ends with definitions from Hippocrates, Aristotle and Galen and contains the gloss 'spasmus ... .s. crampe' (f.33r), concluding (f.33v) 'Explicit epistola Aristotilis de regimine corporis'. This treatise is included as *.a.* in the Index on ff.9ra–11ra.

ff.33v–75r [first hand] The medical compendium beginning *Pur le vertun de chef* printed below. From f.55r the receipts seem essentially miscellaneous and are numbered individually (as opposed to in unified groups) at the top of the page. These numbers correspond to the index on ff.9r *et seq.* The numbers go up to 100 (f.62v) and the numbering then recommences with roman numerals i–xlix (f.75r) which include two prognostic texts which are apparently intended to be part of the compendium. At the beginning of the third series of numbering on ff.62v–63v the receipts have received additional individual numbers in the margin, from .x. to .xvii. Towards the end the compendium exhibits increasing heterogeneity of content, including the Hippocratic facies in severe illness

[8] See T.Hunt, "Old French Translations of Medical Texts", *Forum for Modern Language Studies* 35 (1999), 351–52.

[9] See H. Suchier, *Denkmäler provenzalischer Literatur und Sprache* 1 (Halle, 1883), pp.473–80, 530–31 and P. Möller, *Hiltgart von Hürnheim. Mittelhochdeutsche Prosaübersetzung des 'Secretum Secretorum'* (Berlin, 1963); L. Thorndike, "John of Seville", *Speculum* 34 (1959), [20–38] 24–27; M.A. Mazalaoui, *Secretum Secretorum: Nine English Versions* 1, EETS 276 (1977), pp.xix–xv.

(f.65r), 'signa mortalia'[10] in Latin and French, and a range of preparations involving individual plants, waters, ointments, in a somewhat muddled order, with an increase in the amount of Latin material. The final elements (ff.73v–74v) are three prognosticatory texts in Latin: a brontology, instructions based on the wind daily from Christmas Day to Epiphany, and observations drawn from the day in the week on which Christmas Day falls: *Incipiunt significaciones tonitruorum et conjectura eorum que evenire solent in singulis mensibus anni*; *Significaciones ventorum in nocte natalis Domini et in ceteris .xii. noctibus usque ad Epiphaniam*; *Hec quoque sunt annotationes et opiniones diversorum atheniensium super diversis diebus natalis Domini in ebdomada contingentibus*. To these are added (ff.74v–75r) two charms: *Ut quicquid volueris accipias et quicquid petieris gratum fiat*; *Ut non timeas aliquem inimicum ...*

ff.75r–82r [first hand] Peter of Spain's 'Thesaurus pauperum', *Incipiunt flores thesauri pauperum, et primo contra casum capillorum* (ThK 1443)[11] with sections numbered at the top of the page from i–xxix.

ff.82r–84v [first hand] *Incipit practica puerorum* (ThK 1028), numbered .xxx. at the top of the page, as in the index, concluding 'Explicit practica puerorum'.

ff.84v–866 Miscellaneous receipts, charms, instructions on bleeding still numbered .xxx. as if forming part of the previous treatise, no doubt as the result of the rubricator's error.

ff.86v–87v A treatise on phlebotomy inc. 'Minucio alia fit per metatesim alia per antipasim ...' (ThK 875), ending 'Amen, explicit'.

f.87v 'A man is mad of .vii. thingis: erthe and water, sonne and wynde, cloudes and ston and of the holi gost'.

Erthe blod sonne breth cloudes bon
Water flessh wynd bowel ston wit
Of the holy gost the soule etc.

Ossa hominis sunt numero .ccxvii. Vene autem sunt .ccc. et .lxv. Dentes vero in perfecta etate .xxxii. Memoria eius est in cerebro, intellectus in fronte, ira in felle, avaricia in jecore, amor in corde, anelitus in pulmone, leticia in splene, cogitatio in corde, sanguis in corpore, spes in anima, mens in spiritu, cor in mente, fides in corde, Christus in fide.

10 See Hunt, *Popular Medicine*, p.102 and n.17, and *Anglo-Norman Medicine* 2, p.250.

11 See M.H. da Rocha Pereira, *Obras medicas de Pedro Hispano* (Coimbra, 1973), pp.77–301.

In the MS certain headings are underlined in red and these are italicized in the edition which follows, since they largely coincide with the titles in the indexes. Under these headings are grouped receipts which are preceded by red paragraph marks. The scribe seems to have been systematic in executing such divisions.

For ease of reference I have numbered the receipts and identified them by number (in square brackets) in the opening list of headings. Receipts in Latin are marked by an asterisk.

Incipiunt capitula[12]

[f.9ra]
Primo de regimine corporis .*a*. [–]
De capite .*b*. [1–31]
De infirmitatibus oculorum .*c*. [32–50]
De auribus .*d*. [51–63]
De dentibus .*e*. [64–77]
De naribus .*f*. [78–95]
De fetore oris .*g*. 96–107]
De infirmitate jecoris [corr. gutturis] .*h*. [108–10]
De umeris .*i*. [111–2]
De brachiis .*k*. [113–20]
De mamillis .*l*. [121–32]
De dolore pectoris .*m*. [133–70]
De ventre et intestinis .*n*. [171–93]
De infirmitatibus ani .*o*. [194–203]
De genitalibus et cura .*p*. [204–16]
De infirmitatibus natum .*q*. [217–9]
De pedibus .*r*. [220–6]
Nota quod corpus hominis .*s*. [f.44r]
De antrace qui dicitur felon .*t*. [227–59]
De rancle .*v*. [260–82]
De festre .*x*. [283–6]
De cancre .*y*. [287–304]
De malo mortuo .*z*. [305–15]
De morphea ⁊ [316–9]

[12] The section letters are in red. Roman numbers relating to another reference system which is no longer visible have been entered in a small hand beside most of the items.

[13] Above has been written 'quartana' in a small hand.

Pur oster dens de la bouche *.71.* [490]
Si quis secum habuerit *.72.* [491]
A saver si femme port mal ou noun *.73.* [492–3]
[f.10ra]
Pur conustre quant homme doit seygner *.74.* [494–5]
Medicine au goute enussé *.75.* [496]
Encontre canker *.76.* [497]
Pur estancher vomys *.77.* [498]
Pur menisoun *.78.* [499]
Pur dolour des espaules *.79.* [500–1]
A freide goute *.80.* [502]
A goute enfestré *.81.* [503]
Medicine que vous ne sentez froid *.82.* [504]
Medicine a face leprouse *.83.* [505]
Pur roses que cressount en face *.84.* [506]
Pur celi que est semblable mesel *.85.* [507]
Medicine encountre toutz manere de rune *.86.* [508]
Medicine a celi que ne ad point de barbe *.87.* [509–10]
Medicine pur enfaunt letant costyf *.88.* [511]
Medicine pur festre [corr. fevre] *.89.* [512]
Item pur festre [corr. fevre] tercein *.90.* [513]
Encountre jaunis *.91.* [514–5]
Pur oster a femme maladie pryvé *.92.* [516]
Ut mulier cito pareat *.93.* [517–8]
Ad guttam caducam *.94.* [519]
[f.10rb]
Qui non potest dormire *.95.* [520–1]
Ad eos qui sensum amittunt *.96.* [522]
A fer chival neir blanche *.97.* [523]
Pur ventosité *.98.* [524]
Pur beauz colour aver *.99.* [525–32]
A homme que ad chaudepisse *.100.* [533]
Medicine que chevus devenent noir *.i.* [534]
[two receipts 535–6]
De playe *.ii.* [557–65]
Pur estauncher sanc de playe *.iii.*[14] [566–73]
Signa mortalia *.iiii.* [574–7]

[14] Nos..iii.–.ix. occur in the text after .xvii.

Pelotes a boir pur playe *.v.* [578]
Autre boir pur playe *.vi.* [579–80]
A nerves tranchez *.vii.* [581]
Comune bature a playes *.viii.* [582–3]
Autre entret bone *.ix.*[15] *[584]*
Unguentum pro salso fleumate *.x.* [537]
Oignement pur arsure *.xi.* [538–9]
Uncore pur enflure de gorge *.xii.* [540]
Uncore pur rune *.xiii.* [541]
Pur teter tuer *.xiiii.* [542]
Pur morsure de irayne *.xv.* [543–4]
Uncore pur brisure ou que il soit *.xvi.* [545–6]
Pur morsure de serpent e de chen *.xvii.* [547–56]
A dures overtures *.xviii.* [585]
Emplastre pur saker e entrere espine *.xix.* [586]
[f.10va]
Autre coloine [corr. ceroyne] pur playe *.xx.* [587]
Une autre ceroyne *.xxi.* [588–9]
Oignement pur garer checun playe *.xxii.* [590]
Oignement a playe *.xxiii.* [591]
Autre oignement pur plaiez *.xxiv.* [592]
Uncore autre [593]
Pur fere boire a playé *.xxv.* [594–5]
Item autre [596]
[Item pur fere oignement 597]
Entractum Gracia Dei *.xxvi.* [598]
Oignement Nerval *.xxvii.* [599]
Pur fere populeon *.xxviii.* [600]
Emplastre pur enpostume *.29.* [601–4]
[oils and ointments f.68va et seq.]
Bone emplastre pur playe *.30.* [605]
Pur fere sauve *.xxxi.* [606]
Item auter sauve [607–8]
Potus Antiochie *.xxxii.* [609]
Aqua vite *.xxxiii.* [610]
Aqua ardens *.xxxiiii.* [611]
Aqua tartari *.xxxv.* [612]

[15] This is separated from the next by a wavy red line.

Aqua mellis *.xxxvi.* [613]
Ad faciendum claretum *.xxxvii.* [614]
Aqua lac virginis *.xxxviii.* [615]
De signis lupi *.xxxix.* [616]
De signis noli me tangere *.xl.* [617]
Ignis infernalis *.xli.* [618]
Diversitas operandi in vulnere *.xlii.* [619]
[f.10vb]
De impedimentis sanacionis vulneris *.xliii.* [620]
[canones]
De unguento albo *.xliiii.* [621]
[Unguentum frigidum 622]
Unguentum ad vulnus *.xlv.* [623]
[swellings in wounds 624–7]
Nota quod emplastrum *.xlvi.* [628]
De nuce muscata *.xlvii.* [629–32]
Significaciones tonitruum *.xlviii.*
Significaciones ventorum *.xlix.*

There follows a list of chapters I–XXIX of the *Flores thesauri pauperum* (text on ff.75r–82r).

.b.

[f.33v] (1) *Pur le vertun de chef*: Pernés averoine od mel e od eisel, triblez sovent e li donez a boire.

(2) Item triblez rue od olie e si oignez les tenples.

(3) Item fel de levere triblez od mel si que mout seit triblé e que il resemble rouge[16] colour e tant en eit de l'un cum de l'autre. De ce oignez le frount e les tenples. E tut la dolour vous en osterat, qar mout est precious oignement.

(4) Item le puliol od sa flour triblez e si li donez a boire jun od ew chaude, si sei tigne de manger dekes a noune. Ce est pur le vertun.

(5) Item averoine, sauge, cerfoile, ere terestre od ewe temprez, si li donez a boire.

(6) Item rue triblez od sel e od mel, e mis cum emplastre al chef mout profite.

(7) Si vous est avis que le chef lasus seit afoundré eins cum une fosse,

[16] MS *argue*.

pernez lé foiles de egrimoyne e lé quisez od mel e metez l'emplastre desus, si garra.

(8) Item celidoine quisez ben en bure e pus le colez parmi un drap, si le gar[f.34r]dez en une boiste. E de ce oignez le chef e pus le lavez od ewe ou celidoine seit quit.

(9) *A felun de chef que fet enflure*: Pernez le gresce de cerf e novele ferine de orge e ere e morele, triblez tous ensemble, pus si oignez le chef al malade. Si metez ceste emplastre en une almuce, si eschaufez ben le almuce od l'emplastre e le metez ausi chaud desus le chef cum vous porrez suffrer e seit ileques dekes il seit garri.

(10) *Pur tous maus de chef*: Pernez rue e fenoil e les quisés bien en ewe, si en lavez le chef.

(11) Item triblez bien rue e metez le en fort eisel e de ce oignez ben le chef desus.

(12) Item pernez la neire bete e la triblez ben, si pernez le jus e en oignez ben la frunt e les tenples.

(13) Item betoine e verveine, aloine, celidoine, plauntaine, rue, eble, sauge e de l'escorce de seu e mel e vin e greins de peivere, triblez les tous ensemble e le quisez ben en vin, si en bevez checun jour au matin e al cocher deqes vous soiés garri.

(14) *Pur dolour de chef que longement ad duré*: Pernez un poigné de rue e un autre de ere terestre e la verte foile de lorer ov nef bayes e quisez tut ensemble en ewe ou en vin e de ce oignez le chef, si garra.

(15) *Item autre pur dolour de chef*: Pernez gyngivere, si le triblez. E pus pernez vin egre e quisez les ensemble e bevez le chaud cum vous porrez suffrer, e ben garrez. Ceste medicine est prové.

(16) *Pur le malade que pert sun sen e reve*: Donez li a beivere la semence de rue destempré od eisel e versez le jus en ses narils.

(17) Ou destemprez celidoine e semence de rue od eisel, si li donez a beivere.

(18) *Pur homme que pert sa* [f.34v] *memorie*: Pernez solsequie e averoine e sauge e triblez ensemble e lui donez a beivere cink jours, ou plus si mester est.

(19) *Pur homme que pert la parole en enfermité*: Distemprez aloine od ewe, si li versez en la bouche, si parlera. [Destemprez savine] e les foilles de pin e si metez piaine e peivere, medlez ensemble, si lui donez a beivere, si garra.

(20) *Pur homme que reve e parle en dormant*: Destemprez averoine od vin, si li donez a beivere.

(21) *Item lilium in vino vel servisia bibat.

(22) *Pur teine de chef*: Pernez fel de tor e eisel e triblez ensemble e oignez

la teste. Pus pernez su de tor e ail e sel ars en pudre e oille de olive e fetez oignement e oignez la teste.

(23) Item pernez pis e cere e fetez boilir ensemble. Pus raez le chef e metez l'emplastre sur un drapel tenve e pus le metez sur le chef .ix. jours sauns oster, si garra.

(24) *A ceus que les chevus cheunt*: Ardez la semence de lin medlé od oile, si oignez le chef.

(25) Ou pernez verveine e aloine e les essuez ben e les quisez e sovent lavez le chef.

(26) *Item pur fere les chevus crestre*: Quisez malwe od tote la racine en ewe, si lavez le chef.

(27) *Ke les chevus ne seient chanus*: Quisez racines de cholet en ewe deke a la moité, si en lavez le chef sovent en bain, e jamés ne serrunt chanus.

(28) *A ceus que sunt chanus, pur fere muer lur barbes ou lur chevelure e les fere bruns*: Pernez en esté les nugaces tutz vertz, sicum il sunt el noer, od tutes les escorches, pus si pressez entre deus peres, si emplez un pocenet auque grant, e si metez plein poin de sel e pus de ewe, que le pot seit tut plein. E pus le fetez quire au fu deke a la terce partie de ceste ewe. [f.35r] Mettrez sur tous les chevus. Mes vous le mettrez en ceste manere: Primerement vous moilerez des estupes delyés en cele ewe e de les estupes moilez ben les chevus taunt que homme veie que il seyent mués. E ce checun jour deus foitz ou treis e jamés ne plus ne devendrunt chanus.

(29) En yver fetez autretele medicine. Pernez l'escorche de noer aprés, trestut sicum est devisé – en esté de nois fetez, en yver de l'escorche – mes ewe ne metra homme. Iceste medicine est verraie e provó.

(30) * *Ad faciendam barbam crescere vel pilos ubi non sunt*: Accipe mel cum pulvere olearum, misce simul et talpam combustam redige in pulverem et super id sparge et inde unge capud calvatum et maxillas. Mirabiliter crescent.

(31) Item les foiles [de saus] quisez od oile e metez la ou les chevus failunt.

.c.

De infirmitatibus oculorum

(32) *Si sanguis in oculo fuerit ex percussione: Cuminum pistatum cum cera sepius calefac ad ignem et multociens pone super oculos. Hoc fac donec sanguis fugiat.

(33) *Ad oculos lacrimantes*: Pernez un foile de cholet, si le oignez de gleire e metez sur les oils la nut quant vous irrez dormer.

(34) *Item pur la teye des oils veez medicine esprové*: Pernez la fel de levere e mel owele mesure, si destemprez ensemble e oignez les oils.

(35) Item la grece de tous pessons de flum eschaufez al solail deques il eit seim, e pus metez de mel e oignez les oils.

(36) *Item as oils que a la fetz dolent e a la fetz nent*: Medlez ensemble mel e jus de centorie e oignez les oils.

(37) Item mangez betoigne jun, si amendera mout la vewe.

(38) Item pur la maele des oils ne dei pas celer: cele maladie vient de divers humours. [f.35v] La curaciun de ce mal si est tele. A comencement seignez le malade de la veine capitale que vous eiez del sank. Aprés si pernez del jus de pimpernele e le jus de olive owele mesure, si en oignez les oils.

(39) *Item oignement esprové a la maele e a la teye*: Metez eisel mout egre en un vessel de arein e le jus de prunels dé bois e plum e alum e medlez tut ensemble, si lessez estre le vessel covert bien lungement. E kaunt mester sera, si le metez es oils.

(40) **Item ad caliginosos oculos*: Accipe pulverem zinziberi et misce cum succo feniculi et albo vino, mitte coagulatum et mitte in oculos cum dormitum ibis.

(41) *Item accipe succum absinthii et mel ana, mixta reddunt oculos claros si inde ungantur.

(42) *Item comede rutam omni die. Vel unge oculos succo rute et succo maratri et melle et felle galli equaliter mixtis.

(43) *Item comede feniculum et cum succo radicis eius et melle mixtis oculos unge.

(44) *Item succus marubii mixtus cum melle et vino fugat caliginem oculorum.

(45) *Idem facit succus celidonie.

(46) **Item ad eos qui habent claros oculos et non vident*: Serpillum in aqua coque et inde oculi sepe abluantur.

(47) *Item ad sanguinem oculorum tollendum: Accipe herbam vocatam anglice 'ravenesfot' .i. pes corvi et tere et appone modicum vini albi. Deinde exprime succum et tantum recentis sanguinis porcini appone et conmisce et fac bullire fere usque ad medietatem. Et inde oculos unge.

(48) *Item ad oculos: Accipe celidoniam vel flores eius et tere et succum misce cum melle et oculos unge et accipies maximam claritatem.

(49) *Item ad oculum rubeum pro sanguine attracto: Accipe plantaginem et bene tere, postea appone de albumine ovi, illa duo bene misce. Et postea fac emplastrum et liga ad oculum. Sanguinem et dolorem tollit.

(50) *Item versus [f.36r] Feniculus, vervena, rosa, celidonia, ruta, / Ex istis fit aqua que lumina reddit acuta.

.d.
De infirmitatibus aurium

(51) Pur dolour des orailes e pur verms: Pernez le jus de mente e le eschaufez e le mettez as orailes, si garra.

(52) Item pur verms dedeins les orailes: Distemprez le mentastre od vin, pus la colez parmi un drap, si fetez teve e mettez es orailes.

(53) Ou le jus de aloine, ou le jus de semence de seu, ou le jus de la semence de fenoil teve, ou le jus de eble teve donez a celi que ad esté sourd.

(54) Item pernez le jus de senichun e su de motun e fetes emplastre.

(55) Item pernez seim de anguile blanc, si metez es orailes e le verm s'en istra.

(56) Item pernez le jus de planteine teve, si metez en le oraile.

(57) *Item pur oraile sourd*: Pernez le ewe que decourt de frene vert quant homme le art, si en quilez plein escale de un oef e autretaunt de mel, si le quisez tut ensemble. E pus le mettez en un vere e metez en la oraile. Ceo amende mout le oir e estaunche la fenge que decourt.

(58) *Item pur dolour de oraile*: Pernez jus de coriaundre od let de femme e seit mis en la oraile e ceo oste la dolour.

(59) **Item ad surdum qui noviter auditum amisit*: Accipe acetum et fac bullire et bene despumare cum penna, et dimitte refrigerare ita quod infirmus possit bene sustinere. Et postea infunde in aurem cum qua bene non audit et illa aure sursum versa sic iaceat tota nocte et ita usque ad septimam noctem. Et quando infundis, calefac.

(60) **Item ad auditum recuperandum*: Accipe succum rute et cum sagimine anguille conmisce et in sanam aurem quando vadit dormitum mitte. Probatum est.

(61) **Item contra infirmitatem aurium*: Valet fumus absinthii decocti et supponatur auribus herba trita cum melle vel oleo.

(62) **Item ad aurem percussam* [f.36v] *vel vulneratam*: Micam panis calidam cum melle tere et frequenter auri suppone.

(63) *Et nota quod nichil debet auribus instillari nisi tepidum secundum Avicenam.

.e.
Hic incipit medicina contra infirmitatem dencium

(64) Et primo pur neir dens: Pernez un branche de vine, si en fetez de ceo charbun e frotez ben les dens od ceo charbun sovent e les lavez aprés de ewe.

(65) Ou quisez betoyne en eisil ou en vin deques a la terce partie, si tenez ceo ben chaud en vostre bouche, e ceo fetez sovent e ben garrez.

(66) *Medicine a dens que se movent*: Pernez le corn de cerf, si le ardez en poudre e de ceo frotez les dens, si s'afermerunt.

(67) Item pernez la poudre de la baye od un poy de encens, si triblez en vin e de ceo frotez ben les dens e pus le tenez en la bouche, si se afermerunt.

(68) **Contra dolorem dentium*: Vinum et piper tritum et tepefactum in ore teneat.

(69) Item pernez encens e blanc de l'oef e triblez ensemble. Pus metez un poi sur parchemyn e le metez sur la jowe de cele part ou la dolour n'est pas.

(70) Item triblez bien la primerole deske vous en eyez le jus, si le metez en la narile de cele part ou la dolour n'est pas.

(71) *Item accipe herbam que vocatur dens leonis et conquassetur et denti dolenti interius superponatur et curat.

(72) **Item ad dentes candidandum*: Farinam ordei, mel et sal misce et inde dentes sepius frica.

(73) *Item accipe corticem interiorem nucis, desicca et fac pulverem et zinziber similiter et pone hunc pulverem et illum simul super pannum lineum et frica dentes.

(74) **Item ad dolorem dentium carmen*: Christus sedebat super petram marmoream. Petrus stabat manus ad maxillas tenens et interrogabat eum Christus dicens 'Quare tristis es, Petre ?'. 'Domine, dentes mei dolent'. Et dixit Dominus 'Cesset dolor'. Unde adiuro te, emigra[f.37r]nea gutta, per Patrem et Filium et Spiritum Sanctum, per celum et per terram et per .ix. ordines angelorum, per .xii. apostolos et per .iiii. evangelistas, qui sunt Matheus, Marcus, Lucas, Johannes, et per .xxiiiior seniores qui Deo placuerunt, ut non possis nocere amplius huic famulo Dei .N. in dentibus nec in naribus nec in auribus nec in oculis nec in ullis compaginibus menbrorum vigilando nec dormiendo. In nomine Patris et Filii et Spiritus Sancti, Amen. Et dicitur hec oratio: 'Deus qui de beate Marie virginis utero' cum tribus Pater Noster et tot Ave Maria.

(75) **Item ad idem oratio*: Proficiat, quesumus, Domine, hec institutio tua anime famuli tui cassiani .N. ad compescendum dolorem horum dentium et totius capitis. Pater Noster ter dicatur. Post dicantur nomina patris et matris et nomen infirmi, ceie.leie.cato.naqui.aufer celo fecit. Et dicatur ter Pater Noster.

(76) *Pur enflure de jowe*: Pernez primerole e la triblez, pus pernez le jus e le metez en la oraile de cele part ou la maladie n'est pas.

(77) Item quisez osmunde, jubarbe od seim de ver e metez sur l'emflure.

.f.

As narils puantes que avient del cervel

(78) Pernez le jus de mente e de rue, si medlez ensemble e metez es narils sovent.

(79) Item pernez le jus de here, si le metez es narils.

(80) Item triblez ben la rose, pus la quisez ben en vin rouge e un poi de mel. Pus le colez parmi un drap. Pus le metez es narils.

(81) Item fetez pudre de les escales de les oefs dunt les pucins sunt forsclos, si les sufflez es narils e endementers que vous frez celes medicines avantdites fetez li beivere aloine triblé od mel.

(82) *Item medicine bone pur estauncher sanc de playe ou de nes*: Pernez de meme celui sanc e escrivez od un penne a homme ou a femme ces motz: si il seit homme + betonix + , si ce soit femme + betonixa + e od la croiz devaunt e aprés.

(83) *Item ad idem: Recipe sanguinem fluentem in [f.37v] testa ovi et bulli ad ignem et statim restringetur. Probatum est.

(84) **Item contra fluxum sanguinis per nares vel per vulnus*: Scribe 'alleluia' in fronte pacientis de sanguine illo et cessabit.

(85) *Item sume fimum porci recentem et involve sindone et sic applicetur naso profluenti et si non cessat, exprime succum eiusdem in nasum pacientis et stabit.

(86) *Item lini frontem de succo urtice.

(87) *Similiter plantago vel succus eius.

(88) *Item succus rute fundatur in naribus et timpora eo liniantur.

(89) *Item succus salvie idem facit.

(90) Item si le nes vous seigne, [...]lez ensemble les jointes dé deus petitz deis e le sanc cessera.

(91) *Charme bone pur estancher sanc*: In nomine Patris et Filii et S[piritus] S[ancti] Amen. Jesu en la croiz fu mis, de un tirant fu feru que fu Longis, en la destre coste fu feru. Auxi vers cum Deus es tu, estanche tu sanc[17] en nun del Pere e de[l] Fiz e del Seint Espiritz. Ditez .v. Pater Noster e .v. Ave Maria.

(92) *Item in nomine Patris et F[ilii] et S[piritus] S[ancti] Amen. Conjuro te, sanguis, per sanguinem qui de latere Christi exivit et per .v. vulnera que in cruce passus est pro nobis, ut cesses sanguis.

(93) *Adiuro te, sanguis, per quatuor nomina Christi, Adonai, Sabaoth, Emanuel, Ensaday, libera hunc famulum tuum .N. et sicut mulierem a fluxu

[17] MS e. sanc tu.

sanginis liberasti, ita hunc sanguinem cessare facias, Jesu Christe, Dominus Noster. In nomine Patris et F[ilii] et S[piritus] S[ancti] Amen.

(94) *Item In nomine Patris et F[ilii] et S[piritus] S[ancti] Amen. Sancta Maria iuxta Christi crucem stabat, filium suum servabat, mortem et penas eius plangebat. Longinus miles latus suum lancea perforavit, continuo exivit sanguis et aqua, sanguis redempcionis et aqua bapstismatis. In nomine Patris et F[ilii] et S[piritus] S[ancti] Amen.

(95) *In nomine Patris stet sanguis et Filii cesset sanguis et Spiritus Sancti non exeat gutta + et sicut sanguis Domini Nostri Jesu Cristi ex plagis in cruce cessavit, ita sanguis .N. prece sancte Marie et omnium sanctorum cessare [f.38r] videatur, Amen.

.g.
Incipit medicina pro fetore oris

(96) *Ad oris fetorem: Pulegii semen manduca vel costam jejunus bibe.

(97) *Item semen apii jejunus manduca.

(98) Item mangez sovent les foiles de fou e lavez la bouche de eisel.

(99) Item bevez puliol destempré od vin aprés manger e ce mut sovent.

(100) Item destemprés peivere od blanc vin, si le tenez chaud en vostre bouche. Par cestes medicines le puour osteretz.

(101) Item triblez comin en mel, si en bevez.

(102) Item mangez puliol sek ou cerfoile e lavez sovent la bouche od eisel.

(103) A homme que pert la parole: Triblez .iii. racines de rouge urtie e les destemprés od ewe, si li donez a beivere.

(104) Item pernez chenlange e le distemprés od servoise, si li donez a beivere.

(105) Ou donez li a beivere aloine distempré od vin, si parlera.

(106) **Ad cancrum oris*: Accipe succum celidonie, quantum testa ovi potest capere aceti et mellis tantumdem, piperis longi grana .v., coque ad medietatem, ore tene. Probatum est.

(107) *Pur enflure de lange*: Pernez sauge e grein de perecil .ii. poignés e de ceo fetez pudre e defossez le en mel e en electuarie e donez al malade a beivere en un bain.

.h.
Incipit medicina pro infirmitate jecoris [corr. gutturis]

(108) *Ad illud valet potio apii, feniculi, salvie cum melle.

(109) *Pur esquinancie*: Pernez mel e mies de gasteal ou de blanc pain e

pudre de comin e friez ensemble. E fetez emplastre e metez a la jowe e le fetez seigner de la veine capitale ou desoutz la lange que meut vaut.

(110) Item li donez jus de columbine ou la semence a manger.

.i.

Incipit medicina pro infirmitate humerorum

(111) Pur dolour des espaules: Pernez herbe beneite e quisez la ben en eisel e pus la treez fors, si la mettez sur un [f.38v] linge drap e metez teve sur la dolour.

(112) Item pernez vin veuz e veuz oile e seim de porc male e boillez tut ensemble sur le feu tanque il seit remis. E pus pernez la leine de berbis ben carpé, si la moilez dedeinz, e pus la premez que ele rende partie, e pus la mettez ou que unques la dolour serra, si entrera tut hors.

.k.

(113) **Ad inflationem brachii de sanguine post minucionem*: Semen lini et mel simul bene coque, deinde super lineum pannum pone et brachio applica.

(114) *Item fabas coque in vino vel in aqua donec resolvantur. Addes etiam semen lini quod sufficiat ponesque in lineo panno et appones calidum.

(115) **Item si quis minutus percutitur per medium vene et periclitatur*: Sume salgiam cum enula campana et apio, et exprime succum super vulnus. Et deinde liga residuum super vulnus et cotidie debet renovari istud super vulnus.

(116) *Item accipe micas panis ordeacei vel frumenti frixa in sepo ovino recenti et liga istud calidum super vulnus.

(117) *Item a veine trenché*: Pernez la rue, si quisez en oile e oignez de ceo le bras. Probatum est. E de ce memes metez e liez sur la veine ou sur le bras.

(118) *Item pur bras emflé aprés seigner*: Pernez ache, si triblez e destemprez od l'aubun de l'oef e fetez une emplastre e lessez l'emplastre deus jours sur le bras.

(119) *Item a nerfs custreintz*: Pernez piz e cire e su e meslez ensemble e le eschaufez e metez sur.

(120) **Item si nervi incisi fuerint*: Vermes terre combure et pulverem cum melle misce et superpone.

.l.

Incipit medicina mamillarum infirmarum et primo contra inflacionem mamille

(121) *Contra quod accipe semen lini et coque donec frangatur et superpone et interim bibat oculescunse e morele.

(122) Item pernez les pummes de chene e triblez od oile ro[f.39r]set e metez sur. E aprés pernez le jus de la morele e de la menue consoude e de coriandre e linois ben molu e les lies de eysel e les oefs quitz durs od les escales. Si les triblez e bulez ben ensemble od la farine de orge e fetez un emplastre e metez sur.

(123) *Item folia persice .i. 'pecher' tere et impone ut emplastrum.

(124) *Item succus apii cum succo feniculi vel ungantur oleo in quo hec decoquntur.

(125) **Item ad dolorem mamillarum:* Salgiam et urticam in servisia coque et bibat.

(126) *Item accipe radicem ebuli et tere cum uncto porcino et superpone.

(127) *Si vous voletz que femme eit assetz leit:* Mange sovent la letuse, kar ceo fet mout crestre let e restreint luxurie.

(128) *Item a emflure dé mameles aprés enfaunter*: Si ceo seit de leit, fetez le trere de un persone que le sache estracher de sa bouche.

(129) Item pernez farine de aveine ben munde e su de motun ben colé e leit de vache, si boilez tut ensemble e metez chaud cum emplastre.

(130) Ce memes vaut a rancle dé bras aprés seigner.

(131) **Item ad cancrum mamillarum*: Urticam cum sale modico mixtam impone.

(132) Item pernez pudre de arnement e veuz oint de pork e triblez forment ensemble e metez l'emplastre sur, si garra.

.m.

Incipit de infirmitatibus pectoris

(133) Pur dolour del piz e pur la tusse e la maladie de coer: Pernez un noef pot e fetez en le found un lit de maroil e de ache e de senechun e de lovache e de ysope e de lange de chen e de heihove e pus un autre de lard fresch e pus un autre lit des herbis susdites e ensi de lit en lit tanque le pot seit plein. E pus coverez ben le pot de une covercle desus e le liez de paste ensi que le chalour ne pusse issir. Pus emplez un chaudrun plein de ewe e pendez le pot en cele ewe ensi [f.39v] que le ewe ne puce entrer par desus. E ensi seit quit dekes les herbis seient remises e pus le colez parmi un drap. Pus pernez une quileré, si metez en vin ben chaud ou en servoise. E kaunt vous irrez cocher, si le bevez e en jun sovent.

(134) Item pernez .iii. bayes de lorer, si les quisez od vin e od mel, si en bevez qant vous irrez dormer.

(135) *Item al mal e a l'emflure*: Triblez ben ache e metez od la myure de

blanc pain e metez en veuz vin, si fetez une emplastre e metez a l'emflure.

(136) Item distemprez planteine od eisel e metez sur.

(137) *Item si il ad clous en le piz*: Pernez surele e metez en foile de cholet e quisez en les breses. Pus triblez od veuz oint e metez sur, si garra.

(138) **Item ad pectoris dolorem*: Accipe succum marubii albi et rute, ysopi et apii equali mensura et tantum mellis quantum succi et duplum optimi vini. Et fac bullire usque ad spissitudinem mellis et utere mane et sero.

(139) **Item ad pectus purgandum*: Ysopum et neptam tere et exprimens in lacte ferventi cum sagimine vel butiro et jejunus bibe mane et vespere, quod etiam tussim purgabit.

(140) *Item encountre tous maus de piz*: Quilez une bone partye de pruneles dé bois .i. 'slon' e metez les en un fort vessel, si les triblez ben. Pus pernez servoise sitost cum ele ert culé, si le medlez ensemble od les pruneles anglice 'slon' e metez en un noef pot, si fetez en la tere un fosse e mettez leins le pot e le cuverez ben de une nette esquele. Pus jetez la tere desur, si seit ileoc .ix. jours e .ix. nuitz. E pus pernez une petite hanapé de ceo, si le donez a beivere al malade, le seir chaud e le matin freis e en jun, e ceo fetez deque il seit garri.

(141) **Item contra tussim que habet multum fleuma*: Utatur apii semine et feniculi et rute et folia, simul tere et marubii succo ovum plenum da bibere. Omne fleuma ligatum resolvit.

(142) Item [f.40r] contra tussim siccam: Pernez la semence de ache e de fenoil e de anis owele mesure, si en fetez pudre. Pus le quisez ben ensemble od mel e od vin, si le bevez le seir chaud e le matin freid.

(143) *Item a la tusse perilouse*: Pernez la racine de fenoil, si le triblez ben e medlez od vin, si bevez jun.

(144) *Item a la tusse e a la pomun malade*: Pernez la semence de ache e de anis e moilez ben ensemble e peivere e mel medlé ensemble e auques de vin e distemprez tut ceo ben ensemble, si le quisez al fu deques il seit ben espés. Pus le metez en boistes e mangez .iii. esquilers de ceo al seir e al matin deke vous seietz garri.

(145) *Item encontre glette*: Pernez deus parties de jus de fenoil e la terce de mel e quisez ben deke il seit espés. E usez de ceo a matin e a seir, si vous vaudra mut a l'esplen e al pomun, si vous ostera la glette. Si en fetez pus en ewe e kant vous la quisez, metez une bone quileré de cele pudre, si en mangez sovent de ceo, si garrez pur voir.

(146) **Ad vocem et pectus exclarandum*:[18] Tremuli corticem et ebuli radicem

[18] In the righthand margin a 15th C. hand has written 'pro cantatoribus'.

equali mensura tere et in aliquo vase repone cum optimo vino et per .v. dies mane et sero bibe.

(147) **Item ad vocem*: Salviam cum vino calefacto bibe cum dormitum ieris.

(148) *Item savinam cum melle et vino bibe.

(149) *Item accipe ysopum et marubium et apium et rutam et rauge [sic] liquorys et coquantur cum servisia vel aqua et bibatur cum mensura sero quam calidum bibi potest et mane frigidum et impinguatur apposito butiro.

(150) *Pur le mal que l'en ad entour le coer e pur oster venim*: Pernez la osmunde .i. 'horsehove', si la triblez. Pernez pus gruel de aveine e metez od ceo, si la quisez od la bure de Mai tanque il seit ben quit. Pus li donez a manger .iii. quilers al vespre quant il irra cocher. [f.40v] Si face checun jour tanque il seit garri.

(151) **Item ad infirmitates que circa cor sunt*: Pulegius bibendus est cum melle.

(152) *Item al mal de de coer que tout a homme talent de manger e fet aver abhominaciun de viaundes*: Pernez centurie e la quisez mut ben en estale servoise ou en vin e quant il serra ben quit, le ostez de feu, si la destemprez ben, pus la remetez en le pot e la lessez durement quire. Pus la colez parmi un drap. Pus pernez mel e le boillez ensemble deque mut seit espés. E pus le metez en une bele boiste e fetez le malade manger de ceste eleituare checun jour .iii. esquilers deke il seit garri. E ceo lui ostera la glette de coer e lui fera aver bon talent de manger e de beivere.

(153) *Item centauream cum aqua calida bibe per triduum.

(154) **Item ad omnes dolores cordis*: Pimpinellam cum aceto bibe.

(155) *Pur fere un homme vomer*: Pernez l'escorche de la racine de wrti e la triblez ben, pus la quisez en servoise e pus si coverez ben le pot e lessez estre tote nuit. A matin donez celi a beivere que vodra vomer e quant il avera assez vomé e ne vodra plus, mange de la rouge cerfoile.

(156) *Encontre ceo que homme vomist e ne put retener viaunde*: Pernez puliol e maroil e peivere e quisez ben en ewe, si li fetez sovent beivere.

(157) **Item ad eos qui nec cibum nec potum retinent sed vomunt*: Millefolium tepidum bibant.

(158) **Item ad eos qui sanguinem vomunt*: Apium, mentam, rutam simul cum lacte ebuli bibant.

(159) **Item ad vomitum stringendum*: Coquatur pulegium, martefelun, vetonicam et succus ad bibendum detur.

(160) *A homme que est empusoné*: Pernez une herbe que est apelé confirie, si en pernez le peis de un dener e destemprés od urine de femme, si li donez a beivere, si vomera hors tut le mal e tut le venim. Pus mangetz .iii. plantes de cerfoil e [f.41r] beive leit de vache ou de chevere.

(161) Item pernez la racine de dragaunce, si la tailez menu e la sechez a fu ou a solaile e en fetez pudre. E pus pernez de cele pudre le peis de .v. d[eners] e metez en ewe tedve e ensi lessez estre tote nuit. E l'endemain jetez fors tute l'ewe e metez i vin e le quisez ben, pus li fetez beivere, si garra.

(162) Item pernez luvache e andre e anis, si triblez ben ensemble e quisez en centorie e en vin, si li donez a beivere si chaud cum il le purra suffrir. E delivrement vomera hors le pusun e tut le venim.

(163) Item bevez la racine de fugere .i. 'farn'.

(164) Item bevez tormentille.

(165) Item encuntre tous maus venims: Quisez leit de chevere tanque a la terce partie od semence de chenve vel careué e bevez .iii. jours. Soutz ciel n'ad beivere si bon encuntre venim for triacle.

(166) Item ki ad bu venim beive jus de maroil od veu vin, si gettera hors le venim e sanera.

(167) **Item quicumque venenum biberit*: Betonice trite tres sciatos bibat et venenum eiciet.

(168) **Item ut potio mala non noceat tibi*[19]: Accipe semen lactuce et cum aqua jejunus bibe. Aut nuces jejunus comede.

(169) *Item trifolium bibe quia si araneam biberis, per os cito exibit.

(170) Item encuntre ceo que homme vomist sanc e escope: Pernez la crote de cheivere e fetez une pudre. Pus pernez pure farine de orge, si en fetez pous en ewe e kaunt vous le quirez, metez i une bone esquileré de l'avaunt dit pudre, si mange sovent de ceo, si garra.

.n.

Incipit medicina infirmitatum ventris et intestinorum

(171) Et primo contra vermes in interioribus existentes: Beivere a celui que coluvere ou nule beste venimouse ad dedeins le cors: Triblez averoygne en un morter, si donez le jus a beivere, kar ausi tost cum il le avera bu quele [f.41v] chose qe dedeins lui seit en haste murra.

(172) Item pernez un chival tut sor e taunt le facez coure que il escume. E pernez cele escume e leit de chevere ensemble medlé e donez al pacient a beivere e tost rendra hors quele chose que dedeins lui seit. Aprés, si vous dutez de ren que seit demuré dedeins lui, donez lui a beivere leit de asne jun, si rendra hors ceo que est demuré, e sei garde que il ne mange, si seine viande nun.

[19] In the righthand margin a 15th C. hand has written 'regula bona'.

(173) Item fetez pudre de la mene escorche de sautz e de la racine autresi e un poi de savine. Pus seit ben triblé en un morter, aprés quit en servoise e doné al pacient.

(174) *Si serpent ou coluvere seit entré dedeins le ventre de un homme*: Triblez rue e destemprés od vostre urine memez e bevez.

(175) Item destemprés arnement od vostre urine meme e fetez ben espés e bevez, si gettrez hors le venim.

(176) **Item ad eos quibus serpentes per os intraverint aut alios vermes in se habuerint*: Atramentum spissum bibant et statim liberabuntur.

(177) *Item si verms seient en le ventre de homme*: Pernez le corn de cerf e ardez le en pudre e destemprés le od eisil, si lui donez sovent a beivere, e ceo occira les verms.

(178) **Ad dolorem ventris et duriciam et inflacionem*: Succum quinquefolii bibe vel plantaginis et maxime foliorum duo coclearia.

(179) Item triblez rue od vin ou od servoise e bevez sovent.

(180) *Encuntre custivesun veez si medicine verraye*: Pernez la semence de lin e quisez la ben en ewe e pus si ostez l'ewe e pernez le linois, si freez beau seim en une paele e pus li donez ceo a manger ben chaud.

(181) Ou pernez fugerole .i. polipodie de chene e le lavez ben e le triblez od lard e aparailez ben un geline desplumé e overte e seit ben farcé de cele chose. Pus seit ben quit en [f.42r] ewe e grant partie de l'herbe oveke. E quant la geline ert ben quite, colez cele ewe parmi un drap e le humez a mesure. Pus fetez une cuminé ben espesse e grasse e le destemprez od cele ewe e mangez la geline, si garrez.

(182) *Encontre*[20] *menisun veez si medicine verraye*: Pernez milfoile, si la triblez tanque vous en eyetz le jus. Pus pernez la farine furmentale, si fetez un turtel e le quisez en breses, si la mangez ben chaud.

(183) *Si saver volez de homme que ad fort menisun si il puce vivre ou nun*: Donez lui a manger le peis de un dener de semence de cressun que crest en curtil .iii. jours e nent plus. E beive aprés un tret de ewe tedve ou de vin. E si il estancher[a], garra, si nun, murra.

(184) *Item pur menisun sanglaunte*: Pernez milfoille e plauntayne e frasere taunt de l'une cum de l'autre e triblez les bien ensemble, si les gardez. E kaunt vous en oindrez, si destemprez od vin ou od ewe, si le donez al malade .iii. jours a beivere le matin e le seir, si garra pur veir.

(185) *Item pur menisoun*: Pernez feves e les quisez en un pocenet od su de motun, si li donez a manger.

[20] MS *encentre.*

(186) Item pernez furmage, si le quisez en vin ou en ewe, si li donez a manger.

(187) *Uncore pur dolour des entrailes*: Milfoile quit en leit oste tote la dolour des entrailes e des autres enfermetés dedeins le cors.

(188) *Item ad lumbricos .i. vermes in ventre anglice voca[n]t[ur] 'ffiches'. Ipsos necat decoctio abrotani, rute, absinthii, plantaginis, ysopi sepe potata cum melle et aqua pluviali et oleo.

(189) *Item savinam et absinthium tere simul et accipe succum earum et distempera cum berziza .i. 'wort'. Deinde cola per lineum pannum et bibe. Tamen caveatur ne misceatur savina huic pocioni si debeat dari alicui [f.42v] mulieri.

(190) *Pueris vero medicandis de lumbricis cum succo abrotani .s. domestici cum pauco zucaro. Nota quod lumbrici occiduntur cum omni re amara sicut absinthio et similibus ut supra dictum est.

(191) *Uncore pur verms*: Pernez rue e blanc vin e quisez ensemble e donez a beivere jun par matin.

(192) Item pernez perches, si les ardez en pudre e metez cele pudre en fort eisel e lessez le un poi boiler, pus lui donez a beivere.

(193) Item pernez jus de maroil destempré od vin vermail e donez a beivere.

.o.

Incipit cura de infirmitatibus ani et primo pur le fy que ist hors de fundement

(194) Pur lui triblez tresben l'ameroche .i. 'maithe' e bevez le jus e metez le pasteal desus, ou metez desur la pudre de aloine, si mura le fy.

(195) *Item pur fundement que ist hors*: Pernez la rouge yere .i. [...] e metez en un nef pot e versez le pot plein de vin, si le quisez desque a la terce partie e le bevez le seir chaud e le matin freis. E pus pernez les foiles de yere quites e liés al mal.

(196) Ou pernez sanicle, violete, tanesé, chanevere e la mere des herbes e quisez les en servoise e bevez, si garra.

(197) *Item pur le fy que mange le homme dedeins le cors entour le umbil*: Pernez le neir limasun, si liez en la fosse de umbil tut vif, si le lessez estre tute nuit; si le limasun est mangé,[21] li homme garra, si nun, si metez un autre tanque il seit mangé.

(198) *Uncore pur le fy que fet homme vomer*: Pernez l'aresteboef e jus [de]

[21] MS *m. si est li h.*

coudre e .ix. plauntes de planteyne, si triblez ensemble e quisez en serveise e en beive li homme .ix. jours e un saul(?), si est garri.

(199) *Pur peine de ameroudes*: Pernez 'thunderdokke' e malve e les quisez en leit de vache en un poket e seez sur le poket autresi chaud cum vous purrez suffrer, issi que le poket seit mis desoutz la [f.43r] maladie.

(200) Ou pernez semence de line e fetez en meme la manere.

(201) Ou pernez porret, si le trenchez menu sicum ferez potage, si le friez en bele grece de motun, e pus le metez en un poket kaunt il est frit e tut chaud le metez a la maladie e fetez ser desur.

(202) *Item pur emeroides*: Pernez paritorie, horhune, grund-ivi, wormod e boilez ensemble en un pot e quant il serrunt ben boilez, fetez le malade ser [sur] une sege ou seit fet un pertus cum la sege de un garderobe e lui fetez lever ses dras. Pus pernez le pot e le coverez ben, que nul eir pusse issir forque a un pertus que serra fet desus ce de quei le pot serra covert e que celi pertuz seit encuntre le pertus de fundement, e lessez le ben estuer si chaud cum il le purra endurer. E ceo fetez .iii. foitz ou quatre ou taunt que il seit garri. Esprové est.

(203) **Item ad idem*: Succus persicarie cum vitelli ovi et oleo rosaceo facto quasi unguento valet contra emeroidas.

.p.

Incipit cura de infirmitatibus genitalium et primo contra inflacionem eorum

(204) *Pur enflure de genitaile*: Pernez la ruge limasun, si le ardez a feu e fetez un emplastre e metez sur le mal.

(205) **Item ad inflacionem virge ex calore coitus*: Recipe folia salicis et coquantur in aqua et balneetur virga. Deinde circumligentur folia. Vel semen lini coquatur cum foliis malve cum quibus pistacio cathaplasmetur.

(206) *Item*: Pernez un rouge oynun e rostez le ben e pus quisez le en leit de femme e metez sur le mal.

(207) **Uncore ad inflacionem testiculorum*: Recipe malvam, artemesiam, jusquiamum, et caules veteres. Et si non potes habere hec omnia, accipiantur absinthium et malve tantum, et decoquantur et in illa decoctione epithimentur testiculi. Postea terantur dicte herbe parum[22] et cum melle bulliant et superponantur testiculis in modum emplastri.

(208) **Item* [f.43v] furfur tritici coquatur et superponatur testiculis.

(209) *Item fabe fracte coquantur usque ad spissitudinem et post

[22] MS *parum et parum*.

coctionem terantur cum melle et cera et superponatur testiculis in modo emplastri.

(210) *Item paritoria frixa in patella et testiculis superposita removet inflationem testiculorum.

(211) *Similiter fimus columbinus et bovinus cum aqua coctus et superpositus.

(212) **Item* contra inflacionem virilis membri: Recipe wimave et coque et ex succo lavetur et ipsum tritum apponatur.

(213) **Item* ad veretrum inflatum: Fac emplastrum de gruello avene et sepo arietino et bene calidum impone bis vel ter.

(214) *Item emplastrum factum de caseo qui super servisiam venit quando illa inicitur.

(215) *Item ad veretrum pertusatum: Fac pulverem de vetustis lineis pannis et appone et lavetur cotidie de sua propria urina.

(216) Item pur membre naturel: Pernez semence de line e la racine de lilie e quisez mut ben e triblez ben ensemble e fetez emplastre e liez tut envirun. E ceo esswagera la dolour e trera hors le venim, e garra.

.q.

Incipit medicina de infirmitatibus natum et primo pro dolore eorumdem

(217) Pur dolour dé quises: Triblez la crote de berbis od ail, si en oignez les quises sovent.

(218) Item si les quises desoutz les genuls ou desus seiunt enflés ou que la pel seit despessé, bevez eble triblé od servoise .ix. jours, si garra.

(219) Item as genuls enflés ou que dolunt: Triblez rue od sel e od mel, si metez l'emplastre sure.

.r.

(220) *Contra dolorem pedum ex nimio labore: Teratur plantago cum aceto vel acro vino et inde bene fricentur pedes et superponatur pedibus.

(221) *Item fricentur pedes subtus cum sapone.

(222) Item pur mal dé pes e pur clous: Pernez la parele ov les foiles de rouge cholet, si quisez les en breses e pus les triblez od viel oint, si metez e ben garra.

(223) Item [f.44r] pur surbature dé pes: Triblez rue od oile e oignez les pes desoutz.

(224) Uncore pur genuls enflés: Pernez rue e mel e quisez ensemble e mettez as genuls.

(225) Item pur pes emflés: Pernez eisel e su e triblez ensemble e mettez sur.

(226) Item pur verms desoutz les pes: Pernetz 'sowthistel' e triblez e mettez desoutz les pes cum emplastre.

.s.

*Nota quod corpus hominis ex .iiii. humoribus consistit. Hii sunt: sanguis, colera rubea, colera nigra, ffleuma. Omnia dominantur in suis locis. Sanguis intus circa cor; colera rubea in dextero latere in epate, quod jecur vocatur; colera nigra in sinistro latere, hoc est in splene quod etiam lien dicitur; ffleuma in capite, alia pars in vesica. Sanguis est calidus et humidus et dulcis et crescit in vere. Colera rubea amara, viridis et sicca et crescit in estate. Colera nigra acida, acra et fervens et crescit in autumpno. Ffleuma frigida, humida et caro mellina et crescit in yeme. Isti humores dominantur sive per diem sive per noctem. Sanguis ab hora noctis .ix. usque in horam diei .iii. Colera rubea ab hora diei .iii. usque in horam noctis .ix. Colera nigra ab hora diei .x. usque in horam noctis .iii. Ffleuma ab hora noctis .iii. usque in horam diei .x. Hec omnia habent respiraciones per singulas partes corporis: sanguis per nares, colera rubea per aures, colera nigra per oculos, ffleuma per os etc.[23]

.t.

Incipiunt medicine contra antracem .i. felun

(227) *Consolida minor extracta sine ferro trituretur inter duos lapides cuius succus detur ad potandum.

(228) *Item vellum ovi cum sale tritum et morbo appositum juvat.

(229) *Item jacea nigra .i. 'martefelun' in potu data idem facit.

(230) *Item capud allecis rubei in aqua benedicta distemperatum et bibitum ad idem valet.

(231) *Item tyriaca probata cum aqua decoctionis jacee nigre [f.44v] distemperata celeriter prodest.

(232) *Item radix lilii cum aqua distemperata et eadem speciei non nunc cum auxungia porcina loco applicata juvat.

(233) *Item circumdetur locus saphiro, postea trahatur tractus per medium et juvat.

[23] This passage, often in inaccurate form, is commonly found in Salernitan medical compendia, as for example in MS Princeton University Library, Garrett 131 (s.xiii) f.29v (shortly before a French translation of the *Circa Instans*).

(234) *Item succus maricii[24] .i. 'maithe' anglice potatus celeriter juvat. Sed caveatur ne aliquis homo sit ibi presens dum potatur sed brutum animal.

(235) *Item ostria viva juxta locum apposita et postea iterum paulatim remota et sic iterum et iterum eodem modo apposita ducit antracem usque ad ultimum locum.

(236) *Idem facit lapis adamantinus.

(237) *Item ad idem valet herba sancti Cristofori .i. oculus Cristi. Distemperata cum aqua et in potu data idem prestat beneficium.

(238) *Item anus galline vive loco applicatus juvat, ita tamen quod gallina per rostrum teneatur ne anelitum aspiret, quia sic venenum extrahit. Et si illa moritur, alia applicetur parti infirme eodem modo quod si plures moriantur, signum est mortis.

(239) *Item contra antracem quando capud est rubeum: Superpone salem et vitellum .i. 'le moeal' mixta simul.

(240) *Quando vero capud est album pone saponem .i. 'savun' super capud.

(241) *Quando vero capud est nigrum extrahe sanguinem .i. pinguedinem allecis et vitellum ovi. Cum sit mixtum in omnibus, pone gruellum factum de avena cum sepo ovino recenti super locum et exiet illa putredo. Deinde curetur ut vulnus.

(242) Item pur felun: Pernez le jus de morele e de chiverefoil e de planteine e vinegre e metez sur le mal, si garra.

(243) Item braez scabiose e la petite consoude od viel oint de porc e metez sur le mal.

(244) Item pernez chaus vif e savun e la poudre de peivere e sel e medlez tut ensemble e metez sur le mal, e garra.

(245) Item kaunt le felun serra brisé, pernez le jus de ache e mel e le moeal de l'oef e le aubun e flur de furment e encorperez [f.45r] ensemble e metez sur le mal. Pus metez desus pudre de mastic e de franc ensens.

(246) Item pur rancle e felon: Boilez flur de orge e semence de lin en eisel ou en vin e si metez su de motun. Ceo occist rancle e felun.

(247) Item pur felun que nest al cors par boces: Bevez la plauntaine e la morele e metez l'emplastre desur.

(248) Item pernez maroil, si triblez ben, pus si le eschaufez, si metez tut chaud sur le mal, si garra.

(249) Item pernez maroil e savoun, si triblez ensemble, pus metez tut chaud sur le mal.

[24] corr. amarusce ?

Uncore medicine pur quatre manere de feluns que vienunt dé quatre manerez dé humours de homme

(250) Checun felun, ou il est neir, ou il est de colour de saphir, ou il est blanc, ou il est enfossé. Le blanc, que est apelé la liuer(?), ou le mal est rayé, ceo est la medicine encuntre: Pernez le solsequie e jubarbe e consoude petit e batez ensemble e liez sur la vescie.

(251) Encuntre le neir felun de quele vient festre, fustole ou cancre fetez ceste medicine:[25] Pernez la petite consoude e launcelé e testes de heranc sor e batez ensemble e destemprez de ewe beneite e colez parmi un drap e bevez le jus. Pus pernez le gros que remaint e metez sur le felun en lu d'emplastre.

(252)*Encuntre felon enfossé de quel vient sovent mort subite*: Fetez mesme la medicine cum devaunt [dit] est, tenge sei a pain e ewe e a gruel, e fetez en ewe beneite le licur de tutes treis medicines. E pus metez plaunteine e vif sablun e pudrez sur le mal.

(253) En[f.45v][cuntre] le felun que ad colour de saphir que est apelé noli me tangere veez si medicine: Bevez en ewe beneite martefelun, egrimoine e morele e la cervele de heranc sor. E pus pernez sel e le moeal de l'oef cru e les batez ensemble e metez sur le felun en lu d'emplastre.

(254) *Item pur felun*: Pernez la petite consoude e solsequie e la teste de harenc sor e les batez ben ensemble e donez a beivere.

(255) Item pur le neir felun: Pernez maroil, si triblez ben, pus metez, mez chaufez le primerement e pus metez tut chaud.

(256) Item autre: Pernez maroil e seim .i. 'sope', si les triblez ensemble, pus metez de l'urine al malade, si eschaufez ben, pus metez tut chaud, si garra ben.

(257) *Item pur felun tuer*: Pernez un bon saphir, si le lavez en ewe beneite e donez a beivere a celui que ad le felun e pus donez li a beivere matefelun. E pernez la teste de heranc sor e le batez e le medlez od celui jus e lui donez a beivre e liez la drache desur le felun e ben garra.

(258) *Item pur felun*: Pernez un charbun de chene e le moal de l'oef e un poi de sel e les batez ben ensemble e metez desus le felun.

(259) Item pernez chenlange e la racine de gletoine e lange de cerf e les triblez od ewe beneite ou od bone servoise e li donez a beivere.

.v.

Ici comence medicine pur rancle

(260) Pernez ache e mel e flur de furment e metez sur, si garra.

[25] MS *felun f. ceste m. de quele vient.*

(261) Item pernez farine de orge e la mye de payn de orge, si boilez en vin ou en eisel, si metez desus.

(262) Item boilez groce farine de aveine e su de motun, si metez.

(263) Item racine de urtye quisez en vin, pus triblez od viel oint de porc.

(264) Item encuntre enflure e rancle: Pernez un esquele e demye [f.46r] de aveine e une esquele de semence de lin e su de motun e .ii. oynons tailez menu e quisez mut ben en eisel, si metez tut chaud.

(265) *Item pur rancle occire*: Pernez la mye de payn de furment od ewe e od gleyre de l'oef, si triblez e metez sur.

(266) Item pernez aloine e tanesye, si triblez od mel e metez sur.

(267) *Item a rancle: Marubium cum vino coque et calidum bibe et cooperi te ut sudes.

(268) *Item marubium et tritici farinam cum vino misce et turtellum superliga et sedabit.

(269) Item pur rancle de femme: Lyetz desur foile de cholet.

(270) Item pernez drap de chaminere e mulez en ewe e metez sur.

(271) Item pernez flur de segle, si en fetez past od le jus de eble e de ceo past fetez .ii. turteus, si les quisez en breses. Pus pernez les myes des crustes si chaudes e lyez sur le mal e kant serra refreidi, si metez un altre e ensi deke vous seiez garri.

(272) Item pernez plaunteine e solsequie e la surele e la parele od les racines e launcelé od sa racine e les foiles de sauz e la [...] de gletonere. Tut ceo triblez forment ensemble, pus quisez en ewe deke a la terce partie e donez al malade a beivere le seir chaud e le matyn freid.

(273) Item encuntre rancle dedeins le cors: Pernez les greyns de genevere e boilez en blanc vin e bevez de ceo le seir chaud e le matin freid.

(274) Item pernez chenlange e boilez en servoise de brais en un noef pot, si le coverez ben que le chalour ne puce issir, e donez al malade a beivere, le seir chaud, le matyn freid.

(275) Item pur rancle: Pernez herbe beneite, ache, e chikenemete owel porciun e friez ensemble od su de motun e metez tut chaud sur la rancle, si garra.

(276) Item quisez bren de furment en espés lyes de vin ou de servoise e medlez ben [f.46v] ensemble e metez sur le mal.

(277) *Item pur rancle de egreté de playe*: Pernez bugle e sanicle e pimpernele e les triblez ensemble, si le donez a beivere al malade e ben eswagera la dolour.

(278) *Item pur emflure de bras e rancle en quele manere que se set*: Pernez le fynte de berbis le plus noveles que vous purrés trover e le medlez od su de motun

e le chaufez ensemble. E pus l'emplastrez sur un drap e metez sur le bras, mes ne coveretz mye la playe ové l'emplastre, mes liez l'emplastre en deus parties deske l'emflure seit eswagé.

(279) Item pernez ache e le triblez, pus le fryez od seim e metez si chaud cum il purra endurer.

(280) Item pernez flur de furment e jus de ache e le quisez od su de motun e liez el emflure.

(281) Item flur de orge ou semence de lin quisez en eisel ou en vin ou en serveise estale e quisez tant cum il deit quire e fetez emplastre e metez tut chaud.

(282) Item flur de furment od un poi de mel occist le rancle sauns countredit.

.x.

Ici commence medicine pur festre e primerement coment homme le conustra de cancre

(283) Pur conustre quel est festre e quel est cancre: Pernez furmage e fetez emplastre, mes primez oignez le mal od mel e pus lyez l'emplastre sur le mal al seir. E l'endemain ostez l'emplastre e si le furmage est entamé, sachez que le cancre ad esté sanz nule doute. Mez pernez bone garde kant vous garderez la playe, car le cancre mange la pel e le fet tut neir e tute la playe, mes festre fet tut autrement, kar la playe fet profundement juste les nerfs e juste le os fet les jointes croysé en travers.

(284) *Pur chaude festre que ad petit pertuz medicine*: Pernez petitz roches e les metez tut vifs en un pot e les ardez tut a poudre. Pus pernez [f.47r] le jus de avence e medlez ensemble e de ceo emplez les pertuz.

(285) *A freide festre covent autre medecine*: Pernez le jus de lancelé e un poi de flur de segle e le aubun de l'oef e encorporez ensemble e metez a la festre. E quant il serra secche, le renovelez e metez.

(286) *Item pur festre e cancre occire e tutes playes curer*: Pernez le oile de moaels de oefs e seim de porc par owele mesure, si medlez a ceo un unce de vert alum e atant de blanc alum e .ii. unces de savun e en ceo moilez les meches, si les metez al mal. E sache[z] trebelement garra.

.y.

Ici comence medicine encuntre cancre

(287) *Encuntre cancre e mortmal*: Pernez la teste del grue e les pes e les entrailes e fetez seccher en un fourn, si fetez pudre e metez sur le mal, e ben garra. Icest poudre est bone a tutes playes.

(288) Item pernez le oef de la geline que est faili desouz lui kant ele avera cuvé e le despessez, si moilez estupes de lin en ceo e metez sur le cancre, si garra.

(289) Item pernez chiverefoil, ceo est 'wodebinde', que crest en haut e lyé, si ad un flur blanc que l'em prent (suchii) que ad a nun ligustrum en latin dunt li auturs dit 'Alba ligustra cadunt / vaccinia nigra leguntur' [Vergil, *Eclog.* 2,18]. Pernez cele herbe, si en fetez jus, si medlez od farine de orge e fetez paste. Pus si pernez furmage frez, si metez primes tut un jour a la cancre. Pus le seir ostez le furmage, si metez cele paste la nuit: si troverez l'endemayn le verm del cancre mort e si est tel cum le verm dedeins une nus, pus si metez autre, kar plusurs verms isserunt.

(290) *Item pur cancre*: Pernez cire virgine demi livre, char de porc chastré .i. livre, ceo est assaver la pece par le pisel, [f.47v] ars en pudre, mel un quart, franc encens .i. livre, .vi. neirs crapaudes sauns meins ars en pudre en un pot de tere que unke ne fut usé, bure fres demi livre. Bulez ewe de funtaine vif e kant est freid cele ewe, lavez ladite bure e metez tut en un pot de tere que unke ne fut usé. E pernez un linge drap quatreble mis ensemble en seli pot e lessez le boiler deke le drap eit assez bu. Pus pernez le drap freid, si le metez a le cancre e ceo le degastera. Pus pernez puliol, rue, sauge, peluete, jubarbe, e atant de warence cum de tutes les autres peisent, e le quisez en un galun de estale servoise deske il seit gasté a un quart, e quant il serra freid, si donez a beivere. Si il seit trop sech, en versez une quantité de mel e lessetz le boiler un poi de hure, pus lui donez.

(291) *Item pur cancre tuer*: Fetez emplastre de oef e metez sur le cancre.

(292) Item pernez poudre de arnement e le triblez od vel oint e fetez boiler en un bacin. Iceo emplastre vaut mut e que il seit mis tut chaud a la maladie.

(293) *Item pur occire cancre a force*: Pernez l'escorche de oser e de freine e neir espine e de chene e de trembler e de pruner e de bolacer e de pomer e lé decopez e les fetez ben boiler tanke il seient quites e que le ewe seit ben espés. E pus pernez le mel e le metez parquire ben e pus fetez emplastre e metez al mal.

(294) Ou fetez autre medicine: Pernez char cru de geline e le metez tut chaud e pus le lavez de cele ewe que vous [troverez] dedeins un trunc que seit chete de pluvie e de cele ewe le fetez nette. E si ne avez cele ewe, pernez ewe de tan, car meinte foiz y ad valu, e le pudre de tan ben ba[f.48r]tu, e jete[z] sur le cancre.

(295) *Item stercus humanum combustum et pulverizatum cancerosos sanat et cancerosa ulcera et omnes putredines corrodit.

(296) *Item beivere pur cancre e pur festre que mut vaut*: Pernez senchun, centorie, avence, bugle, betoigne, peluette, tanesie, calketrappe. Pus pernez la rasure de corn de un vif boef e bure e fetez un beivere e lui donez.

(297) Item pernez un oef de geline e le aubun y metez e sel e su tut owelement e flur de segle e arnement e pudre de verre e orpiment. E sachez que la pudre est mut corrosive e pur ceo occist cancre e festre.

(298) *Item pur cancre*: Pernez la coquile de un oef de geline e le emplez de gros sel e le ardez a poudre e cele poudre vaut cuntre cancre.

(299) Item pernez verre e chaus e de savun e emplez les pertus. Ceo garist cancre e festre ens que il purra nestre.

(300) Item pernez quintefoile, planteine e bure de Mai e un poi de vert de grece, si fetez un oignement e metez sur le mal, si garra ben.

(301) *Autre pur cancre sur mamele de femme*: Pernez novele fienz de berbis e metez sur le cancre e il espurgera e clora.

(302) Item pernez pudre de arnement e vel oint de porc, si triblez forment ensemble e metez l'emplastre desus, si garra.

(303) *Item pur tuer water cancre*: Pernez mel e alum de glace e pudre de peivere e vin egre, de checun de owel porciun, e pus le boilez un poi e plus le colez parmi un drap. E kaunt il serra freid, lavez la maladie ben sovent.

(304) Item pernez herbe Roberd e avence e cerfoile, si les triblez ensemble e les medlez od vinegre. E pus les colez parmi un drap e fetez tener en sa bouche plein esquiler si lungement cum il purra endurer. E ceo face sovent e si la maladye seit en un [f.48v] autre lu que en la bouche, fetez sovent laver.

·ʒ·

Ici comence medicine encontre le mortmal

(305) *Malum mortuum dicitur a quibusdam vulgariter quod sit ex melancolia et nascitur in extremis partibus corporis cuius signa sunt hec: latam habet crustulam et duram cum humiditate et pruritu. Cura hec est: prius materia digesta cum oximelle per .xv. dies utatur. Oximelle illo purgetur, postea cum benedicta, mirra, yeralogodion cum oleo nigro, et hoc facto post tercium diem purgationis stuphentur tibie cum calidis herbis bullitis in vino forti. Postea ungatur cum unguento fusco et unguento ad salsum fleuma simul mixtis et acutis et utroque oleo per .vii. dies cotidie bis.

(306) *Unguentum predictum ad salsum fleuma et ad morpheam: Recipe unguentum ad salsum fleuma, unguentum al[bum] et citri[num] ana uncias .iiii. conmisceantur et acuentur ana cum .ii. dragmis utriusque aluminis

utriusque sulphuris subtilissime pulverizati[26] utriusque auripigmenti[27] [utriusque] staphisagrie utriusque ellebori ana dragmam unam.

(307) *Item ad malum mortuum: Accipe testitudines in forti vino vel lexiva coquantur et illa pinguedo que supernatat accipiatur et tibie inde ungantur.

(308) *Item accipe testas nucum magnarum et pulveriza cum fuligine et stercore caprino et distempera cum sagimine ovorum.

(309) *Item accipe fumum terre[28] et salem assum et distempera cum succo paritarie. Postea terendo et pistando cum auxungia vetustissima fiat emplastrum et calefac super tegulam ad ignem et appone quam calidum paciens poterit uti.

(310) *Item fiat stupha de feniculo et de omni genere petrosilini et de sambuco et ebulo et fimo terre et origano et absinthio et de unguento th[eodericon] sto[machon?], de unguento citrino et fusco et de unguento ad salsum fleuma equaliter et acuatur de utroque alumine [f.49r] et utroque elleboro et utroque sulphure cum uncia .i. de qualibet cera alba, staphisagria, fumum terre, spatulam fetidam, lappam inversam, nigellam equaliter terantur et cum auxungia porcina. Postea pone in olla rudi et appone olium et acetum et per pannum exprime fortiter et de illo fiat unctio precedente stupha.

(311) **Item unguentum contra malum mortuum*: Recipe viridis eris uncias .iii., auxungie veteris uncias .ii., confice et ute.

(312) *Item ad idem: Fortius quod postea debet fieri. Recipe celidonie, lappatii acuti, fumi terre, marubii, omnium succorum ana libram unam, fellis taurini, porcini, yrcini, caprini ana uncias .iiii. vel .iii., uncti veteris libras .iii. et viridis eris uncias .iii. confice et ex hoc unge locum dolentem donec caro putrida cadat per se.

(313) *Item ad idem: Quod ultimo debet fieri et hoc unguentum membrum sanat et carnem novam inducit: Recipe litargirii unciam .i., aceti et olei ana quod sufficit, totum incorporetur et per .ii. vel .iii. dies moveantur in mortario.

(314) Item pernez gros nois e triblez e forment a ceo jetez un poi de pis neir, pus triblez les .ii. ensemble ben, pus metez de vif argent tant cum vous verrez que ben seit. Pus triblez tut ensemble oveke oile de olive e de ceo oignez le mal. E pus metez sur le mal foiles de plaunteine vert. E l'endemain le lavez de ewe chaud e autre fois oignez le mal e fetez cum vous fistez devaunt deske vous seyez garri.

[26] MS pulverizatis.
[27] MS auripigmentum.
[28] MS terram fumi.

(315) Item pur mormal jaune: sauterole uint ov plus une pece del flanc de truye que est en sanc ensemb[l]e ars en poudre e le jus de sperewort .i. libram, archaungele .i. libram ou plus, cire virgine .i. libram, code .i. libram nent fete, demi quart de vin blanc, diaquilon .i. unce, tous mis en un pot de tere e quitz e triblé e le jus de tous mis al mormal. Stoncrop e herbe Water, semen[f.49v]ce de fenoil .i. livre, comyn demi livre mis en un pot od un potel de servoise e boilez a un quart e lui donez freis.

.7.

Ici comence medicine pur le morphé

(316) *Morphea alia est alba, alia nigra, quedam curabilis, quedam non curabilis ut nigra, rubea quoque semper incurabilis. Illius vero que curabilis est hec sunt signa: locus cum acu pungatur et si sanguis purus emanaverit, curabilis est. Si vero appareat alba vel humiditas nigra, incurabilis est.

(317) *Illi igitur que est curabilis tale facimus unguentum quod valet morphee omnis coloris: Recipe tapsie condisi, sinapis, nigelle, seminis radicis piretri, rubee ana dragmas .iii., costi, coloquintide, ellebori nigri, capparis .i. denarium, staphisagrie, vitri ana dragmam .i. et semis, euforbii dragmam .i., scamonee, salis armoniaci, sandarice, ameos, ana dragmas .ii. Fac pulverem temperans cum aceto et ungatur eo.

(318) *Item medicine bone pur morphé*: Pernez argoil, si le metez sur nettes charbons ben alumez, si ardez ben le argoil deke il devient tut blanc. Pus les triblez en un morter de fust. Si le destemprez od bon vinegre ensi que il seit ben espés e que le argoil eit le mestrie. Pus le metez tut ensemble en un poket de canevas e le pendez sus e metez desoutz un vessel de arein ou de verre que puce receivere le licour que issera hors de ceo poket de canevas. E de ceo licour lavez e oignez le mal ou que il seit e ceo sovent nut e jour .iii. foitz ou .iiii. deske vous seiez garri.

(319) Item pernez deuté un quart e .iii. deners peisaunt de coperose e le fetez ben moudre. Pus meslez oveke le deuté e de ceo oignez le morphé, pus metez desus cotun ou leine.

.1.

Ici comence medicine pur jauniz, contra ictericiam .i. jauniz

(320) *Recipe rasuram [f.50r] eboris et da pacienti bibere in vino vel servisia.

(321) *Item accipe fimum aucarum et distempera cum servisia vel vino

et da pacienti bibere. Probatum est.

(322) *Item bibet frequenter succum urtice, absinthii, apii, arthemesie, que mater herbarum dicitur, vel semen earum cum vino vel servisia.

(323) *Item accipe de radice asperime urtice et tere bene et cum aqua succum inde exprime et bibe sicque solucionem habebis et galmum(?) expelles.

(324) *Item accipe feniculum et plantaginem maiorem, celidoniam et rasuram eboris et crocum et tempera cum urina pacientis et bibat per .iii. dies vel .v.

(325) Item donez un unce de betoigne en vin teve.

(326) Item bevez celidonie en blanc vin.

(327) Ou lavez .iii. foitz le cors od le ewe ou aloine seit eins quit.

(328) Item pernez grecam urticam od planteine, si le destemprez od sa propre urine, si lui donez a beivere.

(329) Item pernez la racine de la parele e la triblez, si la destemprez od sa urine de meme, si lui donez a beivere nuit e jour, si garra ben.

(330) Item lui donez a beivere la aspre urtie destempré od estale servoise par .iii. jours, c'est asaver le primer jour .ix. sumetes, le .ii. jour .vi., e le .iii. jour .iii. triblé e destempré od servoise estale, e garri est.

(331) Item pernez le maroil chenu e celidoine e les triblez ben, pus pernez de la urine al malade a beivere par .ix. jours.

.2.
Hic incipit medicina contra lapidem

(332) *Accipe sanguinem hircinum recentem, sed oportet esse plene etatis qui occidendus est scilicet .iiii. annorum nec plus nec minus. Et antequam occidatur oportet ut comedat folia feniculi et edere ut sanguis sit boni odoris. Ego autem Ypocras huic sanguini hircino mirice tertiam partem sicque eis dedi qui nimios paciebantur dolores et qui nullatenus [f.50v] poterant facere urinam magnitudine lapidis et accepta pocione mox conminutos proiecit lapides cum urina et confestim pocionem bibendo minutatim proiectus est lapis nec ulterius permissi sunt renasci. Anodi .i. minutissima hec potio dicitur quia et lapides minuit et alios generari non permittit.

(333) *Item accipe urinam verris et fac duos focos, unum ad dextrum latus et alium ad sinistrum infirmi. Et postquam calefactus fuerit nimium adhuc jacenti inter focos dabis bibere urinam illam infirmo qui pro magnitudine lapidis urinam omnino facere non potest qui lapidem statim proiciet per menbrum in partes confractum.

(334) **Item ad lapidem in vesica*: Sanguinem leporis super tegulam coque et fac inde pulverem et pellem ipsius tende diligenter et desicca ad focum et de illis pilis fac pulverem, et de pelle similiter si potes, et pulverem de auripigmento, scalam mangne nucis plenam, et similiter de sulphure. Postea in testa ovi conspersa de forti aceto da[29] bibere et si vis probare, mitte cilicem in ipsam potionem et statim confringetur.

(335) *Item folia tenera ebuli trita et cum vino potata calculum expellit.

(336) *Item gromilium et petrosilum et rubeam urticam et nucleum de petra serasi tere simul et distempera cum medone vel servisia et da ad bibendum donec convalescat.

(337) **Item ad calculum virorum vel mulierum*: Urina de hirco tepefacta coclear plenum viro jejuno dabis. Si mulier fuerit, urinam de capra dabis. Et tantum valet presens remedium ut continuo lapides frangantur.

(338) *Item baccas edere in vino tritas bibe diebus .iiii. mane et sero.

(339) **Item ad lapidem*: Sanguinem vulpis recentem super pubem lini, lapidem in vesica frangit et per urinam foras proicit. Si vis probare, sangui[f.51r]nem vulpis super aliquem lapidem pone. Statim frangitur.

(340) **Item ad petras frangendas que in vesica fuerint*: Saxifragii semen .i. silvaticum, milio .d. .ii., castorei .d. .ii., mirre .d. .ii., hec omnia musa et cribrata cum melle distillato, hec collige et in vase vitreo repone et cum nocte fuerit, accipe et inde quantum nucis avellane magnitudo est distemperes. Sed qua hora accipere vis in balneo sive ad solem, calidum plenum coclear bibat. Post balneum super renes panset, deinde caballo birro caballizet.

(341) *Item lini seminis solidum .i. pensatum bene triti, adde mel coclear .i., tere fortiter et fac potionem et cum vino tepido dabis bibere.

(342) **Item ad petram in vesica frangendam*: Lac caprinum bibe calidum cum mulsum fuerit, aut tepidum fac ad ignem statim enim ut bibitur. Lapidem frangit et urinam expellit.

(343) **Item medicina pro lapide*: Accipe sanguinem hirci et lac de alba capra et acetum et gromilium tritum et atramentum equali mensura et mitte in vesica apri ac coque vitellam ut spissa sint omnia que in vesica sunt. Et distempera unciam in aqua tepida et bibe mane jejunus et cibis utere quasi accepisses potionem.

(344) **Item ad lapides frangendos et eiciendos*: Recipe feniculi dragmas .iii., seminis alexandri ad duplum, canele ad duplum duorum precedentium, petrosilii domestici dragmas .ii., milii solis .i., gromil ad quantitatem omnium, liquiricie unciam semis. Fiat pulvis et detur in potu.

[29] MS *et da*.

(345) **Item ad petram in vesica*: Recipe apium, feniculum, et petrosilium cum radicibus eorum et foliis, eas fortiter in aqua coque, da bibere jejuno.

(346) Item quisez ben mave e aloine ensemble en bon vin deske a la terce partie.

(347) *Item lactucam cum vino veteri bibe.

(348) Item pernez gromil, rouge urtie e persil, semence de fenoil e peivere e fetez un beivere ben boili en vin. E metez [f.51v] la pudre e la pel de levere ars en un noef pot e fetez boiler oveke les choses susdites.

(349) Item pernez la racine de radich e tranchés .lix. petite peces a la grant de un dener e metez les en mel e les usez par .ix. jours en ceste manere: le primer jour mangez .ix., le secund .viii., le terce jour .vii. pus .v. pus .iiii. En tele manere les devez abatre.

(350) Item pernez .ix. bayes de yere e braez e destemprez od vin e donez a beivere.

(351) *Item ad eos qui sanguinem mingunt: Bibat quinquefolium distemperatum cum aqua frigida.

(352) Item quisez la teste de ail od tute la racine en ewe deske a la terce partie.

(353) Item bevez la tere de nis de arundes od ewe chaude.

Incipiunt medicine pro febribus

.3.

(354) *Pur fevre ague*:
Pur[30] le rethour de fevere ague
Que sa chalour auques remue
Si lui doint homme fumitere a beivere
Ky le mal dechace e deceivere.
Qi la senechun beivera
Ja pus ne recherra.
Ky lui durra pur le retour
De consoude beivere le flour,
Pus le suour,[31] si il boit aprés,
Il ne recharra jamez,
Ou la semence de parele
Ben garist male e femele.

[30] MS *Pus*.

[31] MS sucur.

.4.

(355) *Uncore autre*
A homme que ad fevere ague
Ce est le retour kaunt homme sue,
Il deit jus de alisaundre beivere,
Par taunt purra l'em parseivere,
Se il sue ben, si deit garir, [f.52r]
Si nun, fort lui est le suffrer.
Ky dunke avereit ewe rose,
Iceo lui serreit bone chose
Laver ses temples e sun frunt,
Le pouz, les jointes que unkes sunt
Pur la suour que homme deit oster
E les pores desestoper
E fere la suour issir
Ke ein[s] ne poit hors venir.

.5.

(356) *Uncore autre*
Si prenge foile de pecher,
Peirer, pruner, e seriser,
En ewe fetez boiler
E pus ses pes dedeins tener.

(357) *Uncore autre*
Ou emplastre lui vaudra
Pur le grant chalour que il a:
Prenge flur de orge ben passé,
Plaunteine, jubarbe e la faucé
E cherville, hennebane ensement
E la morele owelement.
Le flur de ceux pestelez
Sur un drap linge e cochez,
A le destre part le devez mettre
Sur la feye, si dit la lettre.

.6.

(358) *Pur fevere terceine*
Ben sai que la fevere terceine

Mut malement plusours demeine,
Beive .iii. plauntes de plaunteine
Devaunt les accés, si ert seine,
Treis al matin e treis al seir, [f.52v]
Nef jours si il vodra saunté avoir.

.7.

(359) *A fevere cotidiene*: Pernez un oef que seit ben quit e versez hors un petit de l'aubun e fetez une femme que norist enfant male deguter .iii. gutes de sun let en le aubun e fetez le malade beivere, que il ne sache quei ceo est.

(360) Item a fevere terceine: Quilez .iii. plauntes de plaunteine aprés le rescunce de solail e dite[s] .iii. Pater Noster e .iii. Ave Maria en quilant, si li donez a beivere a comencement de l'accés.

(361) Item bevez le jus de betoine e ne usez nule autre chose icé jour.

(362) Item pernez .iii. oistes de moster e en la une escrivez iceo + el + eloy + sabaoth +, e en l'autre + adon + ay + alpha + messias +, e en la terce + pastor + agnus + on +. E donez al feverous a beivere en ewe beneite, si garra.

(363) Item pernez .iii. oistes e escrivez en la primer + Pater est alpha et omega + e la crois devant e aprés, e en la secunde + Filius est vita +, e en la terce + Spiritus Sanctus sit tibi remedium +. E ne obliez la crois devant e aprés.

(364) Item pernez jus de ache e de fenoil par owele mesure, si lui donez a beivere par .iii. jours. E fetez li garder diete de rost e de vin e de autres charjauntes viaundes.

(365) Item pernez un herbe que est apelé palma Christi e la destemprés od vin, si le donez al malade a beivere par .ix. jours.

.8.

(366) Item ceo est le experiment a cuntesse Mareschal encuntre fevere: Pernez .iii. oblés e escrivez en l'un 'qualis Pater alpha et omega', e en l'autre 'talis Filius vita', e en la terce 'talis [f.53r] Spiritus Sanctus remedium'. E donez le primer en le comencement de l'accés e l'autre .i. le secund en le secund accés, e le terce en le terce accés. E dye checune foitz .iii. Pater Noster e .iii. Ave Maria, si garra.

(367) *Item pur quarteine*: Pernez pudre de sené e pudre de sauge, de chescun demi unce, e seient medlé od ewe chaude ou od servoise. E donez a beivere le matin prochain aprés le accés e issera a chaumbre .ii. foitz. E en la secund accés il n'avera point de freid, ou si il ad, poi en avera. E dunke autre foitz

li seit doné le matin aprés le secund accés e n'avera pas la terce accés. E si rien seit, donez lui autre foitz en meme la quarteine, si garra, kar prové est.

(368) Item autre: Le pacient ou autre en sun noun isce hors le vespre en tens cler kaunt le firmament est esteilé e garde(z) sus a les esteiles. E sitost cum il verra une esteile, ausi tost dye en cheaunt cesti psalme *Deus in nomine tuo* [*Ps*.53,3] e Pater Noster e Ave Maria e pus ne lui grevera la quarteine.

(369) *Item pur terceine*: Aprés la terce accés pernez un herbe que est apelé nimpha aquatica e seit triblé e mis sur le pouz de ambesdeux bras e lyé devant le accés.

(370) Item pernez la racine de yreos .i. glajol .i. unce, seit secché e pudré e destempré od vin e od ewe mellé, si le bevez sovent .ii. hures devant le accés, si garrez.

(371) *Item autre*: Pernez aloine e plaunteine e sauge par owele mesure e mettez boiler en vin blanc une bone espace e donez a boivere al malade bone porciun checun jour jun .ix. jours.

.9.
Hic incipit medicina pro ydropisi

(372) Pur freide ydropisie: Pernez un herbe que ad nun muge dé bois .i. 'woderove' en engleis, si le fetez quire en estale servoise, si le bevez .ix. jours ou plus. Si mester est, [f.53v] mangez kersuns de funtaine.

(373) *Item pur ydropesie*: Pernez racine de eble, si la estampez ben. Pus pernez le jus e le me[tez] en un vessel e le lessez ensi estre une pece tanque il seit assis. E quant il serra asis, ostez ceo que il ad de cler e le metez en un autre vessel e le espés que remeindra quisez en une paele. Pus fetez un grant fu e un lit encost le fu. Pus fetez le malade oster tous ces draps e gesir desus ceo lit. Pus pernez le jus espés que vous avez quit, si oignez tut le corps del malade, si le gardez ben de freid. Aprés pernez treis esquilers de le jus cler e i metez de bure ou de seim a la mountaunce de la quarte partye del jus. E pus pernez .xl. greins de peivere e une racine de gingivere bone, si le molez tut a pudre. Pus metez le jus que est medlé oveke la bure quire un petit e kaunt serra un petit quit, ostez le de fu. Pus i metez vos pudres avauntdites, si li donez a beivere tedve e ensi fetez par .iii. jours si mester est. E gardez que il eit une cele percee prés de lui, kar il avera soluciun e vomite.

(374) *Item pur freide ydropesie*: Pernez archaungele .i. 'blinde nettle', stonore[32]

[32] MS stomere.

e lorele, betoine, turmentille, herbe beneite, saxifragie, gamalie, feliure, foile de coudre, þe rode[33] de honi-pere tre, hayrive, violete grant, gyngivere, plaunteine, weybrode, launcelé, egremoine. Metez les tous en un vessel e les quisez ensemble. E metez le homme en un estu[v]e ne pas trop chaud e le estuez checun jour. E pernez un galun de blanc vin e demi unce de clous e ataunt de canele e tant de gingivere, si les quisez ensemble deske il seient demi gasté, si lui donez a beivere le matin chaud e le seir freid.

[f.54r] (375) Item pernez fumetere e quisez la ben en servoise estale e [don]ez a beivere matin e seir, e ben garra.

(376) *Pur chaude ydropesie*: Pernez un quart de vin blanc e demi unce del plus prés escorche de ellerne, turmentille .ii. unces, a[..]ouse .iii. livre, saxifrage .ii. unces, peluete demi livre, jubarbe .ii. unces, wort douce .i. galun e que ele seit fet de brez de orge. E metez tut ceo en un pot de tere e quisez les herbes oveke le wort tanque il seit demi gasté. Pus i metez le vin e le lessez un petit boiler ensemble. Pus le colez parmi un net drap e le bevez a matin chaud e al seir freis.

(377) Item pur ydropesie: Pernez la racine de lilie e destemprés od bon vin, si fetez beivere le quart jour, si ert segurs.

(378) Item pernez le jus de cressuns de funtaine e porrez owelement e done[z] al malade a beivere, e garra par tens.

(379) Item pernez endive, letuse e petite morele owelement e les triblez ben ensemble e les fetez quire en bon servoise estale e le lessez desque il seit ben refreidi. Pus pernez gingivere, galingale, grein de Parys, clous, macis, quibibes, de checun demi unce ben pudré, pus les quisez en vin blanc, mes nun pas trop, kar il est chaud de lui mesmes, e ceo donez a beivere al malade kaunt il avera talent e nun pas autrement.

(380) Item pernez la racine de gladene e donez al malade checun jour a manger ou a beivere le peis de .ii. deners que mut vaut desque il seit garri.

(381) Item pernez cressuns de ewe e fetez potage od grece de porc ou fetez vert sauce.

(382) Item pernez chardon .i. 'souethistel' un bon partie e le triblez ben e premez hors le jus e donez le malade a beivere chescun jour, e ben garra.

(383) Item pernez le jus de cressuns de ewe [f.54v] e boilez sur le fu e l'escumez ben e nettement e donez al malade a beivere sovent, e ben garra.

[33] MS rerode.

.10.

Hic incipit tractatus de speciebus lepre et quibus nominibus vocentur

*Ex corruptis humoribus lepra consurgit in corpore, unde sicut .iiii. sunt humores, ita et quatuor sunt eius species videlicet allopicia, elefancia, leonina, tiriasis. Est autem allopicia de fleumate et vulpi assimilatur quia quemadmodum vulpes depilantur, sic qui hanc speciem habent pati consueverunt. Elefancia autem fit ex sanguine. Ab elefante sic nominatur, quia sicut elephans omnibus animalibus maior existit, ita et sanguis maior est aliis humoribus. Leonina autem fit ex colera naturali et dicitur sic a leone quia [ut] ceteris animalibus calidior esse iudicatur, ita et hec passio aliis calidior esse prohibetur, vel quia ut leo varius est colore, ita et hec in suis est variata. Tyriasis autem fit ex melancolia que tyro assimilatur, nam sicut tyrus per compressionem et confricacionem spolium amittit, ita isti cum tali humore paciantur tota die simul se scalpere et confricare desiderant. Quibus hoc unguentum facimus.

(384) **Unguentum ad elefanciam*: Recipe saponis gallici uncias .iiii., picule libram .i., cere uncias .iiii., semp[er]vive, farine lupinorum amarorum et siliginis[34] ana uncias .iiii., succus vitis uncias .iii., panis porcini uncias .iii., succi fumiterre uncias .iii., auxungie pernecis uncias .iii., olibani et capitelli quod sufficit, conmisce sic omnia in vase fictili, ad ignem pone. Preterea que teri debeant terantur quousque liquefiant et liquefactis ceram adde. Deinde pulverem terendorum pone et sic tepide juxta ignem omni die usque ad .vii. diem eo paciens ungatur et post ad balneum eat et abluatur ut consuevit. Cumque hoc factum fuerit, post tercium diem testi[f.55r]culi abscidantur et paulo inter humerum et cubitum ubi frons dicitur coquantur et supra utramque auriculam in frontibus [ponantur]. Valet aut[em] hoc unguentum contra elefanciam.

(385) **Unguentum contra allopiciam.* Contra allopiciam tale unguentum fiat: Recipe piperis, sulphuris, vini ana uncias .iii., piretri unciam .i., olei fialam .i., succi porri, saponis gallici libram .i. Confice sic: pulverizanda terantur et cum oleo bulliant, deinde terantur, saponem adde et conmisce et parum dissolvantur ad ignem. Sed prius lanuginem ubi est abradas, poste[a] cum lana fortiter frica et ad balneum pergat paciens et eum in sicco balneo diligenter inungas et in eo sudet. Et sic de tercio in tercium diem faciat donec sanus existat et sic semper abrasus existat.

(386) **Item unguentum contra pustulas qui solent fieri in faciebus leprosorum*: Recipe unguentum ad salsum fleuma quartum .i. et cum hoc .i. unguenti

[34] MS suliginis

citrini ponantur dragmas .iii., pulveris plumbi usti, picis liquide, pulveris litargirii ana uncias .ii.

(387) **Item unguentum contra fissuras et foramina que solent fieri in leprosis*: Recipe litargirii, plumbi usti ana uncias .ii., confice cum aceto et oleo apponendo nunc de aceto nunc de oleo parum alternatum.

(388) **Item unguentum ad mundificationem cutis*: Recipe lupini, amigdalarum dulcium excortica[ta]rum, seminis eruce .i. alba sinapis anglice 'hwit mustard-sed', stercoris soricis, seminis melonis, costi, fabe fracte, nitri, lentis mundate, aluminis, gummi arabici ana [...], pulverizentur et conficiantur cum aqua rosata et albumine ovi et pauco aceto.

(389) *Item pro allopicia*: Pernez la fente de chat e mel e grein de mustarde e lé destemprez od vin egre, si fetez emplastre, e verrement garra.

(390) *Item pur elefantin*: Pernez la belette, si trahez le sanc, pus ardez le cors e fetez pudre. E destemprez cele pudre od le sanc e od fort vinegre, si oignez le cors.

(391) *Pur mal dé reins*: [f.55v] Pernez la racine de la gletonere e la triblez ben e versez sur servoise u vin e bevez le freid al matin e chaud al seir.

(392) Item versez ben chenlange e morele en servoise en un noef pot e bevez al seir chaud e la matin freid.

(393) U fra quiture desus les garez.

.12.[35]

(394) *Pur les glaundres oster*: Fetez cendrez de trus de cholet e temprés od mel, si en oignez le mal sovent.

.13.

(395) *Pur oster pules e lendes*: Fetez cendre de l'aniz salvage e medlez od olie e oignez le cors sovent.

(396) Ou pernez rue, si la triblez ben, e de jus vous oignez ou cors ou teste, e ceo les osterad.

(397) Ou la cendre[36] de l'anis salvage od seim de owe e od vif argent, si vous en oignez.

.14.

(398) *Pur oster roine*: Pernez fumitere, si le lavez e le destemprez od servoise ou od vin, si la bevez sovent.

[35] Chapter 11, on kidney ailments according to the opening list of chapters, is missing.

[36] MS *ceindre.*

.15.

(399) *Encuntre mangue e degrature*: Pernez la rouge parele e ostez la racine, si la triblez od bure de May e od vel oint de porc. Pus culez parmy un drap, si vous en oignez ben al fu.

.16.

(400) *Pur fer ou espine que el cors saili*: Pernez egrimoine, si la triblez od vel oint; ou diptaine metez en la playe ou bevez la ou mangez la.

.17.

(401) *Pur estancher sanc medicine esprové*: Triblez ben les foiles de alne, si les metez e ceo mesmes estaunche la gutefestre si il eyt a ceo sel e urtie.

(402) Ou bevez le jus de sincfoile.

(403) Ou bevez ache, si frotez ben le frunt od ceo e ceo est encuntre le cours dé narils.

.18.

(404) *Encuntre la pere medicine verraye*: Bevez la tere del ny de l'arunde od ewe chaude, si garra.

.19./.20.

(405) *A femme que travayle de sun ventre*: Pernez ditayne, si la triblez ben, si li donez a beivere. Si l'enfaunt seit [f.56r] mort dedeins le ventre, donez lui a beivere ysope od ewe chaude e tost le gettra fors.

.21.

(406) *Encuntre ceo que leit defaut a femme*: Pernez cristal, si en fetez pudre, si lui donez a beivere od leit.

.22.

(407) Ore pur saver del malade lequel il deit vivere ou nun: Pernez un oef que est pount mesme le jour que il enmaladist, si escrivez desur cestes letres + .d. e .go.s.p.r.x.g.y.x. e q.e. Pus metez le oef hors encuntre le cel savement e l'endemeyn le despecés e si sanc en ist, yl mura, si nun, il garra.

.23.

(408) *Qui ad le pomun malade*: Use noys mugate e si il eit taunt del pomun enter que il poreyt mettre une agule, yl garra.

.24.

(409) *Qi ad brisure sanz playe*: Yl deyt bayner e mettre en le bayn lemke e walwort e pus trere hors la membre ou le mal est e oyndre la de mel e pus remettre la en le bayn e ensi deque il seit tut las. Pus aprés fere une emplastre de mel e de cire e de sui e de oynt de porc madle e encens e vyn e piz e walwort e lemke e ache e fere ben quire e fere dunque l'emplastre e mettre a la dolour.

.25.

(410) **Pro quibuscumque brisuris sanguineis ad cito sanandum*: Recipe folia sambuci .i. 'ellerne' et terantur minute et cum albumine ovi misceantur et sic cum tota pressura foliorum apponatur loco leso et statim sanabitur.

.26.

(411) **Ad maturandum apostema*: Recipe ossa bovis vel equi vel cuiuscumque quadrupedis assata et pulverizata et misce cum auxungia porcina et calida superpone et cito maturabitur. Probatum est.

.27.

(412) **Propter adustionem*: Recipe ache multum, fencresses multum, consoude, senchun, hove, crop de rouge[37] urtye e de rouge cholet, herneles cum butiro [f.56v] recenti et sepo ovino conmisceantur simul et ungatur locus adustus et cito sanabitur.

.28.

(413) **Ad occidendum felun ubicumque fuerit*: Accipe linguam canis, radicem gletonie et cerlange et tere cum aqua vel servisia et da ei bibere.

.29.

(414) **Propter unum wenne quando primo crescit*: Frica cum plumbo donec calefiat plumbum.

.30.

(415) **Ad inflacionem virge virilis ex calore coytus*: Recipe folia salicis et coquantur in aqua et balneetur virga in ea, deinde circumligentur folia vel semen lini coquatur cum foliis malve cum quibus pistatis cathaplasmetur.

[37] MS route.

.31.

(416) *Pur podagre*: Pernez l'escorche de truis de rouge cholet e triblez le ben e pernez jus de charduns e eisel e metez ensemble e bevez vin.

.32.

(417) *Pur homme que pert la parole sodeinement*: Donez li a beyvere jus de fenoil triblé od eisel e le jus metez en ces narils.

.33.

(418) *Pur teine oster*: Pernez fente de columb triblé en vin egre, ceo oste la teyne.

.34.

(419) **Contra omnem tumorem et inflationem*: Arthemesia .i. mater herbarum, allea et plauntago et radix wimalve bene trita et mixta cum uncto porcino veteri ad modum emplastri superponantur calida. Vel ista trita cum vino potentur.

(420) *Item fiat emplastrum de succo apii, plantaginis et mica panis frumenti.

(421) *Item savina trita cum melle superponatur.

.35.

(422) **Contra ulcum qui nascitur iuxta oculos vel in naribus et capite*: Fiat unguentum de succo apii, rute, plantaginis, betonice, cerusce, oleo rosarum, oleo olive et aceto et inde ungatur vel fiat emplastrum per .ix. dies de succo plantaginis cum molli lana vel lino.

(423) *Item contere vel coque violam, absinthium, plantaginem, rutam cum aceto, melle, oleo olive vel roseo et inde perunge.

.36.

(424) **Ad pulmonem*: Fiat decoctio apii, [f.57r] urtice, rute, viole, abrotani, ysopi cum melle vel ungatur oleo in quo ista cocta sunt. Valent eciam allea cruda vel cocta in lacte.

.37.

(425) **Contra pediculos et lendes*: Lava corpus tuum cum succo rute et absinthii et cadent vermes.

.38.

(426) **Contra morbum caducum*: Utatur plauntagine.

(427) *Item pocio viole cum aqua vel vino et maxime in pueris.

(428) *Item decoctio betonice cum melle vel vino.

.39.

(429) **Contra adustionem*: Succus plantaginis cum albumine ovi.

(430) *Item viola trita.

.40.

(431) **Ad menstrua provocanda*: Valet arthemesia bene trita cum vino et potata.

(432) *Vel urtica ligetur per noctem super alvum et abrotanus et absinthium bibitum cum melle.

(433) *Item potio rute et salvie cum melle vel vino tepido.

(434) *Item savina trita vel cocta cum vino frequenter sumpta.

.41.

(435) *Entrete pur apostume e emflure que vient de curs*: Pernez oint de porc e su de motun frez e franc encens, piz, rosin, cyre virgine, de checun pernez owele mesure. Pus pernez quatre herbes .i. orpin, avence, aloigne, egremoine, si les triblez ben e metez eins vos gummes avauntdites e lessez ben boiler e a tret. E aprés seit colé e quant il freid est, ostez le ordure que vous troverez desoutz, ceo est a dire la lye.

.42.

(436) *Emplastre pur saker fer ou espine ou ceste ou autre chose hors de playe*: Pernez la racine de rosel, si la triblez ben en un morter e metez mel e taunt la brusez que a gresce seit turné. Pus le metez sur un linge drap auque espés e dunque seit mis sur playe, kar l'emplastre est de tele force que sovent ad l'em trové l'espine dehors la playe desus l'emplastre.

.43.

(437) *Oynement pur palesye*: Celi que est feru de parlesye face sei oignement de tous chaud oignement [f.57v], ceo est a saver de marciaton, agrippe, oile laurin, arrogon, asa fetida e dunque seyent tous ben medlez outre le fu. E aprés seit mis a ceo la pudre de castorie e de euforbe e de soufre vif.

.44.

(438) *Encuntre rupture quant les boeals sunt avalez en la quice*: Metez le malade en un bayn e fetez lui trere sus les boeals en lur lu ou deivent estre e bendez les ben de un drap linge duz. Pus pernez frescon, confirie, osmunde, menu consoude, e brusez ben en un morter e destemprez le od novele servoise e donez al pacient a beivere en sun bain. Isci le fetez .v. jours, ceo est a saver checun jour une foitz. E garde sei de femme .ii. moys e garde sey que il ne beive trop e que il se tygne en repos sans travail.

.45.

(439) *Autre beivere*: Fetez le pacient trere sus ses boels, pus pernez l'entrus de l'ulmentel, que est apelé 'elm' en engleis, e triblez le. Pus le destemprez od novele servoise e donez al pacient checun jour .iii. foitz al matin jun aprés manger e al seir quant il irra dormer e fetez le bayner sovent e gisir en pes jour e nut. E ceo face .xv. jours.

.46.

(440) *Beivere a homme forsené*: Pernez genciane e la semence de rue, si les quisés ben en vin egre vermail fort e donez al pacient a beivere. E pus seit la teste rese e un neir cok mis desus fendu tot chaud e seit lyé al chief un jour e une nuit e al terce jour seit seigné en la frunt dé .ii. vein[e]s.

(441) Item pernez averoine e solsequie e les triblez ben en un morter. Pus les destemprez od blanc vin e donez al malade a beivere .v. jours.

(442) Cestes herbes sunt bones as boces e feluns destrure e tutes autres emflure quant il comencent primes a mover: Solsequie [f.58r] od sa flur, morele od sa baye .i. 'nizteschode', matefelun, columbine. Racine de pele enverse vaut as bubons.

.47.

(443) **Ad capillos crescendos ubi volueris*: Coque malvas cum radicibus vehementissime et de ipsa aqua capud lavetur vel locus ubi volueris ut pili nascantur.

.48.

(444) *A fere chevelure lunge*: Pernez le uy que crest al fou, si le quisez mult en blanc vin ou en servoise, si en oignez le chef primerement un poi e aprés si le lavez de ceo sovent.

.49.

(445) *Uncore esprove si le malade deit garir ou nun*: Oynez ses plauntes de pees od lard e pus jetez le lard a un chen, si il le mange, si vivera le malade, si nun, si murra.

.50.

(446) **Ad pediculos et lendes*: Perunge capud tuum beta viridi, mox cadent.

(447) *Item ruta trita cum oleo capud frica et calefac corpus et unge.

(448) Item fetez cendre de vine savage e medlez od oile, si ly oignez le cors ben sovent e ceo oste pules e lenti(l)s.

(449) Item triblez ben la rue, si oignez sovent le chef del jus.

(450) Item medlez ensemble la cendre de la vyne savage e oint de owe e vif argent, si oignez la teste.

(451) *Item de ruta cum melle trita corpus perunge.

(452) *Item cum felle vituli capud perunge.

(453) *Item succum raphani bibe.

.51.

(454) *Uncore si fer ou fust seit sayli en le cors ou en le pee ou aylours*: Triblez la dytaine e metez la u la playe ert, si en bevez. Ou mangez de la ditayne.

(455) Item triblez la polipodie .i. 'evervarn' de chene od vel oint de porc e lyez sur la playe e tost en istera queqe seit dedeins.

.52.

(456) **Ad sanguinem stringendum*: Scribe in fronte de eodem sanguine 'Sanguis Christi venam defluentem stringat'.

(457) *Vel urticam tritam od arcyl mixtam ustula[f.58v]tam superpone.

(458) *Aut fimum ovis cum aceto tritum et calefactum pone super venas.

(459) *Aut bibe succum apii.

.53.

(460) **Ad partum mortuum eiciendum*: Vervene succum cum aqua frigida bibat et mox liberabitur.

(461) *Item satureyam cum semine suo bibe.

.54.

(462) **Medicine esprové a femme que travayle d'enfaunt*: In nomine Patris et Filii et Spiritus Sancti, Amen. Sancta Maria, vera Mater et vera Virgo, verum

infantem genuit peperitque Jesum Christum + Elizabet + Johannem Baptistam sine dolore + ita + tu .N. per ipsum Jesum Christum + infantem tuum pareas + Deus + deorum + et Dominus locutus est et vocavit terram + Christus vincit + Christus regnat + Christus imperat + Christus famulam suam ab omni dolore defendat et infans Christus te vocat ut nascas + A + g + l + a + In nomine Patris + et Filii + et Spiritus + Sancti + Amen + sator + arepo + tenet + opera + rotas + et fac eam portare mugwort et liga istud breve ad dextrum femur interius littera exterius versa et videas ut deponas breve ab ea cum festinatione quam cito infans natus fuerit et facias illud cremari.

.55.

(463) *Encuntre parlesye*: Pernez la racine de pioyne e de fenoil e de peresil e de amer foil, totes seyent quit ensemble jekes a les .ii. partyes, si usez ceo beyvere, e ben garrez.

.56.

(464) *Pur menbre endormye*: Pernez la furmye od tute la tere, si metez en un drap linge e le quisez tant que cele ewe seit blaunche e de cele ewe lavez sovent la menbre, si garra.

.57.

(465) *A saver si homme seit mesel ou nun*: Pernez la foile de cholet e metez en sa urine tute une nuit. L'endemayn pernez la sus e si y aperunt greins en la foile, il est mesel, si nun, sein est.

.58.

[f.59r] (466) *A homme que pert la parole*: Triblez .iii. racines de rouge urtye, si destemprez e li donez a beivere.

(467) Ou pernez chenlange e destemprez od servoise, si li donez a beivere.

(468) Ou de ewe ou maroil seit eins quit.

(469) Ou beve centorie od ewe chaude.

.59.

(470) *A homme que ne put tener sa urine*: Pernez les ungles de chevere, si les ardez a pudre, si bevez sovent de ceo.

(471) Ou mangez ungles de porc ars en pudre ou bevez.

(472) Item bevez le entrerus de la neire espine, si garrez.

.60.

(473) *Pur esprover si ceux que ne poyunt dormer murrunt ou nun*: Pernez la chenilé, si la triblez od le jus de la mente e lyez al frunt de celi que ne put dormer e si il ne dort, yl murra. Probatum est.

.61.

(474) **Qui dormiendo loquitur*: Bibat abrotanum cum aceto.

.62.

(475) **Ad verucas tollendas*: Agrimonia cum aceto trita verucas frica et siccabunt.

(476) Item triblez solsequie od sel e metez sus.

(477) *Item accipe urinam canis et sanguinem muris et misce simul et unge.

.63.

(478) *A homme roynous*: Lavez la royne de l'ewe ou maroil seit einz quit.

.64.

(479) *Pur arsure*: Destemprez aloine od eysel, si oignez le arsure e la dolour s'en irra.

(480) Item la pudre de orge arse e destempré od le blanc de l'oef sayne tost.

.65.

(481) *Pur ydropesie*: Donez lui a beivere centorie e ail quit en vin.

(482) U li donez a beivere planteine destempré od ewe chaude ou a manger vache ou betoyne od vin ou ysope.

.66.

(483) *Item pur chaud ydropesie*: Pernez turmentille, 'horoune', 'houndestonge' e les triblez ensemble ben. E pus les fetez quire en un galun de bon vin tanque il seit la moité gasté. E pus le colez parmi un drap e bevez checun jour matyn un bon porciun de ceo. [f.59v] Devers le seir beverez un autre beverage que sera fet en ceste manere. Pernez un galoun de jus de plantaine e le metez en un novele pot de tere. Pus pernez un drap linge e lyez sur le pot e metez dé cendrez sur le drap ben espés e gardez que le drap ne touche le jus que est en le pot. E pus le fetez boiler outre le feu tanque la moité de

jus seit gasté. Pus le colez ben parmi un drap e gardez que les cendres ne touchent le licour que est boili en nule manere. E de ceo bevez le seir quant vous irrez cocher.

(484) Item pernez le jus de cressuns de funtaine taunt cum vous purrez aver e de ceo lavez tut le cors enterement .ii. foitz le moys e usez cestes choses e serrez mout amendez.

.67.

(485) **Ad eos qui sunt nimis grassi*: Feniculum frequenter bibant.

[–]

(486) **Ne sis ebriosus*: Betonicam comede vel bibe.[38]

.68.

(487) *A homme irous*: Donez lui a beivere le jus de ache, le jus de egrimoyne, si estanchera la ire.

.69.

(488) **Medicine encuntre la goute kayve*: Mox ut ceciderit occide canem et extrahe fel eius et da ei bibere et nunquam amplius cadet.

.70.

(489) **Pur suffrer de estre tranché ou ars sans grant grevance*: Accipe radicem pionie et tere fortiter et confice sicut piper cum aqua parumper et da homini bibere quem secare vel coquere volueris. Poterit enim postea quam optime pati cocturas vel cissuras.

.71.

(490) **Pur oster dens de la bouche sauns dolour*: Si dentes canino lacte tetigeris, sine dolore cadent.

.72.

(491) **Si quis secum habuerit solitariam herbam .i. luciam*: Ferratura aliqua sibi non obsistet. Hec eadem eicit infantem infra corpus mulieris vel bestie mortuum si potetur.

[38] Not included in the opening list of chapters.

.73.

(492) *Medicine pur saver si femme enceinte porte madle ou femele*: Pernez la let de la femme en un [f.60r] net vessel, si metez de l'ewe od tut e si le let flote, si porte male, e si le let voit a funs, si est file.

(493) *Autrement: Si dextera mamilla mulieris pregnantis sicca sit, masculum habet, si sinistra mamilla, feminam.

.74.

(494) **Pur conustre quant l'em ne deit seyner ne pociun prendre par phisike*: Tres sunt dies in quibus nulla necessitatis occasione liceat homini vel pecori sanguinem minuere vel pocionem accipere, videlicet prima die lune post .viii. Aprilis, secunda dies lune intrante Augusto, et tercius dies lune exeunte Decembrio, quia tunc omnes vene plene sunt. Qui autem in hiis diebus incisus fuerit homo vel animal aut infra .vii. dies aut certe infra .xiiii. moritur. Et si pocionem acceperit, ante .xv. dies morietur. Et si quis de auca manducaverit, ante .xl. dies morietur. Et si masculus vel femina natus [sc. in hiis diebus] fuerit, absque dubio mala morte morietur.

(495) *Item in anno sunt tres dies et noctes in quibus qui genitus fuerit sine dubio corpus eius integrum manebit usque in diem iudicii scilicet Kalenda Aprilis, Idus Augusti, et tercio Kalenda Februarii.

.75.

(496) *Medicine a goute enossé e a tutes maneres de goutes*: Pernez le linoys e quisez taunt que la ewe seit espesse, pus triblez ben le linois e pernez la fresche fente de berbis, si la triblez e medlez od tut le jus de la chenillé, pus pernez le pastel tut chaud e metez sur le mal, si garrez.

.76.

(497) *Encuntre cancre medicine prové*: Pernez un oef e metez hors ceo qu'il y ad dedeins. Pus pernez greins de segle e sel e mel e de mesme l'aubun de l'oef, de tous owelement, e metez a la teste arere, si fetez poudre e de cele poudre metez sur le mal, si garra.

.77.

(498) *Pur estancher vo*[f.60v]*mis*: Pernez le jus de la mente e l'aubun de l'oef e la pudre de franc encens e la farine de orge, si medlez ensemble e de ceo fetez mole paste, si la metez sur un drap e liez entour la gorge.

.78.

(499) *Pur menisun*: Si liez mesme l'emplastre sur le umbil, si garra.

.79.

(500) *Pur dolour des espaules*: Pernez herbe beneite e quisez la ben en eisel e pus la trahez hors. Si la metez sur un linge drap e metez teve sur la dolour.

(501) *Autrement*: Pernez veuz vin e veuz oile e seim de porc madle, e boilez taunt sur le fu que il seit remys e pus pernez la leyne de berbis ben carpé, si la moilez dedeinz. Pus la premez que ele rende partye. Pus la metez ou que unkes la dolour sera, si en trera tut hors.

.80.

(502) *Pur freide goute e pur nerfs blessés e a paralesie medicine esprové*: Pernez sauge, savine, rue, foile de lorer, si fetez ben tribler, pus pernez bure, si triblez ensemble, si lessez en pes gesir ensemble quatre jours ou .v. Pus metez tut vostre gresce en une paele e friez ben tut ensemble, pus colez parmi un drap e al quire metez de aysel.

.81.

(503) *Pur goute enfestré beiver[e] esprové*: Pernez avence, herbe Jon, herbe Water, egremoine pur tost warir, bugle, sanicle, herbe Roberd, pimpernele, pelusete, la tanesie, e chanve a duble des autres herbes, la savonere, e matefelun pur defendre des autre maus. Tous cestes herbes quisez ensemble en un pot de tere tut noef e bevetz .iii. foitz le jour. E de ceste beivere lavez les [...] e de memes les herbes fere oigndre les playes, si garra.

.82.

(504) *Medicine que vous ne sente[z] freid en alaunt ne en chivachaunt*: Quilez la urtye devant le solail levé e pus la quisez en oile, si en oignez vos [f.61r] meins e vos pees e, si vous volez, tut vostre cors, ja n'averez celi jour freid.

.83.

(505) *Medicine bone a face leprouse*: Pernez oynt de ver e jus de kersun e le jus de urtye owelement e medlez ensemble, si oignez la face al seir e al matyn e pus la lavez e ceo fetez .ii. foitz ou .iii. ou plus, si mester seit.

.84.

(506) *Item medicine pur roses que crescent en la face de homme*: Pernez le furmage

freez e que ne seit lavé e triblez le ben e fetez une emplastre e metez sur la face, si garra.

.85.

(507) *Autrement a celi qi est semblable a lepre*: Pernez .ii. unces de suffre e autretaunt de mel cum covient e triblez ensemble e oignez la face, si garra.

.86.

(508) *Medicine a toute manere roigne e a la mangue e a ledesse del vis*: Pernez les escopeals de l'urtye e les escopeaus de maroil owelement e la racine de parele e la racine de aile owelement, ici que plus i ait dé racines que des herbes. E dunc les triblez tanque eles seyent moles e metez de la celidoigne e de la fumitere. Pus metez de veuz oint de porc plus que tout l'autre, pestelinez e dunc le metez fermement ensemble. E aprés si metez suffre un poy molu e de la resyne autretaunt e de sel doubletaunt. E dunc le batez de rechef e au darein si metez vif argent assez. E dunc le rebatez ensemble taunt que il seyunt ben medlez e pus de cele oignement oignez le malade a sa maladye treis foitz le jour e la nuit, si garra.

.87.

(509) *Medicine a homme que n'ad poynt de barbe ou poy de chevus*: Entreles quisez de anesse, trancherez un des urilouns cum duresses que lui crescent en yver sanz peil e en esté lui cheunt. Pernez les, si les ardez e fetez pudre e pus le destemprez od tré vel oile [f.61v] e de ceo oignez les hommes la u vous volez que il eyent peil.

(510) E sachez que ceste oignement est tant vailaunt que si vous oignez le menton a un femme, ja seit iço que nature lui vee, il i crestra de peil assetz.

.88.

(511) *Medicine a enfaunt letaunt costivé*: Oignez les mameles de la mere de la mangure de levere e ceo lui fra certeinement aler avant.

.89.

(512) *Medicine pur fevere jevene*: Pernez le jus de ache e de fenoil par owel mesure e lui donez a beivere treis jours. E fetez lui garder sa diete e de rost e de vin, si garra tost.

.90.

(513) *Item encuntre fevere terceine*: Pernez licorice, si quisez en vin e en ewe meité a meité tant que il seit demi quit, si fetez al malade garder sa diete. E encuntre la hure que il le devera prendre fetez le juner .viii. jours e quant il le prendra, si li donez a beivere, si garra.

.91.

(514) *Medicine encountre jaunice*: Pernez une pome, si tranchez en quatre e jetez la quarte partye en ewe ou la fetez manger a une beste. Pus aprés en la primere des autres treis escrivez 'In nomine + Patris + Jesu + et Filii + Nazareni', e en la secunde e en la terce 'Spiritus Sancti, Amen'.

(515) Ou beive la pioyne ou la racine de l'urtye, si garra.

.92.

(516) *Medicine pur oster a femme sa maladye privé*: Pernez la graunde rave, si le metez en un pot e la ardez. Pus metez la pudre en un saket, si la porte le femme a sa seynture. E si vous volez prover que ceo seit veir, pernez un poi, si la pendez al col de une geline e a l'autre jour la tuez, si ne istera point de sanc.

.93.

(517) **Ut mulier cito pareat*: Liga ad ventrem eius in lintheo os quod invenitur in corde cervi.

(518) *Item liga athanasiam ad inguinem illius et statim pariet.

.94.

(519) **Ad guttam caducam*: Accipe grana pionie et fac potionem et da ei bibere per [f.62r] dies .v. mane et sero.

.95.

(520) **Qui non poterit dormire*: Semen papaveris tritum cum vino bibat.

(521) *Item agrimoniam pone sub capitale eius. Non evigilabit nisi eam abstuleris.

.96.

(522) **Ad eos qui sensum amittunt*: Has .iii. herbas tere cum vino .s. solsequium, abrotanum, salviam et da ei bibere diebus .v., et sanabitur.

.97.

(523) *La mestrie de fere, si vous volez, de un chival neir blanc*: Pernez la taupe e la quisez en ewe e pus la lessez gisir en mesme le breu treis jours e treis nuis. E pus metez de cele ewe desus le col u la ou vous volez, si encherra le neir peil, si devendra blanc.

.98.

(524) *Medicine pur ventosité*: Pernez semence de anis /.ii. pars/ e persil /.i. part/ e semence de fenoil /.i. part/, aniz encuntre les deux, comyn encontre tous les autres, e bevez e ceo vous vaudra.[39]

.99.

(525) *Medicine pur bele colour aver*: Bevez sovent betoine quit en vin ou en servoise, si averez bele colour en la face.

(526) *Item pur colourer la face cum rose*: Qui sovent mangue lupyn au matin, colour de rose en la face avera.

(527) *Item pur colourer la face*: Pernez le salgemme, si en raez de ceo plain escale de oef e fetez boiler sur les cendres, si ostez la escume e del remanant oignez la face.

(528) Item pernez sigillatam, ceo est seele, e frotez ben le viz, si averez beal colour.

(529) *Item pur aver la face bele e blaunche e les mains*: Pernez la racine de luvache e la quisez ben en ewe, si lavez le viz de cele ewe e les meins par .iii. jours.

(530) *Item pur aver la face bele e blaunche*: Pernez la racine de luvache e destemprez od ewe e de ceo sovent lavez le viz, si fra la face mout blaunche e clere.

(531) Item a la face lentilouse: Oignez la face de sanc de levere, si purgera tut le vis.

(532) *Item pur oster tecches del vis*: Pernez le [f.62v] su de cerf e la meule e medlez ensemble e oignez la face.

.100.

(533) *A homme que ad la chaudepisse*: Beive sovent la gletonere, si garra.

[39] Entries between slashes are interlinear insertions.

.i.

(534) *Medicine que chevus deveinent neir la ou vous vodrez*: Fetes cendres de rouges verms que sunt en tere e medlez od un poi de oile, si oignez la ou vous vodrez.

[–]

(535) **Item ad capillos crescendos qui desunt in capite*:[40] Unge sepe capud de felle anguille.

[–]

(536) *Si vous volez que femme seit sans leit*:[41] Donez lui a beivere la celidoine destempré od vin.

.x.

(537) *Unguentum pro salso fleumate*: Recipe racine de fenoil, de peresil, de wymawe, de alisaundre, de luvache, de liz, de dragaunce, que est apelé serpentine, de checun .iii. unces. Ben lavez e ben mundés, si les batez ensemble en un morter menu. Pus les metez en une paele e un quart de vin blanc, demy lyvere de seim de porc madle, demi livere de su de cerf ou de motoun e quisez ensemble, que tut seit degasté for que les greces. E pus les premerez forment parmi un drap. Pernez pus .v. deners pesaunt de salgemme e autaunt de caumphre e demi unce de nitre, tut ceo batez en pudre menu. Pus pernez vostre gresce freide, si le metez en un morter e la pudre ensemble, si les medlez mult ben. Pus pernez la quarte partye de une livere de vif argent, si le metez leins petit e petit e le batez ben desque ataunt que tut seit cum ynde(?). E pus le metez sur la face al malade e ceste oignement est bon pur la salsefleume.

.xi.

(538) *Oignement pur arsure de fu ou pur eschaudure*: Pernez le aubun de l'oef e le batez ben, pus le escumez, pus le batez autre foitz e le escumez auxi. Pus [f.63r] pernez blaunc seim de porc male e medlez ensemble, pus le metez en une paele outre le fu e le eschaufez un poi. E pernez bone garde que il ne seit trop chaud meque teve. Pus le versez en un vessel e les batez ben ensemble tanque il seit ben espés. Pus oignez .ii. foitz le jour en esté e en yver une foitz. Probatum est.

[40] Not included in the opening list of chapters.
[41] Not included in the opening list of chapters.

(539) Item pernez un porciun de ewe de funtaine e ataunt de oile de olive e les batez ensemble taunt que il seit ben espés. Pus oignez. Probatum est.

.xii.

(540) *Uncore pur enflure de gorge*: Pernez farine de segle e la medlez ben od mel e fetez emplastre, si metez a la gorge.

.xiii.

(541) *Uncore pur roine*: Pernez consoude e blanc grece ou bure de May e la friez ensemble. Pus la colez parmi un drap, si oignez la roigne.

.xiv.

(542) *Pur teter tuer*: Pernez un chaundele de su e la metez tute ardaunte en funs de un bacyn taunque el[e] seit fundue. E dunkes pernez roile de fer e medlez od le su e le roilez ben ensemble.

.xv.

(543) *Pur morsure de yrayne*: Pernez pelestre, quintefoile, matefelun e scabiouse, triblés cestes herbes ensemble od oint de porc, si metez ataunt de pelestre cum des autres treis, si metez cele emplastre sur la playe seir e matin e ceste emplastre garist ensement de felun.

(544) Item pernez lé muches e oignez le morsure de ceo. Pus pernez foiles de radich e boilez ben ensemble e quant il serrunt quit, les triblez e metez sur le morsure e le liez e il tendra la playe overte e ostera le venym; u deux foiles mesmes e les batez od mel e metez sur la playe.

.xvi.

(545) *Uncore pur brisure u que ceo seit*: Pernez malve e grundeswilie, si quisez od lies de vin, pus metez.

(546) U pernez suet u su de motoun brisé menu [f.63v] e pus friez ensemble, si metez chaus.

.xvii.

Ici comence medicine pur morsure de serpent e de chen

(547) Pur morsure de serpent: Pernez une forte curreye de quir de cerf e liez le morsure dé deux pars les nerfs en quel lu que ceo seit e le lyez ben estreit de ces .ii. curreys. Pus pernez une geline e desplumez le cul e metez

sur le pertuz la ou le serpent ad mors taunt que le emflure seit abatu. E don[e]z a beivere serpentine, matefelun e morele, si l'avez.

(548) Item encuntre morsure de serpent ou de nule autre beste venimouse: Triblez centorie, si lui donez a beivere.

(549) Ou triblez rue verte e fenoil e les quisez ben, si lui donez a beivere.

(550) *Pur morsure de chen*: Pernez la urtie, si la triblez od mel e metez al morsure e ben espurgera e sanera.

(551) Item pernez la rouge urtye e morele e lard e let cru e les batez ensemble e plaunteine e chenillé, si vous les pussés trover, e les quisez od bure e fetez oignement, si oignez.

(552) *Item pur morsure de chen enragé*[42]: Destemprez sauce e lavez la playe. Pus pernez plaunteine e la triblez ben od le aubun de l'oef e metez.

(553) Item pernez rue e lessez le malade la mascher. Pus pernez hors de sa bouche e metez a la morsure.

(554) *Item urtica cum melle trita et imposita sanat et purgat.

(555) Item pernez vel oynt e le triblez od plaunteine e oignez le morsure.

(556) Item pernez la rouge urtye, morele, lard e bure e boilez ensemble e fetez un oignement e oignez.

.ii.[43]

Ici commence medicine pur playe

(557) Pur saver si homme naufré murra u nun: Pernez pimpernelle e lui donez a boire en ewe e si il ist parmy la playe, il murra.

(558) Item pernez la urine al malade e la metez en un esquele ou en un ha[f.64r]nap e fetez une femme que norist enfaunt male leter en la urine e si le let flote, il murra, e si il medle od la urine, il vivera e ben garra de cele maladie. E de femme fetez autresi, mez fetez femme que nurritz meschine leter en la urine de femme.

(559) *A playe malement close*: Pernez la crote de chevere e veu vin, si triblez ben ensemble. Pus metez e si ele seit malement overte, si clora ben.

(560) *Pur espurger playe*: Pernez mel e farine de segle e un poi de vin e les boilez ensemble e metez sur la playe.

(561) *Uncore pur playe close overer*: Fetez paste de farine de orge e de l'aubun de l'oef e de mel e fetez emplastre e metez desur, si overad.

[42] MS curage.

[43] Chapters ii – ix are out of sequence.

(562) *Pur ben clore playe*: Pernez farine de orge e le corn de cerf e fetez pudre e la esparpliez sur la playe.

(563) *Pur sanier platte playe*: Fetez pudre de la centorie e esparpliez sur la playe.

(564) Item a playe que ne vut saner: Pernez encens e arnement e les batez a pudre e jetez sur la playe.

(565) Item pur estreite playe que mout greve: Pernez plaunteine e mel e quintefoile e flur de furment e les brayez ensemble. Pus le metez a la playe simplement tut cru.

.iii.

(566) *Ore pur estauncher sanc de playe*: Pernez les siouns de rouge urtye e les mincez menu, pus les medlez od fort eisel e le metez a la playe e gute de sanc ne istera.

(567) Item pernez fente de owe le plus novel que vous purrez trover e le metez tut chaud a la playe, si estaunchera.

(568) Item a playe que non est mye ben sané ne ben mundé, ou si fer ou fust i seyt que ne seit hors treit: Pernez ere terestre e peluete e betoyne, si les batez ensemble e fetez emplastre e metez a la playe e sachez que ben [f.64v] overad e le venim ben jettera tut hors. E si fer ou fust i seit, ne le suffera demurer dedeins.

(569) Item pernez ditaigne e fetez boire le jus e pus fetez lyer le pastel desus quit en viole. E sachez que iserad le fer ou fust ou espine.

(570) *Item pur playe garir sauns oignement*: Pernez la tanesye e le coperun de rounce que est apelé englenter e le coperun de rouge cholet e de chaunvere oveke la semence owelement e autretaunt de warence cum de tutes quatre, si les destemprés od vin ou servoise; u ewe vive seit mis a quatre herbes desus ové la warence. Et ex liquido bibat paciens bis in die et curabitur. Vel fiant pillule et custodiantur per annum. E si sur la playe viegne nule legere char, metez alum blanc. E si morte char leve, metez i coperose e al terce jour le ostez aprés ceo, si metez sur la playe emplastre de oignement e al terce jour le aubun de l'oef.

(571) *Item succus plantaginis cum melle vulnera nimis humida siccat et sordida purgat.

(572) *Item pur playe fresche que est encharné*: Pernez plaunteine u launcelé ben triblé e del jus seit la playe lavé e de se memes mettrez en la playe od la raspe, ceo est la drache.

(573) **Item ad sananda omnia vulnera curabilia fiat tale unguentum*: Sume betoyne e selfhele, plantayne e eble e herbe Roberd e bugle e sanicle e pimpernele

e menu ache e columbine e avence e quintefoile e sauge e averoigne e mel et omnia ista terantur simul in mortariolo et apponatur cera et butirum non salsum quod debet fieri in invencione sancte crucis. Et bulliantur simul et exprimatur succus per medium alicuius panni linei[44] et illud expressum servetur ad omnia vulnera sananda.

[PROGNOSTICS]

.iv.
Signa mortalia sunt hec

[f.65r]

Hiis moriens signis certis dinoscitur eger:
Fronte rubet primo, pedibus frigescit ab ymo,
Decidit et mentum, nasus summo tenus albet,
Decrescit venter, levus minuetur ocellus,
Excubias patitur juvenis de nocte dieque,
Sique senex dormit, designat morte resolvi.

Enmi le front enrugera, le quer de pé refreidera,
E le mentun descherra, le pinoun de nes enblaunchera,
E le ventre decrestera, le oil senestre enmenusera,
Si il est juvene, mout veilera, jour e nuit travaillera,
Si il est veuz, mout dormera; ceo est signe que il murra.

Ista omnia sunt vera et probata.

(574) *Item ad sciendum utrum eger moriatur vel non, Macer dicit quod si quando visitas egrum portaveris vervenam et queras ab eo 'Quomodo est tibi ?'; si respondeat 'Bene', evadet; si autem dixerit 'Male', non est spes liberacionis.

(575) *Item dicit Experimentator[45] quod si arthemesia ponatur sub capite pacientis ipso nesciente vel ignorante, si dormierit, vivet, sin autem, morietur.

(576) *Item si manus pacientis liniatur cum fermento vel lardo et detur cani, si illud commederit canis, vivet paciens, sin autem, morietur.

[44] MS panni teli l., an error for panniculi l. ?

[45] 'Experimentator' denotes an anonymous compilation which is mentioned by a number of 13th C. writers, including Thomas of Cantimpré, the original text of which seems to have been lost.

(577) *Item si urtica fuerit perfusa cum urina pacientis, si die secunda fuerit viridis, vivet paciens, si marcida et sicca, non evadet.

.v.

(578) *Pelotes a boire pur playes saner, ce est la receite*: Fetez prendre la ruge urtie e la rouge cholette, pimpernel, cerfoile, mente, porette, taneseye, averoigne, bugle, sanicle e warance. Ore oyetz la virtue de cestes herbes: urtye e cholet ne suffrent pas playe a saner, de celes deux pernez libram semis; pimpernele e cerfoile sanent, de celes pernez libram unam; mente e poret [f.65v] asswagent dolour en playe, de celes pernez libram semis; tanesye e averoigne ne suffrent venym en playe, de celes pernez libram semis; bugle e sanicle gardent playe de peril e la sanent, de celes pernez libram unam sicum ai avaunt dit de pimpernele e de cerfoile; warance amene le boire a la playe, pernez de cele taunt cum de tutes les autres, si les fetez ben tribler en un morter e pus fetez vos pelotes e les metez a secher, mes que vent ne solail ne avegne pur trop seccher.

.vi.

(579) *Autre boire pur playe que bone est e esprové*: Pernez betoine, sauge, ere terestre, plaunteine, violete, egremoine, melis, e warance. Ore entendez la vertue de cestes herbes: betoine sane e[46] t[o]ut dolour; sauge tout[47] passiun; ere terestre sane e nette; plauntaine t[o]ut dolour; violete sane e t[o]ut fenge, e auxi fet betoigne; egrimoine nette e tout survenues; melis ne suffre pas playe a clore; warance ameyne boire a la playe. Pernez de tutes cestes herbes owelement for que de warance. De cel prendrez ataunt cum de tutes les autres, si les fetez ben tribler en un morter e pus fetez vos pelotes sicum avaunt ai dit.

(580) Item pelotes pur veines ou nerfs tranchés ou os debrisé: Pernez consoude, comfirie, osmunde, chaunvere e rouge cholet, averoine, urtie, betoine, bugle e sanicle, de totes pernez owelement par peis for que de warance, de lui pernez taunt cum de tutes les autres herbes avaunt dites. Pus seyent ben triblez e fet pelotes e secchés sans vent, feu e solaile.

.vii.

(581) *Autre pur nerfs tranchés en playe*: Pernez les verms que se meinent em Mai, lembres de tere, par tute ses[i]es, e seyent ars en un novel pot de tere.

[46] MS de.

[47] MS de tute.

Pus les fetez en poudre e metez [f.66r] de mel e medlez e celui licour metez en la playe e taunt tost les nerfs se affermerunt. Mesme la pudre saunz plus joynt nerfs en playe.

.viii.

(582) *Comune bature as playes*: Pernez jus de ache e blanc de l'oef e mel e flur de furment e medlez, mes que pres de fu ne vigne.

(583) Item pernez jus de arthemesie e de eble e de aloigne e de rouge urtie e de ache, de tous les jus owelement, e metez de mel e le aubun de l'of e menue farine de segle, destemprez tut ensemble en un vessel e quant il ensecchist, renovelez le de ache.

.ix.

(584) *Autre entrete bone e verraye pur playe e apostume*: Pernez su de motun frez, cire virgine, piz naval, galbanum, terbentine, ana libras quatuor, e metez vin blanc a tut e lessez ben boiler e a tret. Pus pernez aloen, mirre, oliban, mastik, ana libras duas, si fetez pudre e metez en vos avauntdites gummes e lessez les boiler ben e a tret autre foitz tut ensemble. Mout est bone entrete a postume e a playe.

.xviii.

(585) *A dures overtures que viegnent par survenue des apostumes*: Pernez avence, tendrun de runce e chaneve, rouge cholet, herbe croisé, cerfoile, averoine, owelement, warance autretaunt cum de tutes les autres e fetez vos pelotes, mes que vent ne solaile ne atouch taunt cum fresches sunt pur trop seccher en haste.

.xix.

(586) *Emplastre pur saker e en trere espine ou ceste ou fer, ou ke il seit, e pur abatre rancle e asswager passiun e venym destrure*: Pernez la mouse de aube espine e metez de vin vermail a tut une graunde partie e lessez taunt boiler desque la moité ou la terce partye seit gasté. E metez dunque sur le anguise ou que il seit.

.xx.

(587) *Autre ciroigne a playe ou a postume*: Pernez colofonie .ii. unces, piz e piz liquide [f.66v] ana unciam unam, olibanum, orpiment, aloum, terebentine ana uncias .ii. Metez a tut bon vin vermail a plenté e lessez ben boiler e a tret e dunke seit colé e refreidi.

.xxi.

(588) *Un autre ciroigne petite a playes*: Pernez oint de porc male e su de motun frez e cire virgine e piz liquid e franc encens e lessez ben boiler tut ensemble. La confectiun est bone.

(589) *Si vous volez fere bone entrete pur en trere ceste ou espine*: Pernez egrimoine e la racine de ros ataunt de [l'un e de] l'autre, si le(m) fetez ben tribler en un morter. Pus pernez cire virgine, su de levere, duble taunt e une partye de grece de sengler seit oveke mis. E metez a vos herbes e lessez ben boiler. Pus aprés le fetez coler parmi un saket linge e quant vous avez ceo fet, fundez le autre foitz e ostez la lye desoutz. Pernez dunque aymaunt, ce est une pere, si en fetez pudre e metez en vostre entrete avauntdite e medlez ben ensemble. Il n'i ad fer ne sete ne espine ne quarel ne fust dedeins le cors de homme ou l'em ne put avener pur hors trere saunz peril, que ceste emplastre mise sur la playe ne le sake hors hastivement.

.xxii.

(590) *Oignement pur garer checune pleye que est doné de arme molue*: Pernez bugle, sanicle, avence, burnette, milfoile, pimpernele, orpin, herbe Water, filete, herbe croisé, de tutes pernez owele peis e fetez le mout ben laver. Ben e lungement les triblez en un morter e dunque seyent mis en un pot de tere e une bone partye de vin blanc. Pus lessez ben le ensi reposer un jour e une nuit en ceste sonsyé(?). Pus pernez une partye de oyle de olive e de cire virgine, gumme, piz, rosine, e metez a vos avauntdites herbes e fetez mout ben boiler. Pus le colez parmi un drap linge [f.67r] e metez sus deske il seit freid. E dunque ostez la lye que vous troverez desoutz e fundez le autre foitz. Le oignement est verray.

.xxiii.

(591) *Oignement a playe ou apostume crevé pur ben saner sanz peril*: Pernez oile de olive libram unam et semis, cire rouge uncias quatuor, colophonie uncias .ii., piz naval, serapinum ana uncias .ii., mastik, galbanum, terebentine, oliban ana unciam .i. Primes seit le oile ben boili, dunke metez la cire, pus la colofonie pudré e le piz naval, le serapinum e la terebentine e au darein seit mis la mastik e oliban ben pudré.

.xxiv.

(592) *Autre oignement pur playe*: Pernez groces anguiles, si les quisez en ewe e pus lessez cele breu refreider. E dunc quisez la grece, e la grece de owe

e de geline seit a ceo mis que il seient tous owel. Mes veez que sel ne seit mys. Pus pernez le jus de rue e de sauge, aloigne, ere terestre, de chenlange e de matecicle, ceo est cheverefoile, le jus de verveine e de sanicle. Dunt pernez franc encens e alum e mirre, armoniac ana unciam .i. e la pudre que chet entour la pere de molyn e os dactili e saffran e sandali e acacia e cire virgine que il seit assetz. Si le metez a vos avantdites herbes e gummes e le fetez ben boiler e a tret. Pus seit colé e quant il est freid, ostez la lye que vous troverez desoutz e autrefoitz seit un poi eschaufé e mis en bone garde.

(593) *Uncore autre oignment pur playes saner*: Pernez bugle, sanicle, avence, herbe croisé, consoude, pigle, pimpernele, plaunteine, osmunde, foile de porret, pervenke, trifoile, herbe Water, orpin, filete, counfirie, verveine, launcelé, faverole, cerfoile, quintfoile. Tutes ces herbes seyent ben triblez e dunc metez a tut bure de May e un partye de [f.67v] franc encens e lessez ben boiler e a tret. E pus seit colé e quant il est freid, ostez la lye desoutz. Entret est e oignement a saner mout noblement.

.xxv.

(594) *Pur fere boire pur playe saner de tutes maneres*: Pernez avence pur ceo que ele seyne e sanicle que seyne outre mesure e bugle que fet la playe swef, herbe Roberd que purge e secche, herbe Water que seyne e garde de ordure, launcelé que seyne, milfoile que purge e oste le sanc, tendrun de runce que fet les herbes issir par la playe e si garde de char morte, consoude petite que fet la char crestre owelement, pimpernele la petite oste la emflure, tansye seyne e destrut venim, senechun seyne outre mesure, ache que retret dolour de playe. De tutes cestes herbes prendrez le jus owelement for que de sanicle e de senechun. De cestes deux averez la terce partye. Pus prendrez le jus de tutes cestes herbes cum ai dit devaunt e les confierez od bure de May que seit pure ensi que la terce partye seit bure bele e nette. E averez boire pur tutes playes saner.

(595) *Item pur fere boire pur playes saner*: Pernez une poyné de parele e de sauge e le siun de violete e betoyne e plaunteyne que crest en chemyns, kar ele oste le venym, e metez peluete, pur ce que ele tynt la playe nette, e here terestre e egremoine. Pernez cestes herbes tutes ensemble, si les triblez ben, pus les quisez en vin ou en bone servoise e mettez de mel pur endoucer le boire e fetez le pacient boire a matin e au seir.

(596) *Item autre*: Pernez semence de cholet e la racine de tanesye ou le sioun, si vous volez, e pernez warence autretaunt cum des autres e les triblez tutes ensemble. E pus les quisez ben en vin ou en servoise e donez al malade a matyn e au seir e coverez la [f.68r] playe de une foile de cholet.

(597) *Item pur fere oignement*:[48] Memes les herbes que ai avaunt nomez pernez, mes ostez la peluete, kar si ele fuce, ele overeyt la playe, e metez mel e oile e cire e su de chatrun e les fetez ben quire ensemble e les colez parmi un drap.

.xxvi.

(598) *Gracia Dei*: Pur fere le entret que est apelé Gracia Dei pernez un galun de vin blanc e une poigné de verveine e ataunt de pimpernele e ataunt de betoine e seit debrusé en un morter e mis en le vin. Pus le quisez taunt que la moité seit degasté e pus pressez hors le jus taunt cum purrez parmi un drap. E pus pernez .i. libre de perrosin e .iiii. unces de cire virgine e .i. unce de mastik pudré e seit ben quit e movez adés de une esclice. Pus si seyent mises les herbes e quant averez ceo fet, ostez le del fu e metez leyns demi libre de terebentine e le movez tousjours de vostre esclice taunt que il seit freid. Adunc le pernez e metez en sauf. E le jus est bon pur laver playes.

.xxvii.

(599) *Nerval*. Oignement que est apelé Nerval est bon pur tutes maners de dolours que vignent de freid e pur parelesie e pur nerfs custrayns: Pernez sauge, ambroise, lavendre, rue, mente, calamente, puliole real, puliole de munteyne, primerole, cousloppe, urtye rouge e greke, paritarie, betoine, verveine, egremoine, avence, camamille, calketrappe, heyhove, ere terestre, averoine, foile de lorer, savine, rosmarine, coste, cressun de ewe e de curtyl, de checune un quarterun, de plaunteine e de launcelé .i. lanceolata vel quinquenervia .ii. libres, grece de porc e de sengler e de chat e de chen e de goupil e de tessun, de checun .ii. unces ou .iii., e de vin blanc demi quart. Triblez en un morter e lessez reposer .vii. jours. E aprés les .vii. jours le boilez sur le [f.68v] fu e le clarefiez parmi un canevas e metez a ceo castorium, oliban, ceo est mastik, que est pudré e le ostez del fu. E pus le movez adés taunt que il seit freid.

.xxviii.

(600) *Populeon*: Pur fere populeon pernez morele, jubarbe, teste de sorice, pavot, tendrun de l'englenter, plaunteyne, violete, osmunde, gletoner, letuse, orpin, endivie, de checun un poigné e de foiles de populer e les batez en un morter. E pus les metez a temprer en vin egre .iii. jours od .iii. libres de bon

[48] Not included in the opening list of chapters.

encens ou .ii. Pus quisez tut ensemble saunz cire, saunz gumme. Ceste oignement vaut a tutes chaudes maladies.

.xxix.

(601) *Emplastre*: Emplastre pur apostumes bruser: Pernez la racine de rouge parele e de la parele de ewe e de la wilde clote e de la grant clote e de grundeswelie e braez ensemble. E pus pernez su de motun e rosine e friez tut ensemble e metez un poi de cire.

(602) Item a murer apostume: Pernez la racine de wymalve e une poigné de semence de lyn e le boilez ben ensemble en ewe. Pus braez le ben ensemble e metez a tut un poi de vin e chaud le metez sur le mal.

(603) Item pernez .ii. testes de liz e la racine de wymalve e le boilez ben ensemble. Pus le braez en un morter e metez a tut secches figes e veil oynt de porc e farine de furment e boilez tut ensemble taunt que il seit espés e metez sur.

(604) Item fente de columb e mel braez ensemble e chaufez e metez chaud.

[Oils][49]

Olea calida sunt hec .s. oleum laurinum, oleum muscelinum, oleum rutacileon, antileon,[f.68vb] camamileon, amigdalarum amarum, oleum nucum, petroleon, [f.69ra] nardinum, yrileon, sizanninum, sambucoleon, puleginum, castroleon, serapinum, sacronium, sicioninum.

Olea calida sunt hec et humida: oleum amigdalarum dulcium, oleum de vitellis ovorum.

Olea frigida sunt hec .s. oleum violarum, oleum rosarum, nenufarinum, oleum de papavere, oleum mandragorinum.

Olea frigida et sicca sunt hec: oleum rosarum, oleum citrinum, oleum jusquiaminum.

[Ointments]

Unguenta calida sunt hec: Arrogon, marciaton, unguentum aureum, unguentum mixtum, siraminum, [f.69rb] Agrippa, dialtea.

Unguenta frigida: unguentum album, unguentum citrinum, populeon, unguentum fuscum, sirupus Galieni, sirupus acetosus, sirupus rosaceus, sirupus violarum, oxizacara.

[49] Oils and ointments are not included in the opening list of chapters.

.*xxx*.

(605) *Bone emplastre a playes garir*. Pernez demi libre de terebentine e un quarterun de cire virgine, e copez la cire ben deliement e pus metez ces .ii. gummes en un pot de tere tut noef e metez sur le fu e fetez fundre e boiler. E quant vous verrez l'oundé boiler, si jetez dedeins le pot une chopine de bon vin egre e fetez autre foitz boiler. Si ostez le pot del fu e lessez cestes choses treben refreider e quant [f.69v] eles serrunt treben freides, si purez hors le vin egre e remetez les dites gummes en le avauntdit pot. E quant vous verrez l'oundé boiler, si jetez dedeins un quarterun de su de motun male tut frez e la quarte partye de un hanap de jus de betoyne e demi hanap de jus de celidoine e un poi de let de femme que ad porté file e fetez tut autre foitz boiler ensemble. E quant vous verrez l'oundé boiler, si le ostez del fu e metez en un esquele de argent ou de peautre e la batez adés de une esquiler tanque il serra freid. E quant il serra freid, batez adés de l'esquiler taunt cum vous purrez, kar quant plus le baterez e meilour le averez.

[Beverages]

.*xxxi*.

(606) *Sauve*: Pernez avence, confirie, spurge, fimetere, pimpernele, senchun, mere herbe, consoude, cerlange, sauge, mente, verveyne, egrimoine, trifoile, tendrun de runce e de cholet, frasere, rue, sorel, chaunvere, lyn, fenoyl, averoigne, tanesie savage, wilde tasel, milfoile, plaunteine, launcelé, reigne dé pré, celidoine, stichewort, herbe Johan, herbe beneite, herbe Roberd, herbe Water, urtie, dragaunce, violete, bugle, sanicle, ere terestre, ysope, feverfoye. De tutes cestes herbes pernez par owel porciun par peys for que de warance – de lui averez ataunt cum de tutes les autres. E cestes herbes serrunt quilez en May e ben molu ensemble en un morter e pus medlez ové bure de May dedeins mesme le morter e dunke le deit homme mettre en un vessel e lesser estre quatre jours ou .v. tanque il seit chaun. E pus deit estre ben fryt en un paele e pus colé parmi un drap linge en un vessel. La bure deit estre fet sanz fu, saunz ewe, saunz sel. E si homme seit naufré, si beive au matin e au seir la mountaunce de un grein de orge e deit homme [f.70r] mettre la foile de rouge cholet ou de rouge rounce sur la playe, si garra ben. Ceste boire est apelé sauve (sauve).

(607) *Item sauve (save), unde versus:
Hec olus, urtica, tribulus, taneseaque canabs,
Et maior rubea plage fiunt medicina.

Has herbas citra Baptiste collige festa,
Summam dant quinque, radicem dat tibi sexta,
Per se quamque tere, tritam conjunge statere,
Pondus idem quinque sed sexta sit omnibus eque.
Hic miscendo teras, per se tritas ponis herbas,
Facque pilas siccas sine vento, sole vel igne,
Fit nux forma pile, cum trite sint simul herbe,
Unam cum potu sano, bibe vespere mane.
Hiis quoque temporibus foliis oleis tege plagas,
Nil appone magis fixis in corpore plagis.[50]

(608) *Vel ista valent contra plagas: Addantur avencia, agrimonia in eadem quantitate qua sumuntur predicta alia quinque et contra ungulam similiter. Ut ungula crescat: agrimoniam impone et ungula recrescet. Ut ungula cadat: tolle medianam corticem fraxini et saponem et super ungulam pone et illam auferet ita ut cadat.

.xxxii.

(609) *Potus Antiochie.* Hic incipit quedam aqua vocata Potus Antiochie: Pernez sauge, spurge, peluette, avence, sanicle, bugle, pigle, consoude la petite, confirie, osmunde, ambrosie, plaunteine, launcelé, betoine, scabiouse, spigurnele, matefelun blanc e neir, ditayne, pimpernele, celidoine, ache, herbe Roberd, moleyne, primerole, saxifrage, herbe ive, eufrase, morele, cholet, urtie, tanesie, runce, chaunvere, de checune une poigné e les [f.70v] racines de waraunce que peisent ataunt cum tutes les autres herbes e fetez les ben boiler en bon vin blanc ou en servoise ou en ewe e metez a tut atauntz de liveres de mel cum vous metez galouns de autre licour. E bevez de ceo le matyn chaud e le seir freid e de tutes ces herbes poez vous fere pelotes.

[Waters]

.xxxiii.

(610) *Aqua vite.* Ewe de vye ensi serra fet: Emplez un pot de vin vermail ou blanc, e ceo del plus fort que vous purrez trover, e metez en celi pot od le vin la poudre de cestes espices: gyngevere, galingale, canele, nois mugace, greyn de Paradis, peyvere lung e neir, clou de girofre, anise, fenoil, carewy,

[50] See Walther, *Initia* 7565; MSS B.L. Sloane 3550 f.219v, Sloane 3018 f.36va, Arundel 332 f.230v.

comyn, saffran, luvesche, par owel porciun une dragme ou plus ou meins. Pus metez a tut la pudre de cestes herbes: sauge, mente, roses, ysope, tyme, rosmarine, origone, paritarie, puliol, camamille, lavendre e avence par owel porciun. Si les metez od les espices. Pus metez sur le pot un alembic ben englué de paste, que la fumosité en nule manere puce yssir. Pus fetez un fu amiable de charbuns e le fetez distiller en une viole de verre. Iceste ewe avaunt dite est de la priveté dé philosofres e si ad tutes les vertues de baume naturel e pur ceo ele est apelé la secunde baume. Iceste ewe bue conforte tous les espiritz a vivauns e ele fet homme jolyf e jevenes. Ele est bone pur checune maladye que vient de freidure, ele est bone pur parelesye e pur tremblure des membres e pur contractiun dé nerfs e pur mal de mariz que est apelé retenciouns, e pur femmes que ne poyunt conceivere par freydure, e pur sourdesse, e tue le verm en la oraile, e ele est bone pur dolour dé dens, [f.71r] ele est bone pur la goute freide en quele liu que ele seit, e pur dolour de l'estomac e des boeals de freidure, e pur constipacioun de ventre, e pur la freide ydropesie e pur l'esplen e pur la pere en la vessye e en les reyns, e ele est bone pur cancre e pur festre e pur orde playe purrye, e ele tourne vin corrumpu e purry en sa primere vertu e ele garde pessun e char saunz poriture e corrupciun si lungement cum homme vodera.

.xxxiiii.

(611) *Aqua ardens sic fit*: Emplez un pot taunt que a la moité de bon vin vermail ou de bone servoise que seit estale e metez sur le pot un alembic ben englué de paste, que la fumosité ne puce yssir. Pus fetez un fu amiable desoutz le pot de charbun e fetez distiller en une viole de verre e assayez de une penne si ele art e dunc est ele bone. E quant ele ne art poynt, recevez cele ewe par sei e cele ewe est apelé ewe de eir pur ceo que ele est clere e resplendissaunte. Cele ewe est bone pur oils.

.xxxv.

(612) *Aqua tartari sic fit .i. ewe de argoil*: Pernez une poyné de argoil ben poudré e metez a tut un poy de vin egre e le metez en une pece de un pot de tere outre le fu, si le chaufez ben. Pus metez le en un vessel de verre e en .iii. jours ou en .iiii. devendra ewe. Iceste ewe est bone pur roigne e pur enblauncher la pel e quivere e argent roilé e remue tecches en cors de homme e morphés e burbelettes en la face de meseals e destrut verrues e tecches en drap linge e tue le cancre.

.xxxvi.

(613) *Aqua mellis*: Ewe de mel sera distillé par un alembic auxi cum l'em fet ewe ardaunt. Ele est bone pur fere crestre les chevus e destrut les verms en la teste.

.xxxvii.

(614) *Claretum*. Ad faciendum claretum: Pernez nois mugette e clouz de girofre, quibebes, maces, cane[f.71v]le e galingale. Fetez une pudre de tous ceux, pus le destemprez od bon vin e la terce partye de mel. Pus la colez parmi un saket, si le gardez.

.xxxviii.

(615) *Aqua lac virginis dicta pro scabie et salso fleumate*: Pernez litarge e fetez pudre de ceo e metez cele pudre en bon vin egre un jour e une nuit. Pus pernez la pudre de sein de verre ou de alom de glas e metez od autre vin egre un jour e une nuit. Pus metez les ensemble, si devendra blanc cum let.

.xxxix.

(616) **De signis lupi et cura .i. le lou*. Signa lupi sunt fetor, festina corrosio et nigredo, contra quod fiat talis pulvis: Recipe sal, mel, et ordeum. Ista comburantur et super locum pacientem ponatur iste pulvis cum aceto vel aliis prius abluto et exsiccato cum panno lineo veteri et sic fiat continue, quoniam multum confert. De oleo violaceo et oleo rosarum et mica panis tritici insimul peroptime mixtis fiat emplastrum contra lupum et ipsum certissime destruit in principio.

.xl.

(617) **De signis Noli me tangere*. Noli me tangere est autem apostema faciei et in ipsa sentitur magna formicacio et processu temporis fiunt carnes nervose .i. dure et quando est recens et parvum, non habet fetorem, sed quando est magnum et iam apertum, magnum habet fetorem et periculosum est ad ipsum accedere. Contra quod fiat talis pulvis: Recipe resalgar, pulverizetur, postea decoquatur in succo plantaginis, caulis rubei, lactuce. Postea ad solem desiccetur, deinde secundo vel tercio vel pluries decoquatur et desiccetur. Postea pulverizetur, deinde apponatur apostemati. Parum de hoc pulvere in illa hora apponatur unguentum frigidum et emplastrum exterius. Et sic per .iii. vel .iiii. dies dimittatur quousque sanies exeat et ibi caro mortua multum invenitur que omnino est removenda. Deinde caro bona est regeneranda

cum unguento fusco et aliis similiter. Vel possumus operari cum pulvere salis gemme que pulverizetur et distemperetur [f.72r] cum succo plantaginis admodum fabe et super locum pacienter tota nocte dimittatur. Et mane cum ungue vel alio instrumento radetur. Postea lavetur locus cum forti lexivio de amputationibus vitis. Postea recipe sal gemme, alumen, tartarum, atramentum, cinerem vitis, ista pulverizentur et cum predicto lexivio distemperentur et cum unguento emplastrum[51] singulis diebus loco pacienti superponatur quousque noli me tangere sit mortuum plenarie. Et quotiens emplastrum removebitur tociens cum predicto lexivio lavetur ulcus quo mortificato regeneretur caro cum predictis. Et nota quod plantago et lanceola et celidonia, acus muscata, absinthium, caulis rubeus, herba Roberti, omnes isti simul cancrum curant et quodlibet per se et similiter pes columbinus. Item vitellum ovi cum tanto sale ponatur super cancrum si sit inveteratum et curat ipsum, si per multos dies fiat et tunc locus paciens primo nigrescit, postea citrinescit et postea emittit saniem. Et hoc est bonum signum in vulnere quando emittit saniem quia magna est presumpcio sanitatis et tam in principio huius operis assignata.

.xli.

(618) *Ignis infernalis.* Pur conustre fu d'enfern: Aprimes pernez jus de letuse e de malve e lavez le mal de ce jus. Pus tranchez une veyne de jaumbe ou de mayn la endreit ou le mal est feruz. Si vous veyez que une simayne est passé, kar il vous covent trancher tute la pece de char envirun le lu ou le mal est feruz, kar il n'ad autre recoverer. Le mal devendra del colour de pere, pus en le .viii. jour devendra neir e pus est la menbre perdu. Jeo vous di la verité, que vous covent la menbre trancher de hache ou de siche jeke en la vive char e pus pudrer la menbre que est tranché en pudre e cele pudre mettre desur le mal e pus entret.

.xlii.

(619) **Nota diversitas operandi in vulneribus.* Quia aliquando operamur [f.72v] in vulnere cum pulveribus aliquando cum ung[uent]is unde pulvis regenerans carnem sic fit: Recipe sanguinis draconis, olibani, sarcocolle, aloe, pulverizentur et vulneri superponantur – sanguinem stringit, carnem regenerat, vulnus consolidat et isto pulvere quamvis quilibet garcio utatur tantum in fine Rasis, Avicenna et alii hoc ipsum ponunt.

[51] MS emplastro.

.xliii.

(620) **De impedimentis sanacionis vulneris*: Nota quod secundum Galienum sanitas vulneribus .vii. de causis differtur. Prima est paucitas sanguinis in corpore existens et malicia eiusdem quia tunc bona caro non potest generari et malicia consistit in grossicie vel subtilitate vel caliditate vel frigiditate.

Ecce canones sine quibus non debet esse cirurgicus:[52] Item caro dura vel caro mortua existens inter labia vulneris. Item os putridum quod est in vulnere sive putredo nimia. Item qui vulnus in se nimis est profundum vel maliciosum. Item nimis contrarium vulneri appositum .i. nimis calidum vel frigidum vel humidum,[53] similiter vel compositum. Unde Galienus in Megategni: Si vulnus multam habuerit saniem et illa sit humidissima et putridissima, medicina apposita fuerit nimis sicca. Item si fuerit vulnus magnum concavum solito et tunc fuerit illud rubeum et medicina apposita fuerit nimis calida. Item si livorem vel virorem habuerit et medicina apposita fuerit nimis frigida. Et propter hoc iste medicine sunt apponende et alie repellende. Et qui hos canones ignorant nesciunt qualiter de uno ad aliud transeundum sit.

.xliiii.

(621) **Unguentum album*. Unguentum album sic fit: Recipe litargirii dragmam .i., subtiliter pulverizetur et uncias .iiii. olei et calefiat in patella et apponatur parum cere ut sit magis tenax et deponatur ab igne et addatur pulvis litargirii et misceatur cum spatula. Deinde recipe olibani, colofonie, [f.73r] sarcocolle ana dragmas .ii., pulverizentur et incorporentur. Postea recipe galbani dragmas .ii. , liquefiat cum aceto in patella super ignem et predictis addatur et totum incorporetur. Isto unguento utendum est in vulneribus qui sanguinem non emittunt.

[–]

(622) **Unguentum frigidum in estate et dum tempus fuerit calidum et calor et rubor fuerit in vulnere*:[54] Recipe litargirum unciam .i., optime pulverizetur et distemperetur modo cum oleo modo cum aceto fortissimo quousque bene incorporetur. Postea apponantur ceruse dragmas .v. et camphore parum et nitrum totum in mortario incorporetur et isto unguento utimur in causis predictis et condicionibus.

52 Not included in the opening list of chapters.
53 Corr. simplex ?
54 Not included in the opening list of chapter headings.

.xlv.

(623) **Unguentum ad vulnus siccum*: Recipe olei, cere, visci quercini, picis nigri ana, oleum et cera liquefiant, pix et viscus pulverizentur quilibet per se et illi pulveres cum aliis incorporentur. Et isto unguento in casu predicto utatur.

[–][55]

(624) **De paritaria.* Nota quod folia paritarie reprimunt tumorem manuum et pedum et aliorum locorum si sint calefacta in patella cum vino calido et sic superponantur.

(625) *Si vero tumor acciderit vel morbus resistendum est ad temperanciam et repercussionem tumoris, propter quod recipe succum ebuli et sambuci et cum istis farina lini vel fenugreci vel utriusque distemperentur et incorporentur et tepidum vulneri superponatur.

(626) *Vel panis bene tritus et cum succo apii incorporetur et vulneri superponatur. Hoc enim tumorem et dolorem optime sedat.

(627) *Vel farinam subtilissimam frumenti cum succo apii distempera, quod idem facit.

.xlvi.

(628) *Nota quod emplastrum est confectio dura ex solidis gummis.

Cathaplasma est quando flores herbe, radices et huiusmodi res teruntur et super menbrum paciens cum tota substantia et succo apponitur.

Epithima est inunctio cum levi fricacione cum aliquo unctuoso succo alicuius herbe.

Embrocacio est cum aqua calida vel lac vel liquor aliquis ab alto cadens distillatur super menbrum paciens.

Fomentacio est ponere menbrum paciens in aqua tepida vel in aliquo [f.73v] liquore ubi herbe vel frondes vel fructus vel radices fuerint cocte.

Subfumigatio est quando species aromatice vel fetide in olla ponuntur et recipit fumum menbrum paciens.

Sinapisma est quando locus paciens inungitur et postea aliquo pulvere super aspergitur.

Encatisma est quando herbe vel huiusmodi decoquntur et postea sedet paciens in illa decoctione usque ad umbilicum.

[55] Items 624–7 are not included in the opening list of chapters.

.xlvii.

(629) *Nota quod nux muscata calida est et sicca in secundo gradu. Fructus est cuiusdam arboris que in India nascitur. Tempore maturationis colligitur. Per .vii. annos servatur. Eligenda est que est plana, in suo genere gravis, que cum frangitur interius non pulverizatur et invenitur acuti saporis. Si ista desunt, non est ponenda in medicinis. Virtutem habet confortandi ex aromaticitate et consumendi ex qualitatibus suis contra frigiditatem stomachi et indigestionem et discoloracionem ex frigiditate. Detur in mane nux media vel integra, si est parva. Per experienciam didici quod multum prodest contra frigiditatem stomachi et epatis et intestinorum. Detur vinum eciam decoctionis macis et nucis muscate.

(630) *Ad idem valet vinum decoctionis eius et anisi vel cimini dolorem stomachi et intestinorum ex ventositate tollit.

(631) *Convalescentibus ex egritudine detur vinum decoctionis eius et mastic.

(632) *Ad confortacionem spiritualium nux muscata naribus apposita cerebrum confortat et spiritualia.

NOTES

1. C27,D10,O1/27,T24. Cf.C23. See Sig. 160.
2. T24. Cf. C37.
3. C29 (lacking the last sentence), T24, Hunt 137/8b & 271/22.
4. LH21,C30,D12,O1/22,T24. See Sig. 160.
5. LH8b,C14,T24, Hunt 271/23.
6. LH9,C10,T24.
7. LH8a,C33,D90,H95,H199,O2/28,T24.
8. LH9a,C34,T24, Hunt 238/36, 271/26.
9. LH10,C35 (lacks 'ere e morele'),D352,T24.
10. LH11,C37,HE83/5,T24. Cf. C48.
11. LH12,C36,D449,HE83/4,T24 & 26.
12. LH13,C38,HE83/6,T24 & 27.
13. LH16,C42,CC7,D7 & 452,H93,HE106/6,M117/9,O2/1,T24.
14. LH8,C26,HE83/15,T24, Hunt 271/21. See Sig. 161.
18. Hunt 192, ll.1375–8 & 287/179.
19. LH97,C150,CC42,D839,HE68/20 & 79/20,O14/17,S200/7, Hunt 139 (LH), 231/73 & 285/167. See Sig. 166.
20. See Hunt 285/167. Receipts 19 and 20 are frequently confused in MSS.
22. T27, Hunt 202, ll.1679–81, 272/37.
23. C66,C72,D778,HE106/15,O3/13,T27, Hunt 132,300/17 & 309/77.
24. LH72,C92,T28.
25. LH73,C93 (has 'averoyne').

26. C78.
27. LH76.
28. Abbreviated in Hunt 290/208.
29. This appears to be a sequel ('aprés') to 28, stipulating that water is not to be used and that in winter it is the bark which is utilised.
31. Hunt 139 (LH).
32. T41 ('ciminum in albo vino').
33. LH30,C120,CC14,D469,O8/12,T46.
34. LH39,C128,H90,T48, Hunt 227/20.
35. LH32,T51, Hunt 232/84. See Sig. 161.
36. LH33,C123,T51.
37. LH35,C125,T46.
38. LH37,C126.
39. LH38,
40. Cf. T47 'Zinziber humectatum in vino albo vel in aceto frica cum cote et quod resolvitur inmitte'.
41. Cf. T49 'Jus de aloine medlé od mel e leit e totz passions des oilz sane'.
45. T41.
46. T47 ('serpillum campanum').
49. Cf. Hunt 154, ll.175–80.
50. T40, Hunt 232/79 & 289/197. See Walther, *Initia* 6423.
51. LH65,T59. Cf.C81/88, Hunt 226/12.
52. LH66,C89,T60. See Sig. 165.
53. Combines LH67–69,T59–60. See C90. See also Hunt 232/96.
54. Cf.C85 ('wit gres of heles'),CC10,HE39/12,O7/9.
56. Sig. 165 'Ad percussuras aurium: Plantaginis succus nuce plena conmiscis et tepefactum cum penna in aurem mitte'.
57. C105,CC9,D18 & 266,H210,HE109,M51/13 & 91/5,O6/23,S195/25. Thes. 133/2, Hunt 159,ll.307–10,232/95. In Sig. 167 the text runs: 'Ad eos qui ex dolore exsurdant: Fustes fraxini in foco mittis et cum ardere ceperint, capita foras focum mittis et aquam que exierit colligas et jus feniculi et ex capillis porcorum similiter et mel optimum. Hec omnia equis mensuris simul colas et tepefactum in aurem que sana est mitte et jaceat super aurem surdam ut de sana ad infirmam veniat. Expertum est.'
58. Cf. C104.
60. In Sig. 167 the text runs: 'Item [sc. 'Ad eos qui ex dolore exsurdant'] accipe rutam et exprime jus illius et misce cum sagen... anguille et tamdiu mitte in auricule sede usque lassus sis. Postea colloca te in latere et mitte in auriculam in qua malum non habueris et sic obdormi, quando evigilaveris sanus eris et auditum habebis. Probatum est.'
64. LH62,C195,T73.
65. LH58,C176,T70.
66. LH51,C191 & 197,HE112/14,M98/3,O18/11,T68/71.
67. LH52.
68. LH61,C189 & 201,T71.
69. Hunt 294/250.
70. LH60,C177 & 194.
72. C199, Hunt 161/11.395ff.
74. T73.

76. See 70 above. LH60,C177. The reading 'oraille' is an error for 'narille'.
78. LH41.
79. LH42.
80. LH43.
81. LH45,C227,T62.
82. C235,T61 & 79, Hunt 237/30. The forms should, of course, be Beronix and Beronixa (cf. Veronica).
85. Cf. C223 and Thes.151/1 & 155/26.
86. Thes.151/8.
88. Cf. C233 & 251.
91. C236,HE71/22,M81/3 & 89/9,T79, Hunt 239/43.
96. Cf. LH47('puliol sec u cerfoil').
98. LH48,C155,T63.
99. LH49,C156,O15/35,S196/18,T63.
100. LH50,C157,T63.
102. LH47,C154,T63.
103. See 466 below.
104. See 467 below.
105. LH97('aloen'),C150,CC42,D839,HE68/20 & 79/20,O14/17,S200/17, Hunt 139, 231/73 and 285/167. See Sig. 166 'Si quis obmutescit, accipe aloen et distemperatum cum aqua infunde illi in os, statim loquitur'.
109. Cf. C170 (second half).
112. C252.
114. T79.
117. C258.
120. Hunt 173, ll.773–6 (lacks 'mel').
122. Hunt 139 (LH). Combines C346 & 347. See O27/7 & 9.
127. Hunt 139 (LH, adding 'humer bure od vin').
129. Hunt 321/72 ('Pur apostumes').
133. LH82 (fewer ingredients). Cf. T137 (containing simply 'maril' and 'bure').
134. C287 & 325.
140. LH86,C290,T137, Hunt 292/222.
142. LH83,C288.
144. C289,T138.
145. T136 (omitting last sentence).
148. T139 'Quisez savine en vin e usez' and 'Savinam coctam cum vino et melle bibe'.
152. C297(with 'fymtorie' for 'centurie') & 324,O19/34, Hunt 285/166. O has 'and drynke .iii. dayes lewke & it purges þe breste & the stomake'. See 153 below.
153. Cf. 152 above.
157. T136.
160. LH88,C291 (with 'symphonie' for 'confirie', 'foyles' for 'plantes', and 'leyt de anesse ou de chevere').
161. C292.
165. LH90,C294 (with 'semense de canve'), Hunt 274/58.
166. LH91,C295.
172. C374 (ending at 'drynke').
174. LH162,C409.

175. C410.
176. C392.
177. LH101,C404.
178. LH99,C402. See Sig. 162 & 165.
179. LH100,C393 & 403. T143 'A estresse del entre: Beivez sovent rue triblé e destemperé od vin o cerveise'. See Sig. 162.
180. LH102,C406.
181. LH104,D183,C408.
182. LH105,C397 (with 'moderwort anglice mougwed' for 'milfoile').
183. LH106,C399, Hunt 226/13, 276/72 & 293/232.
184. LH107,C398 (omitting 'frasere' and '.iii. jours'), Hunt 293/230.
186. Cf. Hunt 276/70.
194. LH109,C242 (with 'amerose', and 'playstre' for 'pasteal', and omitting the last two clauses). See also Hunt 276/75 and 293/34.
195. LH142.
196. LH143.
197. LH112, Hunt 171, ll.685–96. Cf. Hunt 322/76.
198. Hunt 170, ll.675–84.
209. Cf. C336.
217. C518 (with 'ov oynt de porck'), Hunt 139 (LH).
218. C519 & 520 ('.ii. jours'), Hunt 139 (LH).
219. C521,D813, Hunt 139 (LH), 213/32.
220. T107 'si ab itinere pedes intumuerunt, plantago contunsa cum aceto et imposita tumorem tollit'.
223. T107 ('Ke vous ne seiez laz de aler').
224. Hunt 282/132.
225. Cf. Hunt 282/134.
248. See 255 below.
249. Cf. 256 below.
255. See 248 above.
256. Cf. 249 above.
265. LH124.
266. LH125, Hunt 302/28.
269. LH127 ('A rancle de seignee').
270. LH126.
283. Hunt 185, ll.1157–70 & 1181–88.
287. LH114,C640,CC141,O81/27, Hunt 320/61.
288. LH115, Hunt 280/114.
293. Hunt 181, ll.1027ff. 'Mel' refers to the medlar.
294. Hunt 183, ll.1089–98.
297. Hunt 184, ll.1115–24.
302. Hunt 183, ll.1077–80.
323. Cf. 330 below.
332. The use of the first person pronoun in conjunction with the name of Hippocrates indicates that the paragraph has been drawn from a compendium which included excerpts from various authorities, as is the case, for example, with the *Breviarium Bartholomei*.

340. The final sentence remains obscure.
341. Sig. 166 'Item lini semen solidum unum pensante bene tritum et adde mel cocl. .i., tere fortiter et fac potionem .i. et dabis cum vino tepido bibere'.
342. Sig. 166.
347. Cf. Sig. 165 'Ad eos qui urinam non continent: lactuce semen tritum cum <vino> vetere dabis bibere'.
348. Hunt 188, ll.1257–66, 276/76.
349. Hunt 188, ll.1268–80, 276/77.
350. Sig. 166 'Item bacas edere .vi. aut .xi. contritas ex aqua calida et vino potum dabis, cauculos in vessica frangit et per urinam educit'.
353. See 404 below.
354. These and the following verses are drawn from the *Physique rimee* (Hunt pp.142–216), here Hunt 191, ll.1359–70. See also Hunt 286/172.
355. Hunt 190, ll.1301–14 & 285/170. The Rawlinson text is corrupt. In line 10 a number of MSS read 'Les poins, les jointes cum il sunt' and in line 11 'les humours' and 'la savour'.
356. Hunt 190, ll.1315–8 & 285/170.
357. Hunt 190, ll.1319–28. The fifth line in *PR* reads 'Et canellie ensement'. See also Hunt 285/171 (fifth line 'chenulé') and 305/57.
358. Hunt 190, ll.1329–34 & 286/173. Cf. 360 below.
359. 'Derhymed' from Hunt 191, ll.1335–44, 286/174, and 305/58.
360. LH153,C695.
363. Hunt 237/28.
395. It is possible that 'l'aniz salvage' here and in 397 is an error for 'la vine salvage', see 448 & 450.
400. C574 & 590, Hunt 133 (LH),139 (LH) and 140 (LH). Cf. Hunt 227/26.
404. C473,T83 (against 'les verues') & 88 ('Ad petram qui impedit urinam'), Hunt 138 (LH, 'Pur la pere ke teut estaler'),277/78 & 293/234 ('Encuntre ceo ke home ne pot pissir').
436. C592, Hunt 139 (LH, omitting last sentence), Hunt 177, ll.895–8.
444. The MS has *vyt*" *que crest.*
445. Hunt 293,233.
462. Hunt 302/36. See Hunt, p.358 n.100.
463. The name 'amer foil' may be a rendering of 'amorfolium'.
466. See 103 above.
467. See 104 above.
471. Hunt 277/82.
486. Hunt 232/93.
494. The passage is of a type frequently met with in scientific manuscripts the contents of which conform to a number of Pseudo-Bedan texts, see *PL* 90,960D and 955C.
520. Hunt 201, ll.1652–4. See Sig. 166 'Ad somnum: Capita papaveris viridia in lacte infunde in aqua ut cooperiantur per triduum postea, coque ad tertias et per lintheum torque quantum habueris jus tantum mitte mel et coque ad mellis mensuram recende(?) da in aqua calida cocl. .v.'
522. Cf. 441 above.
531. Hunt 140 (LH).
544. Hunt 212/28 & 284/153.

547. Hunt 214/34 & 284/152.
551. Cf. Hunt 212/26 & 304/53 and 556 below.
552. Somewhat abbreviated. See Hunt 284/151 'por morsure de chien enragé: Fetes bien forte sause de sel e de eawe, si vus n'avez sause de mer, e de ceo lavez mult bien la morsure. Pus pernez plantaine, agrimone triblez ensemble. Pus mellez a ceo mel e aubun de l'eof e oignez de cel oignement'.
556. Hunt 283/150 & 304/53.
557. Hunt 181, ll.1019–22 & 308/75.
563. Sig. 167.
569. C591, Hunt 139, 282/130.
573. The Hippocratic facies of grave illness, which follows, is frequently found in medical MSS, in Latin, French or English, and derives from the *Prognostica*, see Hunt, *Anglo-Norman Medicine* 2 (Cambridge, 1997), p.250 and CC181.
574. See *Macer Floridus de viribus herbarum* ed. L. Choulant (Leipzig, 1832), ll.1881–83.
595. 'Derhymed' from Hunt 306/65.
597. 'Derhymed' from Hunt 307/66.
599. Cf. H159, M84/12.
609. Cf. the rather different 'Pocio de Antioche' ('Drink of Antioche') in H177, and in HE77/14,128/10,M83/1.

CHAPTER TWO
THE FIRST CORPUS COMPENDIUM

MS Cambridge, Corpus Christi College 388 is, for the most part, the work of a single hand of c.1320–30. The volume was disbound and restored in 1996. The pages measure approx. 234mm × 152mm, the writing block approx. 182mm × 114mm. The decoration is in red and blue. Coloured capitals are usually red, as are rubrics, whilst paragraph marks are mostly blue. Initial letters of lines are often splashed in red and some marginal indications such as 'Nota' are occasionally in red. There is damage to the parchment as follows: f.14 two holes; f.15 there are no outer margins in the upper part of the page owing to deficiencies in the skin; f.38 a large hole.

The MS comprises a set of medical texts, largely receipt collections, which represent some of the most extensive compilations to have survived from medieval England. On close inspection a number of originally independent treatises seem to have been combined under the attribution to Hippocrates, Galen and Aesclepius, for on f.1ra a metrical prologue in Anglo-Norman is headed *Hic incipit liber Ypocracii, Galieni, Sclepei* whilst a similar rubric introduces a quite distinct collection of medical receipts, exclusively in English, which begins with a list of headings on f.36ra, followed by the text proper on f.36va: *Here bygennes mani a god medecine þat leches han drawn out of þe bokes of Galion and Sclepius and Ypocras,*[1] ending on f.48vb *Expliciunt medicine de tractatibus Ypocracii, Gallieni et Sclepeii etc.* The first receipt collection occupies four gatherings of eight folios and a fifth of three. The second compendium is followed by miscellaneous receipts in Latin and English (ff.48vb–49ra). On

[1] See G. Henslow, *Medical Works of the Fourteenth Century* (London, 1899), p.139 cites MS B.L. Sloane 521 f.232a '**Hic incipiunt bonas medicinas**: Here begynne medicinys þat good lechys have made and drawyn out of here auctorys, as out Galion, Acclepias, and Ypocras, qheche wore þe beste lechys of þe world in here days; for al maneer of sorys, woundys, postemys, cancris, goutys, feestris, feouye(?), wormys, freclys, rede bleynys, causflem and generali for al maledys of þe body wytin and wytout'.

f.49rb there is preserved the beginning of a list of medico-botanical terms with vernacular (Anglo-Norman and English) equivalents. The brief text on f.49va–b is the well known set of Latin astrological verses drawn from the *Regimen Salernitanum*[2], ending *Expliciunt virtutes .xii. singnorum lunacionum*. More medical receipts, in Latin, occur on f.50ra–vb, followed (ff.50vb–52ra) by French receipts under the title *Secreta medicine .H. Sampsonis de Clouburnel.*[3] This collection includes a widely transmitted Christian charm said to have been borne by St Gabriel.[4] On ff.52ra–53vb there is a short treatise *Nomina herbarum et earum virtutes* ('Expliciunt nomina herbarum') which furnishes *synonyma* in Anglo-Norman and English. Finally (ff.53vb–54rb) comes a treatise in English on urines beginning *He[r] mayst you knowen urines be coloures.*

The present edition is concerned with the two collections attributed to Hippocrates, Galen and Aesclepius in the Corpus compendium. The first begins with a crudely versified prologue in Anglo-Norman which incorporates the section on humours which forms part of the introduction to the *Lettre d'Hippocrate.*[5] The second text, a treatise on urines 'secundum Magol', for which only the present witness is cited in Thorndike and Kibre,[6] presents a number of problems, not least the name 'Magol' (James hesitated over 'Magos') which remains puzzling. The French treatise on urines, which follows, is incorporated from the *Lettre d'Hippocrate*[7], as are the introductory lines prefacing the compendium, or 'Practica medicinae', which proceeds *a capite ad calcem.*

In the edition which follows the vernacular receipts are printed in italics, so that they may be distinguished at a glance from the Latin sections. The rubrics in the MS are printed in bold. In those Latin receipts which illustrate code-switching unmarked vernacular words appear in italics, marked ('anglice', 'gallice') vernacular items are placed between single quotation marks. The latter are also used to indicate superscript insertions. To facilitate understanding of the English, French and Latin texts a list of the principal orthographical peculiarities may be useful; the illustrative examples are not intended to be exhaustive.

[2] See L. de Renzi, *Collectio Salernitana* 1, 486. For MSS see H. Walther, *Initia* 11780.

[3] See MS Bodley 761 (s.xiv) ff.11v–21r (*Expliciunt secreta H. Samp' de Clouburnel*) where the second and third sections (f.12r–v) are identical to the first two sections (ff.50vb–51ra) of the Corpus text.

[4] See T. Hunt, *Popular Medicine*, pp.90f.

[5] See Hunt, *Popular Medicine*, p.109 and lines 20–38.

[6] *Incipits* 1610.

[7] See Hunt, *Popular Medicine*, p.109 and *Anglo-Norman Medicine* 2, p.259.

French:

c = *s* cel, celgemme, cenevé, encement, ceel ['salt'], solcicle
e parasitic e: est(e, puss(e, un(e, joures, ceilgemme, pus(e
ei = *e* feith (= 'fait'), bein, ceil ('sel'), cheif, ceilgemme
-is = *-s* greynis, humuris, horis, nerfis
oi/oy = *o* coil/coyl, goyt, oif, un poyt, soir, toir, toit ('tost')
ow = *u* nowil ('nul')
qu = *w* etquagera
s = *c* aforse, cumensement, forse, se, selli, semense, servel(e, ses, sette, seus, sez, sindre, sire, staude ('chaude')
t = *s* cretthre, dettemprer, etquagera, let, metter, mettre; *et-* for *es-* : detstoppez, etchapera, etchaufer, etcorche, etcrit, etcrivés, etcume, etkues, etpesse, etplein, etscorche, etscorchier, etscumez, etspine, etsplen, etspurgement, etstamper, etstancher, etstok, etstoppés, etstreynez, etstuer, etswagera, etthre
th/þ = *t* ethre, eyth, thor, voþre
u = *é* numument
-us = -(e)*s* corus, greynus, illeucus, maynus, memus, novelus, pessounus, vermus
z = *s* lez, dez, narez, pulverez

Latin:

ai = *a* plaistrum/playstrum
c = *s* accescionis, cervicia, cilicet, cepe, cepius, cepum, cero, ciccis, salcis
j = *g* jencianam
ngn = *gn* lyngnum, lingni
s = *c* asmisse, cognossere, cressent, eruse, misse, liquessit, pissium, quiesse, quiesset, sedrum, selidonia/seledonia, sentinodia, serfolium, servicia, sessabit, sissum, sito, warense; *s* = *sc* sindi
v = *b* vacas
w = *vu* wlgariter

English:

ei = ME [*e:*] bleind, caneil, ceilgemme, deid, einde, heveid, kneid, meing, reid, seid, weil,
h- huse (vb.), heycil, hold hurine
oi/oy = *o* bloid, broit/broyt, cloit/cloyt(h), floid, foit, goid, goit, groip, hoik, hoil, hoit/hoyt, loitwort, stoik, stroyng, witstoid, wyrmoid
owi = *ou* nowit, (h)owit

q = *w* quan(ne, quat, quer, querso, quete, querof, queþer, quich, quil(e, quite, quo, quyt, sqwalw, sqwellingge, sqwin(e, sqwollen, squage, squet

th = *t* hoyth

Editorial Principles:
In the English, the scribe's use of *u* and *v* and *i* and *j* has been preserved. The letters *y* and *ʒ* have been realised as *þ* and *ȝ* where appropriate. The expansion of abbreviations is not indicated save in exceptional cases. The manuscript word division has not been systematically adhered to except in the case of imperatives with the enclitic pronoun which the scribe almost always writes as a single word e.g. *drincket*, *medlet*.

[f.1ra] **Hic incipit liber Ypocracii, Galieni, Sclepei**

Ypocras se livere fyt,
A le emperour Cesar myt,
Demandant 'Si vol[e]z vivere,
Entendez ben a moun livere'.
Kar il enseinyt humme
De manere e de custhumme
Cumment il deyt tuzjoures
De humme e femme aver cures.
Par lez ewes regarderés,
Cum aprés etcrit truverés,
Cumment humme detcrira
Si de mort etchapera;
Lez medesinez queus il sunt
Ky a maladez appendunt;
E de lour enfermetés
Cumment il serrunt deliverés.
Kar saun acun manere fayle
Vous lez truverés saun travaile
Cum etcrit est saun demurez
De humme e beste .iiii. humurez.
Ses sunt lez humures
Cum etcrit est par plusurz:
Le primere e[st] chaude, le autre secche,
Le terce moyste, le quarte freyde.

Par chalurez sunt susteynous
Let chosez par let queus vivous;
Lez os sunt secchez, saun fayle,
Ke nous donunt forse a travaile;
Nos entraylez freides sunt
Dunt tuz nos viez suspirunt;
Le sanc e[st] moiste ensie
Ke nuryth tut le vie.
Par lez os ou par le saung ruge e blanc
Cuirunt lez veyne[s] gendrant san[c].
En .iiii. parties de meun cors
Est l'enfermeté deins e hores:
A chef, a ventre, a l'etplein,
A le vesie, regardés ben. [f.1rb]
Ore par singnez vuerés,
Cum en les ewez truverés,
Voit humme lez jugemens
De mettrez e de sage gens.

[f.1rb] *De urinis secundum Magol*

Urina viri sani est pura et aurei coloris.

Urina mulieris sane est alba cum quadruplici pollore.

Urina pacientis calorem est rubia sicud sanguis.

Urina pacientis febrem est brouncus sicud lessiva vetera.

Urina pacientis quartanam est nigra ut oleum lampadis.

Urina rubea et pura multam significat [infirmitatem] pulmonis .a. 'lungus' de nimio calore.

Urina multum emissa, si sit alba et multum pura, significat quod sanies pulmonis tendit ad perfectam maturitatem.

Urina multum tenuis et multum pallida significat quod aliquid in stomaco est indigestum.

Urina multum rubea et multum spissa et multum emissa significat defectum pulmonis.

Urina in febre cotidiana habens parva frusticula et tanquam denigrata significat mortem. Consimili modo si parvum est de urina et eadem nigra est signum mortis.

Urina habens tanquam furfur et parum insubstancia cito [f.1va] transit ad mortem.

Urina in magna quantitate emissa et glauca in febricitante signat mortem.

Urina virida in febricitante ex facili paralisim adquirit videlicet de gutta.

Urina gulcinar est signum bonum in qualibet infirmitate, sed infirmus caveat se a frigore.

Urina modica et clara et gulcinar habens spumam, si spuma decendit, est signum quod homo evasit infirmitatem.

Urina virginis est alba et lucida et quedam grana alba [sunt] natantia interrius.

Quando urina est rufa ut sanguis, sic curabis infirmum : Accipe rosas siccas in apoteca et consue unum saccum panni linei et hoc facto depone infra rosas et decoque in pura aqua et post decoctionem pone calidum super epar pacientis, et hoc cepe, quia frigi[di]tas rosarum temperet calorem.

Quando urina est broncus, si habet nigram lunam apertam superius, spes est de sanitate, si autem clausam, signum mortis.

Si autem luna in summitate urine est aperta, tunc[8] sic curabis pacientem: Respice centauriam, semen absinthei, siccas rosas, equali pondere, istis omnibus adde lavendulam [f.1vb] et decoque in olla cum aqua ut due partes aque consumantur. Post hec ad mediam partem imple ollam aqua et iterum decoque ad modum pissium. Hoc facto ad[de] aliam novam ollam et da pacienti jejuno tribus diebus mane et cero et postquam in cero sumserit. Postea nichil aliud sumat et caveat a potacione magna, comedat pedes porcinos et lac amigdalorum quanto sepius potest.

Quando urina est in febre, sic curabis infirmum: Cape succum de *hellerneberiun* et succum radicis, adiecis succum de *mousere*, et ad istas admisse vaccas lauri .i. *coesloppes* bene trita[s] cum magna quantitate omnium istorum et accipe butirum in vere factum et hec omnia decoque et tempera in vase. Cum unguento isto precordia inunge quatuor diebus et quartana cessabit.

Curacio febris. Item alio modo curabis: Respice rutam erbam et decoque in aqua pura et post decoctionem fac tepefieri et bibe illam aquam ante oram accescionis et hoc fac tribus vicibus, semper ante oram accescionis.

Quando urina est pura et rubea, multam significat infirmitatem pulmonis et sic poteris curare[9] [f.2ra] infirmum: Accipe cardemomum quia confortat stomacum et facit bonam digestionem, vomitum refugit et pectus mundificat.

[8] MS tunc tunc.

[9] At the bottom of the page has been added in a contemporary hand 'Quando nascitur ulcus intrinsecus in corpore alicuius, urina eius est pallida et si habeat superius circulum in summitate apertum, illa vel ille curabilis est, et si clausum, incurabilis est. Qui curabilis est dura et acetosa vitet, omnia dulcia comedat ut poma dulcia et mel cocta et magnos labores non faciat'.

Aqua rosea bene mundata valet ad angustiam pulmonis, pectoris et gutturis. Item decoque quantitatem liquiricie cum anisus et semen feniculi. Ista decoctio valet ad omnia vicia pectoris et pulmonis.

Quando urina est multum tenuis et multum pallida, significat aliquid in stomaco esse indigestum. Tunc sic pacientem curare poteris: Da zeduar pacienti cum sit jejunus. Under versus: 'Zeduar ante datum morbum fugat inveteratum'. Post cibum sumptum facit ut bene digerat illum. Item jencianam[10] comedat et zinziber album deglutiat.

Quando urina est multum [...] et multum spissa et multum emissa, significat defectum pulmonis. Sic curare poteris pacientem: Resspice ysopum, liquiriciam et *hertestunge* et decoquas in aqua et appone zinziberum et paciens bibat mane et cero. Et postea dimittet sanguinem de vena pulmonis et curabitur.

Nota quod cum homo evasit, debet abstinere a balneo et custodiat corpus suum a frigore et ne utatur duris et salcis cibariis et multum piperaciis.

Contra acutam [infirmitatem]. Contra tercianam et acutam et quamlibet infirmitatem provenientem [f.2rb] ex causa callida: Accipe apium anglice 'ache' et farinam ordei et parum de aceto et contrito apio, fac pastam et frigidam pone super epar. Hoc fac cepius et curabitur.

Qui consueverit minutionem et neclexerit debito tempore tercianam incidet. Iste paciens caveat et abstineat a duro cibo videlicet a carnibus bovinis, ciccis, salcis, ovis, butiro, vino et bona servicia.

Quando urina est clara et spuma liquessit, sanus est homo; si autem spuma non statim liquessit, tunc adhuc quiesset in infirmitate et non est penitus liberatus et confortetur donec convalescat omnino.

Quando splen hominis est inflatum, tunc est homo pallidus et urina eius est clara et dolor est in sinistro latere et punture accedunt ad cor, quod vix homo potest trahere anelitum et dolor transit ad scapulas. Sic poteris curare eum: Resspice oleum laureum et unge latus sub costis. Postea accipe *humlock* et tere et misse succum cum farina ordei et pone super pannum, quem pannum madefac in aceto et pone super sinistrum latus. Postea decoque in veteri servicia plantaginem, semen feniculi et paciens illam [f.2va] cerviciam bibat tribus diebus mane et sero. Hoc facto paciens minuat spleneticam in dextera manu circa minimum digitum et curabitur.

Quando urina est clara et alba ad modum fontis, signum est quod stomacus est infrigidatus. Sic ipsum curare poteris: Accipe zinziberum et mala grana[ta], zeduar et vaccas lauri equali pondere. Ista omnia pulverisata decoque in

[10] MS jenciariam.

veteri servicia quam bibat mane et cero. Et deglutias zinziber album. Postea respice furfuros tritici et decoque in aceto et pone super stomacum pacientis quantum calidius sustinere potest. Et hoc fac cepius et curabitur. Comedat autem zinziberum conditum. Postquam autem urina est aurei coloris, sanatus est homo et tunc caveat se a bovinis carnibus et duris, balnea frequentat et novam serviciam bibat.

Item de urinis

Si le urine seyt blanche de tut le matyn e ruge aprés manger, signefiet sainté.

Le urine gras e truble e pua[nte], icele n'e[st] pas bone.

Le urine tenve e[st] nent bone en feveres. Si il est truble, signefiet dolour de chef procheynement a veneyr.

Le urine grasse e moyste e blanche signefie fevere [f.2vb] quartine.

Le urine sanglant signefie le vecie ethre debrucé de acun porture.

Le urine petyt, charnu e grasse e velue signefie mal dé reynes.

Le urine sanglant e feveruse od pecez de sancgk signefie grant maladie e numument deins le corps et en le vecie.

Le urine que cheit par gutes ou nouet[11] desure cum ampules signefie long enfermeté.

Le urine de femme cleer e normal e lusant cum argent, [e] ceste femme suvent vomyth e n'at nowil talent de manger ne de beyre, signefie le femme ethre enseynte.

Le urine de femme blanch e peysant e puant signefie dolour dé reynez e le maris plein de mal e de enfermeté de freyde.

Le urine de femme que ad etcume cum sanck desure e que est cler cum ewe signefie dolour de cheif e aver perdu talent de manger et de dormer pur emflure de stomac.

Le urine de femme que eyth colour de or e cler e peysant signefie femme aver talant de humme.

Le urine de femme que ad colour de faryn a l'etspurgement,[12] si le femme eyt fevere quarteyne, signefie que ele mura deins .iii. joures.

[f.3ra] Le urine de femme ky est sicum peiz e eit colour de plum, si le femme est enseynte, signefie l'enfant ethre mort deins luy, e si ele n'e[s]t pas enseynte, signefie le mariz purri[13], e si il est teil, le urine est pouant.

[11] MS vouez.

[12] MS etspungement.

[13] MS purer.

Le urine de femme ky est emflé, ou ele ait le tuse ou le menisoun, si il eit colour de lyn, signefie ky ne puyt ethre sané.

E si devez cunustre par les urinez lé maus de juene corps e kant vous les avez conous, si poés veer medecines. E pu[r] ce ky hummez sunt de diverse humurez e de qualitez, encountre checun qualité plusurs averés medicinez, a comenssement a cheif e pus a tous autrez menbres.

[PRACTICA]

[The Head]

Pur le chef. (1) *Pernés .ii. unces de betoyne e .iii. unces de here te[re]stre, 'þat is heyhowe,' e .viii. unces de puliole, 'þat ys hulwrt', e les fettis brayer en une morter. E kant sette .iii. herbes sunt ben braés, fettes lez frire en une payele de oyle*[14] *de olive e mettez deins le payele un unce de sire verge e .i. quarterun de fraunc encens ben molu. E kaunt il est ben bulé, culez le parmy un drap e le lessés refreyder e cele [f.3rb] unement mettez en une boyste. E cant la dolour de cheif veint, oigniés la fontayne de la teste en crois, e auxi cum sentés que la dolour sey remue, axi remuez le unement. Aprez si garra certaynement.*

(2) *Item pernez l'etstok de ruge cholet e coupez aveye le racine. E pellez le stoik e le coupez en goubounez e le boylez ben en ewe e camamille e betoyne. E pus pernez wy de pomere, anglice 'winballez', e fettez cendre. E de le ewe boylé e de cele cendre fettez lessive e fettez laver la cheif, si garra e donera bone vowe.*

Pur tremulure de chief e m[ayn]us. (3) *Pernez primerole ov tut le racine e primeveyre ov tut le racine, ce este 'cowesloppez', e sauge ov tut le racine e semense de cenevé, anglice 'carloc-seid', e foyle de lorer, si vous lez poés aver, de checun erbe atant de le un cum de le autre. E fettez lez ben moudre*[15] *en une morter e ben medler ov boure freche e lessés le estre quatur jou[f.3va]res ou .v. e pusse en une payele frire e culier parmi un drap. E cele unement ostera tut le tremulure dé maynus ou de cheif. E humme deit oyndre le col e lé nerfis e les veynes e lez joins dez maynus.*

(4) Item ad vertigines at capitis dolores: Accipe betam viridem bene tritam et cum succo inunge tempera.

Ad idem. (5) Item pulegium coctum in aceto ad narez pone calidum, ut odor intret de ipso et fac coronam de eodem et capiti calidam circum appone.

(6) Item si capud videtur sindi pro dolore: Succum edere mixtum cum oleo et aceto et nares unge pacientis.

[14] MS olyve.

[15] MS mourdre.

(7) Item contra omnes capitis dolores: Folia edere trita molissime aceto[16] et oleo roseo mixta fronte illiniatur.

(8) Item pulegium cum oleo coque et cum eo capud et tempera unge.

(9) Item minta trita timpora line.

(10) Item ruta trita cum sale et melle mixta sanat.

(11) Item oleo facto de nucibus maioribus capud inunge.

(12) Item radicem feniculi tere et cum eo capud inunge.

(13) Item absintheum, rutam et ederam terrestrem tere cum melle et albumine ovi et indutum lintheo capiti appone.[f.3vb]

(14) Item rutam, abrotanum, salgiam, ederam terestrem, trifolium simul tere et distempera cum aqua et bibe.

(15) Item trifolium in aqua coque et tempora illini.

Ad capud purgandum. (16) Item ad capud purgandum et vocem clarificandam et raucas reprimendas voces: Jus absinthei sume, jus marubii, jus feniculi, centum grana piperis, farine[17] fabarum, anglice 'flour-ben',[18] siccate duo coccliaria[19] despumate mellis, tantum quantum de jure erbarum et coque simul in olla ad spissitudinem mellis. Et tunc tolle de igne ut frigeat sicque in pixide pone. Et cum opus fuerit, da jejuno coccliar unum et caveat hiis diebus a lardo et butiro et oleo et ab omnibus salcis.

(17) Item plantaginem et ederam in mortario tere et salem et oleum et vinum misse et calidum super capud pone.

(18) Item ob vertiginem capitis qui pre nimio dolore quasi mentes[20] suas amittunt: Selidonia cum radice sua subfumigetur et infirmus per triduum ipsam herbam circa collum ligatam ferat.

Pro ossibus e[xt]rahere[21] illesis. (19) Item folia vervene cum sale trita ossa illisa extrahunt ex qualibet fractura ac vulneri [et] cum auxungia veteri inposita vulnera sana[n]t et capita munda[n]t.[f.4ra]

(20) Item seledonia cum melle trita et capiti vulnerato inposita optime sanat.

Pro surditate. (21) Item sume recentem angwillam et excoriatam, ossa et sanguinem collige in vase mundo. Ille sanguis ponatur in saniorem aurem surdi et valebit ut probatum est.

[16] MS aceto que.
[17] MS forme.
[18] i.e. ben-flour.
[19] There is apparently an omission, so that as the text stands 'two spoonfuls' could apply to either the bean-flour or the honey.
[20] MS mentas with superscript addition of *e*.
[21] MS ehaere with superscript 'a'.

(22) Item ad vertiginem: Unaquaque die .iii. guttas de urina propria super capud infirmi infunde mane cum sit jejunus.

(23) Item abrotanum bibat et li[berabitur].

(24) Item radix plantaginis collo appensa dolorem tollit.

(25) Item *heit holwrt in eycil and do it to þi nese-þerles þat þe odour cum into his heued and mak a playstre of holwrt soþen and ley it up on þi heued.*

(26) *For ache of þe heued þat lounge haik: Tac a anful of rue and an hanful of heihoue and an handful of þe leues of lorer and seit hem togidere in water or in win and þat playstre ley on hise heued.*

(27) *Item tack supernewode and huni and eycil and put hem togydere and drincket ofte fastande.*

(28) *Item poyne rue wit þe þicke ground of eyerose and smer wit þat þi templus.*

(29) *Item tac galle of þe hare and temper it wit huni so þat it be*[22] [f.4rb] *weil red colured and þat þer be al so michel of þat on as of þat oþer and smere þerwit þin heued before and þi templus.*

(30) *Item poyne holwrt wit his flour and ȝif him to dri[n]gcun in hoyt water an hold him fastinge tyl non.*

(31) *Item tac supernewode and walnote-leues and heyhoue and poyne hem togidere in water and ȝif him to drinken.*

(32) *Or puyn salt*[23] *an honi and ley it al so a playstre to þe heued.*

(33) *Item if þe molde becum [...]:*[24] *Tack þe leues of egremoyne and seit hem in huni and mac a playstre and ley it abouen on þe molde, and þou salt warisse.*

(34) *Item seit celedoyne and wring it þoru a line cloit and do it in a box and þerewit smer þin heued and afterward wasse þin heued in þat selue water þat celodoine was in soþen.*

(35) *Item for þe feloun þat mack þe heued to swellen: Tac gres of þe hert, honi and barli-mele and þe rede docke and poyne hem alle togidere and saif þe heued of þe seke and ley þe playstre al hoit up on þe heued and let it be þer til it be sauf.*

(36) *For iche manere euele of* [f.4va] *þe heued: Tac rue and lei it in eycil and smer þerwit þin heved al abouen.*

(37) *Item seit rue and fenil in water and was þe heued.*

(38) *And tac þe ius of þe blake bete and smere þin forheued and þi templus.*

(39) *Item tac þe grene leues of ivi and rue and poyn hem in eicil and smere þe heued and templus.*

[22] MS be iweil ros coloured and be ..., an evident dittography.

[23] MS it salt an water (expuncted) honi.

[24] *a doun* added in margin.

(40) *Item tac þe ious of her[t]wrt and medlet wit olye and salt bren to puder and smere þerwit þin heved.*

(41) *Item sauge in eycil temperud and oyli rosetk medelud and þerwit smere þin heued.*

(42) *Item verueyne and betoyne, wermoid, seledoyne, weybrede and rue, walwrt and þe rinde of hellerne and hony wit peper-cornus, poyne al hem togedere and wel hem in wyne and þerof drink fastynge ate morwen and last at euen til þou be hoil.*

(43) *For wimmen þat arn sore in þe heueid: Iche day fastende drinck betayne an se schal ben hoil.*

Item pro eodem. (44) Accipe rutam, erbam jovis, que dicitur 'humlock', radicem feniculi et levestici, anglice 'þouþistele', [f.4vb] equali pondere. Postea appone albumen ovi et condiendo simul et postea cola per pannum et fac unum plaistrum cum lino et pone super anteriorem partem capitis.

(45) Item centauriam in vino coctam et calidam bibe.

(46) *Item [pernez] puliole, le quisez en eicil, mettés a nariles que il sente(nt) de le odour.*

(47) *Pur le cheif etspurger: Pernez lesive de primerole e mettez a narilis ov un penne, si garr[e]z.*

(48) Item rutam et feniculum coque in aqua et cum ea lava capud tuum.

(49) *Item tac pulial real and ere terestre*[25] *and rue and camamille and betoyne and lorer-leues and wel al in 'h'uni or in eycil and mack a plastre and ley it to þi temples.*

(50) *Item pur le chef espurger: Tac pellestre and schou þe rote thre dayes and it schal spurgen þe heued and don away þe hete, an waris.*

(51) *Item tac þe fillis and seit hem lounge in water; þis drinck schal drawe þe hete owit at þin mowt or at þi nese or at þin eres*[26] *or at þin eyen withly.*

(52) *Item tac mustard-seid and rue and stamp it*[27] *[and temper it wit water] til it [be] þicke and do to [þe] heued.* [f.5ra]

(53) **For w'o'nde in þe heved.** (53) *ȝif him to drincke pigil, senigle, erbe Robert, auence, reid wrte, tansey, hempe, of ilkon olike michel, but of maddur al so michel os of alle þe oþer, and do þerto ambrose, þat is wilde sauge, burnet, and þe crispe malwe and do hem to þe oþer aforsayd and yif þer be bone broken and þou dars nowit serchen it, ȝif him þis to drincke.*

(54) *Tack þe rede cole-wrte and tansey, hemp, hors-mynte, red nettle, brere-cropus, al so michel of madder os of alle þe oþere greses, stamp hem togidere and seith hem in wyne and ȝif him to drinck. And yif it comet howit at þe wonde, þan is it singne of lyue and*

[25] MS and ercestre.

[26] There appears to be a long 's' before eres.

[27] MS wit.

proued verray, for if [it] come owit and he cast it nowit, þat is singne of lyf and þan is it time to serchen þe [wonde] and [save þe] broken [bones] quenteliche þat þou ne tame nowit þe teye of þe braynes. And if it blede faste, wyp it softely wyt line and sithen tack a softe line cloyt wered þat is qwyt and clene and ley ouer þe wounde. And tack quete flour bulted and strew on þe cloyt þat lyit [f.5rb] *on þe wnde ful softely and litel; sitthen lat a wimun*[28] *þat nurisset a knaue child ful softeli milken þer ouere þe flour þat liet on þe cloit, and sitthen ley anoþer cloit þerupon and strewe þeron quete flour as þou dest on þat oþer and do milken al so þerto, and do so til it be euene with þe fleys and hil þe heued warme and lat it ben til on þat oþer morwe. An sitthen vnhil þe heued ful softeli and yif ye se þeron abouen as it were a burbul þat standit on þe water wan it reinet, þan is singne of ded and also if þou se ouer þe teye al so it were a spinuale webbe, blo or reid, þat is tokene [þat] þe rime ouer þe braynez [is broken] and þat is singne of hasti ded.* **Nota**. *And yif þere ben non of þese singnes, þan ȝif him ilke day to drincken at morwen and at euen [þis drincke] and it schal maken þe broken bones to comen hout and clensen þe rime of þe braynez of bloid and hele þe wounde. And ȝif þe heued be broken þat maser behoued ben doun þerinne, lat remue weil þe broken [bones] of þe heued* [f.5va] *as it is aforsayd and sitthen don þerinne maser and grese þe wounde wit þis vnement: Tack puliole real, bonwrt, ambrose, ribbe, bugle, cheuerfoyle, þe [red] nettle, lekes, hache, weybrede, tansey and morel, matefeloun, betoyne, of ilk olyche mychel, and stamp weil togedere wit wine and freis grees of a sqwyn and a litel of honi and virgine wax and with rosine and quan alle þese þingus ben stampped weil togedere, do hem in a bras poet or in a friing panne and do þerto quit wine and lat it stande so a day and a nyth and upon þat oþer morwen do seith it weil and wringit yourth a cloith wil it is hoyte and gres þe sore þerwith, and it schal waris.*

(55) *For þe heued broken: Stamp clene lek and do it in þe wounde a nyth, and on þe morwen do it away and tac ye of þe hache and al so micul of huni, do togedere and do it in þe wnde and it schal drawn howit of þe heued þe broken bones ȝif þer ben ani inne.*

(56) *For bon broken in þe heued: Tac reid wrtes and tansey and yif him to drincken.*
[f.5vb](57) Ad plagam capitis profundam et [si] testa rupta fuerit in primis: Capillos tunde, deinde mundum panniculum .i. est absque ullo medicamine, vel lardi a linthe juxta plage quantitatem in ipso hiatu ossis, ne sanies iruens in juncturas suas putredinem extendat. Postea inpone broceam usque ad terciam diem. Postea ungwentum fuscum qualibet die apponatur.

Ungwentum. (58) Ungwentum fuscum: Resspice celodonie .vi., de mastic .ii., de mirre .ii., cere .ii., olei libri .vi., quod priusquam in coctura ponatur, dissolvatur (prout mundari poterit) et aliquantulum super ignem in aliquo vase locato prout poterit mundari,[29] cum aqua frigida super asspergatur, et

[28] MS wimuns.

[29] MS mudius.

sic mundatum confice sic in ollam, oleum inponatur et sic adjungatur lento. Deinde semini appone cumque liquefactum fuerit, ceram mitte ea que liquefacta, ceterorum pulverez mitte sub intervallo et tunc dimitte bullire quousque coctum tibi videatur. Hoc facto conditum est.

(59) Pro ossibus inpressis in capite vel in alio loco corporis: Tere agrimoniam et inde fac unum playstrum et appone loco.

(60) Pro ossibus fractis in capite: Bibe betoniam et expelle ossa et sanabit vulnus.

(61) Si plaga sit in capite et fracta sit taga, est incurabilis; set si taga [f.6ra] sit sana, curabilis est.

(62) Experimentum si taga sit fracta cum nuce: Si nucem poterit frangere vel nodum straminis, tunc est curabilis.

(63) *For þe heued þat is broken in þe bone: Tac an hanful of malws and an handful of wyrmoid and an handful of mugwede and stampe hem togedere. And tac .iiii. vnces of quete flour or of barlich-flour and .iiii. vnceȝ of huny and reid wyne an .iiij. vnceȝ of galt-smere, and of þat gres so do in a panne and melt it and maket hoyt, and do mack a plaistre, and ley it to þe heued al warm.*

(64) Item folia vervene cum sale et unco porcino cito[30] ossa fracta extrahunt et plagam sanant.

For þe scalle. (65) *Tack þe de lyun and setit in goid leye and saue þe scalle al away and mac a playstre and ley it þeronne sum del hoyt, and it shal waris.*

(66) *Item tac pick and virgine wax and welle hem alle togydere and do hem in a cloyth sum deel hot and ley it on þe heueid .ix. dayes and .ix. nyth. And þanne do it away and tack wilwe-leuus and seith hem in laumpe-oyle and ley it þer þe heir is away.*

Idem. (67) *Item shaif þe heueid al þe scalle away and tac þe speccus of þe newe sole leder an seyth hem and quanne þei arn soþein, tack and do þeronne brinston grunden ful smal and g'r'esse it.*

[f.6rb](68) *Item tack pick and wax and seith togedere*, ut superius dicitur.

(69) *Or puyne garleck wit huny and ley it þeron.*

(70) *Item tack þe blake [bete] and stamp it and tac þe ious þerof and*[31] *smer þin heued.*

(71) *And for to make þe her to growen aȝein: Seith þe leues of þe wiþi-tre wyt oly and ley þer her wantus.*

(72) *Item pernés scire virge e buliés ben e pus raeȝ le chef e fettus enplaystre e lesseȝ cucher a le tette .ix joures, si garra.*

(73) *For wermis in þe heued: Tac salt and saym and brinston and mack þe salue and smer þin heued þerwith.*

30 MS in po cito.

31 MS a*n*d and.

(74) *For þe her schal nowit growen:* Semen urtice cum aceto distempera et cum eo capud perunge.

(75) Item lacte canis inunge et non cressent pili evulsi.

(76) Item ne pili contrarii nascantur: Ova formicarum, lacrimam edere .i. jus, archeme[se]am equo pondere, hec omnia [f.6va] in vino quiesse et locum vulneris tange et pili nuncquam renascentur.

Ut pili nascantur. (77) Ut pili nascantur: Agrimoniam cum lacte caprino pone [super] locum sine pilis, et nascentur.

(78) Ne cadant pili lava capud decoctione mallwe.

(79) *Pur chevus [...] lavez voþre tetthe ow lessive de lis, anglice 'lilie'. Si vous seis chanue, il ne chaungerunt.*

[The Ears]

Oyraylez. (80) *Pur oraler e tike u pur auter vermyn que entreit le orayle: Pernés jous de luveache e le tenez leins*[32] *oun lué de voye, si tu[e]ra lez vermes e lez fra vener hors de teste mors ou vifs certeynement.*

(81) Ad dolorem aureum: Accipe succum mente campestris, anglice 'hormynte', in aurem mitte.

(82) Item ut vermes eicias: Succum sallvie vel abrotani vel savine in aure exprime.

(83) Ad efugandum vermem ab aure qui dicitur auriculare: Accipe medullam tauri vel vacce et appone tepidum in aure et exiet vermis propter dulcedinem medulle.

(84) Contra surditatem: Accipe viride lyngnum abietis et cum ardet tolle illud quod fluit in posteriori parte lingni et admisse favum mellis. Hoc facto *lokechestre* vivens coque et succum eius adde pre[f.6vb]dictis et mitte in aures et curabitur surditas.

(85) *For qwic þing þat enturit mannes here: Tack þe ious of senchoun of huse and blen'd'it wit gres of heles and do it in þe here.*

(86) *Item tac þe ious of þe wilde tanse and do it in þe ere, and it schal waris.*

(87) *For bolnyng of eres: Tac þe soure-docke and fold it in a wrte-leef and bren it in þe eimeriez and stamp hem and ley þerto.*

(88) *Pernez le jous de mente e feites teve, si mettés en oyrayles.*

(89) *Item si il eyt orayler, detemprés mentastre*[33] *en vin e si colez*[34] *le jous parmy un drap, si mettez teve in oyrayle.*

[32] MS leinnes.

[33] MS menstrare.

[34] MS socalez.

(90) *Item pernés le jous de eble*[35] *e mettez as oyrayles, lequele dounet oye a homme que longement at eté surde.*

Si reues (?) i sunt. (91) *De seus que reues i sunt: Se venunt sovent de feblesse de cors ou de maws humuris, la curacioun est teil: Pernez le poel de serpent e pudrez e mellés ow un poyn de 'hawes', si restreynrunt lé chevus*[36].

(92) *Item pernés semense de lyn,* [f.7ra] *si le ardés e mellés ov oyl, si oynés le chef.*

Ad idem. (93) *Item averoyne, aloyne quissez muyt en leye e suvent lavés le cheef.*

(94) *Item le sindre de vine*[37] *pernez e os de beste e veut oynt de porck, si fettés unement e oynez le chef .viii. joures ou .ix.*

A surdesse. (95) *Item pur surdesse de oyrayl: Pernez le gres de freys angwile e le jous de aloyne e feel de chevere e metez ensemble en un poyt, si lez chaufés a fu tanck'il seyt teve e pus le debutés ov*[38] *une penne en orayle e si garrés.*

Idem. (96) *Item a sourdesse e a dure oye medicine bone e prové: Pernés un blanche unioun, si le crevés en le mylou amount. E pus le emplés a le pertuse de cumyn ben batu e pus en mettez jous de rue e jous de jubarbe uelement e pus mettés gres de angwil freys e neyr, si le mettés en morter e brucés. E pus le fettes streindre parmy un drap en une basoun, si mettez a seyr en le orayle surde e etstoppés le orayl seyne e gissés de cele part dekes* [f.7rb] *encounter le jour. E pus gisés desure le malade partie e lessés curer ores. E fettez vous un bayn meme cele jour e detstoppez vous oyrales en cele bayn e lavés voþre teste de lessive feith de vine, e si garrés.*

(97) Ad illos qui male audiunt: Accipe viperam, anglice 'lokechestre', qui cum multis pedibus vadit, qui cum tangatur, statim reddit se rotondum, et bulle in aqua. Postea pone in aure de aqua.

(98) Ad illos qui nullo modo audiunt: Accipe fel leporis cum lacte mulieris, tempera et in aure pone per triduum et claude aurem cum sicca lana.

Wirmus in hed. (99) *For wirmus in þe heued: Tac salt and saym and brinston and mac þe salue and smer þi heued.*

(100) Ad aurium dolorem: Tolle cepas et tere fortiter et adde cuminum et mitte in frixorium in modum cataplasme et tepidum in aurem inpone.

(101) Ad auditum: Micas panis ordeacei[39] pone ad aures calidas.

Ad idem. (102) Ad idem: Accipe flos de salice silvatica que super flumen pendet, vel siccum vel viridem, tere bene in mortario cum aceto et per

[35] MS tenere.

[36] MS clevus.

[37] MS veine.

[38] MS en.

[39] MS ordeiiceii.

pannum stringe et da cum aceto fortissimo bi[f.7va]bere et sine dubio emuclium(?) faciet per .ix. dies.

Ad imygranas.[40](103) Ad emigranias[41] delendas: Grana piperis .xxx. et in quantum levare potest tribus digitis farine ordei mundate et tere piper nimis et misse cum albumine ovis et mire prodest si posueris in fronte pacientis.

Si aqua in aure. (104) Item si aqua in aure introierit et dolorem fecerit, succus coliandri in aurem inpressus prodest.

(105) *Item quo may nowit wel heren: Tack þe grene bowes of hasse and ley hem on þe fyr and gader þe water þat rennez owit of eindez an ey-schell ful and þe ius of senegrene als mycel honi.*

[The Eyes]

(106) *Tack a goid partie of þe rose-floure and of fenkele, a litel rue and litul cumyn and seith hem alle togedere in clene water and wryng hem þorw a clene cloyth and do it in a lome of led or of glas and do þeroffe in þe heye quan ye gost to bedde. And wasse þin eye at morwen wyt eyerose quan þou rist.*

(107) *For howe in mannus eye: Tac peper and bren it in a cloyt an stamp it to p'o'uder and myng it wyt marw of a gos-weinggus and do it in þe eye.*

(108) *For sore eynne: Tac rose-floures and fenkele and filago [f.7vb] and pympurnel and celodoyne and eufrase and temper al togedere wyt hony and gres of snayles and wyt quite of eyren.*

(109) *For hurtyng of eyne: Tack May-butere and comyn and stamp hem togedere and ley it on line and do it to þe eye and offte new it. And quan þe bolnyng is swaged, tak safron and wommanis melk of a knaue-schyld and do hem alle to droppe in þe sore eye, and it schal warisse.*

(110) Colirium istud visum serenat, sanguinem dispergit, telam rumpit, tineam necat, guttam exteriat: Sal cum melle et vino et ovi albumine de omnibus eque sumens in pelvim mitte ubi simul flagellata quasi glaram ad verniculum faciens per novem dies dimitte. Plurimum valet occulis.

(111) Item contra maculam: Folia albe spine collige et tere et succum eorum occulis inpone.

(112) Item atramentum et meel et ovi albumen omnia eque comisse et occulo alliga.

(113) Ad removendum sanguinem de occulo: Ruta et cumynum bulliantur in vino albo et colentur per pannum subtilissimum et cero occulis inponatur.

40 MS Ad dimygranas.

41 MS demigranias.

(114) Ad lippitudinem occulorum: Accipe atramentum, mel, albumen ovi, simul conficies et sero [f.8ra] super occulos pone et mane lacte mulieris inunge.

(115) Ad recuperandum visum: Accipe collubrum viv[u]m et pone in ollam novam et coque super ignem sine aqua et ex pingwedine que inde exierit unge occulos et mirifice videbis.

(116) *For sore eyne þat ben wateri oþerquile wit swelt and witouten sqwellingge oþerquile brennyngge wit water and blodi and oþer manere: For euele of eye seith þe rede snayl in water and gedere þerof þe gres and smer þerwit þin eye.*

Ad eundem. (117) Item: *Bren þe snayl upon a slat ston and put it in þin eye quan þou gos to slepe.*

(118) *For dryth of eye: Tack arment and hony, quite of an ay, and myng togedere and do þe playstre to þe eye.*

Ad eundem. (119) Item: *Poyne hertwrt and temper it [wit] wite of an ay a[nd] ley it on þin eye quan þou gost to slepe and if þer be ani euele bloid or quitour, it schal be sauf certeyn.*

(120) *For wepende eyne: Tac a wrte-lef þat be reid and smer þeron [quite] of an ay and at euen ley it to þin eye.*

(121) *For reid eyne: Tac þe mychel rede snayl and do him gader al to hepe and do hem* [f.8rb] *in a basene and hole is back ful of holez and iche crum ful of salt and seit a lome vnder þe bassyn þat it mowe kepe þe water and do þat to þe eye and schul war[is].*

(122) *A les oys lermans: Pernez efrasie bone partie, si le temprez mut durement e pernez hors le jous parmy un drap. Si metés en une payele de aremme e oynt de pork mar(i)le e ataunt de su de mutoun ow de gres de geleyn. Si culiez parmy un drap e pus mettés a le seym e le chaufés e ben buliez e ben movez a fount de le payele e mettez ens de rounde pere e pus lessez refreyder. E pus mettez en boystez e mettez a le oyl kant vous irés dormer.*

(123) *Item a les oys que sunt a feye dolens e a la feye seynus: Mellez meel ov jus de centurie e oynés les oys.*

For blodi eye. (124) *Item a lez oys sanglant: Mangés mente e mettés longement sure lez oys.*

(125) *Item mangez betoyne e bevez checun jour l'aun(c)e(lé), anglice rue,*[42] *e mangez, si clarunt muyt les oys isi que vous veyrez let stoyles a soleyl lusant.*

For web. (126) *Item pur macle dé oys, anglice 'howe', ou tele, ne devés mye celer. Se avent* [f.8va] *suvent de diverse umures de cervel, se est a savere de mallencollye e de*

[42] The English gloss is a superscript insertion.

autres humurez. Le curacioun est teil: [Lessez] la ruge vine [e] banier. Sey aforse suvent a chanter[43] *e bevez leyt de chevere. E a cumensement seygnez*[44] *que vous eyez un poy de sanck. Pus pernez la jous de ere terestre e le jous de pimpernole e jous de olyve par meme cel mesure, si oynés lez oys.*

Bone oynement. (127) *Item unement prové pur macle e teye: Mettez eycile mut egre en une vessel de arem e jous de purnelez e plum e mettés tut ensemble, si lessez etthre le vessel cuvert longement e caunt mester sera, en oynez vous oys.*

(128) *Item a le teye, anglice 'pyn', medicine eprové: Pernez feel de levere e meel uelement, si lez temprés ensemble e oynez les oys.*

A le teye. (129) *Item a le teye: Pernés vert sarment de vine e en dolés [...] deins greynus de pever e pus lez friez an une ruge etuele eins un poy de vin e le mettés a oys.*

[f.8vb] (130) *Item pernés le racine de fenule e le foyle de rue e betoyne e egremoyne e aloyne, celgemme e pus mettés tous ensemble ov blanche vin e ov leyt de anesse e se temperez cant vous irrés cucher e mettez en vos oys, e sanera.*

(131) *A emflure des oys e des autrez menbres sudement surevenaunt: Pernés leyt de blanck chevere e si le fettes occiler e culier e pus mett[e]z desure le emflure – il deemflera.*[45]

A le teye dé oyes. (132) *Item a la teye e a la chacie dé oys: Pernez oyle de olyve e blanck vin e meel owelement e jous de fenyle e de rue e de aloyne e de ses treis atant cum des autrez treis e .ix. greynez de pevere e atant peysant de gingere e atans bayes de lorer. De seus fettez pudre e mettés a lez autre chosez en une basyn ensemble e mettés un poy de arment. Pus culiez e lessez epre par .ii. joures ou par .iii., mes ben seyt cuvert. E cant vous voulez oyner les oys si il seyunt chaufés, les oynés de ors ow une penne e si unt de teye, si mettez eins les oys.*

(133) *Item pernez le jous de saveyne ow meel e ow leyth de femme e mettez a oys.*

(134) *A oscureté dé oys, anglice 'gluskynge'*[46]*: Trenchez le coil de arunde* [f.9ra] *e resseyvés le sancg sure vere e lessez curer de le vere a lez oys e il garunt san fayle.*

(135) *Item a sanck ouster dé oys: Pernez le jous de verveyne e sang de columbe e mettez deins lez oys e donez a beyre puliole.*

Pur sangk oster dé oiz. (136) *Item mangés checun jour gencie[ne].*

Pur macle dez oys. (137) *Pur macle des oys un charm:* Adiuro te, infirmitas, per Patrem et Filium et Spiritum Sanctum ne hic remaneas + Absterge, Domine, maculam ab occulo famuli tui + agios + agios + agios + sanctus + sanctus + sanctus + Christus vincit, Christus regnat, Christus imperat. *Et*

43 MS clanker.

44 MS de s.

45 MS do emflera.

46 MED sub *gluskinge* cites a single example from c.1500, with the sense 'looking squint-eyed, squinting'.

ditez .iii. Pater Noster. Etcrivés cel bref e le pendez a coyl par .iii. feiye de la jour e a checun foiye dites cele charm.

A oiz lermans. (138) *A lez oys lermans: Pernez jous de betoyne teve e mettez desure les oys.*

(139) *A lez oys maladis: Pernés cumyn, si le ben batez en pudre e le temprés ow leyt de femme que mal[e] nuryth e mett[e]z a oys.*

(140) *Item mangés checun jour en joun .iii. foyles de betoyne, si vous revendra le vewe e le oye. E si a vous seyt venu par maladie u par autre survenue, pernez le blanche de oyf e le batés* [f.9rb] *ben en une nuvelle vessel e lessez reposer. E pus l'etscumez ben e pernez se que rement de le cler e atant de le clere gute de meel en un autre vesseil neet e atant de arrement en puder ben baté. E pus mettés sé tres chosez ensemble e si mettez sure bele tele e pus sure les oys kant humme vat cucher e ke le tele ne seyt plus graunde que le prunele de l'oyl.*

(141) *Pernez .ii. poynés de eufrase e un poyn de betoyne e un poyn de rue e un poyné de chanette e fettez lez seccher e pudrer. E gettés cel puder sure soun manger ou en soun beyre, e si amendra sa vewe.*

[The Mouth]

For þe canker in þe mowt. (142) *Tack þe wodebynde, þe ious, and of þe rede cole ious, and tunhoue and puder of caneil and coporose and puder of wylde sauge brent, and smer þe kanker þerwit in þe mowyt, and it schal warissen.*

(143) *Item tack sour rie-dowe þat is knedun ouer nyth and mack þerof a playstre and strouyt ful of salt and al so mychel pepur and mack it on a cake and baket weil. And sitthen tack hertis-hornes and res of clene leck and bren* [f.9va] *hem and*[47] *grind hem alle togedere to pouder and ley it to þe kanker and lat it liggen al nyth.*

(144) Item cuius os implicatum est savinam et Jovis erbam atque ederam cum vino simul tritas. Ei da bibere.[48]

(145) Item si quis taliter loquelam perdiderit, violam tritam cum vino bibat ipsamque si in parte capitis sinistra ictus est, in planta pedis dextera liga; si in parte capitis dextera percussus est, sinistram partem liga.

(146) Pro fetido anelitu pulvere pulegii et serpilli utatur.

(147) *For men þat specun in sleyp: Tempre þe seid of rue in eysil and ʒif him to drinken and heild þe ious in to hise nese-þerles.*

(148) *Item tack gencian and temper wyt eycil and wyt honi and ʒif him to dryngken.*

(149) *Item tac verueyne wit wyne and ʒif him dringke.*

[47] MS ad a*n*id.

[48] In the lefthand margin a different hand has written 'alapa sancti Johannis in Alexandria'.

(150) Si homo perdat loquelam in infirmitate, cape *aloyne*[49] et distempera cum aqua et infunde in ore, et sic loquetur.

(151) Contra putredinem gin[g]ivarum et oris fetorem: Lave[n]tur os et gin[gi]ve(e) cum aceto in quo decocta est menta ortolana et cepius curabitur.[50]

(152) *Item pur canker de buche: Pernés alun de glas, si mett[e]ʒ desure vo dens e fretés l[e]ʒ gomus e cant vous mett[e]ʒ* [f.9vb] *le novelus, oustés le veuys e fettus ensi par .iii. joures etc.*

(153) *Item pernés le dulié farine de [b]lé .ii. partieʒ e le terce partie de cel e quisseʒ ov coute de meel deke il seit etspesse e si fetus enplaystre, si metteʒ sure le mal deus foiye de la jour deke il seyt garri.*

(154) *Item pur male aleyne de b[u]che ouster: Mangés puliole secche u cerfoyle ow bevés eycil kaunt tu vas cuchier.*

For wicke onde. (155) *Item [perneʒ] fuyle de rue e lavés le bouche de eycil.*[51]

(156) *Item bevés pulyole detempré ow vin apré manger e se fettus suvent e il retreyra horis tut la poür e fra bone aleyne aver.*

(157) *Item trebleʒ pevre, anglice 'pepur', e medleʒ ow blanch vyn chaude e perneʒ en la bouche longement e garr[e]ʒ.*

(158) *A humme que ne powyt parler pur maladie: Perneʒ eycil e l'echafés. E pus perneʒ un drap, si molleʒ de se e mettés le drap a nariles e par[le]ra.*

Palsé. (159) Contra paralisim: Accipe salgiam et ros marinam,[52] layvendulam, anglice 'bynde', et succum illarum erbarum et tene in ore quam diu poteris et juvabit lingwam.

(160) *For flawn in þe mowyt: Tack hony and alum-glas and ious of plauntayne and*[53] *meing togedere, and noynt þe mo[wt].*[54]

[The Throat]

[f.10ra] **For glandren and quinacie.** (161) *For þe glaundre in þe þrote: Tack þe rote of celedoine and stamp it weel and temper it wyt stale ale and ȝif him to drynken .iij. dayeʒ and he schal bein hole.*

For chingles. (162) *Item for þe chingles: Tac þe blod of a man þat hat addeʒ to a man, and þe blod of a wymman for a wymman, and smer hem þerwit or elles þe blod*

[49] Corr. aloen.
[50] MS c. et c.
[51] LH has 'fou' for 'rue'.
[52] MS rosam martini.
[53] MS a*nd* and.
[54] Final two words in the margin.

of a cat, male for þe man and of a femele cat for þe wymman, and gres þe sore þerwit.

Quinacie. (163) *A quinacie verreye medicine: Pernés le gres de chat e puder de ensens e puder de veer e de rosine e de sauge e gumme de Arabye e sire verge. E tuz seus debrusez e trenchez. E en meme tens*[55] *quissez un grasse owe ouveke tus ceuz chosez e fettes culier le grese qui iset de le owe e si le mettés en boystez e oyn[e]z le mal cant metter sera.*

(164) *Item si veine hastiment: Fettez ly seygner de amdeus lé bras e treblez le erbe ke est apellé orpyn, si donez le jous a beyre hatiment e si gara, cum prové est.*

For glandre. (165) *Item pur glandre: Fettez puder de l'estrounke de ruge cholet e mellez a se meel, si oynés le mal. Prové est.*

[f.10rb](166) Contra quinaciam: Accipe spigurnellam tritam, anglice 'spurge', cum vino vel servicia, mynge et da bibere et sta[tim] curaberis.

(167) Item [si] defecerit spigurnella, accipe lanam que nascitur inter mamillas ovium et fac frixari in butiro facto in Mayo, si exstat, alioquin cum alio butiro, et inde fac emplaystrum circum collum infirmi et statim curabis.

(168) Item idem ad inflationem tibiarum ex causa ydropisis.

(169) *Item pur quinacie de humme e de porck: Pernez spinegre e fettez en pellotes e donez a beyre a le malajous.* Item valet pro cardiacle.

Quinacie. (170) *Item for þe squinacie serteyn medecine: Tac a knyif and groip in þe enturspace betwiþene nese-þirlez ay til þow gete blod and þow salt waris. And gif him sedez of columbyne to dryngken or to hete and if [þou] wilt him lyuere of hise iuele ay quil þow do oþer medicene, bynd him harde in þe grete of þe arm-oles and in þe hamus also quile e be latun blod and he schal warisse.*

(171) Ad idem: *Mangez e bevez suvent* [f.10va] *bugle a seyr dreyne, a primere a matyn, e vaudra.*

Pur malad[i]e de roy. (172) *Pernez royne de pree e fettez jous et fet[e]z beyre. Le malade si garra.*[56]

[The Teeth]

For toyt-ake and sore teyt. (173) *For toyt-ake: Tac peper and rechelez and temper hem wit quite of a ey and spred it on a quit ledur and do þerto quete flour and ley it to þe templus.*

(174) *Item tack þe braynes of an hare and seith hem wel and grece þe sore side of þe chek and þerwit wirmus schul deye.*

(175) *Item tack weybrede and stamp it wit schepus-talwe and ley it to þe soir and werm schal cumen owit.*

[55] MS sens.

[56] There is now a blank left in the MS.

(176) *Item seith betoyn in wyn or in eycil and hold wel often in þi mowit.*

(177) *Item tack ious of þe primerole and do it in þe nese-þerl on þe forþere half of þe soir.*

[f.10vb](178) *Item mack a playstre of ribbewrt and ley it to þe bolnyng longe.*

(179) *Item mack a playstre of þe holy malwe and ley it on þe bolnyngge.*

(180) *Item for bolnyng of toit-ake: Tack þe ious of þe rede nettle and þe quite of an ay and fre rechelez and quete flour and mack a playstre and ley it to þe soir.*

(181) Item ad dolorem dentium: Cornu cervinum bulliatur in aceto et fricentur dentes cum eo. Optimum remedium est.

(182) Item edere terrestris succus in aurem missus in ea parte qua dolet statim dolorem mittigat.

Ad eiciendum vermes. (183) Item ad eiciendum vermes de dentibus: Accipe semen jusquiami et semen porri et ceram novam et pone super tegulam novam ita ut fumus assendat in ore ad vermes. Et postea accipiat infirmus aquam in ore et statim exibunt vermes.

(184) Item tere plantaginem cum cepo arietino et unge maxillam et exibunt vermes.

(185) Item ad cancrum in dentibus sanandum: Accipe micas panis frumenti et coque diu cum melle et canceri inpone, et sanabitur.

(186) Item pro dolore dentium: Cape erbam que vocatur pes [f.11ra] leonis et aliga digito tuo inter juncturam et ungwem, sed non ex illa parte in qua morbus habetur, sed in altera parte. Vel infunde succum in naribus tuis de *humelock.*

(187) Item pro vermibus delendis: Cape cepum nigre ovis et fac candelam et cum semine jusquiami et pone ardentem in ore et exibunt vermes de dentibus.

(188) *Item pur dolour dé dens que veint a le feye par grant bullissement, a le feye ow grant emflure, a le feye ow grant perfusioun de sanck.*

(189) *Pur gute dé dens: Vyn e pever pudre[z] e chaufe[z] e fett[e]z le malade beyre si chaude cum il puyt suffrer.*

(190) Item millefolium vino infusum et da pacienti bibere.

(191) *Pur dolour dé dens: Rayés de corn de cerf e quissez en ewe ben, en ewe ow en vin, e oynés le jowe axi chaud cum put suffrer e humez axi chaude cum vous poez e tenés longement en voþre buche e cum seyt refredi, gettez horis e humez autre.*

(192) *Item quissez ben le racine de chenilé, mes en avant raés ben dehors ow cutelle. E cum il e[st] ben quis, le stampés ben e metez desure les dens deke il seyt refredi. E pus metez autre.*

(193) *Item betoyne quissez en eycil ow en vyn deke a le terce* [f.11rb] *part e tenés ben chaude en la buche e se fettez suvent.*

(194) *Item si il avent par emflure, treblez ben le primerole e mettez en se naryl le jous, mez ne mye en cele ow la dolour est.*

(195) *Item pernez branche de vine*[57] *e fettez carboun e frotez lé dens de carboun ben mollé en ewe e si fettis suvent.*

(196) *Item pernez le fule de ruge cholet, si oynez ow poy de meel e se mettez desure le jowe dehors.*

(197) *Item pur dens que dolierunt:*[58] *Ardez corn de serf a pouder e suvent frotez lé dens desure.*

(198) *Etscrivez en le jowe* 'rex, pax in Christo filiorum'.

(199) *Item pur fer dens blanche: Pernez le farine de orge e meel e se meddlez ensemble e le frotez suvent.*

(200) *Item pur dolour dé dens: Pernez arment e ensens e le blanche de le oyf, si treblez ben ensemble e pus mettez sure un poy de parchemyn e mettez sure le jowe kant tu vas cucher de cele part u le dolour n'e[st] pas. E si fettez deke vous seyez garri.*

(201) Item vinum et piper tritum tepefactum et pone in ore pacientis.

(202) Item millefolium vino infusum idem facit.

[Facial Blemishes]

[f.11va] (203) *For sausefleme visage: Tack*[59] *þe rote of horshelin and seyth it [in] a pot wyt*[60] *quyt wyne til it be almost drie and grind it in a morter wit quick-siluer and brinston and sqwines-grese and mack vnement and gres þe visage.*

(204) *Item for freckenez and red bleynes on þe face: Tack þe webrede-rote and salt and þe crop of þe brere and eycil and stamp hem weil togedere and þerwit was hise face.*

(205) *Item for wymmen þat ben pekelede: Seith pellettre in wyn and ley on þe face.*

(206) *Item for sausefleme: Tac þe rede docke and stamp it wel smail and tac barwes-smere to a man, and gyltez-smere to a womman, and friez in a panne and smer þe visage.*

(207) *Item tac þin owen vrine of þre dayes or of foure and hot it on þe .v. day and þerwit wasse þe erliche and late on þe visage.*

(208) *Item for visage þat semes meseyl: Tack quick-silu'u'r and þe gres of þe bor and black pepur and rechelus and* [f.11vb] *stamp hem alle togedere and þerwit smer þin*[61] *heued and kep þi neb fro cold wynd .iij. dayes and it schal*[62] *ben hoil.*

[57] MS veine.

[58] MS appears to have yokerunt.

[59] MS tack tac.

[60] MS wyt wit.

[61] MS zin.

[62] MS sphal.

For meseel. (209) *Yif þou wylt knowen a mesel, cast salt hon is blod and it wile to þe grond fallen.*

(210) Contra circiam in facie: Accipe nigrum vitrum et minutissime[63] pulverisa. Hoc facto oleum appone olyve et fac unam commixtionem et pone super lecionem.[64] Hoc fac multociens donec curaberis.

(211) *A face leperuse: Pernez pudre de veer e le jous de kersoun e jous de urtilez e vyf argent, si treblez ensemble e oynés le face a matyn e a seyr deke il seit garri.*

(212) *A ruge roseu ke sunt en le face: Treblez freys firmage ow meel, e ky le firmage ne seyt lavé, e fettus un playstre e mett[e]z sure le face.*

(213) *A seus qui semblunt la face lepurose: Pernez de sulphur e veut oynt de pork bone partie, si le treblez ensemble e oyn[e]z le face.*

(214) *A fere blanche face: Pernez le sanck de levere, si oyn[ez] le face e il vadra.*

(215) *A ouster ruge tecches de face: Treblez lé perez que sunt en le feye de bef, anglice 'galle', ow de toir, si le temperez* [f.12ra] *ow oli e de se oynés le face.*

(216) *Item pur blanche face aver: Pernez le racine de loveache, le quissez en ewe e lavez la face de cel ewe.*

(217) *Item pur playez en la face ouster: Pernez meel e leyt de neyr vache e sulfure uelement, si treblez ensemble e pus en oynez le face.*

(218) *Item for þe canker on þe paper of þe eye or on þe lippe: Tac gotes-talw and ious of celedoine and myng alle samne and ley to þe sore and it schal wariz.*

(219) Ad lentulas removendas a facie: Unge faciem tuam in sanguine leporis et evanesset.

(220) Item pro noli me tangere: *Primus ly lavez ow le jous de wermod e ow le jous de rue, mellez le un ow le autre. E pus metez coraisym a icele e lessez giser de[ke] il cheith par soun memus. E pus debrucés puder de crabot ars e medlez ensemble e ow pouder de sulphur e mettez desure le mal e il tuera. E kant ile e[st] mort, [donez] a luy medecine sanatyf e il gara.*

(221) *E si se maladie seyt desure le levere ow desure le oyl e ne tuche pas le papere dé ews ne le surcyl ne les naryles, dunke est il curable.*

(222) Item ad verucas ubicumque fuerint nate: Tollas gurguliones ex tritico cum sanguine muris contri[f.12rb]tum (sic) et modicum selicem (=calicem) ab usto et unctum porci, omnia comisse et unge verucas et in triduo sanat.

[Staunching Blood]

(223) **For stanchinge.** *Tack a squines-tord al hot and ley it to þe wounde.*

(224) *Item: Tac rote of þe rede nettle and ley þerto.*

[63] MS minitissime.

[64] i.e. lesionem.

(225) *Item: þe bolt þat gr'u'et in ȝerde.*

(226) *For nese-bledingge: Tack heschulschines*[65] *a branch and bren hem and mak puder (bren hem) and blow þe puder in þe nese.*

(227) *Item: Bren ey-sellez þat briddes han ben inne and blow puder in þe nes wit a quile of a feder.*

(228) *Item: Tac and bren netles and ey-schellez and do þe puder in þe nose or in a wnde.*

(229) *Item: Tack walleres-eirde þat walleres maken of wallez and temper it with eycil and bynd it in hise forheued.*

(230) Item ad sanguinem restringendum: Tene pervinccam super te et non poterit sanguis exire.

(231) Item ad venam ruptam interius: Purum semen narstucii cum aqua vel serv[ici]a bibat.

(232) Item qui sanguinem mingunt: Utantur vervena et erba que dicitur vulpis cauda.

(233) *For bledyngge at te nese*: Fac pulverem de ruta et in nares per fistulam trahe.

[f.12va](234) Item ad eos qui sanguinem myngunt subbito: Succum porrorum da pacienti bibere biduo vel triduo et liberabitur.

Ad idem. (235) *Item a sanck etstancher de playe ow de nes: Etscrivés de le meme sanck enmy le frount, si il seit humme, 'Beronix', e si il seit femme, 'Bironixa'* + .

Ad idem. (236) *A sanck etstancher cum pruvé est: 'Deu fuyt prys e en la crois mys, Longees le ferit e ewe e sanck en isyt. Si vereye cum vers fuy, etstanche le sanck de seti'. E dittez un Pater Noster e Ave.*

(237) *Item a sanck etstauncher: Treblez le foyle de aunne, si le mettez desure e cele meme chaunge gutefestre si il seit mys ov ceil e ow urtiles.*

(238) **Ad eundem**. *Item bevez quintefoyle e ache e si frés froter le frount de cel herbe encuntur lé etkues des narillez.*

(239) Item ad restringendum[66] sanguinem de plaga: Madefac stuppas in albumine ovi et appone vulneri et sessabit sanguis.

(240) **Ad fluxum**. Item pro fluxu sanguinis: Da bibere succum sipii et cessabit.

(241) Item si ex vulnere sangwis fluat ad interiora, detur ad potandum duas partes [f.12vb] aceti et olei unam partem, simul conmissas.

A sang [a] fundement. (242) *Item a sanck que iset hors a fundement: Temprez*

[65] 'heschuls' is written over an erasure.

[66] MS distinguendum.

ben amerose e bevez le jous suvent e mettez le playstre le fundement desure de le meme erbe.

(243) Item si vis extingwere : Scribe hec nomina cum sanguine in fronte Wn + van + won + et sessabit.

(244) *Item for men þat castun blod: Tac þe tirdeles of þe goit and mack þerof puder and tack buttere and a poyne of barli-mele and do it in water and set it weel and quanne it is wel soþen, cast in a sponful of þat puder þat is maked of þat gotes-terdles and ofte hete þerof and so þou salt ben hole.*

Id [ets]thanc[her]. (245) *Item pur etsthancher sang: Pernez un chapel velie, si ly ardés e fettez en pouder e mett[e]z cele pouder sure le playe e si etstanchera. Or dites 'Sancte Marie, duce Dame, requirés voþre cher fiz que pur la honour de vous e de soun duce sang ke il etspandyt en la crois e pur icele sang que vous plurastez, etstaunchez le sang de selli .N.' Ceste orisoun ditez .iii. foiþe ow .iii. Pater Nostrez e il esthan[che]ra.*

(246) *Item brock-lente and percil and þe quite of an ay and do alle togedere and ley to þi nose and blod schal chanche.*

(247) *Item for men þat pissun blod: Drynk þe erde of þe sqwalws-*[f.13ra]*nest wit hot water and [þou schal] be al hol of þin iuele.*

(248) Item ad extingwendum sangwinem: Cape folia de alisaunder et rubeam urticam et tere invicem et appone vulneri.

(249) *Item pur sanck etsthancer: Pernez de colofoyne un livere e bol armanik .x. uncez e de mastik un unce e de encens un unce e de le racine de confirie un unce e de sang de dragun un unce e de rosez secchez un unce e fettez pudrer tuttez chosez menuement e pus sairer [corr.sauvez ?] e vaut a bone soudure fere de playe e de nervez trenchez e pur festre.*

(250) *Item pur etstancher sang: Ditez 'God was born in Beedlem and ifulled in þe flum Iurdan; as wis as þe floid witstoid, al so stancche .N. þi blod'.*

(251) *Item pernez rue e l'etstampez e fettez jous e pernez le jous e le drache e butez ens le nes e estanchera.*

[The Limbs]

Pur dolour [dé] menbris. (252) *Pernez 'quit uyn' e seym de pork marle, si buliez desure le fu deke il seit remise. E puz pernez leyne de berbis ben carpé, si le mollez dens. E pus pernez un partie de se e mettez la ou la dolour est e si treyra tut hores le dolour.*

Item ad [...]. (253) *Item a dolour dé spaudis* [f.13rb] *e de fundement e des autres menbris: Pernez le seu de buck, anglice 'gres', e meel, si treblez le seu de buck ow le mel e metez desure la dolour.*

(254) *Item pernez coliandre e le feve quith ow meel, si metés desure.*

Ad idem. (255) *Item pernez rue, si le(z) triblez ow oyle e met[e]z sure.*

(256) *Item for werkyng of lendes: Tac an ey-schelle ful of þe ious of betoyne and meyng it wit a sponful of hony and greind .xi. pepur-cornes and myng al wit wine and yif him to drynke.*[67]

Pur royne dé maynus. (257) *Item pur royne dé meynes: Pernez fimterie e avence e treblez ensemble e pus etspurgez parmy un drap e pernez e lavez vos meynes e si gar[e]z.*

Pur veyn. (258) *Item pur veyn trenché de seyné: Pernez rue, si le quissez en oyle e oynés ben le bras e de meme se mett[e]z sure le playe ow su de mutoun e lyez a le bras.*

A veruis. (259) *Item a veruis oster, anglice 'wrottus': Frotés les su*[f.13va]*went de amplette. Cant lé racinez sunt peris, dunke chayrunt lé verues.*

(260) *Item: Pernez egremonie e cel e lez ben frotés e pus liez desure. E le meme pernez ow oynt de porck e stampez e fett[e]z emplaystre e met[e]z desure.*

(261) *Item pur emflure dé bras que avent par seyné: Pern[e]z farine de furment ow meel e ow leyt e fett[e]z enplaystre e metés a le mal.*

A tous roynes. (262) *Item a maus maladies e a tus ruynes: Pernez le racine de ruge parele, si le quissez ben en ewe e kant il est ben quis, si ostez le suvereyne peel e pernez veut oynt de pork e bure de May, si treblez ben ensemble e pus metez en bostez e kant vous vol[e]z, enoyntez encontur le fu.*

(263) *Item for wertes*: Accipe sanguinem de pullis collumbarum, de eorum capitibus et tere verucez (?) et curabuntur.

(264) Item accipe lavendulam,[68] anglice 'bynde', et tere cum illa erba cotidie et postea cum floribus solsequii dum ros super illos fuerit et curabuntur.

(265) *Item for scabbe: Tac þe rote of þe rede docke and þe rote of celodonie and wirmod and lef of lorer* [f.13vb] *and May-butere. Tac and stamp þe rotez and seith hem wyt þe May-butere. And sitthen tac and wring hem þorw a cloith an do in boystez and smer þe þerwit.*

(266) *Item for runiouse*: *Pernez erbe benet, anglice 'humelock', e de ceil ataunt uelement, si treblés ensemble e buliez mut ben en une poth e si chaude cum vous powez suffrer oynez treis foiþe la ruyne de corps.*

(267) *Item pur mangewe e tisike: Pernez mallows e fenyl e foyle de wilw, e(n) fett[e]z ben etstamper en un morter e pus ben etstuer en un poth ow su de mutoun e frez oynt de porck, e ow cel erbeage lavez suvent la ruyne de corps.*

(268) *Item pur tremblure dé maynez e de chef: Pernez primerole e primeveyre*, ut supra in capitulo *Pur dolour de cheif.*

[67] There follows a blank in the MS.

[68] MS lavenenam.

(269) *Item pur dertres garyr: Pernez le racine de rouge parele saun mettre a l'ewe e le nettez, de un cutel en trenchez rounde pecez de la racine e lé fettez estamper en un morter e dettemprer ow un poy de bone vinegre. E pus metez en une petyt drapele e estreynez desure le dertre isi que il seith suvent molle e si fettez .iii. jours, e garrez.*

(270) *Item pur veyn mal seyné si ky le bras seyt degurdié e emflé:*[69] *Pernés aloyne þat is* [f.14ra] *wermod e le(s) facez brayer ow cumyn e le liez entour le bras e met[e]z un draplet entour le playe e la drache que il ne (ne) chet deins e se etswagera le rancle e desgurdera lez nerfis e auxi fra tut autre blesurez que sunt ranclés.*

(271) *Item pur ruyne dé maynus:*[70] *Pernez cire virge e oyle de olive, deuz tant de oylye cum de la cire, e le fett[e]z ben buler ensemble. E pus mettre en un vessel pur refreyder. E pus oyndre lez gans en le vers partie e mettre seus sur lez maynes malades.*

Weruez. (272) *Item pur verwes oster: Pern[e]z un poy de bacun quyt e oynez lez verues qui l'en ne sache de quey il est. E fettes le demayn manger un muscel ou deux de cel meme manger e il garra isi qui ill ne savera ou il sunt devenus.*

Pur[71] **royne dé ma[in]us**. (273) *Item pur royne dé maynnus: Fettez ben bulyer ruge urtilez e fettez etstuer lé maynus ou lez pees en la fume a matyn e a seyr .iii. jours ou .iiii. Si treyra hors le mal.*

(274) Emplaystrum ad fissuras manuum : Jus mente, masticum,[72] farinam ordei, albumen ovi conmisse et fiat emplastrum.

(275) Item qui manus habet tremulas: Marubium album cum vino bibat et statim liberabitur de tremore.

[f.14rb](276) Item ad rugas manuum tollendas: Acipe mel crudum et super ignem bulliatur donec spumam fecerit et cum spuma laventur manus.

Sicca s[cabies]. (277) Item pro scabie sicca vel humida: Accipe elenam campanam, anglice 'horshelme', et coque bene et accipe butirum May et conmisse ad invicem et unge ante ignem ubi est scabiez et sanabit, set custodi bene testiculos et veretrum ne tangat.

Ad brachium dormientem. (278) Item ad brachium dormientem: Accipe smalagium, feniculum et *walwrt* et coque bene.

(279) *Item for scabbe of body: Gader fimter and stamp wit ale and drynk it and it schaue þe fro iueles witinne.*

(280) *Item for scabbud handus or (of) clawyn[g]: Tac þe rede docce and do of þe rote and seith weil wit butere of May and wring it ȝorw a cloith and do it in a box and smer þe þerwit at þe foyr and it schal waris.*

[69] On the inside margin of the column is written 'Nota bene'.

[70] Beside this in the gutter is written 'Nota bene'.

[71] MS For.

[72] MS jus m.

(281) Item pro manibus et ali[i]s menbris *endormés: Fettez quire en veli serveyse trebonez* [...].

(282) *Pernez foyle de luveache e quisez en ewe de fontane e lavez lé maynus si chaude, kaunt vous irés cucher, cum poés suffrer.*

(283) Item pro manibus scabiosis: Accipe pulverem de scalibus [f.14va] osteriorum et conmisse cum argento vivo, cum pingwedine porci et unge manus.

For scabbe. (284) Item pro scabeo fac ungwentum: Accipe spurge erba[m] et tere cum butiro de May. Simul bulliantur et perunge corpus.

(285) *A le dolour de piz e a le tuse e acuntur tuz maus de quer ce est veray medicine e prové: Pernez un nuvele pot, si festez un lyth a fund*[73] *de mariole e puz un autre, esi un a un deke le pot seyt pleyn. E pus metez de vin eins tanck' pora entrer e quissés de[ke] a le terce partie. E pus culiez parmy un drap e met[e]z a boystez. E kant metter serra, pernez un culieré, si metez en vyn chaude ou en serveyse e bevez kant irez cucher.*

(286) *Encement treblez mariole e ysope ensemble e quisez ben en serveyse estale e bure freys e bevez checun jour joun.*

(287) *Item a corpus:*[74] *Pernez .iii. bayes de lorer e quissez en vin ou en meel e bevez kant tu irez dormer.*

(288) *Item a le seche tusse: Pernez le semense de ache e semense de fenul e estampés ben e bevez joun ov vin.*

(289) *Item a le tusse a le pomune malade: Pernez semense* [f.14vb] *de ache e de aniis. Mollés ben ensemble e pevere ov vyn e temperez e quisez ben ou fu deke il seyt etpesse e mettez en boystez e a le seir mangez .iii. culierez deke vous seyez sayn.*[75]

(290) *A etspurgement de doloruse pisz e acuntre tus maws de piz veyrez medicinis verrayiz e provez: Culiez lez purnelez dé boys bone partie e lez mettez en une fort vessel, si lez treblez ben.*[76] *E pernez serveyse si tot cum il sunt coliez e mellez ov les purnelez e mettés en un nette pot, si metés en tere en un fosse e cuverez de un nette quele e jettés terre desure e seyunt illeucus .ix. jors e .ix. nous. E pus pernez un hanap petyt e donez a la malada [sic] a seyr un tret chaude e un autre a matyn freyde e si fettus de[ke] vous seyez garri. E sachez le medicine est veray.*

(291) *A humme que est enpusonné, si averez metter de medecinez: Pernez un herbe que est appelé symphonie e pernez le peys de un dener e temperez ov urine de femme e donez ly a beyre, si vomera tut hors le venym. E pus donés ly a manger tres foylez de seirfoyle e pus bevés leyt de anesse ou de chevere* [f.15ra] *ow de femme, e si garrés veray.*

[73] MS fumere.

[74] MS corumpus.

[75] MS saym.

[76] MS ben t. b.

(292) *Item: Pernés le racine de dragaunce e trenchez mut menue, si le fettez a solail e pus pudrez. Pus pernez le peiis de un dener e mett[e]z en ewe teve e lessés ethre tut le nowit. E a matyn jettez hors le ewe e metés eins vyn e quissez ben, si donés a beyre, e si garra.*

(293) *Item: Pernez luveache e aundre*[77] *e aniis, si quissez ben en vyn e donez a beyre si chaude cum il purra suffrer, e deliverement vomera hors le venym tretut.*

(294) *Item encuntre tu[t]es pusounes ore oyrez leger medecinez: Quissez leyt de chevere de[ke] a le terce part e le semense de canve e bevés de se .iii. jours. Desuz*[78] *ceel n'e[s]t meliour medicine forck [sic] treacle pur venym.*

(295) *Item pur tuus veynimus: Bevez le jous de mariole ov veut vyn, si jectera hors le venym.*

A humme que [ne puyt manger]. (296) *Item a mal ky feyt humme que ne puyt manger ne beyre mes tuz viandus ly sunt encounter:* [...].

(297) **Ad eundem.** *Pernez fymtorie e quissez ben en estale serveyse e kant il est muyt quyt pernez sous e l'etstampez ben e remett[e]z a pot e lessez durement quire. E pus culiez parmy un drap* [f.15rb] *e pernés deus partie de se e la terce partie de meel quyt par sey e ben escummé e culiez parmy un drap e pus fettis bulier ensemble de[ke] il seyt muyt etpesse. E mettez pus en bele boystez e fett[e]z le malade de manger de ceste checun jour un culieré plain e si le usez deke il seyt garri. E si ostera de quer tut le glette e donera talent a manger e a beyre.*

(298) *A le secche tusse: Pernés de pé de puleyn, anglice 'fole-foit', e mynte e treblez ensemble e fett[e]z petyt pellotes. E le mettez desure un chaude tuale e seyt le malade cuvert desure soun chef, isi ky il powyt reseyvre le fumé en soun buche, e si garra si il fettz suvent.*

Pur tuosse. (299) *Item a le tusse e a la dolour de quer e de pis: Pernez le foyle de cabaline terrestre, anglice 'ivi', si le mettez en un pot de terre ov ewe desure fu, e ky le pot seyt cuverte en cele manere que le fumé [ne] put iser hors fors par une pipe. E cele fumé reseyve le malade deins soun bouche e si garra.*

[f.15va](300) *Item: Receyvés le fumé desure un chaude tuele de ysope suvent.*

(301) *Item: Le cler seym de porck bulli ov ewe humez chaude.*

(302) *Item a le tusse: Pernez le puder de sauge e le usés ov le mouele(s) des os freys.*

Ky unt le piz stoppé. (303) *Item a seus ky unt le piz estoppé par gres: Pernez le foyle de rue, si le quissez ben en eycil e donez a beyre e il garra verement.*

(304) *Item a vomissement de sang: Pernés un erbe que est appellé ficoral, pernés le couste e metez en jous de plantayne, si le bevés ov eycil e garra.*

A touse. (305) *Item a grevus tusse: Fettus ben laver vopre pes a seyr caunt vous*

[77] MS saundrez.

[78] MS desure.

irrez cucher e puz riez ben lé plauntes dé pes ov cuteyl e puz lé frotez ben ov doce de aly, anglice 'garlek', ben brusé en un quele e tempré ov leyt de vache. E se tenez longement encuntre le fu e pus bevez muyt chaude de[ke] vous seyes gairi.

A seus que ne unt [digestioun]. (306) *Item a seuz que ne puunt aver digestioun: Fettez cele figure + desure le frount* [f.15vb] *de humme e si oynés de meel e dictus lé .vii. saumus e lé quinte e le letanie, e si garrez mut ben.*

(307) *Item pur vomissement: Bevés mylefolye ov ewe teve ou vyn e le rue que mut profite.*

(308) *Item a humme que ne puyt soun manger tener: Pernez jous de plantayne e de avence e eycil, si fettez enplastre de seus ov flour de segle, si le lyez desure le furcele de piz. E provė est serte.*

(309) *Item a humme qui se sente peysaunt entur le quer e de cors e sey dute de malader: Pernez mauve e morel e fule de blanche pruner e dez auns ov lé coperounes, si lez fett[e]z ben buler en ewe. E pus lavez le piz e lé jambz en se broyt e pus fettez bulier en serveyse furmentale e aloyne, si le bevez tut chaude e alez cucher ov se cure, e si garrés.*

(310) *Item encountur pusoun: Bevez mentanaunt voþre urine demene e vous garr[e]z.*

(311) *Item pur le tusse perlyouse: Pernez le racine de fenoule, si temprez ov vyn e donez a beyre.*

(312) Item ad eos qui cibum nec potum retinent sed evomant: Predictum potum tepidum bibant et curabitur.

(313) *Item pur le tusse*: Gere super te spumam maris et non pacieris donec tecum geras.

(314) Item: Comede particulam muris assati quando tussis et sessabit.

(315) *Item pur le secche tuse e pur detstresse de piz: Pernez de ysope .iiii. branchez ou .v.* [f.16ra] *e metés en voþre serveyse checun jour e use se un moys, e si garez certeynement.*

(316) *Item pur tysike garer: Fettez destiller ewe de le ruge trifoyle flour e cel ewe fett[e]z sureper ov bon sucre blanc e seyt ben le terce part de cel surep e lé deus partiez de ewe buylé ouveke ysope e ov licoris e seit ensi medlé kant homme le boyt. E suffyt a boyre .vii. culierés ou .viii. ou .ix.*

(317) *Item for iuele at þe brest: Tack wyrmod and mynte and sauge and vinegre and stamp hem togedere ful smal. And tac quyt bred and tostet til it be broun. Tack siþen and myit smal and do togedere and mac a playstre and ley to þe brest and he schal waris.*

(318) *Item for stopped at þe brest: Tack rue and seyth in eicil and ȝif him drynk tyl he be hoil.*

Ad tussym. (319) Item ad tussim: Accipe cumynum, rutam, piper, anis[79].

[79] MS ania.

Hoc tere diligenter et adde [mellis] quod sufficit et post calefactionem jejunus mane coccliar .i. accipe.

(320) Item qui nimis grassi sunt: Feniculum bibant per multos dies et ad tenuitatem ducit.

(321) Item ad fistulam: Piper, alium, ficus siccas, radicem percilii misse et simul tere, inpone desuper et occidet fistulam.

[f.16rb](322) *Item for tysike and narw at brest or oþer euelez: Tac hertistunge and violet, cicorie, endiue, pellethre, perok, fenkele, of ilck olyche mychel and þe rote of partyngale and four sedes of duretyk ysope and a party of figus a quarter, and seyt al þis togeder in a galoun of fayr water vnto a potel and siþe porw*[80] *howit þe ious and do it in a panne, and þre rawe eirun, and stamp [hem], chellez and al, and do it in þe panne and do it a lytel over þe feyr and ster it wel. And sitþen wring it þorw a cloyt and lat it saltel tyl it be cold. Pouret in tyl a newe pot an cuuerit wit parchemyn or wit leder and lat it stounden al nyth and sitthen gyf hym to drynken til he be hoil.*

For euele in þe bodi. (323) *Item yif he have mychel euele in his bodi: Seit barly in water and gef him to drynk for þat is cald a tysan and kep him weil fro oþer drynkes and gotuse mete.*

(324) Item contra morbum cordis qui aufert ab homine affectum comestionis: *Tac centurie and seith it wel.*[81]

[f.16va](325) *Item: Pernés .iii. bayes de lorer e quissés ov vyn ou meel, si bevés kant vous irés cucher.*

Pro morbo card[iali]. (326) Item pro morbo cardialy: *Tack vnioun and tack þe g[r]u[e]l þat is mad of þe grotes of þe ote-mele and seith hem togedere in buttur tyl it be weil þicked and ȝif hym to drynke þre sopuus at ewn and .iii. a morwen tyl he be warissed.*

(327) *Item for [man þat] may nowit for castinge holden his mete: Tack hulwrt and heyhoue and pepur and seit hem wel in water and yif him to drynke and he schal sone ben oyl.*

Qui habet cor aquosum. (328) Item habet cor triste et aquosum: Comedat muscatas .i. macis, flores muscatarum, et bene habebit.

(329) Item contra tussym et contra malum latus et contra febrem: Accipe *hulwrt* et tere, cum aqua misse et bibe. Valet ectiam contra frenesym adeps assarina et porcina et conmisseantur cum allio et ponantur super apostemata et sanabuntur.

Contra singultum. (330) Item contra singultum magnum: Accipe aquam pluvialem, absynþium et acetum, ista omnia decoquantur simul et ponantur in lynio panno super pectus singultientis in sua infirmitate.

80 i.e. 'pour', possibly with a bar through the *þ*.

81 In the righthand margin (cropped) are the words 'ut superius in'.

(331) Item contra collicam pascionem: Petrocillum et absyntheum decoquatur et ponatur super ventrem quanto callidius sustinere poterit.

[f.16vb](332) Item contra siccum tussym: Semen apii, semen feniculi, semen aneti[82] equali pondere et piper et omnia ista pulverizata et cum melle coque et cum vino bono bibe et tussis cessabit.

(333) Item contra henemodus: Accipe cornu hircinum, proice in ignem et fumum permitte intrare in nares et melius habebis. Hec enim pascio cito ducit hominem ad mortem.

(334) *Si mamelez de femmus emflunt de leyt ou de autre chose: Pernés le fente de culveres, si fettez un enplaystre de cele e de meel ov le sire verge e mettez un drap desure ov oynt*[83] *deseus.*

(335) *Si vous volez qui femmus eyunt mut de leyt, fettus manger letusez e se le fra*[84] *cretthre leyt e outera leccherie de femme.*

(336) *Item a emflure de mameles ke emflunt plus cum metter est: Fettus enplastre de farine de fevus e si detemprés ov eycil e si friés ov meel e metez desure le mamele. Auxi il vauyt a genitarius de humme ke sunt emflés.*

Pur femme que ad nuel [leit]. (337) *Item pur femme ke ad perdu soun leyt: Pernez la flour de aube-etspine ov le fulye e le fett[e]z moudre*[85] *et dettemprer de ewe benecte ou de autre lycour*[86] *e le face boyre a le femme e ele revendra a soun leyt. E si se soyt en autre sesoun, pernez de mylueyne etscorché, anglice 'hulwr[t]', e de l'aube-etspine e le boyve, si revendra.*

Emflure. (338) *Item pur emflure de mamele: Pernez rouge mente e le festez brayer e mettre desure le mamele ov le jous enterement, si garra.*

[f.17ra](339) *Item pur chaude rancles: Pernez le jous de jubarbe e leet de femme e ewe rose e medlés ensemble e mollez un drap ou estupe e mett[e]z desure le emflure, si etquagera.*

A emflure de mamele. (340) *Item pur emflure de mamele: Pernés betes e lez quissez ben en ewe e aprés etstreynez hors le ewe e friés lez en boure de May e pus metés desure le mal si chaude cum l'em poez suffrer, e se une foiye a matyn e autre foye a soyr tancke il sera crue. E pus pernez autre foiye lé betus e les quissez en ewe e pus etstreynés hors le ewe mut ben e pus friés lez en bure e en friant pudrés desous ben de cumyn molu e lez movés ben e kant il sera ben frit, metez lez e[n] un drapelet, si etstrenez hors e si resemblera un oynement. E quan il sera froyde, oingnez le mamele a matyn e a vespere.*

[82] MS anati.
[83] MS noynt.
[84] MS fray.
[85] MS morudre.
[86] MS lycoru.

Ou metez le unement sure un petit drapelet e le metez sure le maladie, si gara vereye.

(341) *Item pur chaude ranclez: Pernés le jous de plantayne e mollez un drapelet dedens e le metez sure le rauncle, si garra.*

Enseinment de fisik. (342) *Tuz chosez ducez e amers sunt chaudez e tut chosez egrez sunt freydes axi ben de herbez cum de spiseries.*

(343) *Item for bolnynge of tetus and for ouer mychel milk: Tac* [f.17rb] *drestes of eycil and virgine wax and mack a playstre and ley þerto.*

For hakyng. (344) *Item for akynge of tates: Tack mynte and stamp and ley þerto.*

For bolnynge. (345) *Item for bolnyng of tates: Fold*[87] *þe crop of a red docke in a lef of þe sauine and rost it in þe eymerie and stamp it and le it to þe soir and it schal breke. And quan it breke, 3if him to drynken þe crop of þe tansay and brere-crop and red wrtes and of maddur, al so mychel as of alle þe oþer erbes, and er ye 3if him drinken, temper it wit stale ale.*

Idem. (346) *Item for bolnynge of tate: Tack hock-appelus and stampe wit oyle of rose and lei it to þe bolnynge.*

Ad idem. (347) *Item tac þe ious of morele and þe lytel dayezeye and drestes of eycil and an ay hard soþen wit þe schelles and barly-mele. Stamp and seit al togedere and mac a playstre and ley to þe tate and it schal waris.*

For kyl. (348) *Item for kyl on wymmannus tate: Tac jous of morel and þe quite of an ey and bene-mele and mack þerof a playstre and ley þerto.*

For tate. (349) Item ut mamille pusille sunt et ne amplius crescant: In tempore quo crescant porciculum fac castrare et de sangui[f.17va]ne dexteri testiculi unges[88] mamillam dexteram et de sinistro sinistram mamillam.

Pro lacte. (350) Item ut mamille lac habeant: Sicudam viridem, anglice 'humeloc', in aceto tere et mamille appone.

(351) Item ad dolorem et cancrum mamillarum: Stercora omnia recentia et calida appone.

(352) *Item for wymmen þat an þe brest to-sqwollen: Tac þe hock-appel,* ut superius.

(353) *Item for wymmen þat faylen mylk: Tac cristal and brec it smal and mack þerof puder and lat hire dryngken it wit mylk and se [schal] hauen inow.*

(354) *Item mack hire to etun cruden*[89] *sum del hoyt and supen butere wit wyn and dryncken fenul-seid wit wyn.*

Ad ma[millas]. (355) Item si mulier habeat mamillas contractas vel inflatas: Cape lynum tritum cum albumine ovi et pone super mamillam et

[87] MS Tac f.

[88] MS et u.

[89] Written with a nasal bar over the 'u'.

cape succum de ache et farinam de siligine et fac unum playstrum et pone super mamillam et facies illam bebere succum de ache et de endive et si illa amiserit lac, da sibi succum vervenie, anglice 'verveyne', et sic recuperabit plenitudinem lactis.

For brock and byle. (356) *For brock and kylus: Tack þe ȝelke of an ay* [f.17vb] *and hound-fenkelle and bloid of a sqwin and gres of a sqwyn and stamp togedere and ley þerto.*

(357) *Item a clouus, anglice 'biles', que levunt desure le corps de humme: Pernez le fente de chevere, si le quissez en vyn e si metez kersoun, urtile e su de motun, e fettez enplastre e metez desure.*

(358) *Item for biles: Tac egremonie and senchun and fyuelef-gres, of eiþer olyke michel, and wel hem in eicil and ley hem to sore.*

(359) *Item for oncomus, biles and festrus quan it is slayen: Tac saym of lard and rie-mele and hony and recheles and wax and wyn and well it al togedere. Scum it and lat it kelen. And tac þerof and ley it on a cloyth and ley to þe sore.*

(360) *Item for to brecun a byl: Tack rounceval, anglice*[90] *burre, and quyt malwe and pimpurnol and sqwyn-gres and stamp al togedere and wryng owit þe jous and temper it wit hony and bark-dust and rie-mele and ley it to þe soir.*

A vomisse estancher. (361) *A vomys estancher: Pernés le jous de mente e alboun de le oyf e puder de ensens e farine de orge, si mollez ensemble e de se* [f.18ra] *festez un molle past e si met[e]z desure un drap e liés desure le umbryl, anglice 'nouele'.*

Pur culivur. (362) *Item pur culivures que sunt entur [corr. entré ?) le cors de humme, anglice 'wirmus': Treblés rue e detemperez ov urine e donez a beyre.*

(363) Item ad eos qui cibum nec potum retinent sed evomant: Eundem potum da bibere.

(364) Item ad interficiendum ranam in stomaco vel alios vermes: Accipe panem siliginis bene fermentatum et acrem et cum exeat a furno, pone in forti aceto et cum bene biberit de aceto, deinde ponatur in furno et iterum coquatur. Postea extrahe et iterum pone in aceto et ita ter coque in furno hoc modo. Deinde commedat paciens de illo pane et nichil bibat nisi fortissimum acetum, set eum jejunare facias[91] per diem vel duos et item acerimo aceto et ab pane siliginis acerino interficietur. Deinde purga pocione.

(365) Ad idem porros comedat per dies .iii. tamen cum magna quantitate salis et allia cruda et nichil bibat nisi acetum et morientur vermes. Postea da ei bibere pocionem ad eiciendum vermez mortuos.

(366) Item ne vomas in mari: Absyntheum bibe et non facis.

[90] MS *.a.*

[91] 'facias' inserted in a different hand.

(367) Item experimentum ad ficos vermes a medico regis experto: Accipe cardonem [f.18rb] benedictam cum radicibus suis bene ablutam et tere. Per .iii. dies et .iii. noctes pone in vino forti. Quarto die bene cola et similiter proice in vino et pacienti jejuno cotidie propina et liberabitur.

(368) Item contra debilitatem stomachi: Millefolium tritum cum vino bibat.

Contra omnia mala stomachi. (369) Item contra omnia mala stomachi et epatis: Decoquatur absyntheum cum aqua et stet per unam noctem. Mane autem bibatur. Ista aqua valet contra omnia mala stomachi et epatis et contra illam infirmitatem que dicitur vulgariter 'ȝeskyngus'.

Contra nauseam. (370) Item contra nauseam, anglice 'caste': Accipe farinam ordei et panem combustum de siligine et decoque in aceto. Adde albumen ovi, fac totam calidam et pone super pectus.

For boun[den] in stomac. (371) *Item for þat is bounden in þe stomack of grotus, metes and forbrent in þe wombe and may nowit deliveren and also for þe heued þat werkyt and peyrit þe syth, þerto is þis letuarie god and is cald laxatiue for þe stomack and confortatiue for þe heued: Tac ceve a god partie and al so mykel cumyn and neer als michel of cermountayne and do alle togedere and grind hem in a morter of bras and tack siþen and do it in newe* [f.18va] *scured panne and dittet os it were a letuarie and [quan] it is dyth, scure þe botme of a bacyne witowten and hil it þerupon and breid it os it were a litel cake. And quan it is cold, brec it in smale muscelus as to beneȝ and gyf it him at morwe and at euen and lat hym use culiȝ of hennes and drynken tysan.*

(372) *Item for maken a man to casten: Stamp þe barck of þe walnote-tre-rote and hulyn-barck and stoncrop and step hem in warm water a nyth and gyf it him to drynken.*

(373) *Item agayn castyng: Temper rue wit wyn and vsit leuck.*

For snakes in þe body. (374) *Item for man þat ad snacus in his bodi or venimouse wermus: Mack a red hors to renne tyl þat he squete and tac þe squet and mylck of a quyt got and medle hem togedere and yif hym to drynke.*

(375) *Item for cheruing in þe wombe: Tack otes and parche hem wel in a panne and strencle hem wit water and ley it to his wombe in a cloit.*

(376) *Item tac verueyne aboute missumer and driet weel and mack puder þerof and yif him to drinken in ale stale.*

(377) *For apostume in þe side: Stamp* [f.18vb] *wirmod and mynte and camamylle and herbe benet and malues and cheuerefoyle and rose-floures and sauge and do cumyn þerto and breid-crumes and wel it al in wyn or in pisse and mack a playstre and ley to þe sore side and it schal waris.*

Dropesye. (378) *Item for þe colde dropesie: Tac rote of fenkele and þe sedes of brome and nettel-seid and morsus diaboli, and tac of ilk on olike mychel, and tack al so mychel of smalache os of alle þe oþere erbes and radiche-rote, ysope and betoyn, anie[s]-*

sedes and an handful of ote-mele grotes and stamp hem smal and wel alle in a galoun of water til it come to a potel and clarefie it wit sucus and wring it þorw a cloith and yif it to drincken at morwen and at euen.

Pro apostamate. (379) Item ad mittigandum apostematis dolorem et ad maturandum: Accipe radicem lingwe canine et sub cinere coque, et quod durum est inde proice et quod molle retine, et tere in mortario et eidem ad auxungiam porci recentem et tepidam superpone appostamati.

Pro fluxu. (380) Item contra nimium fluxum ventris: Accipe crustam panis ordeacii et permitte in aceto bullire et post tepidam super umbilicum pone.

[f.19ra](381) Item ad fluxum sanguinis mulieris: Scribe has literas et pone super nudum pectus mulieris et sessabit. p. x. v. c. p. o. anexa que y. et hoc g. quod et si non credis quod hoc sit verum, scribe has in man[u]brio cultelli et occide porcum cum eo et non exiet sanguis.

Contra ydropisym. (382) Item contra ydropisym et distemperanciam epatis in infirmitate apposyma: Accipe semen feniculi et apii, petrocilii,[92] asparagi in aceto et aqua ita quod due partes sint aque et tercia aceti, coquantur ad medietatem et ut maioris sit eficacie de eorum seminibus ad bibitum pone.

Ne inebriari. (383) Item [ne] inebriari possis: Semen cauli, anglice 'wrte', et betoniyam bibe cum vino.

Pro apostemis. (384) Item ad omnia appostomata, exteriora sive interiora: Agrimoniam, vervenam, quinquefolium equis ponderibus pone cum aceto et coque. Adiecta sperma, hec simul trita et super posita sanat.

(385) Item ad rumpendum appostema: Fermentum, olibanum, auxengia, lac[93] femineum.

Pro apostema. (386) Item ad maturandum appostema: Accipe fel porcinum et farinam ordei et vitrum tritum conmisse et super pone tepidum.

(387) Item semen narstucii distempera cum melle, appostema maturat et ad superficiem trahit.

(388) Carmen ad fluxum sanguinis: 'Domine Deus meus, adiutor sis famulo tuo .N. sicud strinx[f.19rb]sisti fluvium Jordanis quando Christus baptizatus fuit, sic disstringe venas famuli tui .N. plenas sanguine'. Quo dicto et si absens sit, liberabitur.

(389) Item ad omnem lecionem:[94] Radix feniculi et folia simul tere et

[92] MS petrocilium.

[93] MS loc.

[94] i.e. lesionem.

distempera et cepius sumatur. Mirifice sanat, non solum homines, sed ecciam jumenta.

Ad fluxum. (390) Item ad omnem fluxum: Accipe cornu servi assum et semen urtice mortue, pulverisa et distempera cum aqua pluviali et da bibere pacienti.

Pro ventre. (391) Item ad dolorem ventris: Agrimoniam cum radice coctam bibat paciens.

Pro vermibus. (392) Item vermes ventris ad occidendum: Atramentum spissum bibat.

(393) Item contra malam potacionem: Accipe ruta[m] et tere ac bullire facias in vino vel aqua. Da bibere per novem dies calicem unum. Si vermes sint in corpore, moriuntur omnes.

Si venter inflatus. (394) Si venter inflatus sit, per malam potacionem sanabitur.

[Against Poisons]

(395) Item ad eos qui venenum in potacionibus acciperant: [Accipe] folia fraxini sicca ita quod non sol tangat ea et cum opus fuerit, tere et cum vino veteri da bibere.

Pro veneno dato. (396) Item ad venenum datum: Semen ac folia canobi et jus de mora campestri, calicem unum da bibere. Si moras non habes, lac caprinum da in potu.

(397) *Item for þe menysoun: Tack þe modurwrt, anglice 'mougwed',* [f.19va] *and stamp it til þou have þe ious. And tac flour of quete and kneid it wit þe ious and mack a kake and back it and et it al hot.*

(398) *Item for blodi menisoun: Tac milefoylie and weibrede, and so michel of þat on os of þat oþer, and stamp hem wel togedere and myng hem wel wit wyn or temper hem wit ale, and ȝif it þe seke to dry[n]ken þerof at morwen cold and heuen hoit.*

(399) *And for to witen queþer a man schal leun or deien of þe menisoun: Tac a peniweythe of soud crassen-seid and het it .iij. dayes faste and drynck a drayth after of wyn or of water and it schal eiþer sthanche or it schal turne to an oþer coluur and þanne schal he deye.*

(400) *Item for eueri venym or pusoun: Tac mylk of þe goyt and seit it wit seid of cheranse to þe þridde*[95] *del and drinck it .iij. dayes and under heuene is [not] so god med[icine].*[96]

[95] MS rridde.

[96] MS med'.

(401) *Item for venym: Tac þe ius of maydeil, anglice 'hehoue', and drynck wit hold hurine of man and þou salt castun howit þe venym and þe pus.*

(402) *Item for þe wombe þat is hard and soer: Tac þe ious of fiuelef .ij. sponful and lat him souppun.*

(403) *Item for squellyng of wombe: Poyne rue in wyn or in* [f.19vb] *ale and drinck þat often.*

(404) *Item tack of þe hertus-horn and mac þerof pouder and myng it wit eycil an yif him ofte to drycke.*

(405) *Item ȝif hym to drycke fastinge grene rue sodþen in wyn.*

(406) *Item for costyue wombe: Tac þe lynseid and seit it wit seym wol and lat him etun it wel hoit.*

(407) *Item tac þe rote of þe brake and scher it smal and ley it a nyth in wyn and at morwen drynck it ereliche.*

(408) *Item tac fern þat growet vnder þe hoik and wasse it and poyne a fat henne and seit altogedere til it be wel soþen. And after stamp it wel and siþen wryng it þorw a line cloith and drynck it wit þe broyt.*

(409) *Item ȝif edere or snake be witinne mannus body oþer wimmannus: Stamp rue wit mannus oþer winmannus [urine] or of quat best had iuele and ȝif þe seke to dryncken.*

(410) *Oþer tac vrine of þe selue man oþer best and arrement and mack it sum del hard and ȝif him to drynck and he schal casten al þe venym.*

(411) Item qui biberit venenum bibat succum de *horune* cum vino sanusque fiet.

(412) *Item for þe menisoun þis metus ben gode for to vsen: Asimus panis, wastel oþer sim*[f.20ra]*nel*[97] pissi et (bipe?) ponite in dulcedine et lacte et quilibet panis bis pistus, cilicet primo in furno et postea super prunas, est bonus utendi cum bono vino albo et rubeo. Et hoc optimum quod potest inveniri.

(413) *Item for deid child in wimmannus wombe to delieueren: ȝif hire to drynken þe ious of verueyne in cold water and se schal delieueren hastili.*

(414) Item pro veneno: Cape salgiam[98] et tere mediocriter et pone super corpus ubi venenatur. Simul et succum et folia facias ligari super malum et sic curabitur.

(415) Item si sit venenatus infra corpus: Cape salgiam et sic mundari facias cum vino vel servicia vel aqua et sic bibe ad vesperam et mane.

97 'sim' is repeated at the beginning of f.20ra.

98 MS salgie.

(416) Item ad dolorem et duriciam ventris: Cape .ii. cocclearia de succo quinquefoliorum et da sibi bibere.

(417) Item ad tergecitatem ventris : Tere rutam cum vino vel servicia et bibe frequenter.

(418) Item pro morbo veterno, veteri sive forti: Cape celodoniam et contere et bibe cum vino vel servicia et da sibi bibere.

(419) Item pro morbo veterno vel venticia: Cape radicem de paradella anglice 'docke' et radicem de *glatenere* et sic distempera cum urina hominis et postea da sibi bibere .ix. diebus.

(420) Item contra venenum: Qui biberit da succum de morel cum vetero vino et sic eiciet venenum.

(421) Item statim bibat urinam propriam.

[f.20rb](422) Item pro appostamatibus infra corpus hominis vel foris quamvis sint dura: *Tack webrede and erbe Johan and mushere, seit þis þre togedere and medle hem wit oly and water and drynck þre dayes first and last and it schal passun adoun þorw þe bodi and howit at þe fundement.*

(423) Item contra fluxum sanguinis: Accipe cepum hirci pistum cum ovis et simula in patella et manduca.

(424) Item ad restrin[gen]dum fluxum sanguinis: Accipe vivas angwillas et pone in ollam et decoque super carbones sine aqua et paciens sumat fumum per inferiorem partem corporis.

(425) Item quandocumque nascitur ulcus intrinsecus in corpore alicuius, urina eius est pallida, et si habeat superius circulum in summitate appertum, ille homo curabilis est, si autem clausum, incurabilis est.

(426) Qui curabilis [...] dura et acetosa vitet, carnes porcinas, dulcia poma cocta et mel comedat et magnos labores non faciat.

Contra malum epatis. (427) Item pruritum et malum epatis: Macis, hec est flos muscatarum, est calida et sicca, confortat epar, splen, stomacum et precipue aufert cordis tristiciam si cum vino sumatur.

(428) *Item pur manere de menisoun: Pernez un oyf e hostez* [20va] *le blaunche e pernez .v. graines de poyvre ben mollue e metez deins le oef e le movez ben e rosticez le oef mol e le festez manger a la malade en joun par .iii. jours, checun jour un oef, e si humme seit velz e froid, mett[e]z plus de graynes e si il seit enfant, meins, e il etstanchera si il ne deit murer.*

Contra fluxum. (429) Item pro eodem *e de sanck: Pernez sang de dragoun e pudrez e mettez de la puder dedeins un poy de servoyse estale e le fettes humer sous a un foye e fettez ensi par .iii. jours a matyn e a vespre, si etstan[che]ra.*

(430) *Item pur tut manere de menisoun: Pernez ruge parele e le festez ben brayer en un morter, racine e foyle, e tut ensemble. E le fettez bulier ausi ben cum un joute e pus*

lavez lé pes auxi chaude cum vous poés suffrer taunc que a le chevele[99] *de pé a matyn e si il cumense a stancher,*[100] *fett[e]z le auter feyþe le nowit a my jambe, e la terce foiþe tanc desuus le genoyle e nent plus. E si vous veyés ke il n'estanche mie uncore, fettez meme set chose auxi chaude buliant cum il veint de fu, e mettés desouis* [f.20vb] *un tele partie*[101] *e fettez le malade seer desour, que la chaline puisse entrer amount eins le cors, si garra si il ne mura.*

(431) *Item pur turtele deins le cors: Pernez le fruit qe crest sure le frayne e ostez l'ecorche que est dehors e pernés le fruit dedeins un bone poyné e boylez lez en un quart de vyn ou de servoyse, e pur deus poynez mett[e]z le duble de vyn ou de servoyse. E avant que il seyt mis en le vin fett[e]z le ben brayer en une morter e puis ben boiler tanck'a la terce partie. E pur enducer le beyre metés un poy de sucre ou licoris, pur se que plusores sunt gagé de beyre amer choses, noun que se*[102] *vait meut que le chose seit ewe pure en soy que de autre chose si l'em put suffrer. E lequele ky il soyt, duci ou noun, fett[e]z le clar[i]fier de gleyre de oef. E si vous ne poés aver la fruit de frayne, pernez le vert etcorche de un gevene bletron de freyne e ostez le gris dehors e la seve deins e le mylu de cel escorche fett[e]z myncer mout menu e boyler [en] memez la manere que vous frez le frouyt e usés se, si garés.*

Pur dropesye. (432) *Pur dropesie, froyde e chaude: Pernez l'estomac de un po[r]ck e le fendez de un cutel e metés tut chaude sure* [f.21ra] *les menbris, si pissera tut hors la maladie e auxi de femme. Se chose est prové.*[103]

(433) *Item pur froyde dropesye: Pernés un taupe e le fettez etcorchier e pus boyler e fettez le ydropick manger le*[104] *e boyre le broyt, e il garra.*

Pur veniment. (434) *Item pur enveniment: Pernés un herbe que crest en checun bruere que est appellé tormentine, que porte un petyt flour jaune ow .iiii. foylez, en la sesoun quan la vertue est en herbez, e le fac[e]z braer e gester cel herbe deins [...]. E si il soyt humme, bevez la jous. E si il seyt en la mort seysoun, pernez la racine de meme herbe e destemperez ov ewe benette .iii. foye a matyn e a vespre, si garra. E auxi festez pur croyse e pur tute manere de poynture.*

Pro poynture. (435) *Item si humme soyt ponté d'etspyne: Pernez la muse de la neyre*[105] *espine e le fac[e]z frire en bure de May e le fettez sure le mal auxi chaude cum il pora suffrer, si trera hors l'etspyne e gara le mal. E si vous ne poés aver la muce, si*

99 MS achevele.
100 MS astanchancher.
101 i.e 'cele [for sele] percié'.
102 MS se que.
103 The following words in the MS, 'estomack est male', appear to be displaced.
104 MS manger le manger.
105 MS voyre.

pernez la grece de levere e le metez desure la ponture e se treyra hors l'etspine e gara le mal.

Pur pouson. (436) *Item qui sey dute de enpoussunement: Pernez .iii. figus de Malec ou .v. [ou] .vii. e lé fettes ben laver e pus fendez checun fige e metés en checun .iii. foylez de rue e le mangez en joun. E se jour ne averez garde de puson.*

[f.21rb](437) *Item pur le mal de flanc: Pernez la semense de ruge parele e le donez a beyre a matyn e a vespre e si il use, il garra certeynement, mes qe il sey garde de pommes manger.*

(438) *Item pur garrer de mal de feye: Pernés un poingné de sicori e de serlange un poyngun e de licoris un poyné e les bulez en .iiii. quartez de ewe si longement q'il ne demurge fors un potel. E bevez sele a primere a matyn e a drayn a sere e si garr[e]z le feye, anglice 'galle'.*[106]

(439) *Item pur feloun e postume deins le cors: Pernés espigurnele e columbine e scabiouse e matfeloun e solsicle qe seyt quili en May e fettez lez seccher saunz solayl e quant il sera ben secchi, si en fettez pudere, e qui avera feloun ou appostume dedeins le cors, si dettemprés cele puder en bone vyn ou bone serveyse, si le bevés .ix. foiþe, e vendra hors.*

(440) *Item pur estrandre ventre: Pernez un herbe qe est appellé burnette /.a. tunhoue/*[107] *e fettez en buler e[n] quel lycour ke vous plus amés e bevés le tres foiþe e ill strandera.*

Pur alacher. (441) *Item pur alacher: Pernés un onyon ruge e gros e ostés le coperoun e le quer de le unioun de eins e mettés gres de porck fundue e fres mellé ov cumyn mollue, e pus remettez le coperoun arere e le liez de un fil, si le fettez* [f.21va] *ben rostir tanck'il seit tut mol. E pus le metez sure le umbril auxi chaude*[108] *cum humme le purra suffrer e ly fra lyverance aver par tens.*

Ad eundem. (442) *Item pur alacher: Pernés pleyn poyngné de percil e plein poyngné de malve, e qe il eyt plus de percil que de malve, e festez lez ben bullier e strayndre hors le ewe e liez desure le numbyl auxi chaude*[109] *cum humme le pouyt suffrer, e se delivera le ventre.*

Pur gravel e mal [de flanc]. (443) *Item pur gravel e mal de flanc: Pernés chites ruges e si vous ne lez avés rugez, si pernez de blancches un pongné, e lez lavez ben nettement. Pus lez metez en une nette pot e metez eins de l'ewe un quart e lez lessez temperer de soir deke a matyn. E pus pernez puder de semence de apie e semence de fenoul e semence de percyl e semence de fenegrek, owelement de checun. E pus pernez puder de squinante atant com dé autrez catre desur diz. E a checun foiþe cum vous voudrés user,*

[106] MS anglice galle le feye.
[107] Superscript addition by a different hand which is responsible several insertions.
[108] MS staude.
[109] MS staude.

vous mettez un quilieré de argent de ceste pouder en pot ouveke lez chites en le ewe e le matyn en la jour [a]vaunt fettez lez tant bulier dekez il seit a la manere de purré de peiz. E dunkes bevés un bone tret de cele purré si chaude com vous le poés suffrer. En jour le puit humme user tres foiþe la semeygne.

[f.21vb](444) *Item a tus emflures de ventre e dé reins e de numbril e de quir e pur dropesye: Pernez se que lé chaminnus reunt de lour quiscine, anglice 'squot', e mollés ben tanck'il seyt a la manere de glu e pus gluez un drap e mettez desure le emflure e il deemflera.*

Ad eundem. (445) *Item une mesure pernés de farine de lentilez e un mesure de vyn tel cum vous voudra e fettez puree e quissez amablement e si mete amablement*[110] *e si metez un poy de myes de payn de furment, treblez ensemble en un morter e mettez un poy de ayle. E chaufés e metez desure le emflure e il deemflera.*

Apostume. (446) *Item pur tut postumus deins le corps de humme: Pernez purneles, de le herbe que est apellé 'notisoda-berien' anglice, morel, si lez treblez e donez a beyre. E il fra le cle decrever deins le cors e il le vomera tut hors.*

(447) *Item a emflure que aveint par postumus: Pernez le sulfre, treblez e medlés ov olye e ov coliandre e si oynez la ou la peyne est e le maladie. E se medecine est pruvé veray.*

(448) *Item a le ventre emflé: Pernez la rue, si treblez e mell[e]z ov vyn e de se baynez le ventre e mut profitera.*

A l'etsplen. (449) *Item a l'etsplen de lanck (sic): Pernez le feve freché e met[e]z en eycil e si lessez ethre .iii. jours. E pus le treblez en un morter e metés desure* [f.22ra] *un drap e pus a l'etsplen.*

(450) *Item pernez saveyne, si quissez en ewe deke a la terce partie, pus le treblez e temperés de meme la broit, si ly donez a beyre un hanap plein e medlez ov vyn e fettis ly cucher desure le coste ou le malad[i]e ly teint, si gara.*

(451) *Item pur le menisoun: Pernez eicyl e oynés e friez ben en un nette vessel de aremme e mangez de ceste cant vous irez cucher, mes garde[z] vous de beyre.*

Pur ventre enmoler. (452) *Item pur ventre enmoller: Pernez leger payn e mellez en eycil e mang[e]z.*

(453) *Item pur trenchivesouns, anglice 'freit in þe wombe', chose qui est prové: Pernés cumyn e pevere par uele mesure e festis en pouder e le donez a beyre .iii. culierés ov ewe chaude e il vaudra.*

(454) *Item a moller le duresse de ventre: Pernez la racine ov la foyle de lauriole, si lez treblez e metez de gres de porck e fettus enplastre e metez desure numbryl.*

(455) *Item pernez .iiii. foyles de meme le herbe e liés ferm de un fyl ov un pece de char grasse de porc ou de autre bette, si lessés ben bulier. E puz fettes le malade manger le char e ne mye lé foylez, mes bevera la broyt, e se vadra cum prové est veraymment.*

[110] MS cunablement.

[f.22rb](456) *Item le jous de ache si ly donez a beyre e il vaudra.*

(457) *Item a costivisoun: Trenchez tun musel si long cum voþre deie e le pudrer de ceilgemme e mollez en mel e metez la launge en fundement.*

A vermus de ventre. (458) *Item a tus manere de vermus de ventre occire: Pernés lé lupins e lé bayez de lorer e feel de thor, anglice 'galle', si mellez tut ensemble, si mett[e]z de numbyl asure*[111] *cum emplaystre deus jours e .ii. nouytes.*

Pur reynes. (459) *Item a dolour dé reynes: Pernez centurie ov eycil, si bevés e il heydera mut ben.*

(460) *Item a cely ky trop beyt: Donez ly a beyre centurie ov ewe teve e se tut le fra etspurger le pis.*

Pro fluxu. (461) Item contra fluxum ventris: Decoquatur caseus in aqua vel in aceto et lavetur in aqua donec totum sal exierit et da ei unam dragmam .i. unam potacionem. Si non distingwat, da ei aliam et sic donec curetur.

Ad eundem. (462) Item coagulatum lac caprinum da sibi bibere et idem facit.

(463) *Item encountur costivisoun: Pernez le semense de lyne e quissez ben en ewe e pus ostez le ewe e pernez le lynez e friez ben en un paele*[112] *ov seym de porck freis, pus mangez un culieré ben chaude.*

(464) *Item encountur menisoun:* [f.22va] *Pernés mylefoyle, si l'estampez e pernez la jous e la flour de furmente e fettez un turtele e quissez e brisés e mangez. Set chose e[st] prové.*

(465) *Item for man þat is costiue: Tack gret suur quete-bred and myit smal in vaxe and gyf hym to etun tyl he be hoyl.*

For dropesie. (466) *Item for dropesye: Tack fenul-rotes and percil-rotes and of boþen olike mychel and rote of ache als michel and tack þe herdez, eie rose, anglice pisse,*[113] *and tac an hanful of hauere-mel grotes and stamp smal and .xx. peni-weythe of fenkele-rotes and .xl. of ache and tack a galun of water and do al in a pot ouer þe feyr and lat it seþen to þe haluendel. And tack þanne and clense hem þorw a cloyt and do it in a pot. And sitthen tac þe ious of fenkele and þe oþer iousez and do ouer þe fier and lat it wel pleyen and tac houit .ix. sponful of þe firste and tac .iij. sponful of þe jous of fenkele and do togedere and drynk þat hoyt at ewn and at morwen cold and kep þe weil fro oþer drynk and þe*[114] *salt warisse sone in sertayn.*

(467) Item si vis deliberari ab ebri[f.22vb]etate: Accipe nigrum sedrum et pone in poto et da bibere.

[111] Corr. desure le numbyl.

[112] MS panele.

[113] The text is evidently corrupt here. It looks as if something has fallen out after 'herdez'.

[114] Ms 'ye', apparently for nom. sing. 'you' = 'þou'.

(468) *Item encountre menisoun de ventre: Pernez le foyle de clote e quissez ben en ewe e aprés auxi chaude cum il pouit suffrer mettez a la plaunte de pé e il garra si toit.*

(469) *Item pernez leyt de vache de un colour e un pere que est appellé 'flynt' e mett[e]z en fu deke il seit ben chaufé e ruge. E pus metez eins le leyt e lessez ben bulier ow le pere e pus donés a beire, e il gara verey.*

Pur pere medicine. (470) *Item pur le pere: Pernez le sanck de buck en un ampulie de ver cant la lune sera en le corus de .ix. jour. E en cele meme lunaciun pernez un levere e pernez la peel ov le sanck e le metez a fu e le secchés isi que vous pussez pudrer. E pernez la puder e le semense de aniis un culier plein e treblés ensemble e puse medlez ov vyn e donez a la malade a beyre. E si vous volez icele prover, metez en cele beyre un pere muth dure, quel que vous volez, par .iii. jours e le troverés tut depecee vereyment.*

(471) *Item a femme que ne puit pisser: Pernez alisandrez e serfoyl e sauge e treblez ensemble e dunez a la malade .i. hanap a seir e autre a matyn, e il gara.*

A seus que ne [pount pisser]. (472) *A seus que ne pount pisser:* [f.23ra] *Quisez mauve ov bone vyn u ov eicil deke a la terce part e si dunez a beyre.*

Pur pere. (473) *Item pur le pere: Bevez la tere de ny de arunde ov ewe chaude e il vaudra.*

Ad eundem. (474) Ad expellendam petram: Sume piper, petrocilium, semen spargii, hec omnia mola et cribra et melle paralis (?) et da uti cum lacte. Et si vis experimentum facere, pone lapidem in vitrio vase et pulverez quos dixi et lapides se reminissent in crastino.

(475) *Item a humme que ne pouit pisser: Quissez ben en bone vyn deke a la terce part malws et aly, anglice 'garlec', e donez suvent a beyre, e il vaudra.*

Pro lapide. (476) Item pro lapide: Accipe radicem vervene, mymite, consissa et comisse cum aqua tepida et da bibere et mirabiliter frangit lapidem et quicquid urinam inpedit celeriter discutit.

(477) Item accipe radicem urtiole vel paritorie et fugit lapidem optime.

Ad eundem. (478) Item unge statum tuum cum sanguine vulpis, anglice 'fox', et franget lapidem optime.

(479) Item egrimonia pulverisata idem facit cum potatur.

(480) *Item medicine pur le pere: Pernez saveyne e canel e annis e semens[e] de fenyl e semense de grumele e lez brayés tuz ensemble. E pus mollez en feble serveyse e donés a beyre. E pus mangez un vas de perez, anglice 'a score de cheriz'.*[115] *E prové est verey.*

[f.23rb](481) *Item pur garer de pere: Pernez bardons, polipodie*[116] *de chenne, bayes de ere qui cret en boys e saponoyre e arcaungeline, saxifrage, de checun oelement, demy livre de sucre, lycoriz ou meel, e seiunt ben menus treblez e pus quyt en bone vyn tanc*

115 The text appears to be corrupt.

116 MS p. e de ch.

que a le moyté degastie ou en bones serveyse clere. E beyve le matyn froyd e a vespre tevve, si degaste la pere et sauve le humme.

Pur gravel. (482) *Item pur gravele: Pernés grumile, philibz (sic) et saxefrage, semence de percil macedoyne,*[117] *e le racine de fenul e le racine de percil, lyngua avis e cressoun de ewe e sancg de buck, e de checun taunt cum vous voudrés sol[u]m se que vous veyrez qui la persone seit gre[f]ment malades. E braez tut ensemble e le metez en ses boyrez e en ses viandes sovent, e il gara.*

(483) *Item pur garir de la pere: Pernez des unglez de porck e les fettez arder en puder e donez lez a beyre a malade suvent, e il garra.*

For man [...]. (484) *Item for man þat may nowit stale: Seit wel in god win þe ok-apel and in eicil and garleck al togedere to þe þridden del and ʒif him to drincke.*

Ad eundem. (485) *Item oþer: þe heued of þe garleck wit þe branches poyne and [ʒif] him to drincke.*

[f.23va](486) *Item for þe ston: Bren þe clawe of þe got and yif it him to dryncken in ale.*

(487) Item qui urinam proicere non potest: Decoquat radicem jusquiami in aqua et quanto calidius sustinere potest imponat membrum .i. virgam virilem et hoc faciat .iii. vicibus et curabitur.

(488) Item qui urinam retinere non potest ut sepe accidit pueris lacivis: Semen[118] tritum cum vino, anglice 'senevey', bibat et cum veteri vino bibatur.

(489) Item ad eos quibus semen fluit dormiendo vel vigilando: Jus lactuce in vino coctus et potatus lapsum seminis retinet.

(490) Idem facit canopis silvestris et si frequenter sumatur, aufert facultatem generandi.

(491) Item contra lapidem in vesica: Accipe radicem saxifragie, si fuerint recentes in parva quantitate, si sicce[119] in maiore, radices piricarie rubee, radices pentaphilon,[120] semen ameos,[121] semina granorum simul et radices graminis et de istis fac potum et da tepidum.

(492) Item ad eundem: Accipe cretani nastucii aquatici[122] radices, graminis radices, petrosilii utriusque .s. macedonii et comunis, et semen le[vi]stici et de omnibus istis fac potum et da pacienti bibere.

(493) *Item for man þat may nowit wel pisse: Tac sen*[f.23vb]*chun of house and*

[117] MS marcedoyne.

[118] Before 'semen' the scribe wrote 'semem' (or 'semeni') with a bar over the first syllable. In view of the English gloss 'sinapis' is needed.

[119] MS succe.

[120] MS pontaphilon.

[121] MS aneos.

[122] MS equatici.

schepus-talw and wel it wel togedere and al so hoit as he may suffre ley it in a litel poket up on his menbris.

(494) *Item for man þat had lorn nature for colde*[123] *of himsele in þe body or for siknesse: Tac þe seid of fenkele and þe seid of persile an þe seid of carwey and of cardemoyne, of ilk olike mykel, and tac lyngnum aloes, geloffre an ganygal*[124] *and caneel, of ilk olyke mykel, of ilk a peni-witthe, and iubarbe to dragmes, of alloy .ij. dragmes, of mastic .i.*[125] *dragme, and do alle togedere in a morter of bras. Tac siþen a clene scured panne and cast a god del of sucre þerin and lat it melt and tac al þe grindyng in þe morter and cast þerto. And tac a clise of yren and ster*[126] *it wel togedere tyl it be þicke and ropande. An do it þanne in boystes and husit eni ore fastyng and it schal make þe hoil.*

(495) *Item for þe ston: Tac saueyne, canel and anies-sedes and fenkele-sedeʒ and grumyle-sedes and stamp in a morter and medle hem in his drinck þat he drincket and huse cheri-stones.*

(496) *Item for [man] þat may nowit pissen: Ley galbanum on his pyntul-einde or on a winmannus nouele or drinck croppes* [f.24ra] *of þe rede nettles, an he waris.*

(497) *Item pur privé mal de humme. Pur humme que ad ressu privé maladie par maveyse cumpanie de femme: Perneʒ un os de un humme mort en le semiterie e le face arder e mettre le puder sure le maladie, e il gara hasti[f]ment. E si le festre fuit pris, si gara de cel puder.*

(498) *Item for bolninge of pyntul:*[127] *Tac and scher clote-levus smale and primerole and fri hem in seym, anglice 'gres', and ley it aboute þe pyntul on a lyn.*

(499) Item ad cancrum in virili virga: Aceto et lacte mulieris lavetur locus optime. Et post aspergatur locus morbi de pulvere quiz(?) in trusia(?) lupy. Sepe probatum est.

(500) Item ut penna viri erigatur, anglice 'pyntul': Accipe cerebrum cornicis et illini inde testiculos tuos quando volueris habere veni(?) cum ea incontinenti et nuncquam permittet alium habere cum ea.

(501) Item pro virga virili lesa: Cape succum de morel et semen lyni et ungwentum porcinum et simul bulias et appone virge tue et curaberis.

(502) Item ad libidinem exstin[g]wendum: Accipe rutam et conmisse cum aqua calida et da libidinoso bibere.

(503) Item modicum vervene date ad potandum non sinit virgam virilem erigi per .vii. dies postquam potaverit de eo potu.

123 MS colded.

124 for 'garyngal/galyngal'.

125 MS a .i.

126 MS possibly 'stor'.

127 MS pynt'.

[f.24rb](504) *Item pur la membre emflé: Bevez betoyne, treblez ov vyn e metés a la mal, si garés.*

(505) *Item for soer on þe pyntul: Tac linsed and stamp it smal and seit it in gotes mylk as gruel and ley it warm on þe sair as he may suffer.*

A dolour de fundement. (506) *Item a dolour de fundement: Pernez un lange si long cum voþre deie, si uinés de mel e [metez] puder desure de arnement e liez a fundement.*

A emeraudes. (507) *Item a lez emeraudes: Pernés mulene-gres and stamp it weel wit freis schepus-talw e metez desure un launge a fundement, e il gara.*

Ad idem. (508) Item pro eisdem: Radicina de casso et folia nepite equali pondere, pisa cum pyn[g]wedine, fac inde emplaystrum et pone in ano et sanus efficitur.

Idem. (509) Item ad emerodias: Vade iuxta mare et in vadora, anglice 'gravel', que sunt ibi inveniez erbam que habet folia similia eruse. Colige ipsam herbam et da succum eius ad bibendum et sanat ipsum.

Chaudure. (510) *Item in rotula pur chaudure*[128]*: Pernez tansé salvage e le fettus mou(r)dre e lavez suvent le ar[s]ioun de jus, e il gara.*

Floures. (511) *Item pur floures e restues: Pernez un galun de servoyse e un grant poyné de ermoyse, herbe e racine, tut ensemble, e festez le moiller. E pus bulier tanck' il veine a un potel de serveise, e de se deyt humme beyre un tret a vespre e autre a matyn chaude.* [f.24va] *E que use de se boyre, il garra de maladie. Hermoyse est en englez 'mogwed'.*

(512) *Item pur celoy que est encumbré en soun furcele: Pernez vinegre e le face etchaufer e pregne un esponge e mollés dedeins le vinegre chaude e le metez sure le furcele si chaude cum humme le pura suffrer, si garra.*

(513) **Pur marys.** *Item le mariz, si la maris seyt avalé que il seit hors a fundement: Pern[e]z feþerfoye e le estampez e pernez le jous e mettés en un pece d'un pot de tere un poy chaufé. E pern[e]z une penne e mollez dedeins le jous e de cele penne mollez la marys que est issu de jous counter le fu sovent e si retrayra e turnera arere en soun droyt lou, e si amendra.*

Pro testiculis. (514) Item contra tumorem testiculorum et aliorum menbrorum emplastrum factum de altea et butiro et ex medulla fabarum confecta ex vino vel aqua pro qualitate distemperantie vel ex radice altee et seminibus liny et fenugreci cum butiro.

(515) *Item for werkyng of lendus: Drink þe fyue-leues wit water and it schal al away.*

128 In the righthand margin *chaudere* is written in red with what is apparently an expunction mark under the penultimate 'e'. After 'pernez' in the text the scribe has expuncted '.iiii. pes de porck' by both expunction marks and barring the phrase in red.

(516) **For werkynge.** *Item for werkyng of lendus: Tac an hey-schelle ful of þe ious betoyne and bleind it wit a spon.*

[f.24vb](517) *Item for brusyng and nowit broken: Tac ious of wirmod and betoyne and malweȝ and hache and stamp al togedere and wel hem in gres and wax and hony and heycil and ley to þe sor.*

(518) *Item a dolour de quisȝ: Trebleȝ lé crotes de berbis ov oynt de porck e oyneȝ suvent le quis.*

Pur le quiz. (519) *Item si le quiȝ desure genule seit emflé ou la peel depessé: Bevés eble ov servoyse .ii. jours, e si garés.*

(520) *Item for þius þat ben to-swollen beneþe þe kne or abouen oþer þe fel to broken: Drynck walwrt .ix. dayes so þou salt ben hoil.*

(521) *Item for knowes þat ben sqwollen and hard oþer akyng: Tack rue and poyne wit salt and huny and þerof mack a playstre and ley þer hon.*

For brusing. (522) *Item for brusyng of lendes* ut si quis ab alto precipitetur: Millefolium cum aceto bibat, et curabitur.

Ad eundem. (523) Item si aliquis ab alto ceciderit ita quod corruptus sit in corpore ab aliqua causa vel pondus levavit vel luctaverit ac de quacumque plaga in corpore malum habuerit: Accipe carbones de quercu et facias pulverem et similiter de tegule rubee et distempera cum vino et bibat callidum et manducet [f.25ra] donec sit sanus et cito curabitur.

(524) *Item for broken bon of schanke or oþer lyme: Tack confirie and dayeseye and cheuerfoyle and loytwrt and .ij. sponful of hony and yif him to drincken .v. siþes on þe day and loke þat þe ben sette euene togedere and weel.*

For werkyng of [schankes]. (525) *Item for werkyng and bolnyng of schankes: Tac and seit þe rotes of walwrt and do away þe ouereste barck and stamp þe mydeleste wit boris-gres and ley it to þe schanke.*

(526) *Item for bolninge of schankes or of oþer membris: Tac þe rede hertistunge þat attet serfoyle and miset smal. And tac dresteȝ of ale and quete bren and scepus-talw and do hem in a pot and pley hem alle togedere til it be þicke and ley it on þe sore.*

(527) *Item for hurtyng of schankes þer senwes ben hole and moules and sorews: Tack grete erde-wirmus and stamp and ley to þe sore, and it schal wariȝ wel.*

A os debrusés. (528) *Item a os que sunt debrusé: Perneȝ la servele de una [sic] chaele letant, si meteȝ desure le brisure e si le outtés pur kant que il puse suffrer, e si gara.*

(529) *Item.: Pernés le puder de* [f.25rb] *blanc eicyl, un poyné ou deus, e sel, medleȝ ov albun de le oif e meteȝ desure, si ne ostés par .vii. jours. E en se tens il bevera sauge e violet ov vyn.*

(530) *Item si jambe ou bras seyt debrucé: A comensement fettes spelkeȝ de arbre ben acordans a les os brusés e pus gardeȝ en quel lou il sunt debrucés e remetés arere a sun*

propre lou. E pus pernez tarock e oynt[129] *de porck marle e pus pernez e mettez outer le fu. E pernez un novele drapelyne e mollez ben ens le gras outer le fu e pus mettez entur le jambe ou le bras e desure let spelkes e liés ben e ferment desure lez spelkes. E pernez ses tres erbes e donés a beyre consoude, confirie, erbive, e lez os gardera de festre e des autre maus. E pres le .ix. jour remués let spelkes mut sutilement e anoyntez lez os ov aucun entret sanatyf e respelkés, mes ne mye si durement cum il furunt en avant, e si garderés a icele cum vous veyrés tens.*

(531) *Item pur mortmal: Pernés lé genitras de seyngler e les ardés en puder e auxi ardés un taupe tut enter e medlez ensem*[f.25va]*ble e le mettez desure le mal, e il garra.*

For fot d[isoluid]. (532) *Item for þe foit þat is disoluid wyt bresingge or wytston or of gate: Tack vertegres and arrement and greynd hem togedere and do in þe sore and it schal doun away ded flex and sitthen holyt wit entret ful weel.*

(533) *Item a le pees emflés* ut superius habetur.

For bolnyng. (534) *Item for bolnyng of schankes or oþer lymes: Tac and mise þe rede cresse and do it in a pot and drestez of ale and quete bran and scepus-talw and seit hem wel togedere til it be weel þicke. And sitthen tac a linene cloit þat may ouertaken þe sore and do þe playstre þeron al nyth and it schal squage þe bolye þerof hastely.*

For byt[inge]. (535) *Item for bitynge of wod hound: Tac mynte and clene leck and salt and stamp wel togedere and ley it to þe wounde tyl it be hoil.*

(536) *Item for þe werm: Tac þe roke-ay and do it in a newe pot of erde and bren it al to pouder and do it in þe hole þat þe wyrm made quan þe*[130] *gost to bedde and it scal [...]*

[f.25vb](537) *Item for bytingge of wonde: Stamp clene leck wit alle þe piles, amyng it wit ale and geif him to drinken.*

(538) *Item for þe canker: Seit sloþorn-barck in water tyl it be þicke and blac and do þerto huny and temper togedere. And do þerto flour of rie-mele and mac a playstre and ley to þe sore.*

For to helyn wonde. (539) *Item for helen wounde: Tac auense and betoyne, tansey and hemp-croppus and maddur and stamp hem wel togedere and temper hem wit hold ale and ȝif him to drynke.*

(540) *Item drinck to helen wnde: Tac an hanful of þe lytel dayiseye, als michel of þe rede wrte and als mychel of bugle, pigle, senygle, and al so michel of strawberienwyes, and fiue plantus of auense, .iii. plantez of erbe Roberd, and foure of tansey and þe crop of þe rede nettle, and al so mychel as a þumbe-honde of þe rote of confirie, .vj. croppus of hemp at missumer witouten rotes and .ij. plantes of orpyn, and wel hem in a galun of stale ale in to þe alwndel and let it kelen and* [f.26ra] *clens it þorw a cloit and tac þanne*

129 MS noyit.

130 Another example of 'ye' = 'þe' for nom. sing. 'þou'.

and [seith] it ouer þe foyr and do it seþen to þe þridden del. And tac þe quantite of gres and wel hem togedere and sitthen do hem cold in a uessel and ȝif him .iij. sponful wit .vj. of water to drynken at morwen and at euen and hel þe wnde wit lyne þeron.

(541) *Item for to doun away ded flex: Tac longwrt and huny and rie-mele and mack a playstre and ley to þe sor.*

(542) *Item for rancleinge quer so it be: Tac holy malwe and senchoun and egremoyne and lilie and weybred and stamp alle togedere. And tac þe ious and quete breid-crummes and þe quite of an ay and myng al togedere and ley it to þe soyr.*

(543) *Or tac red-wyn-dregges and quete bryn and ote-mele and ious of ache and scepus-talw and wel hem togedere and ley to þe sore.*

Senewis. (544) *Item for senewys þat arn neyt hewn on to: Tack grete wirmes þat arn in þe erþe quil þei lyn gendring togedere and loke þat þei parte nowit, and stamp hem togedere an ley hem to [þe] sore and it schal helen þe senwes ayen.*

(545) *Item for wnde þat is wrang*[131] *haled: Tack squines-grees and gotes-terdel and melt it togedere and ley it to þe sore and it schal [ben]ole.*

[f.26rb](546) *Item for rancle on festre or on veyne: Pernez hayhove od*[132] *sou de mutoun e treblez ensemble e si chaude cum il le pout suffrer mettez desure e dites set urisoun. Oratio:* Omnipotens sempiterne Deus, sicud potes per sanctam gratiam tuam et per sanctam Mariam Virginem matrem tuam, sana hunc egrotum – ettiam hanc vel hunc famulum vel famulam tuam .N. – ab hac infirmitate tali die, In nomine Patris et Filii et cetera. *E dites set orisoun tres foye e .iii. Pater Noster et .iii. Ave Maria.* Ibant tres boni fratres ad montem Oliveti querentes erbas vulnera sannantes, tollentes langores, et dixit eis Jesu Cristus obviando cum eis 'Quo tenditis, boni fratres ?' Responderunt ei: 'Magister, vemus a monte Oliveti, querebamus erbas vulnera sanantes, tollentes langores'. Et dixit eis Jesu Cristus: 'Conjuro vos, boni fratres, per mamillas que lactaverunt Dominum Jesum Christum et per quinque vulnera eius[133] quod nullam capiatis inde mercedem neque siletis. Ite in monte Oliveti et accipite oleum de arboribus et lanam de ovibus et ponite ista super vulnera, dicentes "Sanantur sicud vulnus quod Longenus milex (sic) fecit in dextero latere Christi et non putrescant nec ullis doloribus conmoveantur". Et dicas "Vulnera quinque Dei sunt medicina mei"'. Vera crux sit super istum vel istam et fac signum crucis in nomine [f.26va] Patris et cetera, Ave Maria, pietatis triduum nobile, in nomine Dei officii et benedicti pectoris. Fac

131 MS wrarg.

132 MS ad', possibly for 'and'.

133 MS acuis.

signum in nomine Patris et cetera et dicat infirmus .iii. Pater Noster et .iii. Ave Maria.

(547) *Item for to slo festre: Stamp mychel morel and crouscipe, erbe Jon, erbe Roberd and celodoyne, fenkele, erbe benet and wring ouit þe jus and temperit wit hony and þe ȝelkes of eyren and barck-dust an rie-flour and ley to þe sor.*

(548) **To knowe fester**. *And here mait þou se querof fester and canker cumet, it comet þer a wnde or a sor is wroing holed and brech ouit ayein, for or it cumet houit of þe flex or of þe senewes or fro þe bon, for yif it come houit of þe senewes or of þe flex, it cumit houit os it were bron leye, and ȝif it cume ouit þe bon, it cumet houit as it were þicke bloid and red quitour. He mayt þou knowe quat fester is and ordeyne medecine þerfore þat fallit þerfore.*

(549) *Item for sores þat arn ay open and wil nowit ben hole: Tack þe recheles and arment and greind al to pouder and do it in þe holes or in þe wnde.*

(550) *Item for wnde: Tack brere-croppus and þe rede wrte-*[f.26vb]*crop, dayeseie, red nettle, bugle and stamp hem togedere and wel hem in quit gres and in butere of May longe. And afterward wring hem þorw a cloith and gres þe wnde þerwit.*

(551) *Item for þorn in foit or in hand: Tack ditayne, stamp and lei þerto.*

(552) *Item or þe quit mos*[134] *of þe haweþorn þou mast ley þerto.*

(553) *Item or bares-grees or egremoyne wit hony ley þerto and [it] sal cumun houit.*

(554) *Item for to drawen howit a þorn or sticke or nayleȝ-stubbe [or] ayny oþer þing of þe foith or of any oþer leme: Stamp sengel and herche, wodebynde, husleck and þe leues of betoyne and temper wit hold ale and late hem drincke non oþer drinck til it be hol.*[135]

(555) *Item for canker: Tack lyme mad of ston vnslecked and black pepur and orpyn and mynte and stroyng eicyl and hony and barly-mele, of ilk olike mykel, and wel hem in a newe pot of herde tyl men may make puder þerof and do þat to þe sor.*

(556) *Item for festre: Tack hemp-seid and ote-mele, and bren togedere to puder. And tack þe ious of ache and hony* [f.27ra] *and mack a tent of linen cloit and wel it weel þerinne and put it in þe festre. And ȝif þe tent be wet quan þe drawist it howit, þan is it nowit warissed, but do ay þe tent þerinne tyl it be hol.*

(557) *Item for canker: Tack hye-schelles and arment and myng al togedere and ley on þe sor.*

(558) *Item god medic[ine] for rancle and for to slo festre and werkyngge of sores: Tack mosse of squet huni-appul tre or of anoþer squet tre and seit it in stale ale to þe haluundel. And tac þanne þe mos and ley to þe sor and it schal to-squagen þe bolye.*

Fo[r] wnde. (559) *Item for peryl of wnde at þe gynningge yif him to drincke: Tac*

[134] MS mois with 'i' expuncted.

[135] MS and hol.

pygel and bugle and senigel, erbe Roberd, matfeloun, egremoing and litel dayiseie, webred and centurie, þat is loitwrt, ambrose, þat is wilde tanse, sauge, cristene malwe, tansay, hemp, þe brere-crop, of ilke olike mychel weyen, and al so mychel of maddur os of alle þe oþer greses, and stamp hem weel togedere in a morter and do hem seþen in quyt wyn and wring hem þorw a clene cloit [f.27rb] *and do wellen hem togedere, an tac and lat it kelen and ȝif it him to drynck leweck. And yif he cast it nowit, þan is it a singne of lyue, and ȝif he cast it, a singne of ded. And ȝif þer be signe of lyve, serche wnde quentely, for þis is cald þe mychil drinck and it is god for canker and festre and alle oþer sores.*

(560) *Si playe seit sursané: Pernez le gres de levere e feinte de gars e fettes frire ensemble e mettez desure le playe auxi chaude cum il pouit suffrer, si overa sicom poés mettre autrez emplaystres par quey humme pusse le mex garer. E si soyt pur femme: pernez la fente de owe ovesque la gres de levere.*

(561) *Item pur playe garer: Pern[e]z pimpurnel e bugle e serfoyle, de checun un poyné, e de avense atant cum dé .iii. autres erbes, e festez lez ben moudre*[136] *en un morter e pus getés de[d]eins un potel de servoyse e lessez lez estre en un vesseel. E checun jour pern[e]z cel[e]z erbes en servoyse auxi gros cum un pombe petit dedeins cele servoyse e bevés checun jour un tret a vespre e autre a* [f.27va] *matyn. E mettés un foyl de rounse ou de ruge cholet sur le playe e il destrura le maveys sanc e gara la playe saun autre chose fere.*

Pur festre. (562) *Item pur le festre: Pernez mylefoyle, avense, spigurnele e peluete [e] braés les en un morter. E pernez le tute ensemble en un vessel e caunt vous le volez boyre, le culiez parmy un drapel. .ix. jours bevés par matyn e a soyr.*

Un crache. (563) *Item pur un crache: Pernés ribwrt e la foyle de cheverfoyle e menu ache e les estamp[e]z ensemble e lez culiez parmy un drap e gardés que ne ad point de ewe e pernez se jous e frotés le mal encontur sovent a matyn e a vespre e si gara en .iii. jours. E auxi ben l'em pouit fere encountre le soleil en esté.*

Encountre kanker. (564) *Item encountur canker: Pernés un oif e metez hores se qui est dedeins e pern[ez] greynis de segle e de ceel e de meel e mollez le alboun de un oif de tuz seus owelement e mettez ensemble e fettez puderer e metez desure le mal.*

(565) *Item a playes: Pernez aloyne e plantayne e lé racinez de fenoule e saveyne e ere e egremoyne* [f.27vb], *si les treblés e le jous de cette quissez en seym tanck' il seyt etspesse. E pus [pernez] la racine de lilie*[137] *e si en mell[e]z ben ov foyle de cholet e le quissez ben e tut ses choses treblés ensemble e festes un plastre e mettez desure. Se est cuv[en]able.*

Ad easdem. (566) *Item pernés jous de aloyne e de savine e de fres oynt de [porck] e de [...] e le farine de segle, temprés ow meel, e de se fettez un enplastre que est mut bon.*

(567) *Item pur rancour abatre: Pernez arement ov albun de oif e fettez enplastre e metez desure un poy de lyn e pus mettez a le enfermeté. E si seit de playe ou de ponture,*

136 MS mourde.
137 MS lisse.

pernez la jous de eble e de ache uelement e de farine de furment e si lez mettez ensemble e le quissez cum potee. E cum voreit arder, si mettez seym de porck freis e duncke le quisez longement e le met[e]z tut chaude cum emplastre cum il pout suffrer deus jours ou tres, e il deemflera.

(568) *Item pur angwisse de playe: Pernez la foyle de poret, si fetez le jous e le pastel metez a la playe, e le dolour pasera.*

(569) *Item pur rancle occire. Treblez ache ov farine de furment e puder de fevus mollues ensemble e metez desure le rancle, e mut profitera.*

(570) *Item faverolez que cressunt entur cressen treblez sulement.*

[f.28ra](571) *Item a gutefestre bone medicine e prové: Pernez pessounus que sunt appellez roches, si lez ardés en un nuvele pot de tere dekez a puder e pernez le jous de avense, si versés eins a la pertuse de pot e mellez ov le puder e quissez dekez il seit secche e dumenteres donez loy a beyre le jous de avense. Gara.*

(572) *Item pur gutefestre qe fet lez menuse pertusez, kar lez unus sunt chaudes e les unus freydes: A la freyde pernez le jous de lenthe e le blanche de oif e poy de flour de segle e de se festez enplast[r]e e metez desure le mal. E lyés ov un drap illeucus dekez il seit secchi, e si mester seit, mettez autre, e si garés sertein.*

(573) *Item a mors de serpens: Treblés centurie e donez a beyre.*

(574) *Item si etspine ou fer ou autre chose seit en aucun menbre par cas: Treblez egremoine ov veut oynt de porck e metez a playe, ou pelipode ou ditayne. E si enfaunt seit mort deins sa mere, donez ly a beire [ysope] en ewe chaude, si jettera hors, ja se ke il seit purri deins.*

(575) Item ut[138] appareat utrum plaga sit curabilis vel non: Accipe serfolium et da pacienti bibere et si retinuerit, curabilis est.

(576) Item aliud melius experimentum: Accipe semen canobi et warense, simul contere et da pacienti bibere in aqua; si retineat, curabilis [est].

[f.28rb](577) *Experiment de humme nuvelement feri: Pernés chervele e treblez en un morter e loy donés a beyre, e si il vomyt hors a playe, il murra, e si il ne face, ben puit estre gari pur vere.*

(578) *Item pur gutte etsquager: Pernés jubarbe, anglice 'husseleck', crowesipe, fane, tunhove, walwrt e les treblez ensemble. E pernez oynt de porck e le buliez tut ensemble e le met[e]z tut chaude la ou la gute plus agreve par .iii. nowis cant il vat cucher, e il gara.*

(579) *Item pur feloun garer:* Accipe farinam frumenti et distempera cum lacte mulieris puerum masculum[139] nutrientis et pone super morbum, et valebit.

138 MS ad.

139 MS masculini.

(580) Item ad omnem dolorem vulneris et ad collectionem umorum: Testa alliarum minutissime incisa[140] decoquatur in aqua et postea tritura(n)tur cum un[c]to porcino veteri vel recenti, bene incorporetur in emplastro et supponatur plage.

(581) *Item for þe canker: Tack lene bakun and brenit and ley to þe sor and got-fen and man-fen, euenely temper hem, and netus-fen, mack in cakes and ley þer he moun drien, or þou do hem þerto and or et gou þerto, stamp hem ful wel.*

Pur tuer. (582) *Item pur fe[st]re tuer: Pernés smalache e cheverfoyle uel porsioun e meel e farine de orge e braés tut ensemble en un morter e fettus* [f.28va] *un playstre e metés a la festre checun jour deuz foiye. E pernez ruge chous e quisés ben en ewe e lavez la festre checun jour deke il seit tué, e si ben. garés par Deu.*

(583) *Item a tous playez venimose clarefier: Tenez la ruge cholet e quissez en ewe e ov set tut lavés la playe e il amendra.*

(584) *Item si volez saver si un play deit garer ou noun: Donez ly a beyre cerfoyl e si il se vomit hors a playe, il gara. E pus ly donez a beyre checun jour ses tres erbez ben treblés e mellés ov bone serveyse pimpurnol, bugle e sanicle. E caunt il lez avera ressu, suus salirunt hors a playe; a etspurgement ben sanerunt dehors le playe.*

(585) *Item medicine pur destrure mort char: Pernés bef de sen Martin e de ceel un bone porsioun ov mutoun salé e de pilgrym salve bone quantité, un petyt porcioun de ver brayé e metés tus ensemble en un drap lyne e ardés en puder e pus braés e pudrés e metez desure le mort char, e il degattera tretut.*

(586) Item contra morsum serpentis seu alicuius vermi venenosi: Succum allii bibe vel assatum allium tantum comede et per vulnus exibit venenum viride.

[f.28vb] **Feloun.** (587) *Item pur feloun saner: Pernez un yolke de oif crue e un poy de ceel e mellez tut ensemble e metez desure feloun, e il tuera le feloun.*

(588) *Item pernez un posseyt fet de let sure, serveyse cha[u]de e ostez le servoyse e pernés cumyn e le brathelez sur carboun e ostez tuz les auges e pus mettez desure le possoyt e pernez foyl de solcicle e mariegolde e treblez e met[e]z tus ensemble e ben mell[e]z e pus metez desure le feloun e cel e[st] bone pur feloun e pur brock. E pus caunt le feloun e[st] debrusé, fettus tel emplastre: Pernez smalache e folefot e treblés ben ensemble. E pus medlez ov oif e ov meel isi qui il seit ben teve e pus pernés farine de orge e metés a icele isi qui il seit ben tempré. Pus fettus un emplastre e metez a la malade a matyn e a vespre e il gara. E cest emplastre e[st] bon pur veyne e pur playe.*

(589) Item carmen pro vulneribus: Precipio te vulnus per virtutem mamillarum beate Marie virginis de quibus lactatus est Jesu Cristus et per

[140] MS incise.

virtutem quinque plagarum Domini nostri Jesu Christi quod neque vulnus doleat neque putreficiat neque siccatriscat plus quam fecerunt vulnera Domini nostri Jesu Christi quando erat suspensus in cruce, [f.29ra] set ita munde laventur et a profundo sicud fecerunt predicta. In nomine Patris et Filii et Spiritus Sancti, Amen. Et ponatur lana et oleum super plagam.

(590) *Item ȝif iren or þorn or tre be in mannus leme: Tack agremonie and poyne wit salt, smere and ley þerto.*

(591) *Oþer: Tack ditayne and drinc.*

(592) *Oþer: Tac þe rote of rosel and wellit wit hony and do it in a cloit of flax and ley it to þe sore and it schal drawn houit þe þorn an al þe acche.*

(593) *Item for senewis þat arn herte: Tack pick and wax and smer and myng togedere and hetit and ley it þerto.*

(594) *Item for þe felun*: Accipe solsequium et albumen ovi et salem et tere invicem et appone morbo et sanus erit.

(595) Item pro carne mortua: *Tac þe curnele of þe walnote and salt and sope and meyng al togedere and ley þeruponne. Witoute dute it schal helen.*

(596) Item ad aperiendum plagam: Cape cerebrum de lepore et mitte super plagam per totam unam noctem et unum diem et plaga erit aperta.

(597) Item optima medicina pro omni genere guttarum: Cape erbam que vocatur 'walwrt' et tere bene in mortario. [f.29rb] Et cape succum et appone in una pixide et claude firmiter et liga cum cordis ita quod aer nequeat intrare. Et postea pone in una plena aqua et bulliri facias per totam unam oram diei ita quod due partes aque deuastentur ita quod tercia aque remaneat. Et pone pixidem in sole ut foris siccatur et quando siccatur, aperi pixidem et aparebit ut unum ungwentum et cape illud ungwentum et unge guttam vel morbum donec sanatur.

(598) Item qui vult scire et cognossere si homo sit curabilis quando vulneratus est periculose: Cape erbam que vocatur 'mushere' et inde facias succum et bibat illum. Si eiciat, est in magno periculo et si non, curabilis est.

(Pro omni genere gutte)[141]. (599) Item pro omni pena ictuum: Cape *welwrt* et semen lyn[i], tantum de uno sicud de alio, et coque in aqua. Et accipe de aqua et tere linum bene in pisa et tunc bene confrixa invicem cum pingwedine porci et appone illud emplaystrum vulneri, sed folium oleris et pyngwedo tangat vulnus inter plaistrum et cutem.

(600) Item contractus que valent *a le festre* et pro omnibus huiusmodi morbis et ad plagam et ad carnem mortuam destruendam et salvandam: [f.29va] Cape seram que nunquam fuit in opere et viridam pinguedinem

[141] Either the rubric is displaced (from 597 ?) or material following it has been omitted.

anglice 'vertegres', code, francus stor, picem, anglice 'pick', tormentine (sic) et cepum de ovibus et sic facias coqui invicem in una patella, et cape satis de cepo[142] ovis cum necesse fuerit. Postea sint compressa et facias colari per .i. pannum et in pixidibus ponas.

(601) Item pro morsura canis rabii, hominis vel caballi vel alterius plage venenate: Tere lyngwam caninam et rutam equaliter in veteri vino et pingwedinem porci et mel. Ista quatuor pone invicem. Istud emplastrum sic extrahet venenum et curabitur.

(602) *Item for manere byil and feloun: Poyn þe rote of þe lylye and þe holy docke and grunswilie and vinegre and linsed, hunyoun rosted and an heuid of garleck rosted, alle þese medled wit hold squines-smere or wit oly d'olyve and het it and ley þe playstre to þe sore.*

Documentum: (603) Item hic docet Ypocras quomodo quodlibet genus plagarum curare possitis per unam platam plumbi, quod neque festra neque cancra poterit remanere in illo dum plata plumbi quadrati et crucis inpressis in quatuor angulis plate .s. una cruce in medio loco et benedic illam platam crucem faciendo et quando facis crucem, dic quinquies Pater Noster in honore Domini nostri Jesu Christi et postea dicas versus: [f.29vb] 'Vulnera quinque Dei sunt medicine mei / sint medicina tui peria crux et pascio Christi'. Et postea dicas 'Jesu Christe ita vere sicud passus es, quinque plagas in vostro sanctissimo corpore pro omnibus peccatoribus, ita vere sana istum hominem famulum vestrum de isto morbo et omnibus aliis malis'.

(604) Item in nomine Patris et Filii et Spiritus Sancti, Amen. Et dic quinque Pater Noster. Caves bene qu[o]d plata non tangat terram. Post benedictionem et removeas pla[tam] tribus vicibus in die et lava platam cum aqua calida. Ad quamlibet remotionem dicas .v. Pater Noster in honore quinque plagarum quas Dominus Noster Jesu Christus passus est pro omnibus peccatoribus.

Pro ossibus sissis. (605) Item ad plagam sito sanandam vel ectiam si os digiti vel pedis sit sissum ac tritum vel aliud os: Primum cola os in proprium locum. Postea circum appone folia virida atquileie integra, et fascia .i. liga usque ad alterum diem et sanabitur. Et si non habueris folia, fac de radice eius similiter bene siccata et trita et sito sanabitur.

(606) Item ad plagam: Piloselle succum da ei bibere; si reiciat, morietur, si non, vivet.

(607) Item ad vulneratos: Semen canobi vel guarancie, radicem tanseti,

142 MS cepe.

cauly rubei equalem [partem] fortiter contrita et vino distempera et coque bene cum parvo melle et bibat donec sanus fiat.

Ad plagam clausam. (608) Item ad plagam male clausam: Tolle stercus caprinum, cum veteri vino misse et fac emplastrum et pone super eam si fuerit [...]. [f.30ra]

(609) *Item for goutefestre. Fyrst þou mait wite ou þou salt knowe a gutefestre fro þe cauncre: þe gotefestre ad a narw hole witouten and wyd witinne, þe canker ad wyd hole witouten and narw witinne; þe festre is seldum þat he ne had mo holeʒ þan on, and þe canker is euermore wit on hole.*

For festre. (610) *Item god emplaistre for festre: Tac weybrede and tansay, nosebledeles, sentinodie, þat is suquines-gres, merch and auense and stamp everyl[k] gres be þe selue and wring owit þe ious and loke þat þou haue of euerich gres olyke mykel of wose .a. ious and þat it be þicke. And tac walwrt and stamp and loke þat þou haue als mykel of þe ious os þou haddes of alle oþer gresus and þat it be ȝicke. And þanne tack virgine wax and freis schepus-talw and huny, May-butere, and hold squines-smere and tack of euerich olyke mykel and [loke] þat it be þicke and loke þat alle þese þinges þat ar last seyde be als mykel os þe ious of þe walwrt and do alle þes þingus in a panne and wel hem wel, but þe quite malwe þou salt welle þerwit, for þou mayt nowit wringen houit þ[e] iouse so mayt of þe oþer erbes, for it* [f.30rb] *is so fat. And quan it al wel welled is togedere, wring it owit þorw a cloyth and do it in boxes. Tack þanne quete flour and a parti of þan oynement þerto an wasse þe wounde at morwen and even wit quit wyn and ley þanne þi playstre þeron and do so ilk a day and gyf him to drincke fastinge wirmod and auense and salt, of ilk olyke mykel.*

Pudur for festre. (611) *Item god pouder for to slo þe festre: Tack benes, ri, hineray, arment and salt, of ic olike mychel, and do al in a newe pot and bren it tyl þou mayt stampen it to puder, a-puder it, and do it þorw a bultyng-cloyth. An tack þanne a stele of þe malwe and weit it in hony, a-walwe þe stele in þe puder til it be cloue þeron al buten, and put it in þe holes of þe gute tyl it cume to þe grounde of þe hole and þane ley þe playstre þerouer þat is befor sayd and quo so wile sclo þis*[143] *fester, him muste done þis stele wit þe puder þerinne .v. dayes or .vij. nyth. And þerafter do a tente þerinne of smal lynene cloith and wet it wit sum salue sanatyf and evere as it gynnet to holen mack þe tente sorter* [f.30va] *and schortere and ilk a day twies.*

Ad eundem. (612) *Item anoþer: Tack lauriole and driet and stamp it wel al to puder, þan tack þat puder and seit it wel in hony tyl þou mast maken tentes þerof. An do in euerilk hole a tente and hile hem wit cloutes and bynd hem so þat he ne go nouit of tyl þou vndost it at morwen. And þanne scourre þe holes wel and wasse hem wit quit*

[143] MS þe þis.

wyn and do so ilk a day tyl ye se red bloid cummen houit. Afftre þis medicine þou mast elen it wit pouder of recheles and wit þe jous of webrede.

Ad eundem. (613) *Item tack also vertegrece, brent lyme,*[144] *arnement and þe puder of þe racine of garleck brent, of euerich olike mykel, and mac puder þerof and do it in þe holes of þe festre to þe botme and do so euerilk [day] twyes, at morwn and at euen. And at euerilk tyme was it wel with hat wyn and do away quitur. þis medicine is god wit canker and goutefestre also.*

Idem. (614) *Item an oþer: Tack egremoyne and stamp it and ley to þe festre twyes on þe day and wase(t) it wit* [f.30vb] *wine.*

(615) *Item tack a plate of copere and wet it wel wit eysil and tack salt and stamp tyl it be smal and softe puder an strowit in þe eicyl on þe plate and spyt þeron. And seit it þanne on quike coles til it be wel brent. þanne weet þe plate eftsones wit eicyl and eft strowe on puder of salt and ley it on þe coles and do so ofte tyl þou hauest a gret del of brent salt in þe plate. þan do þe salt owit of þe plate an driet in þe sunne and þanne grind it smal to puder. And þanne tack to partes of þe puder and þe þrid del of puder of uertegres and myng þerwit, so ilk a day of þis pude[r] do in þe holeȥ of þe festre, doun to þe botme wit teynt and do so ilk a day tyl þou se þe flex waxen red and clene. And þanne do þerto ilk a day apostolycone til it be hol. It is a sicur medecine.*

(616) Sciendum est *þer be tweie guttus festreȥ, þe ton cold, þe thoþer brennande hot: þe cold festre is wit mani holes smale, þe hote is wit brode holes. Item to þe colde festre tack þe ious of auense or þe ious of lauriole* [f.31ra] *and quite of an ay, of everic olike mychel, and tack þe flour of rye and kned it wit þe ious and do it to þe holes so als it were a plaistre and bynd it þerto wit a cloyt and lat it lien þerto til it falle awai be þe self. And do þanne oþer þerto hupon þat same manere and do so euere til þe festre be hol. And ilk a day drynck þe ious of þe auense.*

For brennande [festre]. (617) *Item medicine for brennande festre: Tac þe flour of þe rye and cler huny and meng togedere til it be ard and mack also manie litel cakes as þer arn holes and ley to everi hole a cake and [quan] þei be wate, do hem away and do oþer þerto and do so til it be hoil. And mack sum drinck of auense or of peruincle and gyf it him to drincke.*

(618) *Item medicine for þe canker: Tack a storck body and al hoil os it is, heuid and al, and do it al in a newe erdene pot and do it in to an ouene and driet so þat þou mayt make puder þerof. And do of þe puder to þe canker and in fewe dayes þou salt ben hol.*

Experimentum:(619) *Item ȝif a man be wnded and þou wilt wite queþer* [f.31rb] *he schal leuen or deye: Tac pimpurnole and stamp it and temper wit water and gef him to drinck and ȝif it go houit at þe wnde, he schal deye.*

[144] MS lyne.

(620) *Item ȝif him to drinc letuse wit þe water and ȝif he spewe it, he schal deye witouten fayle.*

(621) Item emplaystrum factum de pulvere thuris et pilis lep[oris] cum albumine ovi vulneri superpositum sanguinis fluxum stringit optime.

Canker. (622) Item ad cancrum verum experimentum: Ponatur primum caseus recens ter vel quater supra. Postea accipe sisimbrium.i. men(s)t(r)astrum et tere cum sale et pone interi(o)us et erbam superpone.

Ad plagam. (623) Item ad plagam male clausam: Tolle stercus capri ut superius habetur. Si fuerit aperta, sanetur; si fuerit clausa, aperietur ut dictum est.

(624) Item ad omnem plagam ubi fuerit apertura: Accipe jus apii, anglice 'hache', et jus radicis rubee parelle et album vinum vel propriam urinam, omnium equali mensura et tantum mellis quantum omnium precedentium et fac bullire ad ignem usque ad spissitudinem et ponatur dum bullit farina(m) frumenti et sic ponatur in vulnere cum mundo lyno et statim sanabitur.

[f.31va](625) *Item for þe felun*: Accipe stercus porci recens et tere cum aqua et postea cola et da egrotanti bibere. Valet utique viro ut detur de masculi et mulieri de stercore suis.

Contra arsuram:(626) Item contra arsuram ignis: Stercus bovis recens superpone. Optimum succum est.

(627) Item ad spinam vel ferrum evellendum de vulnere: Accipe stercus anseris, anglice 'gander', superliga et sine dolore extrahes.

(628) Vel evelle sic: manibus radices arundinis, anglice 'reed', et cum melle tere et per pannum succum exprime et superpone.

(629) Vel sic: caules ranaturos teneros tunde et eorum succum pone super spinam; mitte ut succus non decurrat et sine mora exietur spina, ut probatum est sepeus.

(630) Item ad omnes dolores et tumores et ad plagas sanandas et vulnera: Accipe plantaginem, morellam et apium equaliter frumenti farinam et auxengiam, simul tere et appone ad modum emplastri.

Carmen ad cancrum. (631) Item pro vulneribus et cancris: Primo fiat plumbum tenue ad mensuram plage et fiant .v. cruces cum .v. Pater Noster ut in quatuor angulis plate et una in medio plate ut hic apparet per figuram istam sequentem × + × × × et dicitur istud carmen super plumbum: [f.31vb] 'Domine Jesu Christe, qui precioso sanguine tuo nos peccatores in cruce redemisti, mittere dingneris benedictionem tuam super plumbum istud ut quicquid infirmitas eo tactum fuerit per virtutem sanctissime pascionis tue accipiat sanitatem per Christum dominum nostrum'. Et dicitur ter Pater Noster et non moveatur plumbum usque ad quartam diem et quotiens movetur dicitur ter Pater Noster et sine dubio sanitatem sine dilacione possidebunt.

(632) *Item for þe feloun: Tack matefeloun and solcicle-floures and morel and lylie-rotes and stamp ilk on by em seluen and quich so hat left of ious, tack of ilk als mychel, and myng þerwit and ʒif him to drinck þre sponful. Meyng wit water þries on þe day.*

(633) *Item ʒif þou wilt wite queþer þe goutefestere is hot or cold: Tac þe tendre stalke of a red docke and fold it in on of þe same leuus and ley it in þe hote eymeri of þe fyre til it [be] brent inow and mack puder and ley to þe hole to dayes and to nitthe. And ʒif it ne falle nowit þanne awey be self, þan is þe festre hoyth for soþe.*

(634) *Item god puder for gutefestre: Tack arment and salt and bren to puder. And sith tack vertegres and pepur and wit glas and mustard-seid and mack pudur of hem and wey hem euene and ley on þe sore.*

[f.32ra](635) *Item for rankelling of sores: Tack ious of morel and hot possot and stamp hem togedere and ley to þe rancle.*

(636) *Item for bolnyng of blod-latyng: Yif him to drincken serfoyl, anglice 'red hertistunge', and he schal faren wel.*

(637) *Item for goutefestre: Tac gingere, seit it wel in stroyng eycil. And sitthe tac puder of alum-glas and vertegres and hony, of ilk olike mychel, and meyng hem togedere and ley on þe soer.*

(638) *Item boyre pur festre: Pernés mylefoyle, avence, spigurnele e peluete, e brayés les en un morter. E pernés le jous tute ensemble en une vessel e caunt vos le(s) volés beyre, le culiez parmy un drap e le bevez .ix. jors par matyn e a seir.*

(639) *Item pur caunker: Pernés oynt de porck e meel, si treblés ensemble e metés desure le mal.*

For þe canker. (640) *Item for þe canker god medicine: Tack þe heued of þe crane and þe fot and þe inward an dri em wel in a ouene til þou mast make þerof puder and ley þe puder upon þe canker and on a lytil quile it schal him scle nowit only to þe canker, but for eueri wnde it is god.*

Ad eundem. (641) *Item oþer medicine for þe self: Tac þe rote of dragaunce and schor it smal and mack þerof puder and tac þe puder* [f.32rb] *weythe off .ix. pens and do it in hoit water and ley it þerin al nyth and on morwen cast owit þe water and ley pouder on þe sor.*

Ad eundem. (642) *Item oþer medicine: Tack loueache an andre and aniis and poyne hem togedere wel and seit hem wel in wyn and ʒif him dryncken als hoyt as he may suffren and anon he schal castun al þe venym and al þe pusoun.*

(643) *Item pur feloun: Pernez solsicle e festes frire en gres freis e metés lez sure le feloun a matyn e a vespre, e si gara.*

(644) *Item pur remuer feloun u que il seyt: Pernés pei(d) de lyoun, yere terestre, atant de le un cum de l'autre, e si braés ben ensemble e le metez en un eschale d'un grant noiz*

e le metez par la u vous voliez que le mal veine. E cant vous troverés ke le mal seyt enduri, pernez fenugreck e festez pudrer e puse pernez olye[145] *de olive e gres de porck fres, atant de un cum de l'autre. E pus pernez le puder de fenegreck e medlez ov le su de porck e ov le oyle de olyve en un paele e lez friés isi que il seit espesse. E p[er]nez un pese de lyne teille e mollez deins sette unement e pus le metez desure le mal e la levera un vecie. E puz pur garer le mal pernez le mol de un oyf e atant* [f.32va] *de meel e de ewe benoyte e flour de furment e medlez ensemble tanc'il seit espesse. E puz pernez e le molez en ewe e mettez le(n) emplaistre de le oyf sur le lyn auxi large cum le mal est. E metez a la mal checun jour tanck'il seit gari.*

Pur gairer de feloun. (645) *Item pur garer de feloun: Pernez lé nowés de petyt noiz e surcicle e la petit consoude, e sez .iii. choses mettez owel porcioun, e lez batez ben ensemble e metez desure le mal un jour e un nowit saun remuer. E si tot cum vous le ostez metés un autre de meme sele manere. Ensi fettis tanc que il seit gari.*

(646) *Item for wind in goutes: Tac þe rote of þe clote and do ale þerto quan it is wel stamped and ȝif it him to drincken, at euen hoyt, at morwe cold.*

(647) *Item tac þyck hony and butture and do seþen togedere and smer þe evele aȝein þe fyr.*

(648) *Item: Or tac þe seid of ache and temperit wit wyne and drinck it ofte fastande an þou schal wa[ris].*

(649) *Item for þe goute, boþe hoyt and cold: Tack mannes pisse and hold it in a vessel .viij. dayes oþer more, so þat it be wel rotun, and sitthen seit* [f.32vb] *it wel in to þe haluendel or more and clens it þorw a cloyt and affter tack al s[o mychel] of þe ious of þe rowe and al so mychel of þe rede nettele and do hem togedere and tack and hanful of cumyn and quantite of virgine wax and quantite of barwe-smere and seit hem alle togedere and wryng þorw a cloyt and lat it a-kelen. And þan smer þerwit þe sor querso it be.*

Ad dolorem. (650) Item [pro] dolore ventris: *Tac suþernewode and tansey* et comede cum sale, et exiet.

(651) Item contra guttam caducam: Crudum ovum corvi absorbeat, ovum eius absconditum in sale potest servari dulcissime.

Ad morbum caducum. (652) Item paciens ferat super collum suum tria nomina regum: Jasper, Baltisar, Melchisar.

(653) Item valerianum, hoc est anglice 'wilde sethewale', ferat circa collum suum et tute bibat illum et in eternum sanabitur.[146]

[145] MS olyve.

[146] The MS reading is a jumble as follows: Item valerianum ferat et sanabitur circa collum suum anglice wilde sethewale hoc est tute bibat illum et in eternum sanabitur.

Ad eundem. (654) Item contra morbum caducum anglice 'gute' carmen probatissimum + dealbagut + deglutym + Item caro caduca reputa.

(655) Item morbum caducum + dealbaguth + debangue + deglutym et aliud caro caduca reputa Samuel, Manuel et Paraclitus. Eripe, Domine, ab omni malo, a viro iniquo libera me. [f.33ra] Eripe me de inimicis, Deus meus, et ab insurgentibus in me libera me. Eripe me, Deus, ab operantibus iniquitatem et de viris sanguinum salva me + abra + abraca + abracula + Christus vivit, Christus regnat, et Christus imperat et Christus hunc (hunc) famulum tuum vel famalam [sic] .N. ab omni malo defendat ut nuncquam contra fantasmata et postquam semel claudantur, nuncquam postea aperiantur nec ab egroto maxime et postquam semel circa collum susspenditur nullo modo auferatur sub pena evasionis morbi quoniam probatum est, nec nuncquam comedat de ullo capite et maxime de capite porci.

Gute ossé. (656) *Item pur gute enossé e a tuz autrez gotes volajous: Pernés le lynesed e quissez ben tanck que le ewe pesse. Pus treblez lez lynews e pernez fente de owayle, si le treblés ov tut le jous e pernez le pastel tut chaude e mettés desure le gute, si gaira.*

(657) *Item a gutefestre: Bevez la jous de pervincle e metés le pastel desure le mal endreyt dé pertuz e de la puder de blanck marbye ou de verte ow mel. De se fettes uynement e oynez le tente e mett[e]z a pertus par .iiii. jours e .iiii. nowis, e il gaira la festre serteyn.*

[f.33rb](658) *Item a le gute un bone plastre: Raés veud firmage e plein poygne de fevus fretis e meel e eycil e le albun de le oyf. Si treblés tut ensemble e mettés a dolour de gute.*

Curale. (659) *Item a goute curale: Mangés gingevere e peyvre e bevés un petyt de serveyse ou de vyn quit ov lyneus. E pus alez dormer.*

(660) *Item pur gute cheyve: Don[e]z fant a beyre,*[147] *einz que il ne seyt de .vii. anis, lé peres que sunt en le feye de bef ben debrucés a puder, e il ne avera jammés le gute cheyve.*

Pur cheyve gute. (661) *Item pur gute cheyve: Pernez lé pijounus de corf e le ny tut ensi e gardés que il ne tuchent tere ne ky venunt en nule mesoun e si lez ardés en un nuvele pot e donez se puder a beyre a la malade ov ewe benette, e il gara mout ben.*

(662) *Item pur rancle de gute etquager: Pernés voþre urine demene e bran de furment, ben buliez ensemble e metés le plastre chaude sure le mal e violet ov soun flour, [e] outez le dolour de playe serteynement.*

(663) *Item for lous gute þat is nowit festerd: Tac rue and red brere-croppus and flour of* [f.33va] *þe brome, of ilck oliche mychel, and stamp al*[148] *samne. Tac sithe gres of*

147 MS b. qui vous e.
148 MS as.

sqwin and haweþorn-blomes or þe lews þerof and do al in a panne ouer þe fyr[149] *and let hem wel bulion. And sitthen wring hem þorw a cloith and þerwit smer þe gute and it schal abate þe werck of alle manere gutes sertayn.*

(664) *Item for alle gutes: Tack lekes and seit hem al hoil and stamp hem wel smail and havermele-grotes and schep-talw and do hem togedere in a pot and seit hem wel and ley hem on a cloyth and ley it on þe gute and it [schal] ben ol.*

(665) Item contra guttam ossis: *Querez ambrose anglice 'wilde sauge' e buliez ben en blanccbe vyn e bevez suvent. E pus [ov] olye de rose*[150] *oynez le gute e se festes suvent e il amendra.*

(666) Item ad guttam festinandam: *Pernez pessoun que est appellé roche, si ardez ben tut vives en une nuvele pot tut a puder. E pernez le jous de avence, si versés eins le pertuse de[ke] il seyt ben moyste. E puz met[e]z*[151] *se enplaystre a le gute e festez ly beyre jus de avence.*

[f.33vb](667) *Item pur gute ou que il [seit] sure corps de humme: Pernez le plu cler gute de meel e oyn[e]z le gute contur le fu tanck que il soyt ben enbou de mel. E puz pudrés le ben de la puder de franck ensens par desus le meel e pus pern[e]z un pece de canevas de camfre e le streinez sure le mal si fort cum humme pura [suffrer] e lessez estre un jour e un nowit. E puz enracés le canevas si hastiment cum porra e vous troverés le meel e le ensens que il avera tret hors tut le mal isi que il prittra la char hors a le trere de canevas que lez gutez de ewe apparunt. Ensi gara il de gute si sey face ventuser par desus le mal de gute.*

(668) *Item pur gute froyde: Pernez un chat savage e le fettus etscorchier e rostier ouveke tus lez entrayles e metez un payele ov ewe pur reseyvere le gres e oynez la gute de cele gres, si gara hasti[ve]ment. E si vous ne avez nowel chat savage, pernez un chat privé, e pur humme pernez madle, e pur femme la femele.*

(669) *Item pur gute freyde: Pern[e]z le mowle(s) dez os de chival e(n) mettez deeins un novele boyste* [f.34ra] *en scire .iii. jours. E aprés le terce jour oynez la gute pres le fu le matyn e le so[y]r, e si gara dedeins neif jours.*

(670) *Item pur gute cheyve: Fettez seygner sely que est malade tanc cum il gist en panesoun en la veyne desure nees entur lez .ii. euz, e se le gara a le eyde de Deu.*

(671) *Qui hat gute avivé si boyve erbe yve, si garra.*

(672) *Item for gutefester: Tack flour of rye and kned it wit ious of walwrt-rote and mack lytil cakes and back hem on þe heryth. And sitthen tac þe cakes and do away þe*

[149] MS fyr þan he ben stamped. Either the phrase has been displaced or something has been omitted.

[150] MS rosee.

[151] MS m. de se.

cruste and lay þe crummes to þe soer al so hoyt so he may suffre. And do [þ]is away quan it arn[152] *cold.*

For brenande goute. (673) *Item for þe brennande gutefester: Tack rie-mele and kned it tyl it be ard wit hony and mak þerof lytel cakes and ley on ilck an hole a cake and quan þe arn wete, do hem away and do oþer þerinne.*

(674) *Item for goute, boþe hoyt and cold: Tack þe marwe of an hors ritthe leg and al so mychel of May-buture and melt hem alle togedere and gres þe gute.*

(675) *Item*[153] *for þe same: Tack henbane, mogwurt,* [f.34rb] *sauge, mynte, horsmynte, watercressen, senchun, fenoil, of ilck olike mychel and vinegre, wyn-drestes, ale-drestes and medle al togedere and fry hem weel in scepus-talw and ley þerto.*

(676) *Item for þe gute: Tack May-butere and melt it in a panne and do away þe fom. And tack þe floures of þe brom and wel þerinne and wryng hem þorw a cloyth and gres it.*

(677) Item emplaystrum factum de pulvere thuris et pilis leporis cum albumine ovi vulneri superpositus sanguinis fluxum stringet.

Experimentum. (678) Item experimentum de sanguinis minucione: Accipe de ipso sanguine unam guttam parvam et in vase plena aqua mitte et si gutta integra fundum petat, in ipso non morietur pro certo.

(679) Item si vis extingwere sanguinem, ista nomina debent ascribi in fronte illius qui emittit sanguinem. + geon + gedeon, et statim sessabit.

Pur arsure. (680) *Item pur arsure de fu e pur chaudure: Pernez oyle de olyve e deuz partiez de ewe e lez fettez mover ensemble tanc que le ewe seyt degastie dedeins le oylye e mettez cel oyle sure le arsoun de une penne saun demayn.*

[f.34va](681) *Item pur arsoun de fu: Pernez leyt de vache e farine de furment, si en fettez putee mut ben e kant il e[st] quit e refreydé, fettus un enplastre sur peel de levere e mettés desure tanck que il seyt garri.*

(682) *Item for man þat is scalt on any membre: Lat him bloid on a veyn wel mouble and tack þe quite of an ay and lynen and do þer abuten. And tac siþen puder of elm-barck and puder of wynballez evenely and strou on þe sair and he scal wariz ȝif þe medicine be hoyth.*

(683) Item contra arsuram ingnis: Accipe pilos leporis et sinde eos in multis partibus et misse cum albumine ovi et fac ex istis emplaystrum et ponatur super arsuram et non sublevetur donec sanetur, sed prius accipe salarium quia de facili sanabitur.

(684) *Item fuyt agayn wilde fuyr: Stamp seym and hold chese and stamp tyl it be neysse and sitthen anoynt þe soir þerwit.*

152 The obvious lack of concord suggests an error here.

153 MS Item tack for.

(685) Item ad eos quorum ora serpens intravit aut ad alios vermes eiciendos: Attramentum cum vino bibant et exient.

Pur serpent. (686) Item ad morsum serpentis: Succum calamenti da ei bibere.

(687) Ad pu[n]turam aranie: Mulcam cum fermento tritam et superpone in loco pu[n]ture et venenum expellet sine dubio festinanter.

(688) Item contra morsum serpentis: Tere rutam viridem et superpone.

(689) *Item pur tut manere de morsure: Pernez le coperoun de ruge urtilez e gres de porck freys e fettez batre ben menu ensemble e metez a le morsure e cel le garra.*

(690) *Betoyne chase hors lé querdes dey (sic) os brucés e sire soude lé nerws.*

(691) *Milefoylie axi resoude lé nerfs.*

(692) *Let de chevere ou de vache auxi chaude cum il est aleté restore le servel e leyt de femme plus.*

(693) *Item pur escroyles que est malad[i]e de roy: Pernez reyne de pré e fettus jous e festez le malade a beyre, e si gaira.*

(694) *Item pur ponture de serpent, de humme ou de beste: Celuy ou cele que lé novelus vous portera que le beste est poynté, dites louy que ele querge se que ele vodra beyre en un anap ou en esquele e ly demande que ele vous portera e mettés desure vos .v. deyus cenestres e ceste paroles direz en croysaunt outer le lycour dé .v. deyus de le autre mayn: 'Caro, caro se iu uupite (?) sane vinamet paraclitus'. Ceste choses direz .iii. feye en croysaunt e meme celuy ou cele que le un*[...]

[f.35ra](695) Item pro febre terciana: *Tac þre leues of weybrode after þe sunne be gon doun and sey þre Pater Noster. An tac þerof and temper it wit ale or wit water and gyf him to drincke beforn þe euele him tack.*

For quarteyne. (696) *Item for feuere quarteyn: Tack þe ious of mugwrt and oly and het it togedere and smer þerwit þi bodi al togedere .iii. dayes.*

Knowinge. (697) *Item ȝif þou [wilt] knowe queþer lyf or ded be in man in secnesse: Tac an henne-ay þat be leyd þat iche day þat þe euele him tock first on and wryt wit igke þese lettres on þe ay: g.f.p.x.g.q and after le þe ey in sauf stede witouten house al nyth and at morwen breck þat ay on to and ȝif þer cume owit blode, he schal deye; and if þer is no singne of blod, he schal ben hol. þis is asayd.*

(698) *Oþer: Tac bred and smer it upon þe brest toward þe herte or fat lard of a squyne an do al so and cast þe bred or þe lard to a mastyf or to an oþer honde and ȝif et ete sauourliche, he schal lyue; and ȝif he wil nowit etun it, he schal deye witouten fayle, as ofton ad ben asayd.*

[f.35rb](699) Item qui curabilis est dura et acetosa vitet carnes porcinas, dulcia poma cocta, et mel comedat et magnos labores non faciat.

(700) Item ut bonum colorem post infirmitatem vel ut semper habeas super te: Accipe .iii. vicas et pone in aqua anglice 'wyn-soppe', et quando

debes extraere illas de aqua, calefac aquam cum ferro calido quod sit valde purum et comede illas in vino et ita fac .ix. diebus et habebit colorem valde bonum sine dubio.

(701) Item cave ne minuas ultra modum et oram vir[um] vel mulier[em] quia quisque minuit sibi sanguinem ultra mensuram, isti morbi inde venient: Interiora efficit frigida et facit deesse calorem et morbus glaucus inde pervenit et debilitat cerebrum et facit manus tremere, gutteque multe inde veniunt et inde venit tussis cordis et morbus capitis et multa alia mala inde emergunt.

For boystynge. (702) Item de fleobotomia in tempore idonio facta mentem sincerat, vesicam purificat, serebrum temperet, medullam ... [MS stained] [f.35va] depellit angustiam, bonum sanguinem alit et malum destruit et longiorem lucem in vita tua tenet.

NOTES

3. HE91/3 'For schakyng of hede and of handes'. For 'primeveyre ...' it reads 'lange with alle the rotes' [= 'lange de buef'] and omits 'ce este ... racine'.
4. LH13.
5. LH7,T24. Both omit 'et fac ... appone'. See Sig. 161.
6. LH17, Hunt 271/28.
7. LH14.
10. LH9,R6,T24.
13. T24 omits 'absinthium', as do Hunt 152/ll.97ff & 272/35.
14. LH8b,R5,T24. Cf. Hunt 271/23.
19. 'illisa' for 'illesa'.
20. T41('succus celidonie'). Cf. Hunt 238/36, Thes.101/34.
25. LH7.
26. LH8,HE83/15,R14,T24, Hunt 271/21. The last four witnesses add, after laurel leaves, '.ix. bayes/bays/baiez de lorer'.
27. D10,O1/27,R1,T24. D has 'pound it togedir'. O1/27 has 'aueroyne' and is shorter. H198 also has 'aueroyne' and ends 'ʒyf hym to drynke amorowe and at eue'.
28. D11 reads 'eufras' ('eyebright'), of which 'eyerose' may be a misreading. The comparable receipt D663 has 'oyle of rosis'. As it stands, 'eyerose' is just as likely to represent 'eue rose' i.e. rose-water (see 106).
29. R3,T24,Hunt 137/8b, & 271/22 (omitting the ref. to red colouring).
30. LH21,D12,O1/22,R4,T24. O has 'puliole with þe jeuse of þe floure & braye it in a mortere'. Ogden cites a Latin example with 'puleio cum flore suo' as representing the better reading, which is also that of R and T ('puliol od sa flour/fleure').
31. Hunt 271/23 (adding 'sauge').
32. Cf. Hunt 271/24 (reading 'mel e rue e eysil ensemble').
33. LH8a,D90,H95,H199,O2/20,R7,T24, Hunt 271/25. See 60 below. O begins 'If þe thynk þat þi heuede be tome a-bouen'. The receipt in H95 is longer and the various MSS have the rubric 'For þe molde þat is doune / fallen; For moold fallinge'. In

H199 it has the rubric 'Si palatum ceciderit', in R and T 'Si vous est avis que le chef la sus est afoundré/enfundré cum une fosse'.

34. LH9a,R8,T24 add 'cum burro/en bure'. Hunt 238/36 also adds 'in butiro' and ends 'lavetur capud cum aqua decoctionis celidonie, rute, feniculi et eufrase albe'. See also Hunt 271/26.
35. LH10. D352 has 'sywet' for 'grese' and reads 'barly and mele, heyhoue and the rede dok'. T24 has 'farine d'orge' and is longer.
36. LH12,D449,HE83/4,R11,T24,T26.
37. LH11,HE83/5,T24, and 48 below. D450 combines 37 and 38.
38. LH13,HE83/6,R12,T24,T27.
39. T24 'les moles foiles'.
40. Cf. LH14. D451 reads 'hertwort'.
41. LH15.
42. LH16,D7('rubb' is an error for 'ruw'),D452,H93,HE106/6, M117/9,O2/11,R13,T24. D7 omits 'þe rinde of hellerne'. D7 and M specify five peppercorns, HE and O specify nine, H adds 'hayhoue' and 'red fenel' and substitutes 'nyne bayes' for peppercorns.
46. LH7,T24, Hunt 272/33. Cf. O1/12.
48. LH11,H85,R10. See 37 above.
50. CC5,D6,D690,H66('peletur of Spayne'),M117/7.
51. CC6.
52. CC4 D5('rubb' is an error for 'ruw'),D454,HE37/8,M117/3,O1/15.
53. D92 has 'rede coole', 'hemp-croppis' and 'crispe hocke', and omits the gloss on 'ambrose'.
54. D93–94,HE50,O69/14. Ogden discusses several versions of this receipt on pp.114–5, whilst a full commentary is provided by M. Benskin, "For Wound in the Head. A Late Medieval View of the Brain", *Neuphilologische Mitteilungen* 86 (1985), 199–215 who prints a text from Dublin, TCD MS 158 (D.4.15). D93 has 'hemp-croppis' and 'white wyne'. The reading 'remue' (remove) is found in two MSS, whilst O has 'rounge' meaning to clean out. There is evidence elsewhere of a piece of maplewood being inserted in the skull to replace shattered bone. Most versions refer to the spider's web, 'blo or reid' being a reading peculiar to Corpus. In the final receipt D94 and O have 'baynwort, ambrose, rib(wort)' and D adds 'celydoyne' and omits 'þe nettle, lekes, hache' and 'matefeloun', later adding 'frankyn encens' (O 'fre rekills'). O has 'bubill [corr. bugill], seterib, celidoun, cheverfoil'. The treatment of symptoms is confused, both D and HE describing symptoms of death.
55. HE39/9 abbreviates.
60. See 33 above.
63. D97 has the rubric 'For the hede that is broken and the bone hole', has 'hockes' for 'malwes' and 'mugwort' for 'mugwed'. It omits the reference to barley flour.
65. Hunt 309/76. H96 expands and one of the MSS has 'pedilion .i. staueacre'.
66. D778,HE106/15,O3/13,R23, Hunt 132 (Lat.) & 300/17, Jör. 41/V; all omitting the last sentence of the Corpus text. See 72 below. O expands (see Ogden's note).
68. See 66 above.
69. O3/20(expanded),T27.
70. T24.
71. O4/24 has 'welowe-lefes'.

72. See 66 above.
74. T30. Cf. Hunt 272/46.
75. Hunt 253/125.
76. Cf. Hunt 253/126–7.
77. O4/28,T28.
78. LH73,R26.
80. HE93/17 has 'put þe jus in the ere, and lat it ben so a myle-wey'. 'A myle-wey' denotes a period of twenty minutes, approx. the time to run a mile, see also M136/4. The French looks like a calque on 'mileway', with 'lue' representing 'lieuee', the time to run a league.
81. LR65,R51,T59, Hunt 226/12, all French. See 88 below.
83. Cf. Hunt 233/100.
85–6. Combined in HE39/12 which adds 'jus of rewe' to the first receipt. Cf. R54 'Pernez le jus de senichun e su de motun e fetes emplastre'. HE110/1 substitutes 'jus of sentory' for 'senchoun', has 'gres of a clene ele' and adds 'jus of rue'.
88. LH65,R51,T59, Hunt 226/12.
89. LH66,R52,T60.
90. LH69,R53,T59, Hunt 237/32.
91. LH70 (for hair loss).
92. LH72,R24, Hunt 230/63 ('Ad capillos nutriendos vel confirmandos').
93. LH73,R25.
94. LH74.
95. Cf. HE109/18.
98. T58 has 'fel porcinum' and 'lana succida'. Cf. Hunt 233/103 which adds 'mel'.
101. Cf. R62.
104. Cf. R58.
105. CC9,D18,D266,H210,HE109,M51/13 & 91/5,O6/23(and note),R57. Cf. Hunt 159/ll.307ff & 232/95, and Thes.133/2. This commonly attested receipt varies in length (the Corpus text is the shortest) and in the identity of the tree used.
106. HE40/9.
107. O12/21 (and note). Cf. H210 ('Item þe moyst souereyn') 'Tak mary of ganders whyngges and flour of barly and medle þese wel to geder and put þerof in þyn eye alytel and hyt schal voyde þe pyn or þe web and alle oþer eueles of eyen'.
108. O9/21 stipulates black snails.
109. HE108/3 ('For bolnyng of eyen') and O10/35 add after milk 'þat fedyth/fedis a knaue-child'.
111. See H209 ('Pro lacrimis et sanguine in oculis') 'Tak þe jus of hawe þorn croppes and þe whyt of an ey and medle hem to geder and þen tak cotyn and medle þerynne and ley to þyn eye'.
112. T45, Hunt 289/202. See 114 & 140 below.
113. See Thes.127/89 & 91.
114. LH28. See 112 above.
116. LH27,D476,HE107/6,O10/10,S194/15,T51, Hunt 231/74.
117. HE107/8,T52. Cf. CC23 & Thes.121/50.
118. See 112 and 114 above. CC13,LH28,H85('Pro oculis qui guttant .i. goundi'),T45, Hunt 289/202. Cf. Thes. 127/89 & 91.
119. LH29.

120. CC14,LH30,D469,O8/12,R33 specify 'red caule lefe'.
121. D470 stipulates placing 'a glasse' under the bacin, HE80/11 has 'sette a lome', HE107/10 omits the detail.
122. CC25,D501,H68,HE107/18 (abbreviated),LH31,O11/7,S193/14,T43 & 51. LHRT are in French. Often rubricated 'For the web'. HES lack the reference to the stone, CC25 indicates stirring 'wit a clyse', DHO 'wit a round staffe', T 'de un pere rouge'. LH has 'movez les funz de la paele ben od une ronde pere'. See also Hunt 225/10.
123. LH33,R36,T51.
124. Cf. T47 'Succus floris mente maculam oculi tollit efficaciter'.
125. LH35/36,R37,T46.LH36 has 'l'aune e mangez rue'. The scribe has erroneously inserted superscript '.a. rue' before 'e mangez'. T45 has 'mettez ent jus de lancelé'.
126. LH37,R38 (shorter). For bleeding, LHR specify 'from the cephalic ('capital') vein'. LHR have 'ne dei pas celer'. T47 has 'leschez bainez e vin vermeil, si bevez leit de chevre blaunche attemprément'.
127. CC24,D473('flo' is an error for 'slo'),503 & 995,H90, M112/4,O11/3,R39. See note to CC24.
128. H90(Engl., expanded),LH39,R34,T48, Hunt 227/20.
130. For the use of 'salgemme' in treating the eye cf. H99.
135. T46. Cf. H209 'Pro oculis sanguinantibus: Put in hem blod of a dowe and hyt schal hele hem'.
137. Cf. H98 which ends 'wryte þis charme on a skrowe' (p.99 ll.11–12).
138. T46. See Thes.123/53 etc.
140. Cf.112/114 above. See Thes.127/89 & 91.
142. HE34/1 which has 'honi' for 'tunhove' and 'pound' for 'puder' ('half a pound of kanele', 'a pound of wilde sauge').
150. LH97,CC42(Eng.),D839,HE68/20('avereyne') & 79/20, O14/17,R20 & 105,S200/7, Hunt 231/73.
152. Cf. 160 below.
154. LH47,R102,T63 (contains first part only).
155. LH48,R98,T63.
156. LH49,O15/35,R99,S196/18.
157. LH50,R100,T63.
160. D211 which has 'iii part of vertgresse' in place of 'jous of plauntayne'. Cf. T67 'Item ad mal de la bouche: Lavez le de jus de plantainne'.
164. Cf. M94/15 'For þe quinasy: Take orpyn, and grynde it well, and drynke þe jus þerof. And þou mayst ȝewyn it to bestis þat hawyn þe same ewyll'.
170. Cf. HE113/14 'Take sede of columbyn and þe sede of febrifu and þe leuys of conferi, and dryng it with stale ale and þou sal be hole'.
172. See 693 below.
173. Cf. Hunt 294/250 'Pur la dolur des denz: Pernez blaunc encenz e la gleyre de l'of, si le triblez ensemble e metez sur parchemin e metez cel sur la jowe seyne, si lessez estre tote nuit, si garra'.
174. T68, Hunt 160/ll.355ff. Cf.T70.
175. HE95/21,O17/22,S257/11, Hunt 160/ll.351ff.
176. LH58,R65,T70. See 193 below.
177. LH60,R70. See 194 below.
179. Cf. Thes.147/47.

180. HE45/15('ote-mele') & 112/10('whete-mele'). See Thes.141/10 (with 'aqua' for 'aceto'). See J. Norri, "The Origin of the Expression *Fre rekills* in the *Liber de Diversis Medicinis*", *Notes & Queries* 233 (1988), 301.
181. See 191 & 197 below.
182 See Thes.141/3 & 149/66.
183. D33 (Eng., with 'floure' for 'ceram novam'). Expanded versions in D912,HE8/6, 95/14 & 111/19,H70,M97/7,O17/11, all with (frank)incense replacing 'ceram novam' and all in English. See Thes.141/5 (omits leek-seed).
184. HE95/21(Eng.),T68.
186. Slightly expanded version, in English, in HE45/9, omitting the final sentence.
187. Cf. fuller versions, in English, in HE8/11 & 112/3.
189. LH61,R68(Lat.),T71. See 201 below.
190. T71. See 202 below and Thes.149/71.
191. See HE112/14,LH51,M98/3,O18/11.
192. LH57,O17/19 & 18/8.
193. LH58,R65,T70 & 71.
194. LH60,R76. See 177 above.
195. LH62,R64,T73.
197. CC39,R66. See 191 above and Thes.143/24.
199. R72(Lat.), Hunt 161/ll.395ff.
201. LH61,R68. See 189 above.
202. See 190 above.
203. HE40/15 substitutes 'vynegre' for white wine.
204. O22/21 adds before salt 'and þe rute of burre'.
206. HE40/19 begins with 'þe route of þe docke'.
207. HE41/1 specifies 'pisse þat is 4 dayes or 5 dayes old and hete hit at þe fuyre'.
208. D340 & 791;HE41/3 substitutes 'face' for 'heued' and 'neb'.
209. D534.
211. T34 begins with 'oingt de ver'.
212. T33.
213. T34 specifies '.ii. onces de soufre' and omits the reference to 'pork'. Cf. T33 (Lat.) which adds at the end 'cum foliis rampni'.
214. See 219 below.
215. T33.
216. T38(Lat.).
219. See 214 above.
223. Thes.151/1 & 155/31. Cf. R85.
225. The word 'bolt' remains obscure. An error for 'bol[wr]t' ?
226. I take 'heschulschines' to represent 'astel-shides', that is pieces of wood split off from timber and commonly used for building a fire.
227. LH45,R81,T62. Cf.H214('Pro emeroydis') which simply adds white wine.
228. HE30/1.
229. HE30/2 'take þe erþe þat walkerys walkyth wyþ ...'
230. Thes.153/26. Cf. M90/10. See also Hunt 197, ll.1539–42 (re staunching nosebleed by taking periwinkle in the mouth).
233. Cf. Thes.153/11.
235. R82,T79, Hunt 237/30 ('Veronica').

236. HE71/22,M81/3 & 89/20,R91,T79, Hunt 239/43. Cf.H120.
237. LH163, Hunt 132/163.
238. LH164, Hunt 132/164. Cf.Thes.155/33.
239. Cf. Thes.153/14.
242. LH109,R194 (with addition), Hunt 276/75 & 293/234.
246. 'Brock-lente' 'water lentil' is likely an error for 'brock-lempke' 'brooklime'. Cf.H124 which has 'brooke lempke and smalache and erbe Robert' added to egg white.
249. M70/15(Engl.).
250. Cf. H122,M90/6.
251. Cf. 233 above.
252. R112('vin veuz'). It is uncertain why 'white wine' has been specified in English.
258. R117.
260. M58/11 & M90/13(Engl.), lacking the second sentence. The words 'e cel' may be an error for 'eicel' ('vinegar').
262. T82.
264. On similar use of the marigold (solsequium) see HE45/1.
265. O37/26,T81, both lacking 'rote of celedonie ... lorer'. See 280 below.
268. See 3 above.
271. The ointment is applied to the 'reverse' i.e. inner side of a pair of gloves, which are then placed on the patient's hands.
287. R134('Pur dolour de piz e pur la tusse e la maladie de coer'). See 325 below.
288. LH83,R142.
289. R144,T138.
290. LH86,R140,T137.
291. LH88,R160 (with readings 'confirie' for 'symphonie', 'plantes' for 'foyles', and 'leit de vache ou de chevere').
292. R161. Cf. HE17/16.
293. LH89,R162.
294. LH90,R165(with 'chenve vel careué'), Hunt 274/58.
295. LH91,R166.
297. LH92,324 below (both with 'centurie').
303. O23/28.
306. The reference is to the seven Penitential Psalms (6,32,38,51,102,130,143).
311. O21/4.
315. Cf. O23/11.
319. HE114/18 adds 'sauge'.
322. D116 is closest, but reads 'centory' for 'cicorie', 'peritory' for 'perok', 'persyngall' for 'partyngale'. HE47/11 shares D's readings, but differs in details in the second half of the receipt. 'Perok' is no doubt a miscopying.
324. O19/34,R152. O continues 'and drynk .iii. dayes lewke & it purges þe breste & the stomake'.
325. See 287 above.
326. MS 'gul' I have assumed to be an error for 'gruel'.
334. Hunt 201, ll.1655–8.
336. Cf. R209.
343. HE39/7.
344. O26/32.

345. O27/1 has 'seluen' (?) for 'savine' and 'rede cale-croppe' for 'red wrtes'.
346. O27/7,R122, Hunt 139(C346/7 combined).
347. O27/9(note),R122, Hunt 139(C346/7 combined).
348. D717 & 916,O27/13.
350. O27/16(Lat.,note) & 27/22(Engl.,note).
352. See 346 above.
353. H81, Hunt 133.
358. O54/21 reads 'syfull' and 'pentafilon'.
360. O54/26 supplies 'gronswalle, wymalue, pympernole & fresche grese' and the Corpus text then combines the latter half of O54/28 (beginning 'herbe Robert and celidon'). See too H151 'Tak bausones grece, wylde malwe, grundeswele and pimpernel ...', which continues differently from the Corpus text.
362. D277 ('For eddir or snake in a mannys body') has 'a mannes awn uryn or womans or what best that that evell hath', HE18/5,LH162.
366. S208/20 'For castyn on the see: Drynke þe juce off wormet in wyne or þat þou comyst to þe see. Also þe juce off worme how-euer yt be ete and drunke defendyth a vomytt'.
372. O15/17 and S253/12 have 'and do away þe utter barke' and omit 'and stoncrop'.
374. R171 (expanded).
375. O29/37.
376. O30/3 adds after 'veruayne' 'and dry roses and mak powdir of þam abowte missomer' and omits 'in ale stale'.
377. O35/29 has 'cerefoill' for 'cheverefoyle' and specifies 'white wyne'.
378. O32/38 has 'and fawthistyll and percell' for 'and nettelseid and morsus diaboli', 'auance sede' for 'anie-sedes' and 'suger' for 'sucus'.
388. Cf. Hunt 87/23,25,26 and 93/53,55 and 96/76.
392. R176.
393. LH100,R179(Fr.),T143. See 403 below.
396. See Hunt 248/94 '*Item contra venenum pocio*, pur poysoun: Pernez let du chevre et semence de caumbre e boillez ensemble, ce est le meillour bei[v]r[e] que seit pur poysoun'.
397. LH105 and R182 have 'milfoil'. 'Mugwort' and 'mugweed' are sometimes used together to gloss 'artemisia' (Artemisia vulgaris L.) in lists of 'synonyma herbarum'.
398. LH107,R184 include also 'fraser'.
399. LH106,R183(omitting the change of colour), Hunt 226/13 & 276/72.
400. LH90,HE83/8. The correct reading is 'chanve' (see also Hunt 129/90 'cum semine quercino vel *chanve*').
401. HE83/12 'Take þe juys of morell and herhoune and drynke it with olde vyne; so he shal caste oute þat venym and fro þe poysunn be saued'.
402. LH99,R178.
403. LH100. See 393 above.
404. LH101,R177.
406. LH102,R180.
407. LH103.
408. LH1O4. D183 has 'asshe', but contains a second receipt which includes the oak. See R181.
409. LH162,R174.

410. R175. Cf. CC109.
416. LH99.
417. LH100 ('A l'emflure del ventre' / 'Ad inflationem ventris').
457. It looks as if something has fallen out after 'musel' (a morsel or piece of what ?). The analogy of 506 ('Pernes un lange ...') might suggest that the reference is to a piece of cloth.
466. O32/7 has 'tak owte þe hardest of þe rute', omits 'eie rose anglice pisse', and after 'fenkele-rotes' reads 'xx peny weghte of percell rute and xx peny weghte of ache rute', and specifies nine spoonfuls of 'þe firste confeccion'.
470. T88(expanded).
471. T89.
472. T89, Hunt 132(Lat.,adds 'allium').
473. R353 & 404,T83 (against 'les verues') & 88('Ad petram que impedit urinam'), Hunt 132 (Lat.,'Ad urinam provocandam'), 138 ('Pur la pere ke teut estaler'), 277/78 ('Ad frangendum lapidem in renibus et ad eos qui mingere nonpossunt'), 293/234 ('Encuntre ceo ke home ne pot pissir').
474. T89 after 'sparagi' has 'litus spermi, lufestici at scrupulos .v. Hec omnia tunsa et tribellata cum melle dispumato confice et cum necesse fuerit jejunus cum lacte bibe ...'
475. T88,Hunt 132(Lat.).
478. T88. The blood of the fox is also prescribed for the treatment of warts, see Hunt 263/171.
483. Hunt 189, ll.1291–96.
486. CC82.
493. HE40/3 omits 'of house'.
507. Cf. S242/9 & 13.
511. The terms of the indication are both obscure, 'flours' normally being used of the woman's menses.
516. Cf. CC73(expanded).
518. R217, Hunt 139 (LH).
519. R218, Hunt 139 (LH).
520. R218, Hunt 139 (LH).
521. D813('For suellynge of reyns or of knees'),R219.
525. CC87.
526. O47/12 reads 'þe rute of hertis tonge' and after 'bren' has simply 'ut supra'. The gloss provided for Hart's-Tongue (Phyllitis scolopendrium (L.) Newm.) is erroneous, but sometimes found in 'synonyma herbarum' lists.
540. See H228 with modifications.
547. Cf. O54/28 which omits egg-yolks.
548. D545(cf. 533),O77/17. Cf. H147.
555. D543.
573. LH160.
574. See 590 below.
581. O81/22(note) covers 'Tack ... sor'.
584. Combines LH119 & 118.
590. R400, Hunt 133, 139 & 140. See 574 above.
591. R569, Hunt 139 & 282/130.

592. R436, Hunt 139 & 177,ll.895–8.
609. O77/23.
610. HE20/19 with some changes of detail.
611. CC133,HE21/17,O78/17 (with 'darenell' for 'hineray', 'sarce' for 'bultyng-cloyth', specifying eight nights).
612. CC134,HE22/7,O78/28.
613. CC135 which has 'brent lyne'.
614. CC136. O79/1(note) specifies hot wine.
615. CC137,O79/3. CC has 'seith it þanne as a culiz' instead of 'on quike coles'.
616. CC138,HE22/15.
617. CC139,HE22/22 lacking the final sentence.
618. LH114,CC141,O81/27,R287, Hunt 320/61. See 640 below.
619. CC145,D524. 'þe rede pympernell',HE25/3, Hunt 181/ll.1019ff.
620. D525,HE25/7.
632. O54/18.
640. See 618 above.
645. Presumably 'surcicle' is for 'solcicle'.
650. M113/11('For akynge of a wombe þat trembelyth') adds 'ruwe'.
664. O63/26.
693. The so-called 'King's evil', *morbus regius*,a name which reflects various practices based on the belief either that the illness was caused or else that it was cured by contact with a monarch. See H. François Delaborde, "Du toucher des écrouelles par les rois d'Angleterre', *Mélanges d'histoire offerts à M. Charles Bémont* (Paris, 1913), pp.173–9; M. Bloch, *Les Rois thaumaturges* (Strasbourg, 1924), Engl. translation by J.E. Anderson, *The Royal Touch. Sacred Monarchy and Scrofula in England and France* (London, 1973). See the anecdote contained in *La Estoire de Seint Aedward le Rei* ed. K.Y. Wallace, ANTS 41 (1983), ll.2598–683. A thorough study of the various medical conditions it came to denote incl. jaundice and leprosy, scrofulas and strumas, and diverse wasting diseases is F. Barlow, "The King's Evil", *English Historical Review* 95 (1980), 3–27.
695. LH153,R360, Hunt 249/104.

CHAPTER THREE
THE SECOND CORPUS COMPENDIUM

The second receipt-collection in MS Corpus 388 (ff.36ra–48vb) is composed of 185 receipts in Middle English, with a few phrases in Latin, and one receipt (183) in French. Decoration, including initials and parafs, is in red and blue. There are rubrics in red and sometimes 'nota' is written in red in the margins. Like the other collections printed above it is furnished with an index, but as there are no precise locations provided, I have identified the indications by supplying the relevant receipt numbers in square brackets. The index is a largely accurate list of the receipts in the order in which they occur, but there are some omissions which might indicate displacement of some of the material. The italicised receipts are not included in the index:

31	*(on betony)*
34	*(spewing)*
51	*(dry cough)*
52–3	*(spewing)*
56	*(heart)*
57–9	*(purging)*
62	*(worms in the stomach)*
95–7	*(ache in the wrists)*
106–7,110–1	*(antidotes to poison)*
112–14	*(worms in the body)*
115–17	*(bite of a rabid dog)*
118–20	*(scabies)*
156	*(boil)*
166	*(liver)*
167	*(constipation)*
175	*(tertian fever)*
176	*(rose syrup)*
177	*(ointment)*
183	*(many ills)*

[f.36ra]

For werk of hefed	[1–8]
For werk of eris	[9–10]
For werk of eyne	[11–25]
For werk of nese-therles	[6]
For vanite of þe hefed	[8]
Quo so may nowit here	[9]
Wo so haue blerd eyne	[13]
Wo so hauet rennand eyne	[14]
Wo so hat wermus in eyne	[15,19, 21–3]
Wo so had þe web in eyne	[24–5]
Wo so had euele in his mowt or in his throte	[26–30]
Wo so had drunken venym	[32–3]
Wo so had stinkand onde	[35]
Wo so had stinkand nes-þirles	[35]
Wo so had toyt-ake	[37–8]

Here bygennes mani a god medecine þat leches han drawn out of þe bokes of Galion and Sclepius and Ypocras

[The Head]

For werk [and] turninge braynus. (1) Quo so haues werk and turning in his hed, mack leye of verueyne or of betoyne or of filles or of wirmod, and þarwit wasse þin hed þries in þe woke.

(2) Item tack þe rote of wermod and grindit, and tack wax and rechelus and stamp hem togedere, and quite of an ay, and do in a lyne cloith and wind abute þin heued.

(3) Item tack saueyne and [f.36vb] stamp it wel, and myng þerto olye of rose and lat it wellen a walm. And smer þin hed þerwit, ageynes þe sunne in þe sumere, and be fyr in wyntur, and do so often and it schal doun awey þe werck and þe turnynge in þe hed.

(4) Item tac mustard-seid and rue and stamp hem and tempur hem wit water, þat it be þicke, and do it to þin hed. It is ful god.

(5) Item a clensyng to þe hed: Tac pellestre and chew þe rote þre dayes and it schal spurgen þin hed and don away þe hete.

(6) Item for þe hed werck or for eres or for eyne or for nes-þirles: Tack þe filles and seith hem longe in water. þat drinck schal drawe þe hete out at þi mowith or out at þi nese or out at þin eeres or out at þin eyne.

(7) Item an oþer god drinck for hed werck: Tac beteyne and verueyne and wermod and seledoyne, weybrede and rowe and walwrt and sauge, and fyue cornes of pepur, seith it in (a) water and drinck it fastyng.

(8) Item a oynement for vanite of þe hed: Tac þe ious [f.37ra] of walwrt and salt and hony and wax and recheles and wel hem togedere ouer þe fyr and smer þin hed þerwit.

[The Ears]

For deef. (9) Item quo so may nowit wel here: Tac þe grene bowes of aysche and ley hem on þe fyr. And tack þe water þat rennes out at þe furþer einde, an ey-schelle ful, an þe ious of þe senegrene and als mychel of hony als so mychel of olye, als mychel of þe hed of leck wit alle þe facis þeron, and myng hem togedere and do þerof in þin eres.

(10) Item tack þe gres of þe eyl and þe ious of sengrene, of eþer oliche mychel, and do it often in þin here and witoute fayle þou schalt han helpe.

[The Eyes]

Quo so may nowt [wel se]. (11) Item quo so may nowit wel se: If þin eyne ben rede, tack þe quit gingeure and rub it on a queston or on a basyne. And tac als so mychel of alum glas as hast of puder of gingere and stamp wel togedere and temper it [wit] wyn and let it stounden in þe basyne a day and a nyth. And þan do þat þing in a verre [f.37rb] of copur or of glas or of horn and smer þin eyne þerwit, quan þou schalt sclepe, wit a feþer, and do so often and þou schalt amenden ful sone.

(12) Item tack ious of þe houndestunge or þe ius of centurye or of golde and do þe ious in þin eye and þey schuln ben ole.

(13) Item to eyne þat arn goundi and blered beneþen: Tack arnement and hony and quite of an ay, of alle olike mychil, and temper hem togedere. And tac herdes and wet hem and wring howit þat water and do þes þre þingus on þe herdes as it ware a plastre and ȝif blod or quitour be þerinne, it schal drawen it houit.

(14) Item medecine for rennende eyne: Tack a red cole-lef and smer it wit glaire and ley it to þin eyne quan þou gost to bedde.

(15) Item medicine for wermes þat arn in þe eyne-lydes or þat han sowande eyne: Tac calamynte an bren on þe fyr and do it [f.37va] out and eft bren it and eft do it out and do so .ix. syþes and mayth þou helden þe calamente al þe twelve mound. And quanne þou hauest to-done þerwit, tac a lytil as a bene and greind it on a brede and temper it in an ey-schelle ful of quit wyn and let it satlen. And þan tac a feþer and smer þin eyne þerwit, and [it] schal don away þe wermes and clensen þin eyne.

(16) Item an oþer þat leches callen colure, þat is a god oynement for sore eyne: Tack a bacene and scuret and smer þe botme witinne wit lard of bacun-fat and upon þe lard smer it wit hony, þat þe hony gange ouer þe lard on euery side. And tac a lytel pot ful of pisse and do a parti þerof in þe basyn and lat it stonden þerinne þre dayes and þre nythes. And þe þridde day tac þe basoun and [quat] so þou fynde þerinne do it out clene and do it [in] a verre of copur or of glas or in a clene horn. And tac a lytel and smere þin eyne quan þou gost to bedde.

(17) After þis medecine ne [f.37vb] after non oþer ne was nowit þin eyne, but it be in water þat fenyl be inne.

(18) Item tac selodoyne and stamp it wel and wring out þe ious and driet in þe sunne. And [quan] þou hast so don, tac a lytel þerof and temper wit aycyl and do a lytel in þin eyne þerof.

(19) Item tac betoyne and stamp it wit water and drinck .ix. dayes and it schal driuen out alle wermes [and] evele of þe hed and of þe eyne.

(20) Item tac blod of squannes-briddes and smer þin eyne and schullen euere more ben þe betre.

For wermes in eyne. (21) Item an oþer god medicine for wermes þat eten mennus eyne: Tack salt and bren it and do hony þerto, temper it togedere, and do it to þin eyne witinne.

(22) Item an oþer: Tack turmentille and rowe and seledoyne, ribbewrt and fenyl, and stamp hem wel and smer þin eyne þerewit quan þou gost to bedde.

(23) Item bren þe rede snayl to pouder and myng it wit hony and striket in þein eye.

(24) Item quo so haued þe web or þe macle: Tac [f.38ra] strange[1] eycil and do it in a vessel of bras and tack blak slo in þe wode and lede and wirmod and do it þerto and lat it stounde longe hilled and [quan] it is nede, tack and do it to þin eyne and it schal breke þe web.

(25) Item for te don awey þe web: Tack eufracie a god del and stamp it wel and wring it þorw a cloyt. And tack bor-gres, als mychel of gos- or of chapun-smer, and melt togedere in a bras panne and do þe ious þerto and stir wel þe botme wit a clyse and lat it kelen and do it in boystes. And [quan] þou hauest nede, do to þin eyne a lytil quan þou gost to bedde.

[The Mouth]

(26) For iuele in þe mowit or in þrote: Tack þe five-leued gres and wel it wel in water and quan it is wel stued, hald þin mowit ouer þe pot and cuuer wel þin eued and soupe þerof, and hald it in þi mowit til it be cold. And þanne cast it owt and soup mare til þou haues doun so þries, and do so to dayes, and waris.

(27) Item tack ious of sauge or of þe primerole and do in his mowit and he schal speke as tyt.

(28) Tack [f.38rb] mente, ache, rowe, betoyne and bulyt wel in god-mylk.

(29) Tac puliole and betoyne and mack puder þerof and do of þe puder in to hony, and het it, and do so þre dayes.

(30) Tack .iij. vnces of betoyne and swet milk of a got and temper togedere and drinck it þre dayes.

(31) Nota betoyne is a graciouse gres and ful of gode vertues and holy. Quo so hauet fantem or metyng in slep hang it on his squere and it schal gon away.

[1] MS straunge strange.

(32) Item tack betoyne and temper wit water and drinck fastinge. And ȝif ye drincke venym þat day, þorw þe vertue of þe betoyne þou schalt spewn it out as tyt.

(33) Item ȝif þou haue dronnken venym, tac betoyne and brenit and mack pouder. And tac als mychel of þe puder so þou mayt taken up wit þi þre fingres þries and do it in þe cuppe ful of wyn and bulit tyl þe to parties. And þe þridde part þat byleues tack and drinck leuck fastyng al at ones and [þou] schalt be deliuered hastely and wel sone. [f.38va]

(34) Quo is costif tac lauriole and mack puder þerof and do hony þerto and et a sponful or tweye and it schal so lib'.[2]

(35) Quo so haues stinccande oynde or stincande nes-thirles: Tack þe blake mynte and ious of rowe, of ilk olyke mychel, and do in þi nese-þirles.

[The Teeth]

(36) Quo so haue toit ake or wermus in his teit: Tack þe seid of hennebane and seid [of] lekes, and recheles, and ley þes þre þing on a red glowende tylston. And do mack a pipe þat hais a wid einde and put þe ton eynde of þe pipe in þi mowit and þe toþer in þe fyr þat þe smoik mou cumen in to þi mowit to þi sore toith. And it schal slo þe wermes and don awey þe werck.

(37) Item tac hauere-mele and seith it in god wyn, þat it be þicke, and do it in a lynene cloyth, as it ware a plastre, and bynd it þerto and it schal doun away þe werck.

(38) Item an oþer for toith werck: Tack pepur and stamp it wit god red win and mack wel leuck and soup þerof, and hald it in þi mowit til it be cold, and soup more and so ofton and þou salt waris. [f.38vb]

(39) Item if þi toith rotes: Tack hertis-horn and brennet and do þe asses in a litel clowit and ley to þi sare toyth.

(40) Item for wermes þat eten menis teit: Tack seid of hennebane and þe wermele of þe ache and virgine wax and recheles and mack a candele þerof, and held þi mowit ouer þe candele þat þe smoick and þe hete mow comen to þi toyth. And do so often and þou salt sein wermes fallen out þi teith.

(41) Item smer þi cheke and þe teith wit hors-smere. It is proued for goid.

(42) Quo spekes in his sclep: Tack averoyne and temper it wit wyn and gef it him to drincke and it schal remue[3] him his speche.

[2] One expects 'deliveren hem' (cf. nos.65,66 and 70 below). It is possible that 'lib'' is for Latin 'liberare' and that the receipt has been translated from Latin.

[3] MS reūe.

[Appetite]

(43) Quo may nowit wel ete: Tack centurie and webrede and peper and seith hem in wyn and quan þou gost to þi bed, drinck it leuk.

(44) Quo so delytes nowit his mete: Tack centurie and seith it in water and drinc it leuke þre dayes. þis medecine spurget þi brest and þi stomack.

(45) Item for þrist: Tack þe rote of loueache and stamp it wit wyn or water and drinck it þre nyth quan ye gost[4] to bedde and it schal fordo þrist. [f.39ra]

(46) Letuarie for þat nowit may wel eten: Tack þe ious of þe fenyl, þe to partes, and þe þridde part of hony, and seith hem togedere in a panne to þe þilkenesse of honi and do peper þerto and tack ilke a day þer to sponful.

[The Chest]

(47) Item for ȝeskyngge: Tack sauge and stamp it and temper it wit eycil and drinc it quan ye ȝeskes and it schal gon away ful sone.

(48) Item medicine for hoesed of speche and of voys: Tack sauge, rowe, comyn and pepur and seith it togedere in a panne wit hony and eth a spounful at morwen, an oþer at euen.

Letuarie. (49) God letuarie agayn al manere eueles for hoes, for þe brest, for rutelyng in mannus þrote, for byles, for sor in þe syde, for þe mylte, for þe stomack: Tack horshoue, grunteswale, ysop, centurie, ache, fenyle, rowe, solcicle, puliol, and nepte, of elk olike mychel, and do peper þerto and hony and et þerof morwen and euen.

(50) Item tack pulyol and cumyn, of eiþer ileke mychel, and pepur, and myng it wel wit ale and drincket, on euen oyt, an on morwe cold. [f.39rb]

(51) Medicine for þe drye cowque an hoste: Tac horshelle and confirie and et it þre dayes.

[Haemoptysis]

(52) Item quo so spews blod: Tac ache, mynte, rue and beteyne, of ilk olyche mychel, and wel hem in god wyn, or mylk is þe betre, and drinck þre dayes.

(53) Item tack puliol and mack þerof puder and ete þerwit an eg a. eye. Do so þre dayes and it schal lette þe spuwyng.

[4] Such errors of concord are also found in Corpus 1.

[The Heart]

(54) Item quo so is iuele athe herte and ad lost talent to mete: Tack centurie and seyt it in stale ale and quan it is wel soþen, tack þanne and stamp it wel and do it in agayn in to þe pot and seith it wel. And þanne clensit þorw a cloyth and þerof þanne [tack] þe to partes of þe ious and a þridde part of hony and do seith togedere and do it in bostes. And gyf þe seke man to ete þerof ilk a day þre sponful fastande til he be hoil. And it schal don away þe glette fro þe herte and schal renu him talant to mete.

[Digestion]

(55) Item quo be agruted [f.39va] of to mychel mete in his stomack: Tac þe rote of ache and þe rote of fennyl and stamp it and temper it wel wit wyn and gef þe seke man to dryncke.

[The Heart]

For þe herte. (56) Item tack þe rote of fennyl and þe rote of perscil and þe rote of horshelle, þe rote of radiche, þe leues of hertistunge, lyuerewrt, sicorie, moderwrt, mogwrt, waybrede, puliol, nepte and wilwe-leue, of ilk of hem andful and do þerto a lytel wermod and þe flures of violette, floures of rose, an vnce of lycoris and hony. If it is a straunge man or a wimman, do þerto lesse lycor and þe lesse vny ; if it is a freind man or wymman, do þerto þe mare. For to make squete, þat he may þe betre drincken, tack alle þes þingus and seith hem in wature in an herdene pot til þe þridde part be soþen in and þanne lat it standen in þat pot. Or clense it in to an oþer for to hauen it þe more fayr and ȝif þein þerof ilk a day þe seke to drincke, in morwenyng [f.39vb] cold and at even hoyth. þus[5] many gresus þou mayt seþen in þre galounnus[6] of water.

[The Stomach]

For to spurge. (57) Item medicine for to spurge þe stomack of euele humoures: Tack betoyne and sauge and sissimbrium and dile-seid, of ich olike mychel, and do þerto pepur and hony and do þerto, and stamp it al wel, and temper it wit wyn, and gyf him to drinck.

[5] MS to þus.
[6] MS galoounnus.

[The Breast]

(58) Item for euele in þe brest: Tack rowe and ambrose, of heþþer olyke mychel, and stamp hem and temper wit wyn and drinck it þre dayes fastyng.

(59) Item tack cicorie and isope, of eiþer olyche mychel, horshoue, seyrie, and an vnce of lycoris, and seith hem wel in water þat þe þridde part be soþen in, and gyf him to drincke þat haues nede, on morwen cold, on euen hot.

[The Stomach]

(60) Item for euele in þe wombe, if þi wombe be sor or hard or swelled: Tach housleck and stamp it and tack to spounful of þe jous and drinck it, and it schal don avale þe squellingge.

(61) Or tack þe twelue leues of rue and .ix. cornes of pepur, and als mychel seid of dyle as [f.40ra] þou may taken in þi þre fyngres. Stamp and temper it wit oyt water and drinck it.

(62) Item tac nepte and stamp it and temper it wit oyth wyn and drinck it and it schal caste out þe wermes.

[Constipation]

For costyf. (63) If þou be costyf: Tac malwes and seith hem wel and þan cast in a cuppe ful of newe ale and þerof ete wel and þi wombe schal ben neisse als sone.

(64) Item tac gret grumyle and stamp it wel and seith it weel in freis butere and eet þerof, and it scal maken þi wombe neysse.

(65) Item tac þe galle of a bole and breid it wel and do it on þi novele. It schal deliueren þe.

(66) If man or wimman be to faste bounden þat non of þese þingus may helpun hem: Tac a pipe of elerne as gret as a spyndel or sum del more and do it in his fundement an hanbrede depe. And do þe toþer einde in a bladdere of a squine or of a hoȝ,[7] and fil þe bladere wit oyle, and lat it rennen in als longe as þe seke may þole, and it schal drawen and deliueren him. [f.40rb]

(67) Item tack lynsed and seit it wel in water and [quan] it is wel soþen, do awey þe water and tack and fri et in quith seym, and do þe sike man to eete þerof als hot as [he] may suffren.

[7] The final letter looks like an ill-formed 'y'.

[Diarrhoea]

(68) Item ȝif a man have þe menisoun and þow wilt wete queþer he schal lyuen or deien: Tack a peni-weithe of tuncressen and gyf him to eeten and to drincken affter a teis of wyn or of water and do so þre dayes. And ȝif he stanche, he may leue wit helpe, and ȝif he do nowit, he schal deye.

For menison. (69) Item tack þe mylk of a cu, þe quilk adde no calf þat yer, and tack als so mychel of god red wyn and myng hem togedere and drinck it often and it schal staunche.

(70) Item tack þe seid of percil and stamp it a[nd] mynget wit god red wyn and drinck it hoyt and it schal deliuere þe.

(71) Item tack clene quete and set it tyl it be brosten and stamp waterles in a morter and þanne wring out þe ious. And do it in a pot and seith it and do salt þerto and eet it and it schal helpe þe ful soun.

[Back-ache]

(72) For werck in þe back: Tack [f.40va] egremoigne a[nd] mogwrt, boþe þe leues and þe rotes, and stamp wit eld gres and heycil and ley it to þe back.

[The Loins]

(73) Item for werck in þe lendus: Tack an ey-schelle ful of þe ious of betoyne and an oþer of wyn and an oþer of hony and .ix. cornes of pepur and stamp it togedere, and gef him to drincken þre dayes.

(74) Item tack walwrt as sone as it is drawen uppe and seith it in wyn and stamp it wit eld smere, and myng þerto rie-mele and do it in a cloit and bynd it to þi euele.

[Inflammation of the Liver]

For chaufed [levere]. (75) Item ȝif mannus leuere be achaufed: Tack puliol and stamp it and smer him þerwit and gyf to eten sucre rosette and lat him blod on þe veyn of þe lyuere.

[The Bladder]

For euele in bledere. (76) Item quo so haue euele in his bleddere: Tack ache and fenyl and percil, of ilk olike mychel, stamp hem and temper hem wit water and drinck it and it schal hele þin bleddere and hete þin stomack.

[The Stone]

For ston. (77) Item quo so have þe ston: Tac grumyle and percile, þe rede nettle, violet, recheles and þe kyrneles of cheri-chones (sic) and stamp [f.40vb] hem togedere and temper it wit stale ale and drinck it often.

(78) Medicine for to breke þe ston: Tack þe a koc þat is twel mond old and opne him and þou schalt fynden in his wombe quite stones. Stamp hem wel in a morter wit a pestel of hiren and temper hem wit wyn and drinc it. And ȝif þou have þe herberd, temper it wit water.

[Haematuria]

(79) Item quo so pisse blod: Tack amerose an hanful and percil and stamp it and temper it wit gotes-mylk and gyf him to drinck.

[Strangury]

(80) Item quo so may nowit wel pisse: Tack rowe, grumyle and percil and stamp hem and temper hem wit wyne and drinck it.

(81) Item tack spikenard, fenil, cumyn, ache, percil, grumyle, cassia, canel, sauyne, alysaundre, puliol, aniise, anet, betoyne, luueache, serfoil and þe kerneles of cheri-stones, al þes þingus don a man wel to pisse. Tack als mychel of þese so [þou] may hauen and temper it wit wyne and quo so haues þe horberd, temper it wit water and wring it þorw a cloit and drinck it.

Quo so may no[...]. (82) Item quo so may nowit wel holden is pisse: Tack cattes-clawes an bren hem in a newe pot al to puder and [f.41ra] put þat puder in þi potage, and witouten fayle it schal helpen þe.

[Inflammation or swelling of the Testicles]

For þe balokes. (83) Item for werck and squellynge of ballokes: Tack bygmele and myng it wit hony, and stamp cumyn and myng it þerwit, and do in a cloyt and ley it to þi soor.

(84) Item tack þe ious of walwrt and aycil and hony, of ich olike mychel, and do rie-mele þerto, and seith it tyl it be þicke so a playstre. And do it in a cloyth and bynd it to þin euele.

[The Penis]

For þe pyntul. (85) Item for pyntul scaldingge: Tac lyn cloyth and bren it to pouder and tac þe puder and ley þeronne and it schal hele ful fayre.

[Swollen Knees]

(86) Item quo so haued werc in his knes or squellingge: Tack rowe and loueache and stamp it wit hony and do it vnto þin euele and it schal don awei þe werck and þe squelle.

[Swelling of the Thighs or Feet]

(87) Item for werck and squellyng of schankes or of feit: Tac þe rote of walwrt and seith it in water, and tack þanne and do away þe ouereste rinde, and tack þe mydeleste rinde and stamp it wit bar-smere and do it in a cloyth and bynd it þerto.[f.41rb]

(88) Item quo so haues werck and squellynge in his fet: Tack þe rede water-cresses and scher hem smal and do hem in a pot, and do schepus-talw þerto, and latit leyen tyl it be wel þicke. And þanne tack a cloit þat may wel hillen þe squellyng and do þe plastre al abute on a cloit þer þe sor is and lat it lyne al nyth þerto and it schal warisse ful wel.

(89) Item tack gromelie and seith it wel in water, and þanne tack sengrene and schepus-talw and do þerto and do in a cloith and bynd it al abute þe squellyng, and it schal gon away.

Ad eundem. (90) Item tack þe docke-rote and set it wel in water, and þanne tack it up and stamp it, and do it þanne in a panne and [do] schepus-talw þerto, and seith it til þe talw be moltun. And do it in a cloith and ley it to þin euele.

[Broken Thigh-Bone]

Broken [...]. (91) Item quo so haues his schanke to-broken: Tac þe quite malwe and bren it, and tack þe axsen and bor-smere and stamp hem togedere and smer it þerwyth. And tack þe asche and mack [f.41va] leye and wasse þi theus and þin sankes or þat þou smere þe and afterward, quan þou wilt wassen away þe smere.

[Aching Feet]

For werk in fet. (92) Item quo so haues werk and squellyngge in his feet: Tack mogwrt and stamp it wit eld smere and do it to þin feet.

(93) Item tac rie-mele to partes and þe mele of þe rede lentiles þe þridde part and seith hem in a pot wit eicil and wit hony and do it þerto.

(94) Item quo so haues werck vnder his feet of travayle: Tack cumyn and stamp it and temper it wit oyle and smere þi feet vnderneþen and bynd it vnderneþe þin feet and it schal don away þe sqwellynge and þe werck.

[Aching Wrists]

For werk. (95) Item quo so hauet werck in his wristes or in his senewis: Tack mogwed and stamp it wit old squines-smere and do aycil þerto and bynd to þi sair.

Ad eundem. (96) Item tack wermod and seith wit oyle of olyue or of lynsed and wring it þorw a cloith and do it in a boyste and smer þe soir, [f.41vb] and [it] schal don awey þe werck.

(97) Item tack malws and stamp hem wit old smere and do it þerto and it sch[al] drawen out al þe werck.

[Shingles]

(98) Item þer is an euele þat men callez þe red changel. It wil springen out sum tyme as it were wilde fyr, but it is gretere and red and it wille springe here a rowe and þer an oþer, and if þou byde so longe til it be cumen al bute þe, þer may þe non leche saven. For þis evele to warisse tack douuue-muke and barly-mele and stamp hem togedere and temper hem wit eycil and do it þerto tyl it be hoil.

[The 'Wild Fire']

(99) Item for þe willde fyr: Tack þe leik-heuedes wit alle þe blades and stamp hem togedere, het it wel in scherdes witouten water, and lay it þerto tyl it be hol.

(100) Item tack þe dreggus of wyn or of aycil and temper it wit an ey and bind it þerto.

[Sweating]

For to do squete. (101) Item quo so wile squete: Tack an vnce of cumyn, driet and grind al to pouder, and myng it wit oyle, and þin feet vnderneþen and þin handis [f.42ra] witinne smer, and quan þou gost to þi bed, tack a lef of canelle and ley þeron and hille þin armus and it schal do þe to squete.

(102) Item tack humelock and stamp it and smer þi feet vnderneþen in þi bed and cuuere þe wel.

For sqwet. (103) Item quo so squetes to mychel and wil sese: Tac lynsed and letuse and stamp hem wel togedere and bynd it to þin stomack.

(104) Item tac puliole and salt and stamp hem togedere and temper hem wit win and drinck it and it schal don away þe squeet.

[Jaundice]

(105) Item quo so haues þe iaunes: Tac wermod and seith it longe in water and wasse þe seke man in þat water þries and gef him drincken ivori schauet in vyn and in his pissynge and gyf him to drincke.

[Antidotes for Poison]

(106) Item quo so haues drunke pusoun or venym: Tac dragaunse and gladeren þat growe in þe yerd and mynte, of alle olyche mychel, and stamp hem and temper hem wit wyn and drinck it.

(107) Item tack þe rote of þe dragaunse [f.42rb] and stamp it and temper it wit wyt wyn and het it a[n]d drinck it.

3if a nedere ad [...]. (108) Item ȝif a neddere haues byten a man: Tack centurie and stamp it an temper it wit water. It is als so god to beste as to man.

(109) Item tack þin pissyng and drinck it and it schal castun out þe venym.

Ad idem. (110) Item tack fiue-leued-gres and stamp it and temper wit wyn and drinck it.

(111) Item [tack] rue and stamp it and [do] oyle þerto and bynd it to þe wounde.

Nota. (112) Item ȝif a tode or an oþer werm be cropen in to a man: Tack rowe and stamp it and temper it wit þin owen pisse and gef it him to drincken.

(113) Item tack arment and temper it wit þin ouen pisse or wit wyn and lat it be wel þicke, and drinck it and [it] schal casten out þe wicke wirm wit al þe venym.

For wirm. (114) Item ȝif a werm ad mad an hole on mannus flex or on a beste: Tack at þe begynninge and smer þe hole witinne wit hony and tack þe puder of a gres þat men callun wodesoure and do [f.42va] þerto and [it] schal scle wermes and helen þe wounde.

[Rabid Dog-Bite]

(115) Item ȝif a wod hound haue byten a man: Tack þe sed of þe boxe and stamp it an temper it wyt alliwater and gyf him to drinck.

(116) Item tack þe rote of aristeloge þe longe and stamp it and do it in wnde and it schal helen it wel.

(117) Item tack tun-cressen and pulyol and seid wel in water and gef him to drincke and it schal casten out þe venym and if [þou] may hauen þe houndes smere, lay it þerto and it schal helen.

[Scabies]

(118) Item quo so haues scabbe or clawynge: Tack þe rote of horshelle, þat is to seye scabbewrt, and seith it longe in water and tack þe nesseist þerof and stamp it wit old smere and do it on a lynene cloyt and het it at þe fyr and smer þe scabbe often and it schal away.

(119) And tack it an oþer wey and seith it in a panne wit squines-gres and wring it out into boxes and smer þe scabbe or þe mangewe of an hors or of hany oþer beste and it schal helen it wnderly weel.

(120) Item tack þe rote of þe docke and stamp it wel and seith it wit May-butere and wring it þorw a cloyth in a panne ful [f.42vb] of water and lat it standen and harden þerinne and do it þanne in boxis and smer þe scabbe be þe fyr.

[The 'Falling Evil']

For fallynge euele. (121) Item quo so haues þe fallynge euele: Tack a be and draw out his tounge and do þe seke man to drinck it in ale at þe begynnynge þat he ne wite nowre quat it is and he schal be delyuered for eueremor of þat euele.

(122) Item tack ribbewrt and euerevern þat growet on þe ock, egremoygne, marigolde, nesebledellus, recheles and pepur, of alle olike mychel, and stamp hem alle togedere and mack puder and gyf him to drincke wit water.

(123) Item for gute þat tack man or wimman soum tyme in þe hed or in þe wombe so it ware þe fallande euele: Tack saveyne and stamp it and temper it wit water and quan þe evele tach hym, gef hym to dryncke and he schal warisse wel.

[Varieties of Gout]

(124) Item a god vnement for alle gutes: Tack an owele and do of þe

federes and opne it and do out al þat is witinne and ditz it als þe wldes[8] eten it and salt it wel and do it in a newe pot and hille it wit a tyle-ston and do it in an hot houene tyl it be wel baken and nowit brent. þanne tac and stamp it wel wit hors-smere and smer þe gute be fyr. [f.43ra]

(125) God emplaystre for þe gute: Tack amerose and wilde nep and seith hem and stamp hem wit old smere and smer þe gute be þe fyr and it schal helen þe wnder wel.

(126) God oynement for þe gute: Tack þe broc-smere, þe smere of þe ratounne, kattis-smere, fox-smere and boris-smere and tac feþerfoy and aycil and stamp togedere and tack a lytel lynsed and stamp it wel and myng it wel wit þe smere and het it in a sard and smer þe gute be þe fyr.

(127) Item tack þe rede snayl and do in a vessel and strow salt þerto and þei wiln sone melte. Smere þe gute þerwit be þe fyr wit a feþer and it schal hele þe ful sone.

(128) Item tack a moleward and seith it wel in wax and wring it þorw a cloyth and do it in boystez; ouere þe lengere þat it is witinne, þe betere it is to many manere eueles, als wel as to þe gute.

(129) Item tack hennebane-leues on myssumer-euen and bruse hem a lytel and do hem in a michel pot bretthelud and hole þe pot on þe botme and cuuerit abuven wit a tyl-ston and mack an hole dep in þe herþe and do þat pot þerinne and set a lytel lede[9] vnderneþen þe pot for to reseyue þe olye þat comet fro þe hen[f.43rb]nebane þorw þe pot. And fil þan þe hole witoweten þe pot and cuuerith abouen wit a brod ston and playster it fayre, þat no þing may cumen into þe pot. þat ilke day twelve monþe tack up þe pot, and þat þou fyndest in þe lede tack it up and do it in boxes of glas. þis oyle is wnder god for gute and wit rancle and wit many oþer eueles if he wiln smeren it be [þe] fyr. If þou haue nowt þis olie, tack þe oyle þat is mad of þe seid of hennebane as men maken of oþer sedes and smer þe gute be þe fyr.

Vnement for [þe gute]. (130) God oynement for þe gute : Tack brinston and puder þerof and grind it wit oyle of eiren on a ston so men grinden vermylioun. And þis vnement is god for alle gutes, and gyf a lepurouse [...], smere þerwit hym and it schal ben þe betere.

Gutefestre. (131) For gutefestre here þou may wite hou þu salt knowe goutefestre fro þe canker þus. þe gutefestre as a narw hole witouten and wid witinne. þe canker had a wid hole witouten and narw witinne. þe festre is

[8] The 'd' is ill formed in the MS.

[9] MS lyde with y expuncted and superscript e.

seldom þat he ne had mo holez þan on. A ca[n]ker is eueremore wit on hole. [f.43va]

[Varieties of Fester]

(132) God emplastre for festre: Tack weybrede and tansay, nosebledeles, centoinodye, þat is to seyne squines-gres, merchaunt, avense and stamp eueri gres be þe self and wring out þe jous and loke þat þou haue of eueri gres olyke mykel ious and þat it be þicke. And tack walwrt and stamp and loke þat þou haue as mychel ious of þe walwrt so þou addis of alle oþer greses, and þat it be þicke. And þanne tack virgine wax, fres schepus-talw, hony, May-butere, eld squines-smere and wyn, of euerilk olyke mychel, and þat it be þicke and loke þat alle þes þinges þat arn last seyde ben als mychel os þe ious of walwrt. And do alle þes þinges in a panne and wel hem wel but þe quite malwe þou salt welle þerwit for you mayst nowit wringen out þe ious so þou mast don of oþer greses, for it is so fat. And quan it is al wel wellid, wring it out þorw a cloith and do it in bostes. And tack þanne quete flour and a party of þat oynement [þ]arto and was þe wounde at morwen and at euen wit wyn and ley þanne þi play[f.43vb]stre þerto and do so ilka day. Gyf him to drincken fastynge wirmod and avence.

(133) God puder for to sclo þe festre: Tack benes, ry, huny, arment and salt, of ich olike mychel, and do it al in a newe pot and bren it til þe mouwe greinden it to puder and bult it þorw a cloyth. And tack þanne a stele of þe malwe and wet it in hony and walw þe stele in þe puder al abuten til it be wel þicke clouen þeron and þanne poit it in þe ole of þe gute doun to þe grounde. And lay þe playstre þerouer þat is befor sayd and þis puder. Quo so wile slo þe festre do þe stele þerinne wit puder fyue dayes or seven nitthes. And þerafter do a tente þerinne of lyn and euere as [it] ginnes to helen, mack þe tente schortere and wase it ilka day twies wit quit wyn.

Ad idem. (134) Item tack lauriole and driet and stamp it wel al to puder, þan tack þat puder and seith it wel in hony tyl þou mayst maken þerof teyntes. And do in eueri ole a teynte and hille hem wit cloutes and bynd it so þat it go nowit of tyl [f.44ra] þou vndo it on þe morwen. þan scure þe holes and wasse hem wit wyn quit and do so eueri day tyl þou se þe rede blod cumen out. After þis medicine þou may elen it wit puder of recheles and þe ious of waybrede.

(135) Item tack a lytel vertegres and brent lyne, arnement brent and þe puder of racine of garleck brent, of euerilk olyche mychel, and mack puder þerof and do in þe holes of þe festre doun to þe botme and do so euerilke

day at morwen and at ewn. And at eueri tyme was it wel wit quit wyn hat and do away quitour. þis medicine is god for cancker.

(136) Item tack egremoyne and stampit and lay to þe festre twies on þe day and wasset wel wit wyn.

(137) Item tack a plate of copur and wet it wel wit eicil and tac salt and stamp til it be smal to puder and st[r]ow it on þe eicil in þe plate and spyt þeron. Seith it þanne as a culiz tyl it be wel brent. þanne wet þe plate eftsones wit eicil and eft strowe on puder of salt and ley it on þe coles and do so often quile [f.44rb] þou hauest ani del brent salt in þe plate and þanne do þe salt out þe plate and driet in þe sunne. And grind it til it be puder and þan tack þe to part of þe puder and þe þridde weyth of puder of vertegrece and myng þerwith. And þan do ilka day of þe puder in þe holes of þe festre and put it doun to þe ground wit a tent and do so ilka day tyl þou se þe flex es waxe red and clene. þan do þerto ilka day appostolicone tyl it be hoil. It is a suuereyne medicine.

Goutes. (138) Item þer is to manere of gutes festrez. þe ton is cold, þe toper brennande; þe cold is wit manye smale holes, þe hote is wit holes[10] and brade holes. þanne to þe colde festre tack ious of auence or þe ious of laureol and quit of an ay, of ilk olike mychel, and tack þe flour of þe rie and kned it þerwit and do it to þe holes so it were playstre, and bynd þerwit a cloyth and lat it lye þerto tyl [it] falle away be þe self. And do þanne anoþer þerto on þe same manere and do aycil [til] þe festre be hol [f.44va]. And gef eueri day to drinke ious of auence.

(139) Medicine for brennande festre: Tack þe flour of þe rye and þe cler of hony and mack dow þat it be hard and mack as many smale cakes os þer ben holes o'þe festre and ley on eueri hole a kake and quan he ben wete, do hem away and do oþer þerto and do so tyl it [be] hol.

(140) And zif him drincke pervincle or auence tyl he be hol.

[Varieties of Canker]

For canker. (141) Item for þe canker medicine: Tack þe heued of þe storck and þe feet and al þat is witinne þe storck but þe body and do it al in to a pot þat neuere was noted and do it in to an ouene and driet so þat þou mou make puder þerof. And do of þat puder to þe canker and in feuue dayes þou schalt ben hol.

[10] MS many holes, with 'many' expuncted.

(142) Item an oþer medicine: [Tack] colubrum album and mack al to puder and do it to þe canker.

(143) And tack vertegres and arnement, brenston and brent lede, of ich alike mychel, and bren hem alle togedere an mack puder þerof. þis pu[f.44vb]der strowe on þe canker and wasse þe caunker iche aday wit pisse of a knaue-child þat is a mayden, and þanne strow þe puder þeron; and if it be a winman, wassit wit pissing of a mayde-schild and eft strue puder þeron and þus wassit ilk aday. Or puder be don þeron til þe canker be sclawen. And quan it [...] wasse clene and wax fayr, mack it [dri] wit herdes or þou strowe þe puder þeron. þe canker wil be deid witinne þe ferde day or þe fyfte and quan þe canker is ded, þan salt þou do þus: Tack þe ious of ache and hony and saym and do hem togedere in a panne and lat it pleye wit schlaw fyr and do a lytil[11] þerto of quete flour til it be þicke as gruel. þan do it doun of þe fyr. And tack herdes þat arn witouten schiueres and hechel hem rit smale and ley hem on þe canker and ley first þeronne þi plastre and iche aday do so til it be hol.

(144) Item an oþer medicine: If þou may nowit hole þe canker wit none of þese þingus, þan kerf þe flex wit a rasure [f.45ra] als depe als so þe sor laste. And þanne tack þe ȝelkes of eyren and oyle of rose and myng þerto and ley it þaronne .ix. dayes. þerafter tack sauge and confirie and wrtes rede, of euerich an hanful, of blake benes, of beef brent, of orpiment and of pumice, of euerilk tweye vnces. Of alle þes þingus mac neisse puder and do on þe canker til it be hol.

[Wounds]

(145) Item ȝif a man be wnded and þou wilt witen queþer he schal leuen or deye: Tack pimpurnol and stamp it an temper it wit water and gyf him to drincke. And zif it go out at wonde, he schal deye serteyn.

(146) Item ȝif him to drinke quyth letuse wit þe water and ȝif he spewe it, he schal deye sertayn.

(147) Medicine for wonde at þe beginninge of keruinge, of brusynge of quo so[12] it be: Tack þe heuedes of þe lekes wit alle þe fases þeron and stamp an do þe ious to þe wounde. And tack [lyne] and mack þerof a teynte and wet it in þe ious and put it þarinne and þe substaunce of þe lekes þat ious was done out of, [f.45rb] ley it abouen and bynd it þerto. And do þis

11 MS lytil an a litel.

12 or quo of so.

emplaystre þre dayes, but ich aday remue þe playstre ones. And after þe þridde day tack quete flour and god wyn and do togedere and squynes-gres do þerto and wellit togedere. And tack a lynene cloit and do it to-fald or þre. Tack herdes and do þi playstre þeron and ley it ouer þe wnde and do so ilk aday tyl it be hol. And ilk aday yif him to drincke þese þre gresus wit a lytel ale stale, þat is to seyne, pygele, bugle and sanicle. And quanne he had druncken þes þre greses wit a lytel ale, it schal al cumen out at þe wnde and clensen it witinnen and outen.

(148) Item tack centurie and mak puder þerof and strew upon þe wounde and it schal helen it.

(149) If þi wnde werkes þe or smertes þe: Tack nepte and stamp it and temper it wit wit wyn and gyf him to drinke and it schal don away þe werck.

(150) If þe wounde is loken togedere: Tack bryane, þat is þe wilde nep, and [f.45va] mack puder þerof and do þerof to þe wounde and it schal opnen it.

(151) If þi veyn be corwn oto, here is god emplaystre to knitten hem: Tack brent lyn and mack puder þerof and tack huny and þe quite of an ay and stamp it togedere, þat it be wel meyng, and on þe vrtyng[13] ley lyne and do of þis playstre þerupon þe lyne and eft of þe lyne and eft of þe enplaystre and vndo it nowit or þe þridde [day] and quan þou vndos it, wasset wit þe seke mannes owen pisse for to lese þe emplaystre, for ʒif þou drawe it away, it wil don it bleden eftsones.

(152) For to stanchen blod of veyne: Tack brom and schaf of þe barc wit a knyf and mac balles þerof and ley on þe wounde and bynd it wit a cloyt.

(153) Tac salt and bren it in a scherd and mack puder þerof and do in þe wnde.

(154) Medicine for to spurge and to casten þe blod þat is witinne man of brusure or of wnde: [f.45vb] Tack þe ious of þe nepte and drinck it and it schal casten out þe blod witouten swellynge.

(155) Item tack þe quyte malwe and mack puder þerof and drinck it wit win and it schal casten out þe blod.

[Boils, Ulcers etc.]

For byles playstre. (156) Item god emplaystre for byles: Tack fengrec, mylk-sothen lynsed, and mynte and seith hem wel in water and mac emplaystre and ley to þe byle and it schal rote ful sone.

[13] wttyng.

(157) Item for to don away werck of wnde or of byl or of brusynge: Tack þe fatte bacun of an old squyne or of bore and melt it in a panne and lat it stande stille til þe salt be fallen to grunde. Tack þanne þe schire abouen and do it in to þe panne agayn and tack half so mychel of virgine wax so þer is gres, and tac recheles and do þerto and wellem togedere, but brec þe recheles al to puder or ye do hem in and quan ye maste hete is ouersclaked, tac þe puder of mastic als so mychel os of recheles, [f.46ra] and do þerto and sterit wel wit a sclyse til it be os þike os hony. And þanne do it of þe fyr and quanne it is so cold as þou may holden þi fynger þerinne, þanne do als so mychel puder of brynston os þer is of recheles and of mastic an set it on þe fyr ageyn and ster it wel wit a sclyse til it be þicke os hony and do it þanne in boxes. And quan þou hauest nede, do it on a cloit and ley it to þe wounde and [it] schal drawen out þe werk and quat gute so euere men han, and asmere him þerwit tweyes on þe day. It schal don hym god.

(158) Item tack fet bakun of a boer-hog and melt it and lat stonden an resten til þe salt be fallen to þe grounde. And tack þe schire seym and do it in a panne and do half so mychel wax þerto and als so mychel pick and quan þe wax and þe pick arn molten, do þerto recheles and ster wel and quan it is wel ouersclaked, do it in boxes. It is god to drawen howit þe werck of wounde or of byle, þey þou do non oþer þing þerto.

(159) Item god playstre forto b[f.46rb]yle, quo so haued werck or sqwellynge on arm or on oþer stede on his body and he doute þat it wil ben a byl: Tack lynsed and quete and stamp hem wel and do al in a panne and freys schepus-talw þerto and mak it wel hat and do it on a cloit and bynd it to þe sor and it schal don it away.

(160) Item an oþer: Tac an onyoun and stamp it and ley it al a nyth to þe sore byle al so hat so þou mayst þole, and if it be rip for to brecun, it schal breken it wel and softe.

(161) Item tac bryn and wimmannus mylk and it schal breken it littli and do sape þerto and it schal breken it ful sone.

(162) Item tackyn red snayles or þe blake and stamp hem and ley þerto.

(163) Item here is a god oynement for brock, and eueri soyr þou smeres þerwit, it schal be þe betre: Tac auence, bugle, pigle, sanicle, ache, erbe Robert, herbe John, erbe Water, waybrede, rybbewrt, þe litel consonde, þe rede-cole-leues, þe crop of holy brere, holy-ake and walwrt. Tack and stamp eueri gres be self and tack of euerilk gres as mychel ious and do it in a panne. þe holy-ake it is so fat þat þou [f.46va] may haue þerof no ious, for-þi do þe leues þerto. And þan tack virgine wax and fres schepus-talw, hony, May-butere, old smere of a sowe and win, of euerilk olike mychel, and loke þat

alle þese þingus weyun als mychel so half þe ious of þe greses, and do alle þes þingus in a panne and seith wel. þou may wite be þe leues of þe holyake quanne it is sothen anow. Quan it waxes yelw an nessche, do on þi nayl a drope of þe salue wit a sclyce and lat it þare kelen on and if it is wel grene, þan it is anow. Do þanne recheles þerto and styret wel and do it don of þe fyr and wringit þorw a cloyth in to a bacyne and quan it is sum del cold, do it in boystes.

(164) Here is a god oynement for wnde, for byles, for sqwellyng, for bon broken, for gute and for feloun: Tack bugle, sanicle, auense, violet, ache, waybred, lilye, hennebane, morel, gumme of sour plum-tre, wax, pick, askbirne, freys smere of a sqwyn, hertes-[f.46vb]talw and schepus-talw, of euerilk olyke mychel. Do alle þese þingus in a panne and wel hem wel and do recheles þerto and clens it þorw a cloith in to a bacin and quan it is cold, do it in boystes.

[Fevers]

For feuere ague. (165) Medicine for feuere ague: Quo so haues þe fevere ague þat men clepun þe lente feuere, if þe seke mannes heued werck and he may nowit sclepen, tack heuere-vern þat growes on þe ock, [þe] rote, and seith it wel and mack a playstre þerof and do it to þin fored and smer it wit populion.

(166) Medicine for þe lyuere. If a man aues euele on his lyuere and mychel angwisse, mak a playstre of þe gro[t]s of þe barly-mele and of sengrene and morel and aycil, but smer it fyrst wit popilyon.

(167) For costiue mack a sirope on þis wise: Tack an vnce of violets þan þe floures arn ofe an seith it in water a galoun til to partes ben soþen inne and clense it þorw a cloyth. Do þanne to þe ious a pound of sucre and seith it til it be þicke as hony, þerof gyf him drinck sum time to sponful of sirope in a lytel [f.47ra] cuppe ful of water. An tack þe branche of sauge and flour of barly and malws and hennebane and seith alle togedere in water in a caudrun and in hot water bayt his feet and his schankes and aboun his knes and schaue his feet vnderneþen and it schal don him god.

Fransi. (168) For þe fransi: If he falle in þe franesi, lat schaue his heued and tack a red cock or a quelp and cleuyt in þe myddes of þe back, and also hot as ye may, wit alle þe bueles, wappe it on his heued, but smere it first wit popilion.

(169) Item for þe letargie: And if he falle in þe letargie, schaf his hed and tack mustard-seid and seith it and stamp it and do aycil þerto and bynd it

to his heued wit a cloyth and lat it be þerto al nyth. And tac þe ious of onyounes and do in his nese-thirles wit a quile, or fil a pipe wit þe ious and blowit in his nese-þerles and do a man or a winman to kissen him and ley him to þe lyth and agayn þe sounne and [f.47rb] lat crien and blowen and maken mychel dene and lat pricun him and do pricken him as he were an ox.

(170) Item for a man þat has þe frenesi and may nowit sclepun: Tack gronden rowe and seith it in water. And tack þanne þe leues and stamp hem and do þerto aycil and ewerose and do it in a cloith and bynd it abuten his hed and it schal don him sclepen.

[Fevers]

Cotidien feuere. (171) Item for feuere cotidien: Tack a dragme of þe sed of ache and stamp it wel and temper it wel wit þre sponful of water and gyf þe seke man to drincke quanne þou opes þat it schal taken him.

Tercine. (172) Item for feuere tercine: Tack iubarbe and do in a cuppe ful of cold water and lat it stande al nyth þerinne. On þe morwen gif him to drincken of þat water or it take him. And loke þat it take him þre dayes or foure and schake hym or þou gyue hym þe medicine.

(173) Medicine for þe feuere [f.47va] quarteyn: þat ilke day þat it schal taken him do mak barly-bred of rith clene barly and gyf him to etun þerof als hot als it cumet out þe ouene and als so mychel as a may heten þerof. And gyf him to drincke god wyn gret plente or þat euele take him. þan tack .iiij. plantes of weybred wit alle þe leues and alle þe rotes and quan it is wel wassen, stamp it þanne and temper it wit .iiij. sponful of wyn and foure of water and gyf þe seke man to drincke or þe euele tack him, and do him lye and sclepe and wry him wel warme.

(174) Medicine for alle feueres: Tack þe rote of fenkele, rote of percil, rote of ache, rote of loueache, rote of radiche, of alle olyche mychel, þan wasse hem wel and after schaue hem wel and scer hem on lytel gobetes and do hem in aycil a nith. And on þe morwen temper hem and seith hem in þat ilke eycil til þe þridde part be soþen in, þanne klensit þorw a cloith. Tac þanne þe to partes of þat eycil [f.47vb] and þe þridde part of hony and seith it togedere til it be os þike os þe hony, and, if þe man be costyf, euervern þat growes on þe ock to vnces or þre, and seith þerwit. Atte byginning of þe medicine yif þe seke man to sponful or þre wit a lytil water hot on morwen and on euen, if nede be þerto.

A sirope. (175) Here is a god cirope to terciun feuere [and] to dubble tercine men calles cirope terceres: Tac a parti of spick and a party of iubarbe and do hem in aycil and seith til þe to partes ben soþen in. þan clensit þorw a cloith and do sucre þerto and seith it til it be þicke so hony. þarof gyf him a sponful or to wit oyt water on morwen and on euen.

(176) Here is a cirope þat men called cirope rose: Tack an vnce or to of rose and seith it in water til þe to partes ben soþen in. þanne clens it þorw a cloyt and do sucre þerto, and seith it til it be os þicke as hony.

(177) Medicine for alle feueres: Tack betoyne, amerose, horshoue, ruden, tansey, mogwrt, wirmod, rowe and saueyne, of iche olyke mykel, seith þe greses [f.48ra] in wyn and water til þe þridde part be soþen in and do of þe wyn þe to partes and þe þridde part of water. Herof gyf þe seke man to drinken a lytel cuppe ful byforn þe euele tack hym.

Vngwentum. (178) Item an vnement for herbe: Tac an[14] hanful of lynsed and seith it wel in water and clens it and tack als mychel of oyle of rose and myng togedere. Tack and smer al þe mannus bodi þerwit, but þe heued and þe feet.

(179)Medicine for þe feuere quarteyn: Tack þre heuedes of garlec, þre rotes of radiche and .iij. vnderd of pepur-cornes. Stamp hem wel and temper hem wel wit god red wyn and gyf him to drincken an lat him blod on þe veyne of þe mylte.

[Prognostica]

(180) If a man be seck and þou wilt wete queþer he schal lyue or deye, if þe seke man turne hym to þe wowe, if his nese waxe sarp, if hise eres waxen weyke, if hise eyne waxun holle, if his mouyth be opun quan he sclep but he be wone þerto, if his wombe fallis, if he pute in fyngres in his nese-þirles up and doun, if he may se no brithnesse, if he plucke strawes or his cloþe, if men may bringen no warmynge on his feet.

(181) Item [f.48rb] tack þe seke mannus pissinge and lat a wimman mylke þeron and if þe mylk falle doun to þe grunde, he schal deye, and if [it] flete, he schal leue.

(182) Item if his fored waxe red and his browes falle doun and his lyft eye waxe lytel and þe chin falle doun and þe younge man to sqwelle mychel and þe elde to sclepe mychel but he be wone þerto.

A god medicine. (183) Here is a god medicine to manye eueles þat a man haues for palsy, for gute, for menyson, for eyne, for feloun, for squinacye,

[14] MS and.

for appostumus, for venym, for pusoun, for þe dropesye, for þe hed, for wermes in mannus wombe: Lat gader in þe mone of May alle þes herbes and everich olyke manye, sauge and mynte, scabiose, sengrene, auense, eufrasye, erbe Ion, betoyne wit alle þe leues and alle þe rotes an do hem in a ouene to drie or in þe sunne and rubbe þe leues al to puder bytweþe þin andes and stamp þe rotes al to puder and gyf þe man þis puder to drincken for alle eveles aforsayde.

(184) Contra maculas faciei: Pernés oyle que vent [f.48va] de porck male, le racine de lys ov le jous, si vous ne poés aver la racine, e braés ben ensemble. Pus pernés le peis de .vi. deneres de argent vif u plus e mettés ensemble en .i. quele e movez ben e unés vous de se le vespre e le matyn encountur fu par .v. jors de cet unement tanck'il seyt ben encecchi. E pus pernez la ruse de cherfoyle and wodebynde and vinegre e sape d'Etspayne e mellez tus ensemble e oynés vous de cel oynement a matyn e a soier e ov le vant-dith oynement oynés vous deus joures ensemble a matyn e a seir e de la secunde oynement le terce jour e la quarte jour a matin e a seir encontur le fu e volupés voþre face de un tenve keverché caunt vous irrés cucher.

(185) Item for þe ston: Tack an vnce of black flynt and an vnce of quith glas and an vnce of percil-seid and a quarter of an vnce of geet and an vnce of brom-seid and grind hem to puder and myng hem togedere and eth hem or drinck hem.

(186) Item for grauel: Tack leues of clotes þat berit þe burres and buyl hem in a galun [f.48vb] of water til a potel and þan do out þe leues and buyl it eft wel and þanne set it to kelen. And quan it is cold, tempur ful a saucer of þat water wit als mychel of eld ale mad of barly-malt and drinck it.

Expliciunt medicine de tractatibus Ypocracii, Gallieni et Sclepeii etc.

NOTES

1. D2,HE106/6 & 135/1,M116/36,O1/1. The reference to 'filles' is unique to the present text and to C, which actually has 'or filles of wormod' i.e. leaves of wormwood. The Corpus scribe seems to have understood 'filles' as chervil (see 6 below).
2. D3,M116/39,O1/4. O adds after wormwood 'and yven terrestre, ache ...'
3. D4,O1/8.
4. C52,D5 & 454,HE37/8,M117/3,O1/15.
5. C50,D6 & 690,H66,M117/7.
6. C51.

7. C42,D7 ('rubb' is an error for 'ruw'), O2/11. Only D and O include 'sauge'.
8. H66,M51/10 & 117/12,O2/23. O alone adds 'rose' and has the rubric 'For fantome in þe heuede'.
9. C105,D18,HE109/12 ('an hesil'),O6/23 & 13/9,R57,S195/25 (expanded). D has for 'senegrene' 'the bradys of lekys' and differs considerably in the second half of the receipt (cf.S). See Thes. 133/2.
10. HE109,18 has 'a clene ele', O7/9 'þe fattnes of a blake ele'. Cf. D262 which has an expanded version with '.iiii. culpons of an ele that is fat'.
11. H68,M110/7,O8/20. H has 'on a whestoon in a fayre bacin of metal' and later simply 'in a viol of glas'. M has 'upon a whetston over a basyne of metall' and 'a fyooll of glas'. H,M & O substitute salt for 'alum glas'. O also has 'a ampull of glase or coper', the Corpus variants here being unique. In a second version ('Pro perla in oculo in principio') in H88 we read 'Take whit gyngire, and rubbe hit on a wheston of norweye and wyþ wyne in a pewdre sawcer, and sette þe wheston ende in to þe sawcer, and so rubbe þe race of gyngyre on þe wheston in to þe wyn, and take a feþer and wyþ þat licoure wasshe þe sore eye, an þat shal do awey þe perle and saue þe eye'.
12. O8/29 has 'solsekill' for 'golde'.
13. C118,D473 & 490,H85,HE136/9,O9/25 (and note) & 12/24. For 'hards' D490 substitutes 'flex'. CHHE omit the part of the receipt which includes flax.
14. C120,D469,LH30,O8/12,R33.
15. O9/30. Ogden suggests that 'calamynte' is an error for 'calamine / calamite' (cadmia, or zinc oxide) and refers to D497 where it appears as tutty, commonly used in astringent ointments. See Hunt 227/21 which has 'calaminam'.
16. O10/15 refers to smearing the sides of the bacin with 'þe larde of a galte' and turning the residue in to 'an ampull of glas or in a cle vrynall'.
17. In O this forms part of the preceding receipt and is preceded by *nota.*
18. D25,M85/1,O10/26. DM add 'stamp it well in a mortar, and make thereof a little ball, and wrap it in a little hemp or a little flax and lay it in hot ashes' (transl. Dawson). D suggests tempering the dried, crushed plant with soured ale or malt vinegar ('a lyttell aleger').
19. O10/32.
20. O11/1 reads 'swalow-birdis', which is almost certainly correct,since swans occur in a culinary rather than a medical context.
21. O10/3.
22. O10/7.
23. Cf.C117.
24. C127,D473 ('flo' is an error for 'slo'), 503 & 995,H90,M112/4,O11/3,R39. D503 has 'For the webb or perle'. H specifies 'þe jus of sloon and plom sloen', omitting the ingredients of lead and wormwood. M recommends that the mixture be let to stand for three days, H and M also suggesting that it be stored in a box.
25. C122,D501,H68,HE107/18 (abbreviated), LH31(Fr), O11/7, S193/14,T43 & 51. DHO recommend stirring with 'a rownde staffe', H adding 'oþer a ston'. See also Hunt 227/19(Lat.).
26. H68,HE101/22,O13/22,S199/16. H has 'quintefoyle', HES 'quinfoyle', O 'pentafoyloyn id est quintfoyle'.
27. H69 has simply 'þe jus of betonye'.
28. D837 (combines nos.27–9), H69 (reads 'smalache' for 'ache'), HE10/5,M96/22

(combines nos.27–8), M111/4. The receipt appears without the indication being specified. The witnesses supply rubrics indicating that the remedy is for anyone spitting blood.

29. D837,O14/29.
30. D837,M97/1.
31. D312 ('For fantuns and dwelsynge'), M117/15 ('For hem þat trawaylyn in here slepe'), O26/7 (and note to O26/3).
32. O2/16 & 26/12.
34. H69 ('Purgacio'), M111/7 ('For to make a purgacioun'), O15/10 ('To gare a man spewe').
35. D596 ('For the mouth that stynkyth'), D623 ('Nose that stynkith'), H70 ('Pro fetore a[ne]litus per nasum') has 'red myntes',H105 ('Pro fetore de naribus') has 'myntes' in a slightly amplified version found also in HE96/1;HE8/3,68/5,72/13,110/15,M97/4 ('For stynkynge breth or stynkynge nose') & 116/32 ('For evyll breth'), O15/31,S196/13.
36. C183,D33 which has 'floure' for 'recheles' and omits the details about the pipe, D912 specifying 'a pipe of laton',H70 'a pipe of latin',HE95/14 'a pipe of latoun'. See also HE111/19,M97/7.
37. M97/13 ('ote-mele'), O16/7.
38. O16/32 has 'lewke wyn', S201/8 'wyȝte wyne'.
39. C197. Cf. D27 which prescribes washing the teeth with water in which shavings of hartshorn have been boiled.
40. O18/4 begins: 'Tak henbell & pympernoll, smalache, virgyn waxe, stor and mak a candill of ...'
41. HE8/16 omits application to the cheek. M98/11 omits application to the teeth. See also O16/20 & 18/11.
42. C150,D839 ('For spech that is lost in syknesse ... and sone shall he speke' !), HE68/20 & 79/20 ('Ȝif man for-letes his speche for seknesse ... and so shal he speke'), O14/15 ('and he sall spek sone'), R105 (Cf.R20), Hunt 139,231/73(Lat.) & 285/167. Such contrary indications are fairly rare.
43. HE9/5,M98/16,O19/36.
44. H71 has 'warme þre dayes',HE69/1,M98/19,O19/34.
45. D1008,H71,HE8/18 ('Potionte'), M99/1 & 111/15,O25/28.
46. D1010 has 'seth hem togedir in wyn' and, like HE9/1 and O20/1, recommends three spoonfuls.
47. D1015,HE69/4,O20/13. O adds instructions to the patient to hold his breath.
48. H72,HE9/10,69/11,101/5 ('and make a letwarye'), 114/18,M99/5 & 111/18,O21/15. The almost universal rubric is 'For the perilous cough'. H72 adds to the prescriptions 'medle hem togedir in hony and make a letewarie'.
49. D550,HE9/15,O20/30.
50. D552 (omits 'pepur'), O21/1 (specifies 'alde ale').
51. D191,H72,HE9/13 & 115/4,M99/8,O20/37. The Corpus text alone omits honey as an ingredient. H72 offers an amplified text which prescribes use of the electuary 'fyue dayes or sex'.
52. D837 ('boyle heme wele in gotis mylke'), HE10/5 ('Boyle hit wiþ gotys melke').
53. HE10/3.
54. D1001,H70,HE10/8,O24/27,S207/17.

55. D856 ('For stomak that is bolnyd').
56. HE10/19 ('Pro stomaco'), O25/3 (and note) ('For evyll at þe hert'). The Corpus copy seems to offer the best text. It is alone in including 'sicorie' (HEO 'centurie'). HEO insert 'a little sage' before 'wermod'. For 'wilwe-leue' HE offers 'viflef and centorie', O 'fifleues and saueray'. Note for 'hertis-tunge' HE has 'serlange' and O 'longe de cerfe'. The last sentence in Corpus is corrupt and I suggest suppressing initial 'to'; in HE and O it makes perfectly good sense because following 'grasses' they have 'þou moust do .iii. galons of water' and 'do in galons of water' respectively.
57. O25/24 ('To spourge a man of ill humour'). For 'sissimbrium' O has 'water of mynt', which should be corrected to 'water-mynt', and specifies tempering with white wine.
58. O23/3 adds 'horshoue' to the ingredients.
59. O23/6 has 'centorie' and 'sclary' (i.e. 'eyebright' or 'clary'), of which 'seyrie' must be a miscopying. O concludes with 'A galon of water is ynoghe to sethe it in'.
61. HE12/6 ('Si venter sit durus atque flatus'), 69/17 ('Whoso hat wryngyng in hys wombe') and O22/8 ('For bolnyng of wambe').
62. D376 (and cf.D644), H74,HE70/1,O30/12. A receipt against worms.
63. D555,HE12/9 ('... wolt make nesche þy wombe', with 'maþnes' for 'malwes'), M100/ 9,O28/13 (ending 'sal be soluble').
64. O28/16 has 'hauyrmele', and 'soluble' for 'neysse'.
65. O28/19 (note) has 'and breke it & wete a loke of wolle þerin'. HE12/12 has 'Take þe galle of a bole and breke hit in wolle and bynd hit to þyn ancle, et sanaberis'.
66. D188 has 'a pype of pewtre', 'a spyndell end', 'a bleddir full of oyle'. O28/32 has 'a pype of messynge or of tre or of horne' and 'within a net bleddir or a lether', ending '... into his wambe. þan walke a littill or welter on a bedde a while & he sall delyuer hym sone'.
67. O28/22, Hunt 226/14(Fr.).
68. D527 ('touncresse-seede'), H81 & 116,HE37/11,41/14,82/21, 115/15,O30/34. Most of the witnesses specify red wine, and over half cress-seed. O specifies 'a draghte of gude rede wyne lewke or lewk water'.
69. HE12/16 and O31/11 specify that the cow should not have calved in the previous twelve months. O expands the ending.
70. O31/9 ends the receipt 'quod probatur per R[ector] de O[swaldkirk]'.
71. O31/16.
72. D125,HE13/15,O35/9 all specify 'old swine's grease'. O erroneously has 'bake' (the leaves). S218/16 ('For sore of þe bak and of þe reynes') is slightly amplified and includes 'mowse-ere' and 'barowys-grece'.
73. D583 & 765,HE13/18 (specifies twelve peppercorns).
75. D582,HE14/6 ('For castyng of þy lyvere') omits reference to sugar. M100/13 has 'popillyon'.
76. HE14/9 adds 'hit schal be þyn hele and do þe wol to poysyn' where O44/36 has '& mak þe wele to pys'. See also *Rel. ant.*1,51.
77. H75(amplified), HE14/13 ('chireston'), M100/16 (and note), O45/6. H has 'ache' in place of 'recheles'. See also *Rel.ant.* 1,52. For a similar use of cherry-stones see Hunt, 187, ll.1231ff.
78. HE14/17 has 'in þe mauwe' and 'tempere hit wiþ wyn', as does M101/9 (and note). See also *Rel. ant.*1,52.
79. D730,H76,HE15/1,O44/28,S237/9 all adopt the form 'ambros(e', and add, with the

exception of S, 'sanguinary' (Capsella bursa- pastoris (L.) Medic.) and specify 'parsley seed'. S begins with 'eufrace, ambrose and mylfoyle' and omits parsley.

80. H76,HE15/4,O44/16,S238/4. HE ends 'et faciet te bene myngere'. H specifies white wine (like S) and that it should be drunk warm.
81. S238/6 has 'safron' for 'savyne', 'avance' for 'aniise' and omits 'anet'. The ending, which contains no reference to 'horberd', recommends tempering with wine 'or clene watyr distyllid of saxifrage and bene-coddys and strayne it thorow a clothe and drynke þerof fyrst and laste; þis medcyn ys provyd'.
82. The receipt should read 'goat's claws', see the note to O44/22. H77 has as rubric 'Pro dolore et tumore in cruribus'. See Hunt 189/ll.1291ff ('ungles de porc') & 277/82.
83. H76 (amplified) has 'barly-mele', HE15/10 has 'bene-mele'. Cf. also H128 ('Pro tumore testiculorum') which has 'bene-mele' and S240/23 which also has 'bene-mele'.
84. HE15/14 omits honey.
85. D742 'An oþer for hym þat is scaldide þe which man clepith the appigale: Take lynsede or cloth and brenne it and tak þe poudre and do in a clowt and lay þertoo'. HE15/17 'Whoso his scoldyd on þe pyntal, þat me clepyt þe ape: Take sum cloþ and brend hit and take þe askes and ley hym in to a lynne clothe and bynde hit to þe sore; et est optima medicina'. H76 (amplified) has the rubric 'Pro le scaldynge virge quod vocatur apegalle'. S238/17 begins 'Or take an olde flaxen clothe, þat ys clene waschyd, and brenne yt to poudyr and take oyle of eggis and anoynt ...'
86. D546 & 810,HE16/6.
87. D811,HE16/6 ('Pro prurigine et inflatura super tubias'). See also *Rel. ant.*1,52.
89. H77 ('Pro tumore vel dolore tibiarum vel pedum') begins 'Take otenmele and cow mylke and make grewel'.
91. HE16/10 ('horsegrese' is doubtless an error for 'boresgrece') covers the first half of the receipt. See *Rel. ant* 1,53.
92. H77,HE16/13,M102/3. H specifies 'barewes grece'.
94. H78,HE16/17 ('bynd a coule lyf þerto'), M102/7 ('menge it with may-buttir'). The receipt is for soreness of the feet caused by travelling.
98. D873 ('For the schyngles') has 'tak calid dunge',H78 ('For þe sengles') has 'dowe dryt' in what is an amplified version of the receipt. Also amplified is S216/13.
100. H79 ('Pro sacro igne .i. wildefuyre').
101. H145 in an amplified version prescribes 'druye comyn', 'oyle de olyue' and 'barewes grece', the patient being anointed 'agayne a charkol fyre'. There is nothing corresponding to 'a lef of canelle' in the Corpus text. See also HE17/1 ('alteluda' must be an error for 'alleluia').
102. HE17/6 ('lomke' is an error for 'humloke').
103. HE17/8,S246/5.
104. HE17/11.
105. HE17/13 (erroneous heading 'For þe jambes') concludes 'and ȝef hym to drynke euerey smal schauen in wyn'. M102/10 has 'ywory small schawyn in wyn'. *Rel.ant.*1,p.51.
106. D748,H17/16 ('dragannce oþer gladyne'), O25/39. 'þat growe in þe yerd' is unique to the Corpus text.
107. O26/1 omits 'wyt' before 'wyn'.
108. H84 has 'tempre it wiþ his owne vryne'. HE17/19 ('Si quis sit morsus a serpente')

reads 'with wyn and water' and concludes 'et ita bonum est animalibus sicud hominibus'.

109. HE18/3.
112. HE18/5 ('ȝyf an addere oþer eny ouþer evel worme be y-cropyn in to a manys body oþer to breyde þerin').
113. HE18/9 ends 'et bibe et eiciet vermem cum toto veneno'.
114. HE18/12 has 'woderouue' i.e. woodruff.
115. HE18/16 has 'þe sed of flex',M103/18 'þe seed of þe box-tree'.
117. 'houndes smere' is obviously an error. HE19/1 reads 'hundys here' (i.e. dog hair). M103/21 & 103/24 divide the receipt, the second beginning 'And also take þe same howndis her'.
118. D781,H84,HE19/5,M102/13,O37/18. The gloss 'scabbewrt' is unique to the Corpus text.
119. O37/22.
120. D782 & 789,H201,HE19/9,O37/30. HE and the Corpus text have simply 'dock', the rest 'red dock'.
121. O41/26 ('Tak þe firste tyme þat it takes þe man þat þou may wiete it').
122. D361 ('For the fallyng euell that is clepid the gowt cayne [corr. cayve]',O41/31. D and O have 'solsequy'/'solsekill' for 'marigolde' and 'yarow' for 'nose-bledellus'. D omits 'recheles'.
124. D655,H84,HE19/15 & 102/13,M103/27,O63/30,S234/8. D and H read 'bores-grece',O 'bare-grese',S 'boris-grece'. HE19/15 has 'a ston', HE102 'a lytille stone', M 'a lytill stone'; the detail is missing in DHS.
125. D280 (with the form 'ambros'), O65/15 (with the form 'ambrose').
126. HE20/3,O64/4 (cf.63/36), S234/15. O includes both horse fat and boar fat. S starts with 'bawsons-grece' and includes 'ganatis-grece' (cf.H202), substituting 'verven' for feverfew.
127. O64/9 ('rede snyles').
128. O64/12 ('moldwarppe').
129. O64/16 which has 'bretfull' of which 'bretthelud', which makes no sense, must be a corruption. A short version is found in M37/6.
130. HE20/10,O65/10,S234/21 (abbreviated). HE omits the reference to leprosy; O reads 'and if a leprous man be anoynt þerwith, it will do hym mekill gude and mekill ese'.
131. See for an amplified version O77/15ff. In HE20/14 the distinction between fester and cancer is not quite the same and the cancer is described as 'evermore withoute an hole'. See also S235/12.
132. HE20/19,O77/28 (see note), S235/16. HE has 'wilde tansi', OS have 'white'. O has 'ȝarow' for 'nose-bledeles'. For 'centoinodye' (i.e. 'centinodie'), without a gloss, HE has 'white maþerne' and OS 'white malue' (see later in the receipt). In HE there is an omission due to eyeskip. HEOS all have 'ache' in place of 'merchaunt'. S abbreviates the receipt.
133. C611,HE21/17,O78/17. HE replaces the first reference to honey by 'drauk', whilst O substitutes 'darenell'. O specifies five days or eight.
134. C612,HE22/7,O78/28. HEO specify hot wine.
135. C613 has 'brent lyme'.
136. C614,O79/1.
137. C615,O79/3. The reading 'as a culiz' in the Corpus text in all probability stems from

a misreading of 'colis' ('coals'), since C has 'on quike coles' and O 'on þe qwik coles'.

138. HE22/15,O81/15.
139. HE22/22 & 103/15,O81/10.
140. O81/10 has '& drynk ilk day avaunce or oþer thynge als it is byfore-saide'.
141. LH114,C640,O81/27 (note) has 'stork or of a crane' and 'within .iii. dayes',R287. See Hunt 320/61.
142. O81/32 reads 'olibanum'.
143. O81/38 has 'bronstone brynt', omitting lead, and 'and if þe kankir be on a man, wasche ...', omitting 'þat is a mayden'. O also reads 'Bot when it is weschen, mak it dry' and after heating on the fire 'if þer be any knottis of mele, undo þam with thyn handis and menge þam wele'.
144. O82/25 reads 'mirt' for 'wrtes', 'nete flesche brynt' instead of 'breef brent', and 'pyons' for 'pumice'.
145. D524.
147. HE25/13,M104/6,O70/27.
148. HE26/13,26/21,28/9,M104/24.
149. HE26/15 under the rubric 'ȝyf a wounde akyþ'. HE70/1 ends 'and hit schal caste out þe wormes'; in S221/1 the receipt is given.'For wormys in þe wombe'.
150. HE26/18 has 'wylde nepte', M104/21 'bryon, þat is þe wylde nepte'.
151. HE29/8 ('Ȝif a manys nase ys broke or corve þat þe blood wol noȝt stanche') has 'brent lyme' for 'brent lyn.'
152. HE29/16,M105/3.
153. HE29/19,M105/7.
154. HE30/6.
155. HE30/10.
156. HE30/12 and M105/10 have 'and mellilotum' for 'mylk-sothen'.
157. HE30/18 omits 'Tack þanne þe schire ... panne agayn'. Cf. the opening of H82 ('Ad faciendum bonum entret') 'Take fat bacon and olde bacon, and meelt hit in a ponne, and let hit stonde, til þe salt be falle to þe grounde ...'
158. Apparently a variant of the above.
159. HE31/14 begins 'Take lynnesed and wet hit wel and take holy-hocke ...'
160. HE32/1 has 'roste hit'.
161. HE32/21 has 'berme' (barm or yeast).
162. HE32/3 reads 'snaylis þat crepit in houselese'.
163. HE27/1,O74/9. O has 'raynwort' for 'þe litel consonde', 'þe rede brere' for 'holy brere', and 'þe white maue' for 'holy-ake'. Cf. D654.
164. O54/33 has 'white pik þat þir spicers calles pik album' instead of 'pick', omits 'askbirun', and has 'fresche suete of an hert' for 'hertes-talw'. *Rel. ant.* 1,53 has 'white pik that this spicers calles *pix album*'.
165. D348,O61/10,*Rel.ant.*1,p.54. After 'seith it well' O adds '& tak mynt, of aþer ilike mekill, & stamp þam wele & make a playster ...', as does D. O ends 'Bot anoynte hym firste with popilion, if he hafe anger in his lyuer', whilst D has 'make a pleystir to thi forhede and over the eyen enoynt wit pillial'.
166. O61/17 has 'jubarb' for 'sengrene'.
167. O61/16 specifies a cupful of cold water and 'þe smedes of barly' (l.26).
168. O61/16 specifies 'a ȝonge coke' (l.31).
169. O61/16 has after 'aycil þerto' '& couer his hede þerwith & his foreheued' (l.35), for

quill has 'a pipe of a gose fethir' (l.38), specifies that the patient should be kissed 'ofte on his heuede' (l.39), and that he should be prodded 'with prikkes alwaye for slepynge' (62/3).

171. D349 (combined with no.172), HE37/16,M96/9,O59/26.
172. O59/33 reads 'rubarbe & schafe it'.
173. D349(combined with no.170) reads '.iiii. plantes of waybrede' as does D757; HE38/3 also has '4 plontis' and ends 'hele hym wele and lete hym slepe and he schal fare wel'; O60/21 has 'þe fever þat is callede þe quartane takes a man or a woman ilk thirde day' and 'tak & mak a lafe of clene barly'. Cf. Hunt 286/173 & 305/57.
174. O62/31 ('A gude oximell for all fevers') begins 'Tak þe rute of fynkell & þe rute of percell'. It has 'leches' for 'gobetes' and 'þis oximell' for 'þe medicine'.
175. O60/9 gives the name of the fever as 'omni rapacete'. Owing to eyeskip the Corpus scribe has omitted material after 'seith it' which in O reads: 'to þe twa parties be sothen in. þan clence it thurgh a clathe and do þan suger þerto & sethe it ...'
176. O60/14.
177. HE38/16 has 'ambrosie' and 'solsequie' (for 'ruden').
180. *Rel ant.* 1,54 ends 'this er the takenynges of ethe, forsothe witte thu he sal noght leve thre days'.
181. HE44/13.
182. A translation of a set of Latin verses, the 'Signa mortis', most probably drawn from the *Flos medicinae scholae Salerni*, see Hunt, *Popular Medicine* p.102, and based on the Hippocratic facies, see note to R573 and R.H. Robbins, "Signs of Death in Middle English", *Mediaeval Studies* 32 (1970), 282–98.

CHAPTER FOUR
THE LANGUAGE OF THE ENGLISH TEXTS

by Michael Benskin

A single hand of ca. 1330 A.D. is responsible for both of the compendia printed here, distinguished henceforth as 'T1' (= Hunt's C) and 'T2'(Hunt's CC). The script is unpretentious, debased *textura* varying in quality and consistency within as well as between the separate stints. The English parts of the compendia are not known from earlier manuscripts, but textual errors and corrections indicate that they are copies at some remove from the original compositions. Dialectally, the English of T1 is similar to that of T2, but not identical. Both are stamped with the same orthographic peculiarities, and both are of a distinctively East Midland type.

It is a question how far the dialectal differences between T1 and T2 reflect diverse copying histories in the exemplar(s) behind the present manuscript, where the two compendia may or may not have been copied jointly for the first time. It is a question, too, how far T1 and T2 are integrities: compilations of medical receipts are apt to be expanded by their copyists, whose additions may introduce dialectal as well as textual erratics. Were the exemplars to hand, the Corpus scribe's linguistic behaviour could be assessed in a straightforward way; in their absence, the very features that might explain it can only be inferred from his copy. The dialectal analysis that follows is hence reciprocal, and is in part and perforce directed to finding the simplest copying history that will account for the appearances of the texts.[1]

The outline that emerges is of some interest in itself, not least for what it implies about the local production and circulation of these compendia. But for their English contents, probably nothing of that kind could be established:

[1] The principles of analysis are set out in Benskin & Laing 1981. On 'reciprocal' as opposed to 'circular', see the Postscript on Method in *Atlas* II.xiii–xiv, and references there cited.

regional variation within Anglo-French is yet uncharted, such other versions of the compendia as are known are later by a half-century or more, and comparison with the fifteenth-century compilations, in which erratics and cross-contamination appear to be rife, indicates that conventional stemmata are not recoverable by recension.[2] Moreover, these texts belong to a time when, if the surviving manuscripts be any guide, written English was still far from commonplace, and in secular informational works almost unknown.[3] A substantial English text from this period is hence almost by definition of philological interest, and the compendia, particularly in their orthography, are unusually so. Dialectally they are of special significance in consolidating part of the reconstructed East Midlands pattern, for early as well as later Middle English, and they attest to copying practice of a type which, though long since identified, has been documented by little published work.

The copying practice of the Corpus scribe[4]

In principle, T1 and T2 could be *literatim* copies of the Corpus scribe's exemplars. If that were so, the Corpus scribe's own language could not be known, and a philological analysis that combined T1 and T2 as a single entity would be misguided from the start. *Literatim* copying would hardly be in doubt were the dialects of T1 and T2 radically different (unless, of course, we preferred to imagine a scribe who commanded two very different dialects, and alternated inscrutably between them).[5] But T1 and T2 are not

[2] So much is implicit in the identification of receipts in the present volume. See generally Keiser 1998, p. 3653, and references there cited.

[3] For a conspectus, see Laing 1993 and Keiser 1998.

[4] In textual and linguistic commentary, the system of citations is generally in accordance with the antique and mediaeval doctrine of *litera*: *litera* is a complex comprising *nomen* (the name of the letter), *potestas* (its sound-value), and *figura* (the symbol that represents it in writing). *Literae*, independently of any manuscript rendering, are here enclosed in single inverted commas. The *figurae* of particular manuscripts are printed in italics; to borrow a term from the phoneticians, they are in (perforce) broad transcription. (In citations of Old English, *w* is for wyn.) Such abbreviations as cannot be conveniently represented in an approximation to manuscript form, are expanded into the *literae* to which they correspond, and printed in roman. Within sequences of *literae* or *figurae*, commas and parentheses separate variable elements; hyphens are editorial. *Potestates* are represented by I.P.A. symbols in phonetic brackets; their phonemic status or otherwise is not here at issue. Glosses and word-identities are indicated by printing in small capitals.

[5] For an extreme case of textually-conditioned changes of scribal dialect, some nineteen in all, see McIntosh & Wakelin 1982.

radically different; indeed, their similarities are such that even if, did we but know it, they were exact replicas of their exemplars, an account that recognised no more than that would be deficient as to philology and textual history alike.

Unless exemplars are to be multiplied *praeter necessitatem*, there is a preliminary case against *literatim* copying to the extent that certain of the pervasive spelling conventions, which in principle are independent of dialectal type, are idiosyncratic rather than local or regional usage. Though several of them appear in other manuscripts, the combination does not, and though closely contemporary English writings are too few and too scattered for it to be claimed as decisively personal, it may well have been so.[6] Among these conventions are: (i) abbreviation of IN as *ī*, surprisingly uncommon in Middle English,[7] as also is (ii) *ād* for AND;[8] (iii) the placing of the tilde abbreviating 'm' or 'n' not over the preceding letter, but two letters in advance, which is rare if indeed paralleled in Middle English (so, e.g., *w̄iman* not *wīman* WOMAN); (iv) the use of *i*-digraphs corresponding to etymological long vowels, as in *seid* SEED; (v) the use of *ck* instead of *c* or *k* after consonants or short vowels, as in *drincken* DRINK inf., and *tack* TAKE imper. sg.; (vi) the writing of *w* alone for *w*+'u', as in *wnde* WOUND. These combine with fluent copying in a hand that seems not to be taking its time, and in so far as it is improbable that the whole set was the habitual usage of three individuals rather than one, they indicate that the Corpus manuscript is not a letter-by-letter copy.[9]

6 The taxonomic power of combinations of characteristics, as opposed to uniquely confined (and hence uniquely defining) properties, is fundamental; DNA sequences present a classic case. See further McIntosh 1974, 1975; Benskin 1991.

7 Eight exx in T1, sixteen in T2 (respectively 4.3% and 7.5% of the IN occurrences).

8 In T1×27, in T2×43 (respectively 2.29% and 4% of the AND occurrences). Note also *a'*, very rare in Middle English, in T1×28, in T2×10 (respectively 2.4% and .94% of the AND-occurrences); it is known otherwise from British Library MS Harley 913 (the Kildare poems MS), in which it is regular (×434); and there are two examples in the Cotton MS of *The Owl and the Nightingale*.

9 It cannot be sufficiently emphasised that such combinations of forms, although the forms themselves may be commonplace, identify individuals even from within the same scriptorium; anyone in doubt of the fact should examine the writings of the Privy Seal and Signet clerks, even from as late as the reign of Henry VIII. As it happens, *ād* and *ī* are less unusual in early Middle English than in writings from ca. 1350–1450, but for this period as well, their combination is telling. So much appears from indexes to the 141 texts so far examined by Dr Laing. (The number of scribes is somewhat less than 141: a single copyist's replications of diverse texts in diverse orthographies, are counted by text not hand.) Forty-seven of the 141 texts show *ī*, and 14 show *ād* (another 3 show *āt*); but *ād* and *ī* co-occur

At the same time, it is unlikely, though not of course impossible, that only a few selected orthographical features were superimposed on texts left otherwise in unfamiliar dialectal form. Even less likely, however, is the Corpus scribe's wholesale dialectal conversion from each of the two exemplars, for *ex hypothesi* the textual dialects of T1 and T2 ought then to be the same. In such a case there might admittedly be odd carry-overs from the exemplars' dialects, and over the first few folios of each text, usage might be rather mixed as the copyist was getting into his stride; but T1 and T2 are not identical, and their differences are not clustered at their beginnings, but sustained. They now call for some close attention.

The textual dialects of T1 and T2 diverge mainly in the relative frequencies of the same co-variant forms. For example, in both texts the forms corresponding to IF are *ȝif*, *yif*, and *if*, but between the texts their distributions are markedly skewed:

T1	ȝif 18	yif 8	if 7		= 33
T2	ȝif 19	yif 1	if 41	gyf 1	= 62
	= 37	= 9	= 48	= 1	= 95

Between T1 and T2, the proportions of *ȝif* and *if*, *yif* and *if*, are reversed. (The remaining form, *gyf* in T2, cannot be presumed absent from the dialect represented by T1: on this evidence, thirty more writings of IF might well have produced it. It may be relict from an exemplar, though it could well be a misreading of IF as GIVE). Similarly striking cases are the following.

For GIVE (all are imperative sg., save subj. sg. *ȝif* ×1 in T1):

T1	ȝif 23	yif 16	gyf 7	gef 2	gif 1	= 50
T2	ȝif 3	yif 2	gyf 21	gef 8	gif 1	= 36
	= 26	= 18	= 28	= 10	= 2	= 86

(T1 has additionally *geif* ×1, T2 *gyue* 2sg. pres. subj. ×1.)

For the suffix of the 3sg. present indicative:

T1	-t 19	-d 7	-s 2	-ȝ 1	= 29
T2	-t 10	-d 17	-s 35	-ȝ 1	= 63
	= 29	= 24	= 37	= 2	= 92

in only 7 (or 10, if *āt* be admitted). Fifty-three of the 141 show *ck*, which is found in 32 of the 47 texts showing *ī*; only 4 texts combine *ck* with *ī* and *ād* (or 7, if *āt* be admitted). When relative frequencies are taken into account, the practice of the Corpus 388 scribe is set apart even by these three criteria, for in the comparators, *ck* is not sustained, but only sporadic.

For ARE:

T1	arn 8	ben 6	be*n* 1	ar 1	= 16
T2	arn 6	ben 1			= 7
	= 14	= 7	= 1	= 1	= 23

For EVIL:

T1	euele 8	iuele 4	= 12
T2	euele 30	iuele 2	= 32
	= 38	= 6	= 44

(T1 'euele' includes *evele* ×1, *euel'* ×1; T2 'euele' includes *heuele* ×2, *euel'* ×1. On the forms, see pp. 214–15 below.)

For HAS:

T1	(h)ad (2)+4	hat 2			= 8
T2	(h)ad (11)+3	hat 2	(h)aues (16)+1	h' 15	= 54
	= (13)+7	= 4	= (16)+1	= 15	= 62

(What letter sequence underlies the abbreviated form *h'* is indeterminable; the representation may rather be logographic. T2 has additionally *haued* ×3, *(h)as* ×2, *hais* ×1.)

For HEAD:

T1	heued-*type* 43	hed 1	= 44
T2	heued-*type* 12	hed 16	= 28
	= 55	= 17	= 72

(T1 'heued' includes *heueid* ×2, *heuid* ×1; T2 'heued' includes *eued* ×1. T2 has additionally *hefd'* ×2, *h'd* ×1.)

For MAY 2sg.

T1	mayt 5	mait 2		mast 4			= 11
T2	mayt 2		mayth 1	mast 1	mayst 3	may 9	= 16
	= 7	= 2	= 1	= 5	= 3	= 9	= 27

For THESE:

T1	yese 5	yes 1	yis 1	= 7
T2	yese 6	yes 10		= 16
	= 11	= 11	= 1	= 23

Dialectally, therefore, T1 and T2 can look very different, and but for the handwriting probably few scholars would be persuaded that they are the work of the same scribe. Critical here, however, is the extent to which these and the remaining forms of T1 and T2 can be localised as a single dialectal assemblage, and it turns out that nearly all of them are known from the same small area of West Norfolk and Ely. Absolute differences between the Corpus texts involve only small attestations, as for example with the two forms of ENOUGH, a word found only four times: T1 has *inow* twice,[10] T2 has *anow* twice.[11] More frequent use might have shown both in each text, and only if their geographical distributions appeared to be entirely separate could they be taken to indicate different dialectal histories for T1 and T2; as it happens, the domains of *anow* and *inow* overlap where, on all other criteria, the scribal dialect of Corpus appears to belong.[12]

The two textual dialects need therefore be no more than different selections, constrained by the forms of the exemplars, from substantially the same local assemblage: all were part of the same scribe's passive if not active repertoire, and he wrote one form rather than another according as he was prompted by the text in front of him.[13]

This assessment is borne out by the first scrap of English in the Latin texts immediately following T2 (f. 48vb), which are undoubtedly in the same hand. The rubric of the third receipt is *for to maken a blac hors qwyt*: in T2, WHITE is spelled with *qu-* throughout (14 exx.), but with the change of text, *qw-* enters. In the same word, T1 has *qu-* ×21, and *qw-* ×1 (*qwyt*); and that *qw* is the only instance of *qw-* corresponding to OE *hw-* in either T1 or T2, against over a hundred instances of *qu-*, and a like number of *q* with 'u' in abbreviation. Constrained selection once more, unless between times the scribe's own spelling practice had changed.

The hand of T1 and T2, debased *textura* throughout, continues from the receipts on f. 48v into the upper part of both columns of f. 49r, with Latin and English plant synonyma; these afford no useful material for dialectal comparison. Added afterwards in column *a*, however, is a nineteen-line English receipt *For [he]meraudes*, in a much less careful version of what appears to be the same hand; its proportions and some of its letter-forms are not *textura* but *Anglicana*. It is in the familiar T1/T2 orthography, save for *qwete* 'wheat'.

Also in English is the short treatise on urines at the end of the manuscript (ff. 53v–54r, not printed here). Its script is fully *Anglicana*, and does not at

[10] In receipts 354 and 633.

[11] Both in receipt no. 162.

[12] *Atlas* I.482–3, maps 744 & 746; IV.161a, 313b. *a(-)now* is restricted to Norfolk, Ely, and Suffolk; note also *a(-)nowh* in Norfolk and Cambridgeshire.

[13] See further Benskin & Laing 1981, pp. 72–5; *Atlas* I, pp. 18–19.

first sight resemble the work of the T1/T2 scribe. The receipt on f. 49r, however, is an instructive palaeographical link, and close comparison shows that all three are most probably by the same hand.[14] If they are, the treatise affords further evidence of selection constrained by an exemplar. Its language is of the same local type as T1 and T2, but it reverts decisively from T2 usage to that of T1 in excluding *-s* from the 3sg. pres. indic. (*-t* ×15, *-d* ×4), is independent of T1 in having *sche* (×4) and *he* (×1) for SHE,[15] and is independent of both T1 and T2 in sustaining *qw-* not *qu-* as the reflex of OE *hw-*.[16]

In sum, the manuscript looks to be the work of a scribe copying from exemplars in forms of language very similar to his own, a conclusion which implies (though it does not entail) that they were produced in the same locality. The two compendia afford evidence for at least three writers, more or less contemporary, whose habits of written language were acquired in much the same place; the treatise on urines, and the receipt on f. 49r, are evidence for one or possibly two more. And all belong to a time when, if manuscript survival be any guide, the writing of such texts in English was far from common practice.

Local origins

The local origins of the whole assemblage in the Corpus MS are fairly firmly established by comparison with the generally later material (ca. 1350–1450) in the *Linguistic Atlas of Late Mediaeval English*;[17] the most likely area, which

[14] Of the six orthographical peculiarities shared by T1 and T2 (pp. 195–96 above), the treatise shows: (i) abbreviation of IN as *ī* (×1 in 14 occurrences); (iii) (occasional) leftward displacement of the tilde; (iv) *i*-digraphs for etymological long vowels (×4); (v) *ck* for *-c(c)* or *-k(k)* (×4 in 5 possible occurrences). There is no textual opportunity for *w* corresponding to *w* + 'u'; AND occurs only×9, so the absence of (ii) *ād* is hardly telling. The receipt on f. 49r shows *ād* AND (×1), the displaced tilde, *i*-digraphs (×3), and *ck* (×9). Although the layout of the receipt on f. 49r is less regular than in T1 and T2, it shows the same spirit of word-division at the line end: *r'* | *de* RED, *to ge* | *der'* TOGETHER. Note also regular *signe* SIGN, written with a tilde variously over *i*, *g* or *n*, common to all texts save f. 49ra (where the word is wanting).

[15] Beside *se*×1. T1's sole form is *se* (×3); T2 lacks the word.

[16] Five exx., all in WHITE. T1 has *qw*×1, against *qu* fully written×40, and with abbreviated 'u' (as in *qᵃn* WHEN, *qⁱl* WHILE)×25; T2 has only *qu*, fully written ×58, and with abbreviated 'u' ×45.

[17] For the principles of localisation, see McIntosh 1963; Benskin 1991a, 1991b, pp. 219–40.

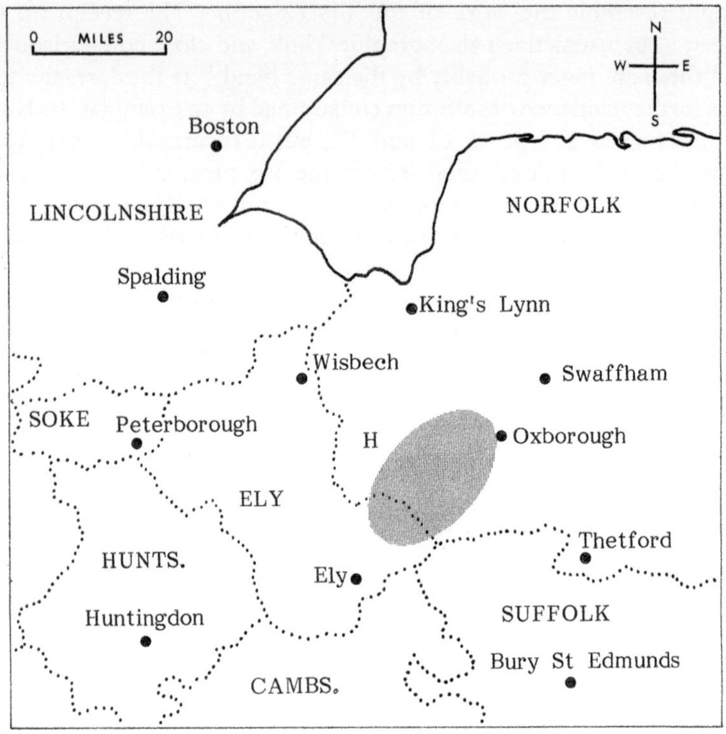

The local origins of the scribal dialect of the Middle English texts in Corpus Christi College, Cambridge, MS 388. The stippled area represents the most likely area of origin in terms of the configuration, necessarily schematic in part, presented by A Linguistic Atlas of Late Mediaeval English. *H, north-west of the stippled area, represents Professor Angus McIntosh's placing of the scribal dialects of the extant versions of* Havelok the Dane *(McIntosh 1976).*

is devoid of other placings, is bounded by *Atlas* LPs 232, 4565, 4041 (John of Grimestone's Preaching Book), 735, 150 (Oxburgh Gild Returns, *anno* 1389), 4566, 574, and 281. Corresponding linguistic profiles ('LPs') for T1 and T2 are printed as an appendix to this chapter, and though nothing is to be gained by rehearsing the innumerable mappings and collations that have led to the present placing, it may be useful to draw attention to the salient forms.

For origins in Norfolk or its East Midland borders: *o, oy, oi* (though with rare *a, ay, ai*) for the reflex of OE [a:] not before *w* or lengthening groups (see pp. 215 and 217–18 below); *qu* for the reflex of OE *hw*; *hire* HER; enclitic *-it*, *-et* IT (e.g., *drincket* DRINK IT; *yei* THEY, *hem* THEM (THEIR wanting); *ilk(-)*, *ich(-)* EACH; *u* as the root vowel in SHALL pl.; *wer(c)k* sb. & vb., with *-k* not *-ch*; 3sg. pres. indic. *-et* (beside *-es*, etc., cf. p. 196 above); pres. indic. pl. *-n*; pres. part. *-ande* (beside *ende*, *-yng*, etc.); *dede* DEATH; *(h)erde* EARTH; *ferde* FOURTH; *eld* OLD; *nouele* NAVEL;[18] unetymological (non-)use of *h-*; interchange of *-t* and *-th*; *th* (with rare *t(t), tth*), never *(g)ht* or *ȝt*, for the reflex of OE *ht*.

More narrowly delimiting, in combination with the preceding set, are: *als(-so)*, *os* AS (beside *as*, etc.); *s-* and *sc-* (beside *sch-*) in SHALL; sb. pl. & gen. sg. *-us* (beside dominant *-es*, etc.); pres. indic. pl. (and rarely as strong ppl.) *-un*; wk. ppl. *-ud* (beside dominant *-ed*); vbl. sb. *-ygge*, *-ingge* (beside dominant *-yng*); *be-twiyene, betweye* BETWEEN; *flex* FLESH;[19] *vnderd* HUNDRED; *to(-)gedere* TOGETHER (note the suffix, as well as the root vowel); *weel* adv. WELL (beside dominant *wel*); *wit* (rarely *with*) in WITH(IN, -OUT).

The relatively few forms in Corpus that are not shown by *Atlas* for this area (among which the sporadic *a*-reflexes of OE [a:])[20] are perhaps all to be accounted for by the discrepancy in date. In earlier generations some of these residual forms were undoubtedly used there, and in the Corpus scribe's day quite possibly still were, even if they were obsolescent and he himself did not normally use them. There need hence be no great time depth in the textual history of T1 and T2, even if these forms are relicts from earlier copies.

Attestation, moreover, may be unusually sensitive to conjunctions of time and place. For example, though *Atlas* (IV.81c–84b) lists over 120 variants for NOT, it has no record of *nowit*, regular in T1 (×20), T2 (×20) and T8 (×4); even *MED*'s twenty-seven columns (s.vv. *not* and *nought*), spanning ca. 1100–1500 A.D., have it only from Laȝamon A (ca. 1225, N.W. Worcestershire),[21] and *Maximian* (ca. 1300, South-West Midlands).[22] But *nowit* is well-formed,

[18] Cf. *Atlas* I.544 (map 1138), IV.314c.

[19] Cf. *flechs* FLESH in *Atlas* LPs 619, 4565 (both Ely). T2 also has *axsen* ASHES (×1), *askbirne* (×1), beside *asche, asses* (×1).

[20] See below, pp. 205, 217–218.

[21] Beside *nawiht*, s.v. *nought* n. 4(a). Etymologically, *not* n. and adv., *nought* n., pron. and adv., are all of a piece. On the hands and localisation, see Laing 1993, 70.

[22] s.v. *nought* pron. 1a(a). Cf. northern *nawit*, recorded only from the Edinburgh MS of the *Cursor Mundi*, s.v. *nought* adv. 1(a); *nohutt*, from *Vices and Virtues* I, ibid. 1(i); *nohut*, from *Thrush & N.*, ca. 1300, ibid. 1(g); these appear to exhaust quotations of the disyllabic type lacking (or possibly lacking) the spirant. On the *Maximian* MSS, see Laing 1993, 92–5, 129–30.

and the implied [nɔ(:)wɪt], if only as a short-lived transitional variant between [nɔ:(-)wɪçt] and [nɔut], must have been commonplace in areas showing early reduction of [çt,xt] to [t] - among which Norfolk, Ely and South Lincolnshire, where *no(-)wiht* > *nowit* > *nowt/nout*, rather than (or in addition to) the widespread *no(-)wiht* > *nowht* > *nowt/nout*. It is at least likely that *nowit* would be very much better recorded if early fourteenth-century manuscripts were known in quantity from these areas.[23] In the Corpus dialect, *nowit* (beside T1 *nouit* ×1, T2 *nowt* ×2) was seemingly entrenched, since other words with etymological or acquired *-out* (*-owt*) show decisively analogical spellings:

		T1	T2		T1	T2
OUT	(h)owit	(7)+10	3	(h)out	(1)+0	(0)+36
	(h)ouit	(10)+3	1	owt	0	1
MOUTH	mowit(h)	1(+0)	5(+1)	mouyth	0	1
	mowyt	2	0	mowt	2	1
CLOUT *sb.*	clowit		1	cloutes	1	1

In no other words do T1 and T2 show unetymological *oui*, *owi* (which may but need not imply [w]-glides): the reflexes of OE (as of OFr.) [u:] are otherwise *ou*, *ow* or *u*. Conversely, *owit(h)* et var. appear in all the Corpus vocabulary (though it is admittedly not extensive) where [u:t] or [u:θ] is etymologically word-final; in ABOUT and WITHOUT, where they are absent, earlier *-en* is still largely preserved. Neither *Atlas* (which excludes MOUTH), *MED*, nor (so far) Dr Laing has recorded the analogical type.

Even so, it remains uncertain how far differences of time rather than of place are rightly invoked to account for such discrepancies as do appear between the Corpus language and the *Atlas* record for the area to which, in all its essentials, the Corpus language belongs. The copying history need not have been wholly confined there, and there are hints that behind the immediate exemplars, though only for parts of them, the dialectal transmission involved South Lincolnshire. Paradoxically enough, the very source that confirms most of the residual forms as from West Norfolk, *nowit* among them, raises

[23] For early Middle English from these parts, Dr Margaret Laing's collections so far add *nowit* only in St John's College, Cambridge, MS A.15, f. 72r (?Bury St Edmunds, ×1). Western sources to be added to *MED*'s lists are Bodleian Library MS Digby 86 (*nowit*, *nowiit*); British Library MS Egerton 613, ff. 7r–12v (*Poema morale*, *nowit* ×1), British Library MS Titus D xviii, ff. 133v–147v (*St Katherine*, *nawit* ×1; Trinity College, Cambridge, MS B.14.39 (323), ff. 81v–82r, 85r–87v (*nowit* ×1).

also the possibility that some do indeed derive from Lincolnshire. That source is the early fourteenth-century manuscript of *Havelok the Dane*, Bodleian Laud Misc. 108, which, apart from the 58 lines in the Cambridge fragments, Cambridge University Library Add. 4407 (19), is the only surviving copy; the scribal dialects of both can be localised, again by extrapolation from the *Atlas* configuration, in West Norfolk near the Ely border.[24] The dialect of the Laud manuscript is a little earlier (or more conservative) than that of Corpus, and on present showing stems from within probably ten miles; overall, their agreements are remarkable, and it would not be surprising if they turned out to belong to the same place.[25] *Havelok*, however, is a verse composition undoubtedly of Lincolnshire, and some of the Laud copy's usage may well reflect Lincolnshire rather than Norfolk. Self-evidently this is true of the rhyme forms, and for present purposes they can be ignored, but metre likewise could perpetuate forms marginal or even foreign to the repertoire of a Norfolk copyist. Lincolnshire *euerilkon* EVERY ONE, for example, cannot well be replaced by *ilkon*, still less by *ilk* or *iche*, even though *everilkon* is absent from the later fourteenth-century Norfolk and Ely material; on the other hand, a good many Norfolk writers must have known *eueri(ch)* and *ilkon* as local forms, and so might have copied *euerilkon* unthinkingly even from a prose exemplar. It is possible, too, that *euerilkon*, by origin an emphatic compound, was earlier used in parts of Norfolk, but never became established there.[26]

Notable among the correspondences between the Corpus dialect and that of the Laud *Havelok* (cited as 'H') are the following:

[24] McIntosh 1976, fundamental to the ME dialectology of this area. For an edition, with invaluable glossary and apparatus, see Smithers 1987, a work which seems never to have received the credit that is its due.

[25] These are placings within a configuration that is partly and inevitably schematic, and the geographical correlations are offered with due reserve (cf. *Atlas* II.xi–xxiii). Though it is axiomatic that geographical distance implies dialectal difference, however slight, the corollary does not hold: small differences must be expected within any community.

[26] On the etymology, see *OED* s.vv. *every*, *ilk*, *ilka*, and *ilkane*. It is also in *Genesis and Exodus*, a verse text which may be of Norfolk origin. The one copy extant is probably of the early 14th century, though it is notably old-fashioned in its spelling; extrapolation from the *Atlas* configuration shows the scribal dialect to be of Norfolk. On the basis of the draft maps for *Atlas*, Professor McIntosh placed this dialect in West Norfolk (McIntosh 1976), where it is now proposed that the Corpus dialect belongs; the revised maps published in *Atlas* lead Dr Laing to think that origins schematically some 12–15 miles to the north-east are more likely (i.e., between *Atlas* LPs 734, 4103 and 4569).

ilk(-)on (T1 ×3), *ilckan* (T1 ×1) EACH ONE (H *ilkon* and *ilkan*); *euer(-)ilk(e)*, EVERY ONE (T1 ×3, T2 ×7); *eueryl* EACH (T1 ×1, H *eueril*);[27] *mykel* (H *mikel*) GREAT; *ware* WERE (T2 ×3); *þey* THOUGH (H *þey*); *yif* IF; *al-so* AS; *ageynes* AGAINST (T2 ×1); *aȝein* ×2, *ayein* ×1 AGAIN(ST) (T1 only, H *ayeyn*); *nowit* (H *no-with*) NOT;[28] *þar(e)* THERE (T2 only, H *þare*); *befor(e)* BEFORE, lacking *-n* (H *bifor*); *iuele* (H *iuel*, *yuel(e)*) EVIL; *yif* ipv GIVE.;[29] *oþer* OR (H *oþer*).

Some of these may show chronological rather than local proximity, notably *nowit*, *oþer*, and the forms with *i* or *y* (as opposed to *e*) in open syllables (so *mykel* and *iuele*, in Corpus beside *e*-forms). Nevertheless, much of the Corpus language, particularly in T2, would not be out of place in South Lincolnshire, and from the preceding list only *þey* THOUGH would be anomalous. Some forms would perhaps be better accommodated there, though on present evidence there is nothing to pull the dialectal history of the Corpus texts decisively northwards. T2's *quilk* WHICH (×1) is not altogether convincing for South-West Norfolk, and would square better with North Ely or South Lincolnshire;[30] but the early fourteenth-century *Genesis and Exodus* has *quilke*

[27] Comparable forms in early Middle English are found additionally in *The Bestiary* (*euril* ×1), Dulwich College MS XXII, *La Estorie del Euangelie* (S. Lincolnshire, Spalding area, *il* ×1). The only western sources are Hand A of the Lambeth Homilies (N.W. Worcestershire, *uwil(-)* ×3, *elene* ×1), and Laȝamon A (N.E. Worcestershire, *eulne* ×1).

[28] The *Hav.* spelling may, however, correspond to [çt] rather than [t]: for the reflex of OE *ht*, *th* is 'by far' its commonest spelling (so Smithers 1987, p. lxxxviii), with variants *ct*, *cth*, *cht*, *t*; but *th* is written also for etymological [t] (ibid.). See further McIntosh 1976, p. 47 n. 3, no. 4.

[29] The only imper. sg. noted in Professor Smithers's glossary. Otherwise in *Hav.*, the present stem of the *y*-type (always with root vowel *e*) has *u* not *f* as the medial consonant (so imper. pl. *yeueþ*); the *g*-type (always with root vowel *i*) similarly has *u* only, but lacks imper. sg. forms. For the relevant parts of Norfolk and Ely, the Corpus variants are not well attested in the *Atlas* lists (IV.181b–182b), but their mismatch with predominant *ȝeue*, *ȝeu-* is less than appears: all save two of the Corpus examples are imper. sg., which in ME genres other than medical receipts is generally ill-attested. (i) *The consonant.* In the imper. sg., as not in the rest of the conjugation, [f] is historically word-final, and so not susceptible to voicing (except in sandhi); phonetically, its correspondence to intervocalic [v] in the suffixed forms is regular, and the paradigm remained until the phonological redistribution of [f] and [v] attendant on the loss of final [ə]. (ii) *The root vowel.* Later ME present stem forms of the type *yiue(-)*, *ȝiue(-)*, are uncommon in face of *yeue(-)*, *ȝeue(-)*, as is predictable from the etymology; in Northern England and East Anglia, moreover, their antecedents were vulnerable to open syllable lengthening, whence [e:] < [ɪ]would be established throughout, except in such forms as had already lost a following inflexional vowel, or (which is to say the imper. sg.) had never had it at all (cf. Luick §§393–4).

[30] Cf. *Atlas* III, map 11.

(beside dominant *quilc*), and whether or not its language belongs in quite the same part of West Norfolk, it seems not far removed.[31]

The sporadic *a*-spellings for the reflex of OE [a:] (not shortened and not before lengthening groups or [w]), more frequent both relatively and absolutely in T2 (×8) than T1 (×4), may point more strongly towards Lincolnshire, depending on what date they entered the textual history; the later they did so, the more likely that they came from outwith Norfolk. Dr Gillis Kristensson's onomastic material from the Lay Subsidy Rolls establishes *a* in neither Norfolk (*annis* 1327 and 1332) nor Ely (*anno* 1330), but shows it in part of South Lincolnshire (*annis* 1332 and 1337);[32] *Atlas* shows it still surviving there in the fifteenth century, though only as a minor variant.[33]

It is of interest that in T2 the *a*-spellings cluster: receipt no. 157, and the very short receipts 159–61, contain four of the eight (158 lacks relevant vocabulary), which may reflect a copying history independent of the main compilation; no. 157 also contains five of T2's ten instances of *os* AS.[34] In T1, such clusterings are more prominent, though the reflexes of OE [a:] are only marginally involved. Three of the four *a*-spellings are in very short texts, nos. 505 (*sair* adj., beside *soer* sb.), 545 (*haled* ppl. HEALED, beside *ol'* inf. HEAL, and *sore* sb.), and for lack of relevant vocabulary nothing is to be made of them. In no. 613, however, *hat* HOT combines with *mykel* MUCH (×1) and *euerilk* (×2), *euerich* (×1) EACH, themselves forms of very uneven distribution. In T1 and T2, the MUCH-variants occur as follows:

T1	mychel 23	michel 10	mychil 1	mykel 10		= 46
T2	mychel 41	michel 1	mychil 1	mykel 2	mekel 1	= 52
	mych' l 5					
	= 69	= 11	= 2	= 12	= 1	= 98

(T1 has additionally *micul* ×1, *myc'l* ×1; T2 has *mych'* ×1.)

The incidence of the *k*-forms is more skewed than appears, for which reason MUCH was not invoked in the initial comparison of T1 and T2. Five of T1's

[31] Arngart 1968, glossary s.v. *quilc*. On the localisation, cf. p. 203, n. 26 above.

[32] Kristensson 1967, pp. 17–37, maps 11–13 (pp. 277–9) and 17 (p. 283); Kristensson 1995, pp. 7–15.

[33] *Atlas* I.464, map 633, and IV.85b, from LPs 62, 38, 75 and 198; for discussion, see Laing 1978, vol. I, pp. 237–40. The North-West Norfolk entry *ay* in *Atlas* LP 67, Wiggenhall Gild returns, is in error: the source appears to be *tway* "two", which has *ay* from *twegen*, not *twa* (cf. *twey* in the same text).

[34] T2 has 67 occurrences of AS. Forms in co-ordinated constructions (AS ... AS) are included in the count provided they reflect *als(-)*; co-ordinated SO is excluded.

ten occurrences of *mykel* are in receipt no. 610; this also contains two of T1's four instances of 'eueric(h)' (no. 613 contains a third), beside *eueryl*, the manuscript's sole occurrence.[35] Overall, *mykel* and 'eueric(h)', 'euerilk' et var., tend to co-occur:

T1

Receipt no.	610	612	613
mykel (10)	5/5		1/1
eu*er*ilk (3)[36]		1/2	2/3
eueryl (1)	1/3		
euerich (4)[37]	2/3		1/3
os (11)	2/2		
OE [a:][39] = *a* (4)	0/1	0/1	1/1

(In the left-most column, the parenthetical figures are the total occurrences for T1. Figures after virgules represent the number of occurrences possible within the vocabulary of the receipt; blanks indicate that such vocabulary is lacking.)

T2

Receipt no.	132	135	144	156	157	158	159	160	162	176
mykel (2)	1/4	0/1		0/3	0/2				0/3	1/1
euerilk (7)[38]	1/3	2/2	1/2						2/4	0/1
os (10)	1/2			5/8						
OE [a:][39]=*a* (8)	0/1	1/2	0/1	1/4		1/3	1/2	1/1	0/3	

Note also no. 26 in T2, a short receipt which combines *hald* HOLD (2 of T2's 3 exx), *iuele* and *mare*.

These observations are admittedly informal and *ad hoc*, but the text of itself frustrates systematic analysis. Receipts may be interpolated en bloc (as perhaps

[35] Though rare, the form need not be in error for *euerilk*: it is in both *Havelok* (1335 *euere-il del*, 2333 *eueril*) and the Lynn Gild Returns of 1389 (*eueril*, *eueryl*). The Lynn occurrences are *Atlas*'s only record (IV.24b–c, from LP 776 in III.331). Compare also *Bestiary* (W. Central Norfolk) *euril* ×1, and London, Dulwich College MS XXII, ff. 81v–85v (*La Estorie del Euangelie*, Spalding area of S. Lincolnshire) *il* ×1.

[36] The form without abbreviation is not found.

[37] Includes *euerich* ×2, *euerich* ×1, *eueric* (no. 616) ×1.

[38] Includes forms with and without abbreviated 'er', and with *euer* and *ilk(e)* written separately or conjoined.

[39] Not before lengthening groups, not shortened, and not before [w].

T2 no's 156–62), but are just as likely to be added as singletons. In either case such erratics may be impossible to recognise, for most receipts are very short, and the relevant vocabulary recurs too irregularly for extensive comparison to be sustained; even so, a computer-aided analysis of distributions and co-occurrences might reveal more than has yet come to light.

To summarise. The textual distributions of Middle English dialectal variants indicate that T1 and T2 were copied from exemplars whose dialectal histories were not the same, and hence that in the Corpus manuscript T1 and T2 were quite possibly conjoined for the first time. The English of these compendia belongs to the borders of the East Midlands and East Anglia. Its local origins can be narrowed down to a small area in Ely and West Norfolk, though it does not follow that the manuscript was written there. Some variants, however, appear to derive from further north, in South Lincolnshire,[40] and they cluster, so implying that the receipts which contain them are textual erratics. These few forms apart, the present placing within the *Atlas* configuration seems secure, and is confirmed repeatedly by incidental local detail.[41] The language is admittedly somewhat heterogeneous, even by Middle English standards, but in the scribal dialects of these parts, internal variation is characteristic. This arises not as local linguistic aberration, or from some putatively abnormal concentration of dialectally complex textual histories: few of the variant forms are peculiar to the district, and they belong to geographically cohesive sets. Here, on the western borders of Norfolk, one widely-distributed dialect-form after another is replaced by some similarly widespread functional equivalent, as the dialects of the East Midlands give way to those of East Anglia. This belt of displacement has hardly been noticed by philologists, their fixation with dialect boundaries notwithstanding, yet, running southward from The Wash, and some fifteen miles from east to west, it is one of the most striking that is demonstrable in Middle English.[42] Writers from those parts could scarcely have avoided knowing an unusually large range of local variants, and, regardless of their spontaneous usage, they need not have balked at reproducing them from an exemplar.

[40] A familiar pattern: Norfolk and S. Lincolnshire are prominent in the dialectal associations of ME medical manuscripts (cf. Keiser 1998, p. 3564).

[41] E.g., *tth* rather than *th* or *þ(þ)* in *sitth(en)* SINCE, cf. *Atlas* LPs 281, 4566; *fiir* FIRE (T8 ×1), cf. LP 735.

[42] Cf. Benskin 1994.

Orthography

Certain orthographic conventions pervading T1 and T2, not of themselves entailed by any corresponding spoken forms, are of variously local currency; some appear to be idiosyncratic, though local assessment is blurred for lack of closely contemporary manuscripts.

1) The letters 'þ' and 'y' are not distinguished. The letter-shape is nearly always *y*-like, its tail recurved strongly to the right. This is a regional trait, the norm in later Middle English from northern and much of eastern England.[43] In the compendia, word-final 'þ' is nowhere written, but *t(h)* (sometimes *d*, occasionally *ȝ*) is used in its stead.[44] Exclusion of ME 'þ' from final position is a very common scribal practice, and from the rarity or absence of [ð] in final position may lead to regular 'th' instead of 'þ' for word-initial [θ].[45] In the compendia, initial *th* is rare, and with one exception (T1 *thother* THE OTHER) is for [θ] not [ð]: T1 *thre* THREE, T2 *throte* THROAT, *theus* THIGHS, *nese thirles* et var. NOSTRILS (×3). Otherwise, word-initial 'þ' is regular, both for [ð] and [θ]: so *yicke* THICK, *yorn* THORN, *yrote* THROAT, beside *yei* THEY, *yanne* THEN, *yer* THERE. Medially, *th* is again rare: T2 *sothen* ppl. SODDEN (×2), T1 *sithe(n)* adv. SINCE (×2); but SINCE (only in T1) normally has *tth* (16 exx) for the historically double consonant. Compounding with *t* or *h* is responsible for *th* in T2 *ath*e AT THE (×2), *witholde* inf. WITHHOLD (×1).

2) The letters 'ȝ' and 'z' are not distinguished; *figurae* with or without a tail are used for both, and the barred type does not appear. Both *ȝ* and *ʒ* are used sporadically in place of 'þ' or 'th', a practice common in (though not confined to) East Anglia; these represent not yogh (from 'g' in the Insular script), but the originally syllabic abbreviation corresponding to -'et' in French and Latin usage.[46]

3) For *c(c)* or *k(k)* after consonants or a short vowel, *ck* is very frequent, beside conventional *k*. Only few and scattered writers of Middle English write *ck*, whether early or late.

[43] Benskin 1982, with map. Subsequent analysis of several hundred local documents requires only minor changes to the regional pattern there shown. See further Doyle and Benskin in Laing & Williamson 1994, pp. 96 & 115–6 respectively.

[44] T8 has *boy* BOTH ×1.

[45] Benskin 1982, p. 18.

[46] Cf. *Atlas* III, xvb.This accounts far better for the regional distribution than that given in Benskin 1982, where *ȝ* for 'þ' is treated solely as a back-spelling based on the interchange of both *ȝ* and *þ* with *y*. This will be treated more fully in a forthcoming paper.

4) *squ* and *sqw* appear regularly for initial and etymological [sw]. Since the reflex of OE *hw* is here regularly *qu*, with *w* as an occasional variant, it may be supposed that *squ* for [sw]- is generated by simple extension of a rule '*qu* = *w*'. Formally such an explanation is possible, but it hardly meets the present case. First, for OE *hw* the texts show very few examples of *w* at all, and of *w* for ME [kw] of whatever origin there is no sign. There is hence no basis for analogical extension of an unpremeditated sort. Secondly and more compellingly, *qu* for [w] appears only where [w] stands etymologically in the combination [sw]: otherwise, *w* is regular, a distribution for which simple back-spelling cannot account.

Explanation is possibly to be sought in the combinations of letters that are permissible in writing mediaeval Latin and Anglo-French. Although either language may use *w*, initial *sw* is hardly to be found; this merely reflects the two languages' phonological structures. A mediaeval writer whose English spelling was not so much *sui generis* as a transfer of system from his accustomed literary languages, might well have balked at writing *sw-*, regardless of his English phonology: in Latin principle it is ill-formed.[47] Even a limited interchange of English *w* and *qu* in OE *hw*-words, however, permits a premeditated *squ* for the offending *sw*: as Latin spelling, *squ* is well-formed, and as English spelling it is lexically transparent. Although in principle [sw]-words and [skw]-words could then be confused, in practice very few homographs could arise; contextually, it would take some ingenuity to confound them.

The spelling of etymological [sw] with *sq* is distinctly rare. Early Middle English examples are known from Bodleian Library MS Ashmole 360, in a dialect probably of South-East Lincolnshire (*squete* SWEET and *i-squingen* ppl. SWUNG, each once); *Genesis and Exodus* (West Norfolk, ca. 1300) shows the reversed spelling in *swinacie* QUINSY×1 (OFr. *esquinacie*). When not in combination with [s], northern and eastern *w* for etymological [kw] is well known in both early and later Middle English (cf. Benskin 1988, pp. 28–9). Examples near to the Corpus manuscript both in time and place appear in *Genesis and Exodus* (*wað* SAID×2, with reverse spelling *qu* for historical [w] in *quake* VIGIL (OE *wacu*)), and *Havelok* (*hwat* SAID×2 and *wat*×1, beside usual *qu* forms (OE *cwæð*)).

5) *scl* for etymological [sl]- is a by-spelling in T1 (2:9), but dominant in T2 (15:5): so *scle* SLAY, *sclep* SLEEP, *sclyse* SLICE. T8 has only *sclepe* SLEEP ×1. In

[47] Lest this seem far-fetched, consider the later and literary proscription of English cumulative negation, in face of the Latin rule that two negatives cancel each other out.

Middle English generally, such *scl-* occurs sporadically, without (save in Sussex) obvious coherence of region or date (cf. *Atlas* IV.322a). It has yet to be explained: a sound-change [sl] > [skl] would be an obvious motivation for it, and is not inherently improbable, but in the modern dialects there is no certain trace. T2 also has *schlaw* SLOW (×1), again seemingly without later trace.

6) Initial [ʃ] (OE *sc-*). Beside regular *sch*, one or two instances of *s* are found, T1 *saif* SHAVE, *sellez* SHELLS, T2 *sarp* SHARP, *sankes* SHANKS (once each). Error cannot be discounted, but they could be intentional: John of Grimestone's Preaching Book shows similar spellings (*sarpe*, *sort* SHORT). The reflex of OE post-vocalic *sc* is written *ss* and *s* almost without exception. These may show French spelling practice extended to English, with [ʃ] corresponding (cf. frequent *warisse*, etc., HEAL); in unstressed forms it is possible that the correspondence was with [s]. Post-vocalic *sch* is found only in *a(y)sche* ASH(TREE) (T2 ×2).

s- in SHALL, a minority spelling in both compendia, is a different case: SHALL is the one word in which OE initial *sc* corresponds regularly to ME forms implying [s]; mostly these are confined to northern and eastern dialects, either as sole usage or beside other forms implying [ʃ]. The [s]-forms are conventionally regarded as having arisen from lax articulation in unstressed position, and it is true that SHALL is particularly liable to such use; moreover, it is the only OE *sc-* word that was so. But the handbooks' notion that [s] developed from unstressed [ʃ] is phonetically indefensible, for [s] requires *more* articulatory energy than [ʃ], not less. If [ʃ] were the starting point, then the product of lax articulation should have been [j] or a high front vowel. Accordingly, the [s]-variants must have developed at a time when the stressed form still had [sx] (or [sç]) < WGmc. [sk] (cf. the present correspondence in Dutch); and since the [s]-variants are not known from Old English, it follows that the correspondence of OE *sc* with [ʃ] came relatively late in those areas showing ME SHALL with [s]-variants.[48]

Besides *sch* and *s*, there are odd cases of initial *sc*, rare even in the earlier East Midland and Norfolk material: *scal* 'shall' (T1 ×2), *scer* SHEAR v. (T2 ×1).

7) Loss of *h*. Initial *h* is variously omitted in words not especially likely to have had distinctive unstressed variants; examples are notably commoner in T1 than T2. In the following lists, occurrences are once per form, unless otherwise stated.

[48] This will be treated more fully in a forthcoming paper.

Native English words lacking *h* are:
T1 *alwndel* HALF, *ard* HARD, *an-* HAND, *attet* IS CALLED, *ole* inf. HEAL; T2 *alli* HOLY, *an(d)-* HAND (×3) *eued* HEAD, *vnderd* HUNDRED.

Reverse spellings (including those in words of French origin) are:
T1 *hakyng* ACHING, *hey* and *hye* EGG, *herde* EARTH, *here* and *her'* EAR, *het(-)* EAT (×3), *heuen* EVEN, *heycil* VINEGAR, *heye* EYE, *hoik* OAK, *hold* OLD, *hon* ON, *hou(i)t, howit* (×18) OUT, *hup on* UPON, *hunyon* ONION, *hurine* URINE, *huse* USE; T2 *hany* ANY, *herye* and *herdene* EARTH(EN), *here* EAR, *heuele* EVIL (×2), *heuere-* EVER-, *heycil* VINEGAR, *hiren* IRON, *houene* OVEN, *howit, houit* OUT (×4); T3 *heyren* EGGS.[49]

In view of these, it is surprising that the unstressed variants familiar from other Middle English are not well represented here. In HAVE (all inflexions), T1 has *h* ×12 and lacks it ×5; T2 has *h* ×60 and lacks it ×7; T8 has *h* 11 and lacks it ×1;[50] overall, eleven of the twelve forms without *h* are monosyllabic. Other cases are far to seek: T1 has *e* HE ×1 and *is* HIS ×2; T2 has *a* HE ×1. On enclitic *-em* THEM, see p. 220 below.

The instability of initial *h-* in Middle English is commonly attributed to the speech-habits and spelling practice of Anglo-French, as a simple contact phenomenon. Latterly, it has been held that [h]-loss in early Middle English was an affectation, a prestige-marker transferred from French,[51] and that may in some part have hastened its demise. It should be noted, however, that weakening and effacement of [h] is the continuation of a long Germanic history, without regard to contact with French: OE [h] is itself a reduction from Gmc. [x], and as present-day dialectal usage, that [h] is preserved mainly in East Anglia, the south-west, the north, and in Scotland.[52]

8) Use of *w*. In mediaeval orthography, *w* is properly not one letter but two, a ligatured form of the separate *figurae* for 'u' ×2. In the compendia, *w* corresponds regularly to [w], but also, as not uncommonly in Middle English, to [w]+[u(:)], so (as in the compendia) Latin *wlnera* and ME *wnde* WOUND, ME *wrte* WORT. The practice was already of long standing: in Latin of the pre-Conquest period, [w] in Anglo-Saxon personal or place names was regularly *uu*, but where [u(:)] followed, *uu* and not *uuu* was written.[53]

49 Note also the irregular use of the indef. art. ‹*an*› as a hiatus breaker: T1 *a anful of rue & an hanful of heihoue*, T2 *an herdene pot.*

50 This excludes the 15 cases of *h'*.

51 Milroy 1981.

52 There is some evidence for [h]-loss even in Old English; see further, Scragg 1970.

53 Benskin 1982, pp. 19–20.

Apparently the triple sequence was unacceptable, and in so far as later mediaeval *w* continued to be regarded as two *literae*, *wu* remained open to objection.[54] Hence ME *w* for [wu(:)], a spelling favoured by economy of pen-strokes as well.

In T1 *alwndel* HALF SHARE (no. 540), *w* is for consonantal 'u' + vocalic 'u', i.e. [v]+[u] (cf. T1 *haluundel*, *haluendel*). In T2 *feuue* FEW (no. 141), *uu* is for [w]. T2 *douuue muke* (no. 98) is PIGEON DUNG (OE **dūfe*), admitting diverse readings: *ou+uu*, corresponding to [u:]+[w]; or *ouu+u*, corresponding to *ow+u*, [u:]+[v].

Word-final *w* after consonants (as in *talw* TALLOW, *yorw* THROUGH, *yelw* YELLOW) may be for ME [uw], or for doubled [u] corresponding to ME [u:] < [ux] or [uw]. Though not in this manuscript, Middle English vowel length is commonly indicated by doubling, as *ee*, *oo*; less used are *ii* (usually written with *i*-longa, as *ij*) and *aa*. Visually these are transparent, but the four minims of doubled *u* would often impede word-recognition. That is no doubt why *uu* for [u:] is rarely found; T1, even so, has one example, *suur* SOUR (no. 540), beside *sour(e)* twice.

9) Etymologically long vowels, in the French as well as the English receipts, in closed syllables are commonly marked with diacritic *i* or *y*, as in *ceil* SALT, *feith* MADE, *hoil*, *hoyl* WHOLE, *goyt* GOAT, *seid* SEED. A similar convention is well-known from Middle Scots and northern Middle English, though in the latter it is not widespread until the later fifteenth century;[55] it is also prominent in Lincolnshire, where it may be of partly independent origin. In the native vocabulary of the compendia, most examples are *ei* and *oi*, which are common; *ai* is rare.[56] Diacritic *y* is confined almost wholly to *oy*, which is frequent;[57] *ey* and *ay* are nearly always for a historical diphthong;[58] *ui*, *uy* are not found

[54] Note that *vv* rather than *w* persists as 15th-century (and even late 15th-century) usage. It is not uplandish: it is characteristic, for example, in the official writings of William Toly, clerk to Henry V's Signet, and of Henry Benet, Privy Seal clerk and clerk to the Council during the 1440s.

[55] So Luick §434, 'Beseitigung der *i*-Diphthonge im äußersten Norden'; cf. Laing 1978, I.147; Benskin 1988, p. 16, *Atlas* I.465, maps 637–8.

[56] In T1: *sair* SORE sb./adj. ×2, *haik* ACHE v. ×1. In T2: *sair* sb. ×1, *hais* HAS ×1. Cf. *Atlas* I.465, map 637. In so far as OE [a:] had generally become [ɔ:] in this dialect, *ai* corresponding to a monophthong is hardly to be found in closed syllables of the native vocabulary. Except for analogical re-formations, [a:] was not re-established there until the loss of final [ə].

[57] E.g., *cloyt(h)* CLOTH T1 ×15, T2 ×16; *hoyt(-)* HOT T1 ×13, T2 ×1.

(for ME [u:], *ou* is written). Usage here is hence at odds with the northern pattern, where *ai* for [a:] > [ɛ:] is the earliest and most widely attested spelling, and *ui* (in French loan words) is also established. Diacritic *i, y* in the compendia appears therefore to be of independent origin, perhaps to be linked with the sporadic southerly *ei, ey* for ME [e:];[59] occasional southerly *oi, oy* for ME [o:] is also found.[60]

Luick (§427) describes English monophthongisations of [-i] (and [-u]) diphthongs as taking place over much of England (though excluding part of the North-West Midlands and the North), towards the end of the thirteenth century. The evidence is said to be found generally only in Norse and French loan words, but Luick's many examples are almost exclusively French. The three Norse words cited are poorly attested in the dictionaries, none with a monophthong until nearly 1400, and of these only two involve [-i].[61]

It is accordingly remarkable that Pope (§1125) should cite Luick's account as authority for the levelling (monophthongisation) of [-i] diphthongs *in English*, this allegedly among 'the English sound-changes which affected Anglo-Norman most strongly' (§1118). Affected were Anglo-Norman [ai, ei, ui, üi] before [tʃ, ntʃ, ʃ] and [s] + consonant, but of these neither [ui] nor [üi] even belonged to native vocabulary. Moreover, as Luick recognised (§427, Anm. 4) the widespread development of [aʃ, eʃ] in native words to [aiʃ, eiʃ], that is, precisely to [-i] diphthongs, goes right against the monophthongisations seen in the French loanwords.[62] On present showing,

[58] T1 has *ayny* ANY ×1, *feyr* FIRE ×1; T2 has *bayt* imper. BATHE ×1. In words of French origin, notably PLASTER, *ay* is frequent; occasional *plastre* implies that the original diphthong had indeed given way to a monophthong, or was at least in process of doing so.

[59] *Atlas* IV.317c, with four attestations for Norfolk, the nearest (schematically) some 20 miles away towards the Suffolk border. The collection is limited to the southern half of the survey.

[60] *Atlas* IV.318c.

[61] Namely *cōpen* v. DEAL, *bask* adj. BITTER, and *gasp* v. GASP. For *coupen* v. > *cōpen*, contamination with *cōpen* from Low German is likely: *OED* (s.v. *coup* v.3) reports that the senses of the Norse-derived word run parallel to those of the Low German 'so that it [sc. *coup*] is often treated merely as a northern dialect form of this word'. For *coup(en)*, neither *OED* nor *MED* shows forms with simple *o*.

[62] 'Dieser Lautwandel ist der Entfaltung eines *i* in der Lautfolge *aš, eš* in Wörtern wie *aische, fleish* (§404) gerade entgegengesetzt' – for which he had no remedy beyond suggesting that differing geographies or time spans might explain them. The native vocabulary of the compendia shows a few instances of such diphthongs: *aysche* (T2 ×1), *fleys* (T1 ×1), *freis* FRESH (T1 ×3, T2 ×1), *neisse* SOFT (T2 ×3), *neysse* (T1 ×1). With simple vowels are *fres* (T2 ×1), *nesseist* SOFTEST (T2 ×1), *nesch* (T2 ×1).

therefore, the Anglo-French levellings are better regarded as internal to Anglo-French, without appeal to English origins at all.[63] And if that is right, the digraphs in the native vocabulary of the compendia are extended from the French, a further step towards a common vernacular orthography.

10) Lengthening in open syllables. Where final *-e* is still written, lengthened [a, ɛ, ɔ] need not be spelled differently from the corresponding short vowels. T2 has occasional *ee* in EAT, but this may be levelled from the preterite, rather than [ɛ] lengthened: inf. *eete* (×1), *eeten* (×1); ipv.sg. *eet* (×2).[64] Otherwise, save in *eeres* EARS (T1 ×1), *ee* is confined to closed syllables, and even there is little used;[65] *oo* is found once only, in *soor* sb. SORE (T2); *aa* is absent. Diacritic *i*, the Corpus scribe's usual marker of vowel length, indicates lengthening in T1 *haik* ache v., *s(h)aif* SHAVE, *smail* SMALL (×2), cf. T2 *bayt* ipv. BATHE.

Lengthenings of [ɪ] and [ʊ], which merge with ME [e:] and [o:] respectively, are seldom attested outside Northern England and East Anglia. For these lengthenings orthography is a less inadequate guide, though the lexical incidence, as generally in Middle English, is very uneven.[66] Lengthening of [ʊ] is indicated by *woke* WEEK (T2 ×1); and perhaps by *comen* inf. COME (T1 ×1, T2 ×1), 3sg.pres.indic. *comet* (T1 ×2, T2 ×1), 3sg.pres.subj. *come* (T1 ×3), though forms with *u* are more frequent.[67] For [ɪ] the evidence is more extensive. In MUCH, lengthening is indicated in only one of ninety-seven

[63] This is the line taken by Jordan, §§233–40, under 'Bis 1400: das romanische Element'. That this is the origin of diacritic *i* in Middle Scots was established by Kohler 1967 (see esp. pp. 52–61), which disposes once and for all of the idea that M. Scots *ai* depended on a monophthongisation of [ai] and its convergence with the reflex of Early Scots [a:]. (I am indebted to Mr Derek Britton for drawing attention to this paper.)

[64] Cf. *OED*, s.v. *eat* v. In the compendia, inf. *ete(n)* and *etun*, and ipv. *et*, are the usual forms.

[65] The remaining 37 instances are largely accounted for by *weel* WELL adv. (T1 ×10, T2 ×2) and *feet* FEET (T2 ×12).

[66] Lengthening in open syllables is probably to be understood not as the single, well-defined sound change of traditional accounts, but as one of several tendencies in a complex of quantity adjustments. Cf. Ritt 1997, who isolates (pp. 33–8) features which correlate significantly with lengthening or non-lengthening in the apparently eligible lexis; the material from the Corpus compendia fits unremarkably into these patterns. (It should be noted, however, that what Ritt regards as probabilities are mostly outcomes: the probablities co-aeval with the engendering of these outcomes are not themselves accessible. Astonishing, in the table on pp. 129–35, is the near-absence of *u*-words, and absence of *i*-words altogether.)

[67] In T1: inf. *cumun*, *cummen*, *cumen* (each ×1); 3sg.pres.indic. *cumet* ×4, *cumit* ×1, 3sg.pres.subj. *cume* ×2, *(be)cum* ×2. In T2: *cumen* inf. ×4, ppl.×1. It is commonplace that *o* replaces *u* before *m* and *n* for purely visual reasons, namely to avoid minim clusters, but

clearly disyllabic occurrences: *mekel* in T1, against regular *mychel*, *mykel*, et var. In GIVE, *gyue* 2sg. pres. subj. in T2 (×1) is the sole eligible form; LITTLE shows *i* and *y* only; WITEN ('know') inf. is *wete* ×2 in T2, beside *wite* ×2, *witen* ×1, and 3sg.pres.subj. *wite* ×1; T1 has only *wite* inf. ×3. EVIL regularly has *e*; though it is possible that this reflects [e] (lengthened or otherwise) from OE [y] (*yfel*), evidence for [y] > [e] in these texts is otherwise lacking.[68] Most occurrences (see above, p. 197) are substantive singulars, *euele* or *iuele*; the indefinite adjectival singulars in T1 *ani euele bloid* (no. 119) and T2 *quo* so is *iuele* (no. 54) show *-e* generalised in this word regardless of grammatical function. On the traditional view, lengthening failed if two or more unstressed syllables followed the open syllable,[69] and substantive plural *iueles* (T1 ×1), with [ɪ] not lengthened to [e:], is supposedly predictable as the trisyllabic form. But T1 shows *eueleȝ* as well (×1), and T2 shows only *e*-forms (*eueles* ×5, *heueles* ×1).

11) *d* for etymological *þ* appears mainly in the suffix of 3sg. pres. indic.; HAS accounts for most examples (*(h)ad*, *haued*, p. 197 above). In view of the restricted range of occurrence, a phonetic correspondence to [d], with origin in unstressed forms, is reasonably inferred; orthographic interchange, with *d* for [θ], is hardly at issue. Otherwise, *d* for *þ* appears in *ded* DEATH,[70] *erde* et var. EARTH,[71] and *ferde* FOURTH.[72] These are widely attested in north-easterly and East Anglian dialects of Middle English,[73] but though their distributions are of strikingly Scandinavian type, no good case for Norse derivation has been established.[74] In ME MONTH, *-d* is hitherto unrecorded: T2 has *mond*, *monnd* (×2), beside *monye* (×1) (the word is lacking in T1).

---

neither the script nor the distribution of *o* and *u* in this manuscript favours such an interpretation here.

68 Except before *r*, where *e* may be by way of *i*, not directly from *y*: T1 *feyr* (×2).

69 Cf. Luick §§393–4; contrast Ritt 1997, esp. pp. 95–105.

70 T1 ×4; *deþ* or *deth* are not found.

71 T1 *(h)erde* ×(1)3, *eirde* ×1, adj. *erdene* ×1; T2 *herþe* ×1, adj. *herdene* ×1.

72 T1 ×1, the only instance of FOURTH in these texts.

73 Cf. *Atlas* I, pp. 480 (maps 728–9), 481 (map 735), and 488 (map 780).

74 On *ded*, see *OED*, s.v. *death*; and Jordan §207, Anm. 3 (where appeal to East Norse [ð] > [d] 'vor 1350' may be some centuries too late to affect developments in the English settlements). On *erd(e)*, see *OED* s.v. *earth* sb. 1, which suggests confusion with *erd* sb. LAND (OE *eard*). Luick (§749, Anm. 1) explicitly denies Norse origins, regarding *erde* (§751) as the product of a native sound-change, 'Wandel von *rð* zu *rd*' (of which another such is *ferde* FOURTH, as in T1). The northern ME forms Luick connects with *rd* for *rð* in the modern dialects of the South-West, but from their distributions it is clear that any such ME 'Wandel' is independent, regardless of its origin.

Scandinavian elements

Some elements are of Scandinavian origin, including such widely-distributed loanwords as *call-* CALL (×9, vs *clep-* ×1), *cast* CAST(×27), and *ta(c)k* TAKE (*passim*), but the language in general is not heavily Scandinavianised. To *þei* THEY (ON *þeir*) corresponds native *hem* THEM; beside (ON) *-ande* in the pres. part. are native *-ende* and *-yng*; the one instance of THOUGH is *þey*, which is distinctively non-Norse; ON *at* as relative particle or infinitive marker is absent, as is *þer* THESE; ARE and IS are of native origin, *arn* and *is*, not ON *er(-)* and *es*; prepositional *til* TO is found only twice, beside regular *to*.

Conventionally regarded as of Norse origin, whether by lexical displacement or sound substitution, are *g* (instead of *y* or *ȝ*) corresponding to OE palatalised 'g', and *k* (instead of *ch*) corresponding to OE palatalised 'c': for example (and to cite forms only from the compendia) *agayn* against *ayein* or *aȝein* AGAIN, *gyf* against *yif* or *ȝif* GIVE; *ilk(-)* against *ich(-)* EACH, *mykel* against *mychel* MUCH.[75] In these texts, words of frequent occurrence may show one type to the exclusion or near-exclusion of the other: *wer(c)k* WORK (sb. and vb., ×50) but not *werch*; EGG(S) is *ay* (×17), *ey(ren)* or *eiren* et var. (×21), but *eg* once only, and then seemingly by mistake.[76] Such lexical variation is well documented in the dialects of the former Danelaw, but the Norse origins of all such *g* and *k* have been perhaps too readily assumed. Vernacular writings are lacking from most of Scandinavian England until well into the fourteenth century, and it is accordingly possible that in some districts ME *g* and *k* reflect what in any event would have been the native outcome – an outcome perhaps to be inferred from the seeming lack of palatal diphthongisation in some of the attested varieties of Old Mercian.[77] Moreover, the OE antecedents of ME [j] (*y*, *ȝ*) and [tʃ] (*ch*) were commonly liable to displacement by paradigmatic levelling, from inflexional forms in which palatalisation was impeded by an adjacent back vowel or another consonant: so, for example, *ilca(n)* beside *ilce* (THE) SAME, *micl-* beside *micel(-)* whence

[75] Cf. Jordan §§177–80.

[76] In T2 no. 53, *ete yer wit an eg a .eye*. The text is well-formed with either *an eg* or *a eye*, but not with both.

[77] Cf. Luick §173. Note, however, that although such diphthongisation presupposes palatal consonants, it is not a necessary consequence of their existence. Note also that palatalisation of [k] does not entail an affricate, whether [tʃ] or some other; these phonetic categories are often confused. Writers on Old English generally assume that if palatalised, OE [k] became an affricate as a matter of course, but though that appears to be the history, it is not an inevitable outcome. Conversely, it is not necessary for a consonant to be palatalised before it can become a continuant or an affricate.

MUCH, *geat* sg. beside *gatu* pl. GATE(S).[78] It is entirely possible that ME *k* and *g* were sometimes over-determined, the result of native analogy and Norse sound-substitution alike.

Phonological reflexes[79]

WGmc [a]+nasal, not in lengthening groups: *a* only, T1 and T2.
-ank: *a* only, in SHANK (T1 ×1, T2 ×4).

WGmc [a] in lengthening groups:
-amb: *o* only, in WOMB (T1 ×7, T2 ×10).
-and: In T1: HAND *a* ×12, *o* ×1; STAND, *a* ×2, with *o* in *on*n ×1. In T2: HAND *a* ×6; STAND *a* ×4, *o* ×2, with *o* in *on*n ×1.[80]
-ang: In T1: LONG *o* ×2, with *o* in *on*n ×2; STRONG *oy* ×2; WRONG *oi* ×1. In T2: HANG *a* ×1; LONG *o* ×3; STRONG *a* ×1, *aun* or *ann* ×2.[81] In T8: *o* in LONG ×2.
-ald: In T1 *o* only: COLD ×17; FOLD ×3; HOLD ×4; OLD ×6. In T2: *o* COLD ×14; TWOFOLD *a* ×1; HOLD *o* ×2, beside *a* ×3;[82] OLD ×7, beside *e* ×6.[83] In T3 and T8, COLD *o* ×1.

In STAND and LONG, probably *onn* not *oun* is to be read; the [u:] implied by *oun* is somewhat implausible. Such spellings, however interpreted, look to have been idiosyncratic: *Atlas* barely records them (IV.206b–c, 300a–301b, 321a). OE lengthening before [ŋg] is indicated orthographically by *oi*, *oy* in T1 STRONG, WRONG; before [nd] in T2 *einde, eynde* END (×1); before [rd], in T1 *eirde* EARTH (×1).

OE [a:] (not shortened and not before [w]): spellings indicating a vowel other than [ɔ:] are rare. *o* (T1 ×65, T2 ×54, T3 ×3, T8 ×1), *oi* (T1 ×40, T2 ×19), *oy* (T1 ×31, T2 ×18, T3 ×2). Implying [a:] are: T1 *haled* HEALED ppl.

[78] Early palatalisation of [g] is only marginally at issue, because OE [g] was at first confined to the combination *ng* [ŋg]; otherwise, early OE 'g' had sound-values [j] and [ɣ], continuants not plosives. In later Old or early Middle English, however, [ɣ] was variously replaced by [g], whence a paradigmatic alternation of [j] and [g] could arise.

[79] The categories here treated are only a select taxonomic list.

[80] The *onn* forms are written *stoñd-*, hardly to be read as *oun*.

[81] *au* may correspond to [ɔ:] as in Anglo-French (cf. Pope §1152), or to [a:] (cf. Luick §414.2); but the correct reading may be *ann*, with *nn* indicating a preceding short vowel.

[82] In no. 26 (×2) and no. 38. No. 26 is further anomalous in having *mare* MORE(×1) and *iuele* EVIL (×1), and may be a textual erratic.

[83] For *eld(-)* see *Atlas* I.500 (map 851), I.544 (map 1141). For other -ALD, I.513–4 (maps 930–32), I.543 (maps 1132–3).

×1, *hat* HOT (×1) *sair* SORE ×2; T2 *brade* BROAD ×1, *hat* HOT ×2, *mare* MORE ×1, *maste* MOST ×1, *sape* SOAP ×1. *yar(-)* THERE (×6) may or may not have *a* from ON [a:]. Unusual is *oe*, found in *boer* BOAR (T2 ×1), *hoes* HOARSE (T2 ×3), *soer* SORE (T1 ×4, T3 ×1).[84] *Atlas* (IV.86a) records *oe* for OE [a:] in only six sources. Three are from Lincolnshire (but only one as far south as The Wash); the others are from Rutland, Shropshire, and the West Riding of Yorkshire.

The reflexes of OE [eo(:)] and [y(:)], whether long or short, are unrounded (respectively, *e* and *i, y*).

In breach are T1 *fuyr* FIRE (×1) and *foyr* (×2, the reading clearly *o* not *e*). In this dialect, *fuyr* is unlikely to show retained OE [y:], but rather to show secondary rounding of [i:] before [r]; the form is rare in Eastern England, though attested in N. Norfolk and S. Lincolnshire.[85] *Atlas* records neither *oy* nor *oi* in FIRE; *MED* lists *foir* among its headforms (s.v. *fir* n.), but without (?) citation. Such forms at this date look to depend on co-variant [ɔi] and [ui] in French loanwords;[86] the spelling hardly guarantees [fɔir]. In *feyr* (T1 ×1), *y* is possibly diacritic, implying [e:] rather than a diphthong, though it is found in other Norfolk texts where *y, i* are not so used.

Note also *herte* ppl. HURT (T1 ×1), possibly reflecting late OE *y* from OFr.[87]

OE *ht*: *th* (T1 ×20, T2 ×13), *tth* (T1 ×3, T2 ×1), *tt* (T2 ×2), *t* (T2 ×1).

OE *hw*: *qu* (T1 ×40, T2 ×58), *ꝗu* (T1 ×20, T2 ×35), *w* (T1 ×2, T2 ×34), *qw* (T1 ×1, T3 ×1, T8 ×5). The lexical incidence of *w* is remarkably skewed: 33 of 34 occurrences in T2 are in WHO, all line-initial in the table of contents. In T2 this word also shows *qu* ×23 and *ꝗu* ×16; T1 has only two occurrences, both *quo*. On *squ* etc. for OE *sw*, see p. 209 above.

Morphology

Inflexional final e

i) In adjectives with monosyllabic base

As a grammatical marker, final *e* is preserved nearly always in the definite

[84] In SORE beside *o* (T1 ×11, T3 ×2), *oi* (T1 ×6), *oy* (T1 ×1) and *ai* (T1 ×2). Otherwise, in native words *oe* is found only in *toed* TOOTH (T2 ×1), beside *toit(h), toyt(h)*.

[85] *Atlas* I.407 (map 412), LPs 62 (Lincs.) and 4571 (Norf.).

[86] Cf. Pope §1161; Dobson 1968, §252–62.

[87] Cf. *OED*, s.v. *hurt* v.; *MED*, s.v. *hurten* v.

forms of such adjectives, that is, where it corresponds to OE weak inflexion: so (def. sg.) *ye rede nettle*, *ye yridde del*, (def. pl.) *ye rede lentiles*, but (indef. sg.) *a red docke*. In breach is *ye cold festre* (×1), beside *ye colde festre* (×1); so also is *quite flour* (×1), beside other indef. sg. *quit*.

In the indefinite plural (OE strong inflexion), *-e* is again nearly always preserved: *quike coles*, *smale cakes*, *brode holes*. In breach are *gret erde wirm*us (×1), beside *grete wirmes* (×1), and *re(i)d wrtes* (×2) beside *wrtes red*e (×1).[88]

In plural predicate adjectives, though there are few examples, inflexional *-e* is mostly preserved: *ye arn wete*, *sores yat wil nowit ben hole*, *yis ben gode*, *heres waxen weyke*, *eyne waxun holle*. The system is breached twice, in *seit hem al hoil and stamp hem wel smail*. In singular predicate adjectives, there is breach of system only in *he schal bein hole*.[89]

ii) Adjectives disyllabic in virtue of etymological *-e*, retain *-e* throughout, whether they are attributive (*a newe pot*, *a clene cloit*, *wilde fyr*, *grene rue*) or predicate (*lat it be ... yicke*, *it is wel grene*).

iii) Adjectives disyllabic not in virtue of etymological *-e*
In some of these, the suffix has become invariable: LITTLE never shows *-e* (*ye lytel dayez eye*, *mani litel cakes*), whereas EVIL (mostly nominal) always has *-ele*. OTHER is variable (*alle oyer sores*, *ye oyer(e) erbes*), but in the plural mostly lacks *-e*;[90] for MUCH, the evidence of *mychel* et var. is meagre, for they are indef. sg. in all but two occurrences, both of which lack *-e* (*ye mychel*, *ye mychil*). Likewise invariable is the pl. *yin* 'thine' before nouns beginning with a vowel or *h*: though most cases qualify the historically neuter nouns EARS or EYES, and so preclude original inflexion, occurrences with (fem.) HANDS and (masc.) ARMS show the form to be fixed.

iv) In nouns, inflexional *-e* is lost entirely, save in occasional compositional datives (e.g., *quete flour*)

[88] In *for reid eyne* (×1), the absence of *-e* may be historical: the noun here is neuter, so OE inflexional *-u* would not attach to the heavy syllable of acc.pl. *rēad* RED, whence ME -Ø not *-e*. Although OE *for* governs the dative (so pl. *-um* or late *-an*, whence ME *-e*), the prepositional case-forms in early Middle English reflect the accusative not the dative, and the rection may have shifted. RED is the commonest definite adjective in the compendia, in which function it always has *-e* (14 exx), whether singular or plural.

[89] The usage is thus very similar to that of *Havelok*, in which marking of the inherited difference between definite and indefinite is 'astonishingly consistent' (Smithers 1987, p. lxxx; but for a full account, see Smithers 1983).

[90] Note that in *ye oyere* + sb. pl. *-e* is historically from the strong (indefinite) declension: OE *ōþer* lacks weak inflexion.

Verbal concord in the 2sg. present indicative

Sporadically, *ye* appears as the subject case of the 2sg. pronoun, apparently THEE in place of nominative THOU: *quan ye gost to bedde, ye salt warisse, quan ye ȝeskes, als ye wldes eten it*, etc. In no case is interpretation as plural YE possible: dialects having *-s* in the plural present indicative replace it with *-e* or *-Ø* when the subject is a personal pronoun next to the verb (so, e.g., *ye ȝesk(e)*, not ***ye ȝeskes*).[91] For THEE as subject case, *OED* has citations from Scots texts of ca. 1375 and ca. 1470, but nothing from English until the 1590s (s.v. *thee* pers. pron., 3). The handbooks record no ME examples, and neither does *Atlas*; the relevant part of *MED* is not yet available. There are ME examples, even so, as in a letter of John Olney, mercer, 'In London', undated but of the mid-fifteenth century.[92] That *ye* represents [ðe:] for THEE, however, is not altogether certain: in the modern dialects, [ðə] is the unstressed form corresponding to THOU,[93] and conceivably that is the basis of nom. sg. *ye* in the compendia.

Cliticised pronoun objects

Cliticised IT is frequent (T1 ×31, T2 ×30, T3 ×2), mostly *-et* or *-it*, rarely *-yt*, *-ith*. Cliticised THEM is found seldom (T1 *-(h)em* ×2, T2 *-em* ×1). All are with imperatives. Such usage is not well-recorded for Middle English, though text-types rather than the state of the language are probably at issue. Such forms are relatively common in medical receipts, because receipts are continually requiring that something be selected and something then done to (pronominal) it: imperative plus direct object is probably the most common verbal construction by far. Other writings in Middle English give much less scope for cliticised object pronouns to appear, but it is they and not the medical manuscripts that have commanded philological attention. The usage may also be regionally variable: Jordan's examples (§155) are mostly from Norfolk (including *The Bestiary* and *Genesis and Exodus*) and South Lincolnshire (*The Ormulum*, ca. 1170 A.D.).[94]

[91] *EDG* §435, McIntosh 1983.

[92] Northamptonshire Record Office, Furtho VII.8, unpublished: four instances, with no use of THOU. Olney is a town mid-way between Bedford and Northampton. For early Middle English, Dr Laing reports eleven sources, scattered geographically and none containing more than two examples. The nearest to the area of the Corpus dialect are probably from N. Central Essex: Bodleian Library Add E.6, Hand A (*Sayings of St Bernard*); British Library, MS Stowe 34, Hand B (*Vices and Virtues*).

[93] *EDG* §404(b).

[94] Of the material so far analysed by Dr Laing, only *Genesis and Exodus* shows cliticised

Nouns: genitive singular and plural inflexion

Genitive singular. T1: -*us* ×14, -us ×5, -use ×1, -is ×8, -es ×5, -ez ×3. T2 -es ×12, -*us* ×9, -us ×7, -is ×5. T3 -us ×1.

Plural. T1: -es ×134, -ez ×30, -us ×25, -*us* ×16, -is 5, -*es* ×2, -ys ×1. T2: -es ×199 -*us* ×11, -us ×7, -is ×5, -ez ×4, -*es* ×3, -en ×3. T3 -es ×1. T8 -es ×9, -*us* ×1.

(i) The -*en* plural is etymological in T2 *axsen* 'ashes' (×1). In EGGS it is not, but ME *eiren* et var. widely displace the historically regular *eire* (OE *ǣgru*): T1 *eyren*, *eyr*en, *eirun*; T2 *eiren*, *eyren*; T3 *heyren* (each once).

(ii) In the dialects of the East Midlands and East Anglia, -*us* is characteristic for neither of these categories, but it is established as a by-form in various texts belonging to West Norfolk.[95] It is notable that the spelling appears unhistorically in the French texts of the compendia as well, perhaps reflecting a convergence of spoken French on the local English. Romance philologists have paid little attention to what may be regional differences within Anglo-French, notwithstanding Prior 1923. Unnoticed altogether, it seems, is Bolland 1914, who observed *u* as the unaccented vowel in the French of the bills in eyre for Shropshire and Staffordshire, 1292–1333, and thought it 'just possible that the native local dialect of these draftsmen had some influence on their French';[96] in the West Midlands, *u* predominates as the vowel of unaccented syllables.

Pres. participle T1 -ande ×6, -a*n*de ×2, -ende ×2, -inge ×3, -y*n*gge ×1, -y*n*ge ×1, -yng ×1, -ing ×1. T2 -ande ×6, -a*n*d ×3, -ende ×2, -yng ×3. T8 -ande ×1, -a*n*de ×1.

Verbal sb. T1 -yng ×19, -y*n*g ×5, -ynge ×8, -i*n*gge ×5, -yngge ×1, -y*n*gge ×1, -inge ×3, -i*n*ge ×3, -y*n*ge ×1, -ing ×2, -i*n*g ×1. T2 -yng ×16, -ynge ×13, -i*n*ge ×3, -i*n*gge ×3, -yngge ×2, -i*n*g ×3. T8 -yngge ×1.

3sg. pres. indic. T1 -et ×11, -it ×5, -es ×1, -*us* ×1, -eȝ ×1 -yt ×1, -ed ×1; *vowel*+ -d ×6, -t ×2. T2 -es ×30, -et ×7, -ed ×3, -it ×1, -eȝ ×1, -is ×1; *v*+ -d ×14, -s ×5, -t ×1. T8 -et ×4, -it ×1, -ut ×1, -ud ×1; *v*+ -d ×15.

---

pronouns as sustained usage (24 exx in lines 1–2108, which is just over half the text); *The Bestiary* (ed. Wirtjes 1991) yields only two examples. Regionally, sporadic occurrences are widely scattered, but among eastern sources note further Merton College MS 248 (N.W. Lincolnshire, 5 exx; ed. Laing 1997) and London, Dulwich College MS XXII (*La Estorie del Euangelie*, probably from S. Lincolnshire, in the Spalding area, 1 ex; ed. Millward 1998, and see McIntosh 1987).

[95] Cf. also the distributions of -*un* in the pres. indic. pl. and strong ppl., and -*ud* in the weak pret. and ppl.

[96] Bolland 1914, p. xxxiii.

Pl. pres. indic. T1 -un ×2, -en ×1; *vowel*+ -n ×3. T2 -en ×5, -u*n* ×1, ?-es ×1; *v*+ -n ×4. T8 -un ×1, -u*n* ×1.

Wk. ppl. (syllabic forms only) T1 -ed ×20, -ud ×3, -id ×1. T2 -ed ×18, -ud ×2, -et ×1. T3 -ed ×1. T8 -ed ×3.

Str. ppl. (syllabic forms only) T1 -en ×20, -un ×3, -e*n* ×2, -in ×1. T2 -en ×29, -e*n* ×5, -un ×1. T8 -en ×1, -e*n* ×1.

i- ppl. The only trace of the OE *ge*- prefix in the ppl., is in *ifulled* BAPTIZED, relict in the 'Flum Jordan' charm (T1 no. 250).

Vocabulary

It may be regretted that the present account does not extend to a study of the vocabulary, but such a work would have enlarged and delayed the edition far beyond the original plan. By the standards of other medical writings in Middle English, the vocabulary of the Corpus compendia seems not unusual, but these compendia are the earliest of their kind, and by a good two generations or more; it would be surprising if they did not provide antedatings for at least some terms of art and botanical terminology, as these are at present recorded in the dictionaries. It is doubtful, even so, whether a lexical study could be sensibly confined to the one manuscript, and to be of any value, it would have to attend to Latin and French as well as to English. It has therefore seemed better to lay the foundations for such a study, by establishing a text, its probable local origins, and something of its textual history, and to leave the study itself to be undertaken by others.

APPENDIX

Linguistic profiles

Separate profiles are presented for T1, T2, T3, and T8; from the foregoing account, it will be seen that relative frequencies cannot be well be combined. As in *Atlas*, these are indicated by parentheses: a single set encloses secondary variants; a double set encloses minor variants; occasionally a triple set is invoked. [ ] enclose variables: e.g., '-ing[e]' stands for both '-ing' and '-inge', 'hau[ed,es]' stands for both 'haued' and 'haues' (but not 'hau'). Abbreviations are as in *Atlas*. The profiles include all the vocabulary of the *Atlas* survey questionnaire; additional items are from the Appendix of Southern Forms (*Atlas* IV.313–25), or are specially discussed in the foregoing analysis of the texts.

T1

THE	ye ((y^e, ya*n*)
THESE	yese (yes, yis)
SHE	se
HER	hire, hir*e*
IT	it (((et))). *Enclitic:* -it, -et ((-yt))
THEY	yei (ye, he)
THEM	hem ((he*m*)). *Enclitic*: -em, -hem
WHICH	quich
EACH	ilk, ilk-a (iche, ilck, ilke, ilkon, eu*er*i, eu*er*ilk, eu*er*ich, eu*er*ic, eueri, euerich, eueryl, ic, ilck-an, ilk-on, ilk*e*)
MANY	mani, manie
MAN	man ((ma*n*)); *gen. sg.* ma*n*nus, mann*us*, ma*n*nes, mannes
ANY	ani, any, ayny
MUCH	mychel (michel, mykel) ((mychil, micul, myc*el*))
ARE	arn, ben ((be*n*, ar))
WERE	*Subjunctive* were
IS	is
WAS	was
SHALL	*1/3sg.* schal (((scal, sal, shal)) *2sg.* salt ((schal)) *pl.* schul
WILL	*1/3sg.* wile, wil *2sg.* wilt, wylt *pl.* wil
TO *prep.*	tyl +h *once only; otherwise* to
TO + *inf.*	to *only*
FROM	+*c* fro; +*v* fro
AFTER	affter, afft*er*, after
THEN	yanne, yan ((ya*n*ne, ya*n*, yan*n*e, yane, yann*e*))
THAN	ya*n*
IF	ȝif, zif, yif, if
AS	al-so, als, as (os)
AS+AS	al-so+[as,os] (als+[os,as], als-so+as, as+as, o+[so,os]
AGAINST	agayn, aȝein
AGAIN	a-yen, ayein, aȝein
ERE	*conj.* or, er
SINCE	*adv.* sitthen (siyen) ((siye, sith, sithe, sithen, sitth*en*, sitthe, sitthe*n*))
WHILE	*conj.* quile, quil, q*ui*l, wil
OE *hw-*	qu- (q*u*-)((w-, qw))
NOT	nowit ((ne + nowit, ne + nouit, ne))
OE *ā*	o (oi, oy) ((oe, ai, a))
WORK	*vb.* werk- ((werck))
THERE	yer, y*er* (yer) ((yere)); *cpd.* yer-, y*er*- ((ye-r+*v*))
WHERE	quer, yer, y*er*; *cpd.* quer-
THROUGH	yorw ((yoru, ȝorw, yourth)
WHEN	q*u*an ((quan, q*u*anne, quanne, wan, yan))
Noun pl.	-es ((-ez, -us, -*us*))(((-is, -*es*, -ys, -e*n*, -un)))
Pres. part.	-ande (-ing[e], -a*n*de, -ende, -y*n*gge, -y*n*ge, -yng, -ing)
Verbal sb.	-yng (-ynge, -i*n*gge, -y*n*g[e], -yngge, -y*n*gge, -ing[e], -i*n*g[e])
3sg.pres.ind.	*3sg.* -et (-it) ((-es, -ez, -yt, -ed, -*us*)); *post-vocalic* -d (-t)
Pl.pres.ind.	-un, -en; *postvocalic* -n
Wk. ppl.	-ed ((-ud, -id))
Str. ppl.	-en ((-un, -e*n*, -in))
y- *ppl.*	Ø-
ABOUT	*adv.* buten *prep.* a[-]boute, a-buten
ABOVE	*adv.* aboue*n*, abouen *prep.* abouen
ADDER	edere
AFTERWARDS	after, aft*er*ward, eft
ALL	al, alle
AND	and ((7)) (((an, a*n*d, a')))
AWAY	away (a-way, awai, awey)
BEEN	ben
BEFORE	*adv. place* be-fore *adv. time* afor-, be-for
BEHOVES	be-houed
BENEATH	*prep..* be-neye
BETWEEN	*prep..* be-twiyene
BOTH	boye, both
BURN	*pres. stem* bren (brenn-,

	bre*nn*-, bren-, bre*n*-)
	ppl. brent (bren)
BUT	but
BY	be, by
CALL	*ppl.* cald
CAST	cast, cast-
DAY	day; *cpd.* day-
DAYS	dayes ((dayez))
DEATH	ded
DIE	*pres. stem* deye (dei-)
DO	*2sg. pres.* dest; *cpd.* -dost
DOWN	doun (adoun)
EARTH	erde, herde, eirde, erye; *adj.* erdene
EGG	ay (ey) ((hey, hye)); *pl.* eirun, eyren, eyre*n*
EITHER	*pron.* eiyer
EITHER+OR	eiyer + or
ENOUGH	inow
EVIL	euele, iuele (euel^{e}, evele); *nom. pl.* euelez, iueles
EYE	*sg.* eye ((heye, eye, eie))
	pl. eyne (eyen, eynne)
FIRE	feyr, fyr, fyre, fier, fuyr, foyr
FIRST	*adv.* first, fyrst
	pron. ye firste
FIVE	fiue, fyue; *cpd.* fiue-, fyue-
FLESH	flex (fleys)
FOUR	four[e]
FRESH	freis
GET	gete *2sg. pres.*
GIVE	*imper. sg.* yif, ȝif (zif, gyf) ((gef, geif, gif));
	subj. 3sg. ȝif
GOES	gos; *2sg.* gost
GOOD	god ((goid, gode))
GROW	grow-, g*ru*-
HAVE	*inf.* hauen
	pres. indic. 2sg. hauest; *3sg.* ad, had, hat
	pres. subj. sg. haue, have
	pret. 2sg. haddes
HEAD	heued ((heueid, heuid, heu*e*d, hed))
HEAR	*inf.* heren
HEAVEN	heuene
HIM	him ((hi*m*, hym))
HOLD	hold[-]
HOLY	holy
IN	in (((i*n*, inne)))
KNOW	knowe (know-, know-)
LET	lat ((late, let))
LIE	li-, ly-, ligg-
LIFE	lyue, lyf
LITTLE	litel (lytel, lytil, litul)
LIVE	leu-, lyue
LONG	longe, lonnge [?lounge]
MAKE	*inf.* maken, make
	imper. sg. mack ((mac))
	pres. pl. maken
	pt. sg. made
	ppl. mad, maked
MAY	*2sg.* mayt, mast, mait;
	3sg. may ((mowe))
	pl. moun
NAVEL	nouele
NEW	newe
NIGH	neyt
OLD	hold
ONE	*adj.* +h on
	pron. on; *def.* yat on, ye ton
OR	or ((oy*e*r, oyer))
OTHER	oyer, oy*er* ((oy*ere*))
	indef. anoyer, an-oyer, a-noyer
	def. yat oyer, ye oyer, y^{t} oy*er*, ye oy*er*, thoyer
OUT	houit, owit (howit) ((ouit, hout))
OWN	owen
RUN	re*nn*e, renn-
THE SAME	ye same, yat sam*e*, yat iche, ye self, ye selue, yat selue
SAY	*ipv. sg.* sey
	ppl. sayd, seyde; *cpd.* -sayd
SEE	se
SELF	self, selue (-sel*e*); *pl.* seluen
SILVER	-silu*er*
SLAIN	slayen
SOME	sum[-], su*m*[-]
STAND	stande, sto*nn*d-; *3sg.* standit
STEAD	stede
TAKE	*imper. sg.* tac, tack

	ppl. taken
THEE	ye
THOU	you ((yow, ye))
THY	+*c* yi ((yi*n*)); +h yin ((yi)); +*v* yin ((zin))
THREE	yre ((thre))
TOGETHER	to-gedere ((to-ged*ere*, togeder[e,*e*], togeder, to-geder*e*, to-gider[e,*e*], to-gider*e*, to[-]gydere))
TWO	to (tweie)
UNTIL	til, tyl
UPON	up-on (upon, hup-on); *cpd.* -upon, ye rup on THEREUPON
WAY	*(in* WAYBREAD, *all)* wey- ((wei-))
WELL	wel ((weil, weel)) (((wol)))
WHAT	q*u*at
WHETHER	q*ueyer*, q*ue*yer, quy*er*, queyer
WHO	quo, quo-so
WITEN	*inf.* wite
WITH	wit ((wyt, w^{t})) (((with)))
WITHOUT	*adv.* wit-outen, w*i*touten, wit-owten
	prep. wit-outen (witoute)
YE	ye
-EL	-el (-ele) ((-ul, -il))
-ER	*(in native words)* -ere, -er (-*er*) ((-*ere*)) (((-er*e*, -*ur*[e])))
-EST	*(superl. only)* -este
-LY	*(adv.)* -ly, -liche (-li)
-NESS	-nesse

T2

THE	ye (((y^{e})))
THESE	yes (yese)
IT	it (((It, et))). *Enclitic* -et, -it ((-yt, -ith))
THEY	yei, yey, he
THEM	hem (he*m*). *Enclitic* -em, hem
WHICH	ye quilk
EACH	ilk-a (ilk, ilke-a, ich[-a], iche[-a], elk, euer[-]ilk, euerilke, eu*er*[-]ilk, euerich, eu*er*[i,y], eueri, euere
MANY	many, manye, mani
MAN	man ((ma*n*)); *gen. sg.* mann*us*, ma*nnus*, ma*n*nes
ANY	ani, hany
MUCH	mychel ((mych*el*, michel, mychil, mykel, mekel, myche))
ARE	arn (ben)
WERE	*subjunctive* ware, were, wer*e*
IS	is. *Enclitic* -es
WAS	was
SHALL	*1/3sg.* schal
	2sg. schalt, salt
	pl. schullen, schuln
WILL	*1/3sg.* wil, wile, wille
	2sg. wilt
	pl. wiln
WOULD	*2sg.* wldes
TO *prep.*	til +*v once; otherwise* to
TO + *inf.*	to *only*
FROM	+*c* fro
AFTER	after (affter)
THEN	yanne (yan) ((ya*n*ne)) (((ya*n*, yan*ne*, yann*e*)))
THAN	yan
THOUGH	yey
IF	if (ȝif) ((zif, yif, ?gyf))
AS	as (als) ((als-so, os))
AS+AS	als+[als-so,als,as,os,so], als-so+[as,os,so], al-so+as, as+[as,os,so], os+[os,as], so+as
AGAINST	agayn, ageynes
AGAIN	a[-]gayn, a-geyn
ERE *conj.*	or (or yat, or y^{t})
WHILE	q*ui*le
OE *hw*	qu- (q*u*-; w- *nearly all in* WHO, cf. p. 218 above)
NOT	nowit ((now^{i}t, -nowit, nowt, ne))
NOR	ne
OE *ā*	o (oi, oy) ((a, oe)) (((*a*, ay, oo))) *excluding* THERE
WORK	*sb.* werck (werk) ((werc))
	vb. werk-

THERE	yer (ye*r*)(((yar, yare, yere))); *cpd.* ye*r*- (yer-) ((yar-))
THROUGH	yorw
WHEN	q*u*an (quan) ((q*u*anne, qua*n*ne, qua*n*, quan*ne*, yan))
Noun pl.	-es ((*-us*, -us, -ez, -is, *-es*, -en))
Pres. part.	-ande (-a*n*d, -ende, -yng, -inge, -i*n*ge)
Verbal sb.	-yng[e] ((-i*n*gge, -yngge, -ing[e], -i*n*g[e], -i*nge*, -y*n*g[e]))
3sg pres. indic.	-es ((-et)) (((-ed, -it, -eȝ, -is))); *v*+ -d ((-s, -t))
Pl. pres. indic.	-en, -u*n*, -un, -e, -es *[?sg.]*; *v*+ -n
Wk. ppl.	-ed ((-ud, -et))
Str. ppl.	-en ((-e*n*, -un))
y- *ppl.*	Ø-
ABOUT	*adv.* abuten, abute*n*, abute *prep.* abuten, abute, abut*e*, bute
ABOVE	*adv.* abuuen, abouen, a-bouen *prep.* abou*n*
ADDER	neddere, nedere
AFTERWARDS	eft (afte*r*ward, after)
ALL	al, alle
AND	and ((7, a*n*d)) (((an, a'))) ((((a, ha*n*d))))
AWAY	away (a-way) ((awey, a-wei, a-wey))
BEFORE	*adv. time* afor-, be-for *conj.* byfor*n*
BENEATH	*adv.* beneyen
BETWEEN	*prep.* betweye
BOTH	boye
BURN	*pres. stem* bren ((brenn-, bren-, bre*n*n-)) *ppl.* brent (bre*n*t)
BUT	but
BY	be
CALL	*pres.* call- (clep-) *ppl.* called
CAST	*pres.* cast, caste, cast-
DAY	day *pl.* dayes
DIE	*pres.* deye ((dei-))
DOWN	doun ((do*n*))
EARTH	herye; *adj.* herdene
EITHER	*pron.* eyer, eiyer, eiy*er*
ENOUGH	anow
EVIL	euele ((heuele, iuele, euel*e*)); *sb. pl.* eueles (e*v*eles)
EYE	eye; *pl.* eyne ((eyn*e*))
FILL	fil
FIRE	fyr ((fyer))
FIRST	*adv.* first, fyrst
FIVE	fyue, five; *ord.* fyfte
FLESH	flex, flex-
FOUR	foure; *ord.* ferde
FRESH	fres, freis
FRIEND	freind
GIVE	*imper. sg.* gyf (gef) ((gif, yif, zif, ȝif))
GO	*2sg. pres. indic.* gost
GOOD	god ((gode, goid))
GROW	growe, grow-
HAVE	haue ((have)) *inf.* hauen, han *2sg. pres. indic.* hauest, haues, hast *3sg. pres. indic.* haues, h', had ((haued, ad, hat, aues, hais, has, as)) *pl. pres. indic.* han *1/3pt. sg.* adde; *2sg.* addis
HEAD	hed (heued) ((hef*e*d, heu*e*d, eued, h*e*d); *pl.* heuedes
HEAR	*pres.* here, her*e*
HIM	him ((hym, hi*m*)) (((hem)))
HOLD	*pres.* hald; *inf.* holden, -holde
HOLY	holy; *cpd.* alli-water
HOW	hou
HUNDRED	vnderd
IN	in ((i*n*)) (((inne)))
KNOW	*inf.* knowe
LESS	lesse
LET	*ipv. sg.* lat ((let))
LIE	*pres.* ly-; *inf.* lye, leyen

LITTLE	lytel ((lytil))
LIVE	leue, lyue, lyu-, leu-
MAKE	*inf.* maken (make, mak)
	imper. sg. mack ((mac, mak))
	pres. indic. pl. maken
	ppl. mad
MAY	*1/3sg.* may; *2sg.* may ((mayst, mayt, mayth))
	pl. may, mou, mouwe, mow
MONTH	mo*n*d, mon*n*d, monye
MOON	mone
NAVEL	nouele
NE+BE	ne was
NE+HAVE	ne had
NE+WITEN	ne wite
NEVER	neuere
NEW	newe
OLD	old, eld ((elde))
ONE	+h on
	pron. on; *def.* ye ton
OR	or (((oy*er*)))
OTHER	oy*er*, oyer
	indef. a-noyer (a-noy*er*, anoyer, anoy*er*)
	neg. non-oy*er*
OUT	out (((howit, houit, owit, owt)))
OWN	owen, ouen
RUN	*pres. stem* renn-
THE SAME	yat ilke, ye same, ye self
SAY	*inf.* seyne, seye
	ppl. sayd, seyde; *cpd.* -sayde
SEE	*inf.* sein, se
SELF	self
SEVEN	seue*n*
SLAIN	sclawen
SOME	sum, soum; *cpd.* su*m*-
STEAD	stede
SUN	sunne (sou*n*ne)
TAKE	*inf.* taken
	imper. sg. tack ((tac)) (((take, tach)))
	imper. pl. tacky*n* *once*
THEE	ye
THOU	you (((yow, ye)))
THY	+*c* yi; +h yin +*v* yin
THENCE	yein
THREE	yre; *ord.* yridde
TOGETHER	to-gedere (to-ged*ere*) ((toged*ere*))
TWELVE	twelue, twel, twelve
TWO	to ((tweye))
UNTIL	til (tyl)
UPON	upon, u-pon
WAY	wey; *in WAYBREAD* way-, wey-
WEEK	woke
WELL	wel (((weel)))
WHAT	quat, q*ua*t
WHETHER	quey[er, *er*], q*uey*[er, *er*]
WHO	quo-so, wo-so, wo-s*o*, q*uo*-so ((quo, q*uo*[-so], quo-, wos*o*))
WITEN	*inf.* witen, wite, wete; *3sg. pres. subj.* wite
WITH	wit ((w^{t})) (((wyt)))
WITHIN	wit-inne (wit[-]inne, w^{t}inne, wit-innen)
WITHOUT	*prep.* wit[-]outen, witoute[n], wit-oweten, wit-oyt
	adv. witouten
YE	ye, y^{e}
YEAR	yer
YOUNG	you*n*ge *[or* yon*n*ge?*]*
-EL	-el (-ele) ((-yl, -il, -yle, -ele, -ul))
-ER (*in native words*)	-er (-ere, -*er*) ((-*ere*)) (((-re, -ur, -*ure*, -er*e*)))
-EST (*superl. only*)	-este, iste
-LESS	-les
-LY	-ly, -li
-NESS	-nesse

T3: receipt on f. 49r.

THE	ye
IT	it. *Enclitic* -et, -it
MAN	ma*n*
TO *prep.*	+*c* to
AS + AS	as + as
OE *hw*	qw-. *Cf.* sqwet 'sweet'

OE *ā*	o, oy, oe
THERE	yer
Gen. sg.	-us
Noun pl.	-es
Wk. ppl.	-ed
y- *ppl.*	Ø-
ALL	al, alle
AND	and (a*n*d)
EGG	*pl.* heyren
FRESH	freys
HIM	hym
IN	in
MAKE	*imper. sg.* mack
MAY	*3sg.* may
ON	on
OR	or
TAKE	*imper. sg.* tack
TOGETHER	to-geder*e*
-ER (*in native words*)	-er*e*, *-er*

T8: treatise on urines, ff. 53vb–54ra

THE	ye
SHE	sche (he, se)
HER	hir*e*
MAN	man
MUCH	mychel
IS	is
TO *prep.*	+*c* to
AFTER	after*e*
THEN	yan
IF	ȝif, if
AS	as (os)
OE *hw*	qw-
NOT	nowit
OE *ā*	o
WORK	*sb.* werck, werk
Noun pl.	-es ((-*us*))
Pres. part.	-ande, -a*n*de
Vbl. noun	-yngge
3sg. pres. indic.	-et (-it, -ut, -ud); *v*+ -t (-d)
Pl. pres. indic.	-un, -u*n*
Wk. ppl.	-ed
Strong ppl.	-en, -e*n*
y- *ppl.*	Ø-
ABOVE	*adv.* abouen
ALL	al
AND	and
BOTH	boy
BUT	but
BY	be
CAST	*pres.* caste
DAY	day
DEATH	deid
EVIL	euele
FIRE	fiir
FLESH	fleyes
GOOD	god
HAS	hat ((had, ad))
HEAD	heued
IN	in ((i*n*))
KNOW	*inf.* know
LIE	*pres. indic. pl.* leyun
LIVE	*inf.* lyuen, liuen
MAY	*2sg.* mayst; *3sg.* may
OR	or
OTHER	*def.* yat oyer
SOME	su*m*
THOU	you
THIRD	yridde, ȝridde
SILVER	siluer
WITH	w[t] *postposed*
WITHIN	*prep.* w[t]inne
-EL	-ele (-el)
-ER (*in native words*)	*-er*, -er, -ere, -er*e*

Acknowledgments

I am grateful to Mr Derek Britton and Dr Margaret Laing, both of the University of Edinburgh, for their commments on an earlier version of this account. I am additionally indebted to Dr Laing for information on textual and dialectal distributions in early Middle English (see further Laing 1991 and 1993).

References

Arngart, O. (1968) ed. *The Middle English Genesis and Exodus.* Lund Studies in English 36 (Lund: C.W.K. Gleerup).

Atlas: *A Linguistic Atlas of Late Mediaeval English*, by A. McIntosh, M.L. Samuels & M. Benskin, with the assistance of M. Laing & K. Williamson (Aberdeen: Aberdeen University Press, 4 vols, 1986).

Benskin, M. (1982) 'The letters <þ> and <y> in later Middle English, and some related matters', *Journal of the Society of Archivists* 7, 13–30.

Benskin, M. (1988) 'Some perspectives on Cumbrian English, mainly mediaeval'. In *Essays on English Language in Honour of Bertil Sundby*, ed. L.E. Breivik, A. Hille & S. Johansson (Oslo: Novus), pp. 13–46.

Benskin, M. (1991)a 'The "fit"-technique explained'. In Riddy 1991, pp. 9–26.

Benskin, M. (1991)b 'In reply to Dr Burton', *Leeds Studies in English* n.s. 22, 209–62.

Benskin, M. (1994) 'Descriptions of dialect and areal distributions'. In Laing & Williamson 1994, pp. 169–87 (discussion pp. 189–94).

Benskin, M. (1997) 'Texts from an English township in late mediaeval Ireland', *Collegium Medievale* 10, 91–173.

Benskin, M., & M. Laing (1981) 'Translations and *Mischsprachen* in Middle English manuscripts'. In *So meny people longages and tonges. Philological essays in Scots and mediaeval English presented to Angus McIntosh*, ed. M. Benskin & M.L. Samuels (Edinburgh: the editors), pp. 55–106; an abbreviated version appears in *Atlas* I, pp. 12–22, 29–33.

Bolland, W.C. (1914) ed. *Select Bills in Eyre A.D. 1292–1333.* (London: Selden Society, vol. XXX).

Dobson, E.J. (1968) *English Pronunciation 1500–1700*, 2nd edn. (Oxford: Clarendon Press).

EDG = J. Wright, *The English Dialect Grammar* (1905. Repr. London: Oxford University Press, 1968.)

Gray, D., & E.G. Stanley (1983) ed. *Middle English Studies presented to Norman Davis* (Oxford: Clarendon Press).

Jordan = R. Jordan, *Handbuch der mittelenglischen Grammatik. Lautlehre.* 3rd edn. rev. H.Ch. Matthes & suppl. K. Dietz (Heidelberg: Carl Winter, 1968).

Keiser, G. (1998) *Works of Science and Information*, being vol 10 of *A Manual of the Writings in Middle English 1050–1500*, ed. A.E. Hartung (New Haven: Connecticut Academy of Arts and Sciences).

Kohler, K.J. (1967) 'Aspects of Middle Scots phonemics and graphemics: the phonological implications of the sign <i>', *Transactions of the Philological Society*, 32–61.

Kristensson, G. (1967) *A Survey of Middle English Dialects 1290–1350. The Six Northern Counties and Lincolnshire.* Lund Studies in English 35 (Lund: C.W.K. Gleerup).

Kristensson, G. (1995) *A Survey of Middle English Dialects 1290–1350. The East Midland Counties.* Skrifter utgivna av Vetenskapssocieteten i Lund 88 (Lund: Lund University Press).

Laing, M. (1978) *Studies in the Dialect Material of Mediaeval Lincolnshire* (unpubl. diss. Ph.D., University of Edinburgh).

Laing, M. (1991) 'Anchor texts and literary manuscripts in early Middle English'. In Riddy 1991, 27–52.

Laing, M. (1993) *Catalogue of Sources for a Linguistic Atlas of Early Medieval English* (Cambridge: D.S. Brewer).

Laing, M. (1997) 'A fourteenth-century sermon on the number seven in Merton College, Oxford, MS 248', *Neuphilologische Mitteilungen* 98, 99–134.

Laing, M. & K. Williamson (1994) *Speaking in Our Tongues: Proceedings of a Colloquium on Medieval Dialectology and Related Disciplines* (Cambridge: D.S. Brewer).

Luick = K. Luick, *Historische Grammatik der englischen Sprache* (1914–40. Repr. 1964: Oxford, Blackwell; Stuttgart, Tauchnitz).

McIntosh, A. (1963) 'A new approach to Middle English dialectology', *English Studies* 44, 1–11.

McIntosh, A. (1974) 'Towards an inventory of Middle English scribes', *Neuphilologische Mitteilungen* 75, 602–24.

McIntosh, A. (1975) 'Scribal profiles from Middle English texts', *Neuphilologische Mitteilungen* 76, 218–35.

McIntosh, A. (1976) 'The language of the extant versions of *Havelok the Dane*', *Medium Ævum* 45, 36–49.

McIntosh, A. (1983) 'Present indicative plural forms in the later Middle English of the North Midlands'. In Gray & Stanley 1983, 235–44.

McIntosh, A. (1987) 'The Middle English 'Estorie del Euangelie': the dialect of the original version', *Neuphilologische Mitteilungen* 88, 186–91.

McIntosh, A. & M. Wakelin (1982) 'John Mirk's *Festial* and Bodleian MS Hatton 96', *Neuphilologische Mitteilungen* 83, pp. 443–50.

MED = *Middle English Dictionary*, ed. H. Kurath et al. (Ann Arbor: University of Michigan Press, 1956–).

Millward, C. (1998) ed. *La Estorie del Evangelia – a parallel-text edition.* Middle English Texts 30 (Heidelberg: C. Winter).

Milroy, J. (1981) 'On the sociolinguistic history of h-dropping in English'. In M. Davenport, E. Hansen & H.F. Nielsen, ed. *Current Topics in English Historical Linguistics. Proceedings of the Second International Conference in English Historical Linguistics, held at Odense University, April 1981.* Odense University Studies in English 4 (Odense: Odense University Press), pp. 37–52.

OED = *The Oxford English Dictionary*, ed. J.A.H. Murray et al. (Oxford: Clarendon Press, corrected reissue 1933).

Pope = M.K. Pope (1934) *From Latin to Modern French, with especial consideration of Anglo-Norman* (Manchester: Manchester University Press).

Prior, O. (1923) 'Remarques sur l'anglo-normand' *Romania* 49, 177–85.

Riddy, F. (1991) *Regionalism in Late Medieval Manuscripts and Texts. Essays celebrating the publication of A Linguistic Atlas of Late Mediaeval English* (Cambridge: D.S. Brewer).

Ritt, N. (1997) *Quantitative Adjustments in Middle English* (Cambridge: Cambridge University Press).

Scragg, D. (1970) 'Initial *h* in Old English', *Anglia* 88, 165–96.

Smithers, G.V. (1983) 'The scansion of *Hauelok* and the use of ME *-en* and *-e* in *Hauelok* and Chaucer'. In Gray & Stanley 1983, 195–234.

Smithers, G.V. (1987) ed. *Havelok* (Oxford: Clarendon Press).

Wilson, E. (1973) *A Descriptive Index of the English Lyrics in John of Grimestone's Preaching Book.* Medium Ævum Monographs, New Series II (Oxford: Society for the Study of Mediæval Languages and Literature; repr. 1977).

Wirtjes, H. (1991) ed. *The Middle English Physiologus* [i.e., *The Bestiary*]. EETS OS 299 (Oxford: Oxford University Press).

GLOSSARY OF FRENCH WORDS

Plant names have been generally excluded because of their bulk, the complexities of identification, and the fact that they can be consulted in Hunt, *Plant Names of Medieval England* (Cambridge, 1989). Middle English terms found in the Rawlinson compendium are included and italicised and marked 'ME', as well as being entered in the Glossary of Middle English Terms. References are as follows: plain numbers refer to the Rawlinson compendium, those preceded by C to the Corpus compendium, by CC to the second Corpus compendium. CU refers to the treatise on urines in the Corpus compendium. For certain composite medicines references are given to their treatment in the *Antidotarium Nicolai* ed. Van den Berg (1917), where numbers refer to receipts. References are comprehensive unless followed by 'etc'.

Abatre v. 349,586 to reduce
Abhominaciun s. 152 distaste, nausea
Acacia s. 592 acacia gum, made from juice of green sloes or plums
Accés s. 358,360,366,367,369,370 onset, attack (of illness)
Afoundré p.p. 7 fallen in, stove in
Agrippe s. 437 an ointment, allegedly used by Agrippa, King of the Jews, *Antidotarium Nicolai* 132
Alacher v. C441,442 to produce a laxative effect (on)
Alembic s. 610,611,613 alembic, still
Aleté p.p. C692 drawn (by milking)
Almuce s. 9 hood, almuce
Alum, aloum s. 286,587,592 common or potash alum (aluminium potassium sulphate) **vert a.** 286 **blanc a.** 286,570 burnt alum **a. de glace** 303,615,C152 crystallized alum
Amer foil s. 463 possibly an error for 'amorfoil' from 'amorfolium' (burdock ?)
Ameroudes s.pl. 199 haemorrhoids
Amiable a. 610,611 gentle
Amplette s. C259 'amblette', unidentified plant, possibly Spurge[1]
Ampulie s. C470 ampulla, phial, small flask
Andre s. 162 ? Betony
Anguile, angwil(e s. 55,592; C95 eel
Anguise s. 586; C568 pain
Anis salvage s. 397 Anise
Apostume, postume s. 435,584,585,587,

[1] See Hunt, *Anglo-Norman Medicine* 2, p.13.

591,601,602; C439,446,447 morbid swelling or inflammation

Archaungele s. 315,374 Dead Nettle

Arcaungeline s. C481 Dead Nettle

Arein, arem(me s. 39,318; C122,127,451 copper, brass

Argoil s. 318,612 argol, tartar of wine, crude potassium bitartrite

Arment, arrement s. C132,140,200,567 vitriol, iron and / or copper sulphate

Armoniac s. 592 gum ammoniac

Arnement s. 132,175,292,297,302,564; C506 vitriol, iron and / or copper sulphate

Arrogon s. 437 an ointment, *Antidotarium Nicolai* 131

Arsoun s. C680,681 burn

Arsure s. 479,538; C680 burn

Arunde s. 353,404; C134,473 swallow

Asa fetida s. 436 var. Umbelliferae esp. Ferula assa-fetida L.

Aubun, alboun s. 245,285,297,359,497, 498,538,552,561,570; C361, 564,567,658 egg white, albumen

Auge s. C588 ?

Auque(s adv. 28 somewhat, a little; pr. indef. 144 a little

Aveye adv. C2 away

Aymaunt s. 589 magnet

Banier s.inf. C126 bathing

Bature s. 582 batter, mixture of egg and flour

Baye s. 14,134; C287,325 berry, fruit of the Laurel; 67 the Laurel; 350,442; C481 berry

Bletron s. C431 sapling

Blinde Nettle (ME) s. 374 Dead Nettle

Boeals s.pl. 438,610 intestine

Boce s. 247,442 a pathological swelling, eruption or lesion

Braer, brayer v. 601,602,603,604; C1,270, 338,430,434,480,482,562, 582,585,638; CC183 to pound, crush

Brais, brez s. 376 malt **servoise de b.** 274 malt beer

Bratheler v. C588 ?

Breu s. 523,592 stock, broth

Brock s. C588 open sore, boil

Broyt, broit s. C309,433,450,455 liquid in which herbs or meat have been boiled or steeped

Bruere s. C434 heath

Bruser, brucer v. 436,438; C96 to pound; 601 to break

Bubon s. 442 bubo

Buck s. C253,470,482 male of a goat or deer

Bullissement s. C188 inflammation

Burbelette s. 612 spot, blotch

Cancre s. 287,288,289,296,297,298,299 etc malignant tumour *water c. (ME)* 303 'water crab', apparently the name of a disease

Canker, kanker, caunker s. C564,639 malignant tumour

Careué s. 165 Caraway

Carpé p.p. 112,501; C252 combed

Cas s. **par cas** C574 by accident

Castorie s. 437 medicament made from dried perineal glands of beaver or their secretions

Ce(i)l, ceel s. C153,237,260,266,294,564, 585,587 salt

Ce(i)lgemme s. C130,457 rock-salt

Cele s. **c. percee** 373 commode

Cenestre a. C694 lefthand

Ceste s. 436,586 arrow

Chacie s. C132 rheum, matter in the eye

Chaele s. C528 whelp

Chaline s. C430 heat

Chaminere s. 270 traveller, wayfarer ?

Chanche v. C246 to cease to flow, staunch (intrans.)

Chanevere, chaunvere s. 196,570,580, 606,609 hemp

Chanu a. 27,28,C79 white(-haired), hoary

Chapel s. C245 hat

Charjaunt a. 364 heavy (of food)

Charnu a. CU containing bits of flesh

Chastré p.p. 290 castrated, gelded

Chatrun s. 597 wether

Chaudepisse s. 533 strangury

Chaudure s. C680 scalding

Chaumbre s. **issir a ch.** 367 to go to stool

Chaun a. 606 ? yellow
Chaus vif s. 244 quicklime
Cheaunt pres. p. 368 falling (to the knees)
Cheith ind.pr.3 of **cheoir**, to fall
Chenve s. 165 hemp
Chikenemete (ME) s. 275 Chickweed
Chite s. C443 chickpea
Chiverefoil s. 289 Honeysuckle
Chopine s. 605 jug
Ciroigne s. 587,588 wax plaster
Clarefier v. C583 to cleanse (of poison)
Cle s. C446 = **clou**
Clore v. 559,562 to close; **clos(e** p.p. 561 closed
Clou(s s. 137,222; C357 boil, aposteme; 379 Cloves
Code s. 315 cobbler's wax, mastic
Coil, **coyl** s. C134,137 neck
Coler v. 52,80,129,133,152,181 etc to strain
Colofonie s. 591 colophony, resin obtained from distilling turpentine
Coluvere s. 171,174 snake
Confire v. 594 to prepare, concoct
Coperose s. 570 copperas
Coperun s. 570,C309,689 top, tip
Coraisym s. C220 unidentified vegetable or mineral substance
Corf s. C661 crow
Corn de cerf s. 66,177,562; C191,C197 hart's-horn
Corpus s. C287 'pulsio cordis', cardiac asthma ?
Corus s. C470 course
Costivé a. 511 constipated
Costivisoun s. C457,463 constipation
Countredit s. **sans c.** 282 certainly, for sure
Cousloppe (ME) s. 599 Cowslip
Couste s. C304 Costmary, or Costus root ?
Coute = **goute** s. C153 drop (of honey)
Crabot s. C220 beetle
Crache s. C563 itching
Crapaude s. 290 toad
Cretthre v. C335 to increase
Crevé p.p. 591 burst
Crop (ME) s. 412 any part of a plant except the root
Crote s. 559 droppings, dung
Croyse s. C434 illness ?
Croysé p.p. 283 see note
Culé p.p. 140 strained
Culier v. C3,122,131,132,163,285,290, 297,562,563,638 to strain; C470 spoon
Culieré s. C285,297,316,453,463 spoonful
Culivur(e s. C362 worm, snake
Culvere s. C334 dove
Cuminé s. 181 stew flavoured with cumin
Curaci(o)un s. 38; C126 cure
Curreye s. 547 strap, belt
Curs s. 435 diarrhoea ?
Custivesun s. 180 constipation
Custreint p.p. 119,599 trapped, pinched, constricted (of nerves)
Cutelle s. C192 knife
Cuver v. 288 to hatch
Darain s. **au darain** adv. 508,591; C438 finally, at the end
Debruser, **debrucer** v. 598; C163,220,660 to pound, crush
Debrucé, **debrusé** p.p. CU; C528,530 damaged, fractured
Deceivere v. 354 to cheat
Dechacer v. 354 to dispel
Decrever v. C446 to burst
Defosser v. 107 ?
Degaster v. 290,537,598; C481,585,680 to consume, destroy
Degrature s. 399 itching
Degurdié p.p. C270 numb(ed)
Deliement adv. 605 finely
Delivrement adv. 162; C293 promptly, at once
Delivrer v. C442 to free, release
Delyé a. 28 fine, delicate, slender
Demayn s. C680 delay
Demene a. C310,662 own
Demener v. 358 to afflict
Dener s. 160,161,183,349,380,537; C291, 292; CC183 penny
Dertre s. C269 tetter
Desestoper, **detstopper** v. 355; C96 to unblock
Desgurder v. C270 to 'unfreeze' (nerves)
Desplumer v. 547 to pluck

Destiller v. C316 to distill
Deuté s. 319 dialtea, medicament made with Marshmallow
Diaquilon s. 49 medicament prepared from litharge, oil and vegetable juices
Doce s. C305 head (of garlic)
Doler v. C129 to trim
Drache s. 257,572; C251,270 dregs, residue
Drap de chaminere s. 270 ?
Dropesie s. 432,433,444 dropsy
Dulié a. C153 fine
Dumenteres adv. C571 meanwhile
Eir s. 611 air
Electuarie, eleituare s. 107,152 electuary
Elefantin s. 390 elephantiasis
Ellerne (ME) s. 376 Elder
Elm (ME) s. 439 Elm
Emeraudes s.pl. C507 haemorrhoids
Empusoné p.p. 160 suffering from poisoning
Enbou p.p. C667 saturated in
Enpoussunement s. C436 poisoning
Encharné p.p. 572 fleshy ?
Encost prep. 373 beside
Endementers que conj. 81 while
Endoucer v. 595; C431 to sweeten
Enfossé p.p. 250,252 entrenched
Enmol(l)er v. C452 to soften, mollify (the belly), relax (the bowels)
Enracer v. C667 to remove abruptly
Enragé p.p. 552 rabid
Enseynte a. CU pregnant
Entamé p.p. 283 eaten into, attacked
Entreles s.pl. 509 entrails
Entret(e s. 435,584,589,593,598 salve or plaster
Entr(e)us s. 439,472 middle bark, 'cortex mediana'
Enveniment s. 434 poisoning
Ere s. 9 Ivy
Escale de oef s. 57,527 eggshell
Eschaudure s. 538 scalding
Esclice s. 598 spatula, stirrer, slice
Escopeal s. 508 cutting
Escoper v. 170 to spit
Escorche s. 28,29,376,416; C431 rind, bark, outer layer **mene e.** 173 middle bark, 'cortex mediana'
Escroyles s.pl. C693 scrofula, the 'King's evil', see note
Escumer v. 172 to froth (at the mouth); 383,538; C140,297 to skim
Esparplier v. 562,563 to sprinkle, scatter
Esplen s. 145,610 spleen
Espurger, etspurger v. 301,560; C460 to cleanse, purify
[Espurgement], etspurgement s. C290, 584 cleansing, purging
Esquele, quele s. 140,264,558,605; C290, 305; CC183 dish, bowl
Esquiler s. 144,152,304,373 spoonful; 605 spoon
Esquileré s. 170 spoonful
Esquinancie s. 109 quinsy
Estale a. 152,281,330,372,375,379; C286, 297,429 stale
Estamper v. 373; C251,267,269,288,297, 464,513,563 to crush
Estancher, etst(h)a(u)nc(h)er v. 401,567; C235–7,245,249,250,251, 361,430 to staunch, cause blood to cease flowing; C428,429 to cease to bleed, flow
Estoppé p.p. C303 congested, constricted, obstructed
Estrandre, strandre v. C440 to compress, tighten (bowels), as an anti-laxative measure; to experience such an effect
Estreyndre v. C269,340 to strain
Estracher v. 128 to extract
Estrounke s. C165 main stem, stock
Estuer, etstuer v. 202,374; C267,273 to take / give a vapour bath; to stew
Estupe s. 28,288; C339 fibres of tow
Estu[v]e s. 374 vapour bath
Etkue s. C238 ?
Etscorchier v. C668 to skin
Etstok s. C2 stock (of plant)
Etsquager, etquager v. C578,662 to soothe, alleviate
Etstopper v. C96 to stop up
Etuele s. C129 bowl, dish
Evervarn (ME) s. 455 Polipody, Oak Fern or Royal Fern
Ewe rose s. 355; C339 distillation of rose petals

Ewe vive s. 570 running water
Experiment s. 366 remedy
Fant s. C660 child
Farcé p.p. 181 stuffed
Farine s. flour **f. furmentale** 182 wheat flour
Farn (ME) s.163 fern
Faucé s. 357 ? unidentified plant,[2] possibly an error for 'favee'
Fe(e)l de t(h)or s. 22; C458 bull's gall
Feliure s. 374 unidentified plant
Felun s. 9,242,245,246,247,250,253 etc sore, boil, tumour
Fencresse (ME) s. 412 Watercress
Fenge s. 57,579 dirt
Fente, feinte s. 38,418,567,604; C334,357, 560 dung
Feru(z p.p. 91,437,618 struck
Festre s. 286,296,297 etc **chaude f.** 284 **freide f.** 285 sore, fistula
Fevre s. 366 fever **f. ague** 354,355 acute fever **f. terceine** 358,360,369,513 tertian fever **f. cotidiene** 359 quotidian fever **f. quart(e)ine** CU quartan fever
Feve freché, f. frete s. C449,658 split
Feye s. 357; C660 liver, gall-bladder
Ffiches (ME) s.pl. 188 fig-worms
Ficoral s. C304 unidentified plant
Fienz s. 301 dung
Fige s. 603; C436 fig; **f. de Malec** C436
Figure s. C306 sign
Filete s. 590,593 Maidenhair Fern ?
Firmage s. C212 cheese
Floures s.pl. C511 unidentified ailment
Fontayne (de la teste) s. C1 fontanel (of the cranium)
For que prep. 579,580,594,606 except
Forsclos p.p. 81 expelled
Forsené p.p. 440 deranged, mad
Fou s. 98,444 Beech
Frescon s. 438 Butcher's Broom
Frez a. 584 fresh
Fu d'enfern s. 618 erysipelas
Fugerole s. 181 Polipody, or Oak Fern
Fumosité s. 610,611 vapour
Fundement s. 193,195; C242,253,422, 457,506 anus
Furcele s. C308,512 thorax ?
Furmye s. 464 ant
Fust s. 318,568,589 (splinter of) wood
Fustole s. 251 fistula, penetrating wound or ulcer creating an abnormal passage between two hollow organs, or a hollow organ and the exterior
Fy s. 193,194 fig-shaped haemorrhoid (perianal haematoma); 197,198 tumour
Fynte s. 278 dung
[**Gairir**], **Gairer** v. C305,645,656,657,693 to cure
Galbanum s. 584,591 galbanum, gum resin
Galingale s. 379,610,614 Galangal, China Root
Gamalie s. 374 unidentified plant
Gan s. C271 glove
Garderobe s. 202 privy
Garet s. 393 ham (of leg)
Gasteal s. 109 bread of the finest flour
Gaster v. 374,483,586 to consume
Geline, geleyn s. 181,288,294,297,298, 516,547,592; C122 hen
Genitaile s. 204 genital organs
Genitarius, genitras s.pl. C336,531 genital organs
Gester v. C434 to throw
Gladene (ME) s. 380 Flag
Glandre s. C165 swollen lymph nodes in neck as a result of throat infection
Glaundres s.pl. 394 swollen lymph nodes in neck as a result of throat infection
Gletoine s. 259 Burdock
Glette s. 145,152; C297 morbid congestion of phlegm or mucus in the stomach or chest
Gleyre s. 265; C431 egg white
Goubounez s.pl. C2 gobbets
Goupil s. 599 fox
G(o)ute s. C658,665,666,667 gout **g. curale** C658 angina pectoris **g. kayve, cheyve** 488; C660,661 'falling sickness', epilepsy

[2] The same name occurs in the text in MS Cambridge, St John's College D.4, see Hunt, *Popular Medicine* p.190, l.1322.

g. enossé 496; C656 gout in the bones **g. enfestré** 503 festering gout **g. freide** 610,668 gout caused by excess of cold humours **g. volajous** C656 erratic gout, passing from one joint or part of the body to an other
Goute de meel s. C667 virgin honey
Grain de Parys s. 379,610 Cardamon (Grain of Paradise)
Grant s. 349 size
Gras s. C530 grease
Gravel(e s. C443,482 small stones formed in the urinary tract
Gre[f]ment adv. C482 grievously
Grevance s. 489 harm, injury
Gris s. C431 grey outer bark
Grue s. 287 stork
Grund-ivi (ME) s. 202 Ground Ivy
Gutefestre s. 401; C237,571,572,657 gouty swelling, fistulous sore
Hanap s. 558,605; C290,450,471 goblet
Hanapé s. 140 gobletful
Hayrive (ME) s. 374 Cleavers
Heihove, heyhove (ME) s. 599 Ground Ivy
Heranc sor, harenc s. s. 251,253,254 red, smoked herring
Here s. 79 Ivy
Herneles (ME) s. 412 ?
Honi-pere tre (ME) s. 374 'honey-pear' tree
Horhune, horoune (ME) s. 202,483 Horehound
Horsehove (ME) s. 150 Coltsfoot
Houndestonge (ME) s. 483 Hound's Tongue
Hove (ME) s. 412 Ground Ivy
Humer v. 181; C191,301 to swallow
Hure s. 513 time
Hwit mustard-sed (ME) s. 388 White Rocket, White Charlok
Ileoc, illeucus adv. 140; C572 in that place, there
Irous a. 487 angry
Jaunice, jauniz s. 320,514 jaundice
Joute s. C430 soup or pottage
Jun, joun adv. 37,143,172; C286,288 on an empty stomach, fasting **en j.** 133,140; C139,428,436
Juste prep. 283 beside, next to
Kersuns de funtaine s. 372 Watercress
Keverché s. CC184 kerchief
Launge s. C457 piece of wool
Leins adv. 537,598 therein
Lembre de tere s. 581 earthworm
Lemke (ME) s. 409 Brooklime
Lende s. 395 nit, louse
Lentils s.pl. 448 error for **lentis** = **lentes,** lice
Lentilous a. 531 freckled
Lepre s. 507 leper
Leprous a. 505 leprous
Lequel conj. 407 whether
Lessive s. C2,79 lye
Letant pres. pt. C528 suckling
Leter v. 558 to release or expel milk
Leye s. C93 lye
Line s. 200,216 flax
Liner s. 250 type of tumour ?
Linois s. 122,180,496 flax
Litarge s. 615 litharge, lead monoxide
Lou s. 616 erysipelas
Lu s. 251,253,304,438,547,618 place, spot
Lué de voye s. C80 'mileway', the time taken to cover a league
Lunaciun s. C470 lunar month, lunar cycle
Lusant a. CU shining
Luxurie s. 127 lust, lasciviousness
Lye(s, lies s.(pl. 276,435,589,590,592,593 lees, dregs (of wine or beer)
Lyverance s. C441 release
Macis, mace s. 379,614 Mace
Maele, macle s. 38,39; C126,127 leucoma
Maithe (ME) s. 194,234 Stinking Camomile
Malader v. C309 to become ill
Maladie de roy s. C172,693 scrofula, tuberculosis of lymph nodes at the side of the neck, 'the King's evil', see note
Mangue, mangewe s. 399,508; C267 mange, scabby skin condition at first applied to animals
Mangure s. 511 **mangure de levere** ?
Marbye s. C657 marble
Marciaton s. 437 a green ointment, *Antidotarium Nicolai* 130
Mariz, maris s. 610; CU; C513 uterus
Marle a. C252,530 male
Ma(r)tefelun s. 229,253,257 Knapweed

Mascher v. 553 to chew
Mastik s. 591,598,599 mastic
Matecicle s. 592 Honeysuckle
Meche s. 286 wick
Melis s. 579 Balm
Membre s. C504 male member, penis
Menis(o)un s. 182,183,184,499; C428,430, 451,464,468 diarrhoea **m. sanglaunte** 184 diarrhoea accompanied by emission of blood (first-degree haemorrhoids)
Menu a. / adv. 161,201,264,546,566 small
Mese(a)l s. / a. 465,612 leper / leprous
Mestrie s. 523 skill, technique
Meule s. 532 marrow
Mie, **mye** s. 109,261,271 breadcrumb
Mincer v. 566 to chop
Mirre s. 592 myrrh
Mo(e)al, **moael** s. 239,245,253,258,286 egg yolk
Moiler, **moller** v. 288; C157,252,289, 339,341,361,444,457,480,511,512,530, 564 to moisten, wet
Moldre, **moudre** v. 373; C561 to grind **mol(l)u** p.p. C1,340,428, 441 ground
Moller v. C454 to soften (the belly), relax (the bowels)
Morele s. 121,242,247 Black- or Deadly Nightshade
Morphé s. 319,612 morphoea, spotty infection of the skin with light and dark patches
Morsure s. 543,544,547,548,550,552,553, 555,689 bite
Mortmal s. 287; C531 a dry-scabbed ulcer, sore or abscess **m. jaune** 315
Moster s. 362 monastery
Mouele s. C302,669 marrow
Mountaunce s. 373,606 amount, equivalent
M(o)use, **muce** s. 586,C435 moss
Muche s. 544 fly
Muer v. 28 to change colour
Muler v. 270 to moisten, wet
Mulueyne s. C337 Mullein
Munde a. 129 clean
Munder v. 537,568 to cleanse
Murer v. 602 to ripen, bring to maturity; C428,430 to die
Muscel, **musel** s. C272,457 morsel, piece of food
Myes de payn s.pl. C445 breadcrumbs
Myure s. 135 breadcrumbs
Naufré p.p. 557,606 wounded
Nerval s. 599 ointment for the nerves or sinews
Ni(s, **ny** s. 353,404 nest
Nizteschode (ME) s. 442 Deadly Nightshade
Noer s. 28 nut-tree
Noli me tangere s. 253,617 erosive ulceration or cancer of the face
Nouer v. CU to float (on the surface)
[**Nowel**] s. C645 kernel
Nowel a. C668 no
Noys mugate, **nois mugace**, **nois mugette** s. 408,610,614 nutmeg
Nugace s. 28 almond nut
Numbyl, **numbril** s. C442,444,454,458 navel
Nus s. 289 nut
Nut s. 33,318 night
Oblé s. 366 host, holy wafer
Occiler v. C131 to shake
Oculescunse s. 121 plant of uncertain identity
Oile laurin s. 437 oil of bays
Oindre v. 33,34,35,36 etc to anoint
Oint s. 132,137,222,243,263,292,302 grease
Oir s. 57 hearing
Oiste s. 362,363 host, holy wafer
Oliban s. 591,599 an aromatic gum resin
Oraler s. C80 earwig
Ord(e a. 610 dirty, foul
Orpiment s. 297,587 arsenic mono-/di-/ trisulphide
Oundé s. 605 boiling
Owayle s. C656 sheep
Owe s. 397,450,567,592; C163,560 goose
Owel a. 34,38,142 etc equal
Owelement adv. 297,357,378 equally, in equal proportions
Paele, **payele** s. 180,373,502,537,538,606; C1,3,463,644,668 pan, dish
Palesye, **parlesye**, **paralesie** s. 437,463, 502,599,610 palsy
Panesoun s. C670 syncope, fainting

Papere s. C221 eyelid
Parquire v. 293 to cook thoroughly
Parseivere v. 355 to see, notice
Paste s. 561 paste
Paste(a)l s. 194,496,569; C568,656,657 paste, poultice
Peautre s. 605 animal skin
Pece s. 373 period, space of time
Pecher s. 123 pear tree
Peiz s. CU pitch
Peiz s. C443 peas
Peis, peys s. 160,161,183,380,580,590,606; C291,292; CC184 weight
Pele enverse s. 442 unidentified plant, error for **lape inverse** ('lappa inversa')
Pelote s. 578,579,580,585,609; C298 pellet
Penne s. C47,95,132,513 feather
Perches s.pl. 192 antlers
Pere s. C470,473,480,481,483 stone (medic.)
Pere de molyn s. 592 millstone
Perfusioun de sanck s. C188 bleeding
Perrosin s. 598 a type of gum or resin
Pertuz, pertuse s. 202,284,547; C96,571, 572,657,666 opening, orifice
[**Pessir**] v. C656 to become thick, viscous
Pesteliner v. 508 to pound with a pestle
Piaine, pioyne s. 19,463,515 Peony
Pijoun s. C661 young bird, chick
Pis, piz s. 23,119,314,409,435,587,590 pitch **p. naval** 584,591 naval pitch **p. liquid(e** 587,588 liquid pitch
Pisel s. 290 penis (of animal)
Piz s. 133,137,140; C285,290,303,308,309, 315 breast
Playe s. C217 sore, blemish
Pluvie s. 294 rain
Pocenet s. 28,185 posnet, pot or vessel for boiling liquid
Podagre s. 416,416 gout
Poigné s. 598,600,602,609; C442,443 handful
Poin s. 28 handful
Poket s. 199,201,318 pouch
Pombe s. C561 probably an error
Ponté p.p. C435 pricked
Ponture s. C435,567,694 prick, sting
Porture s. CU rottenness, decay
Posseyt s. C588 hot milk curds used as a poultice
Potage s. 381 pottage
Potee s. C567 pottage
Potel s. C438,511,561 liquid measure corresponding to half of whatever gallon measure is used
Pount p.p. 407 laid (of egg)
Pous s. 170 paste
Pouz s. 355,369 pulse
Poyné s. 595; C141,431,438,511,529,561 handful
Poyngun s. C438 handful
Poynture s. C434 sting, bite
Premez 112,382 ind.pr.2 of **preindre** to (ex)press **premerez** 537 fut.5
Privé a. C497 intimate
Priveté s. 610 secret possession
Pule s. 395,448 louse
Puour s. 100 stench
Purré s. C443 puree
Purri p.p. CU rotting
Pus(o)un, pouson s. 162; C294,310,436 poison
Putee s. C445,681 pottage
Quarel s. 589 bolt
Quartaine s. 367,368 quartan fever
Quart s. C438,443 a quart (liquid measure)
Quatreble a. 290 fourfold
Quele s. see **esquele**
Querde s. C690 splinter, fragment (of bone)
Quibibe, quibebe s. 379,614 Cubeb
Quice s. 438 thigh
Quil(i)eré s. 133,145; C443 spoonful
Quilir, -er v. 140,360,606; C439 to gather
Quinacie s. C163 quinsy
Qui(s)z, quiz s. C518,519 thigh
Quiture s. 393 prick to draw blood
Raere v. 23,527; C72 to shave; C192,305 to scrape
Rancle s. 130,246,264,265,267,269,273, 275,277,278,282; C270,339,341,662 festering sore
Rancour s. C567 festering
Raspe s. 572 draff, dregs
Rave s. la graunde r. 516 turnip ?
Ravenesfot (ME) s. 47 Polypody
Receite s. 578 recipe, set of instructions

Recherra, **recharra** fut. 3 of **rechoir** 354 to relapse
Remis p.p. 112,133,501; C252 melted
Remuer v. C644,645 to (re)move
Rescunce s. 369 setting (of the sun)
Res(e p.p. 440 shaven
Respelker v. C530 to renew a splint
Restue s. C511 unidentified ailment
Resyne s. 508 resin
Retencioun(s s. 610 retention of menstrual blood
Roche s. C571,666 roach
Roile de fer s. 542 rust
Roilé a. 612 rusty
Roine, **royne**, **roigne**, **ruyne** s. 398,478, 508,541,612; C262, 266,267,271,273 scabies; scabby, irritating skin condition
Roses s.pl. 506 red blotches, acne rosacea
Rosel s. 436 reed, rush
Roseu s. C212 red spot or blotch (on face)
Rosin(e s. 435,590,601,C163 resin
Rostir, **rostier** v. C428,441,668 to cook
Roynous a. 478 scabby
Ruse s. CC184 ?
Sablun s. **vif s.** 252 sharp sand
Sainté s. CU health
Saker v. 436,586 to draw, extract
Saket s. 516,589,614 pouch, little bag
Salgemme s. 527,537 rock-salt
Salsefleume s. 537 swelling of the face accompanied by spotty infection attributed to salty humours
Sanglant a. CU containing blood
Sape d'Etspayne s. 183 a hard, soda-ash soap
Sauf mettre en s. 598 to reserve (in a safe place)
Saul s. 198 ?
Sauterole s. 315 locust
Sautz s. 173 willow
Sauve s. 606,607 salve
Savement adv. 407 safely
Sav(o)un s. 240,244,249,286,299 soap
Seele s. 528 sealing wax
Se(e)r v. 199,201,202; C430 to sit
Segur a. 377 safe
Seim s. 35,55,112,180,279,286 etc grease, fat
Sein de verre s. 615 sandiver, glass gall
Sein, **seyn** a. 172,358,465; C96 healthy
Selfhele (ME) s. 573 Selfheal
Semiterie s. C497 cemetery
Sené s. 367 senna
Senichun, **sen(e)chun** s. 54,133,296, 354,412,594 Common Groundsel
Seriser s. 355 cherry tree
Servoise, **serveise** s. 104,140,152,155, 179,196,218,259,274,276 etc beer
Seu s. 13,53 Elder
Seyné s. C258,261 drawing of blood, bloodletting
Seynture s. 516 belt
Siche s. 618 a cutting implement ?
Sindre s. C94 ash
Si(o)un s. 566,595,596 shoot, scion
Slon (ME) s.pl. 140 Sloes, Wild Damsons
Solucion s. 373 looseness, laxity of the bowels
Sor a. 172 sorrel, chestnut (of horse)
Sope (ME) s. 256 soap
Souder v. C690 to heal, knit together
Soudure s. C249 healing, knitting
Sowthistel, souethistel (ME) s. 226,382 various thistles esp. Sonchus oleraceus
Spaudis s.pl. C253 shoulders
Sperewort (ME) s. 315 ? Spearwort (genus Ranunculus)
Spiseries s.pl. C342 spices
Stamper v. C192,260 to crush
Stancher v. C430 to cease to bleed
Stichewort (ME) s. 606
Stomore s. 374 error for **stonore**, 'stonecrop' ?
Stoncrop (ME) s. 315 Stonecrop
Stoppé p.p. C303 congested, constricted, obstructed
Stoyle s. C125 star
Streindre, **strayndre** v. C96,442,667 to strain
Su s. 119,225,297,542 grease, tallow **s. de motun** 54,129,185, 246,262,264,275, 278,280,435,537,546,605 sheep's grease **s. de tor** 22 bull's grease **s. de cerf** 532,537 stag's grease **s. de levere** 589 hare's grease
Succhii s. 289 Honeysuckle

Suet s. 546 suet
Suffler v. 81 to blow, instil by blowing
Suffre s. 507,508 sulphur
Suour s. 354,355 sweat
Surbature s 223 tenderness, soreness
Surep s. C316 syrup
Sureper v. C316 to make into a syrup
Sursané p.p. C560 scarred over
Survenue s. 579,585,C140 accident, mishap, accidental injury
Swef a. 594 comfortable, gentle
Talent, talant s. 152,379,CU,297 desire, wish
Tan s. 294 (pulverized) bark **ewe de t.** 294 solution of tan
Tarock s. C530 pitch
Taupe s. 523 mole
Teine s. 418 tinea, disease of the scalp
Tele s. C140 cloth
Tente s. C657 tent, pledget, seton
Terebentine s. 587,591,598,605 turpentine
Tessun s. 599 badger
Teste s. 497 eggshell
Teter s. 542 tetter
Teye s. 34,39; C127,128,129,132 leucoma
Te(n)ve, tedve a. 23,52,53,111,161,183, 325,373,500,C87,89 etc warm, tepid
Thunderdokke (ME) s. 199 a plant of uncertain identity
Tike s. C80 grub or small worm in the ear
Tisike s. C267,316 phthisis, pulmonary tuberculosis
Tout 152,579 ind. pr.3 of **tolir** to deprive, remove
Tremblure, tremulure s. 610; C3,268 trembling, shaking
Trenchivesouns s.pl. C453 tormina, gripes
Tret s. (boiler) **a tret** 435,584,587,592,593 at length, unhurriedly
Triacle, treacle s. 165; C294 theriac, 'treacle', antidote to poison
Tr(o)uble a. CU cloudy
Trus, truis s. 394,416 stalk
Tuale s. C298 napkin
Tuele s. C300 pipe
Turtel(e s. 182,271,C464 cake
Turtele s. C431 'cake', a swelling ?
Ulmentel s. 439 Elm
Umbil, umbryl s. 197,499,C361,441 navel
Unement, uynement s. C1,3,94,127, 203,340,657; CC184 ointment, unguent
Uriloun s. 509 ?
Urtie s. 330,348,401 nettle
Uy s. 444 mistletoe ? see note
Vecie s. C644 blister
Veine s. v. capitale 38,109 cephalic vein
Veer s. C211 glass
Veer v. 510 to forbid
Velu a. CU velvety in texture
Ventosité s. 524 flatulence, wind
Ventuser v. C667 to bleed (with cupping glass)
Ver, veer s. 77,505; C163 boar
Ver(e s. C134,470,585 glass
Verrue, verwe s. 612; C259,272 wart
Vers a. C271 reverse
Vertun s. 1,4 giddiness
Vescie s. 250 sore, blister
Vessye, vecie s. 610,CU bladder
Veu(z, veut, veud a. 112,132,135,137,166; C295 etc old
Vif argent s. 314,397,450,508,537; C211; **argent vif** CC184 quicksilver
Viole s. 610,611 phial
Viz, vis s. 528,529,530,531,532 face
Vomis s. 498; C361 vomiting
Vomite s. 373 vomiting
Walwort (ME) s. 409 Dwarf or Ground Elder
Warir v. 503 to cue, heal
Wenne (ME) s. 414 morbid lump, sebaceous cyst
Weybrode (ME) s. 374 Greater Plantain
Wilde Clote (ME) s. 601 Burdock
Wilde Tasel (ME) s. 606 Wild Teasel
Wimave s. 212 Marshmallow
Wodebinde (ME) s. 289 Honeysuckle
Woderove (ME) s. 372 Sweet Woodruff
Wormod (ME) s. 202 Wormwood
Wort (ME) s. 189,376 wort, barley malt
Wrti (ME) s. 155 a plant
Wy de pomere s. C2 mistletoe
Ydropesie s. 373,376,481,483,610 dropsy
Ydropick s. C433 one suffering from dropsy
Ynde s. 537 ? indigo
Yrayne s. 543 spider

GLOSSARY OF ENGLISH WORDS

The glossary includes all English items embedded in Latin and French receipts; otherwise it is selective and excludes plant names which can be consulted in Hunt, *Plant Names of Medieval England*. References are as follows: C indicates the first Corpus compendium, CC the second, and R the Rawlinson compendium. References to the *Antidotarium Nicolai* follow the receipt numbers in the edition of Van den Berg (1917). References by receipt numbers are comprehensive unless followed by 'etc.'

Acche s. C592 ache
Achaufed p.p. CC75 see **chaufe**
Agruted p.p. CC55 glutted, surfeited
Alliwater a. CC115 holy water
Alloy s. C494
Alum-glas s. C.160 crystallized potash alum
Alwndel, haluendel s. C466,540,649 half
Ambrose s. C53,54,559 ['wilde tanse' an error ?]; CC58 Wood Sage
Amerose s. CC79,125,177 corresponds to 'ambrose' in other witnesses
Angwisse s. CC166 pain
Anies-sedes s.pl. C378,495 seeds of Anise
Apostolycone, appostolicone s. C615; CC137 'Ointment of the Apostles', *Antidotarium Nicolai* 44
Apostume s. C377; CC183 morbid swelling or inflammation
Arment, arrement s. C118,410,549,557, 611,615,634; CC13,113,133, 135,143 vitriol, iron and / or copper sulphate
Arm-oles s.pl. C170 armpits
Askbirne s.pl. CC164 an error for 'ascþrotu' (Vervain) or 'askeban' (Henbane) ?
Attet v. C526 is called, known as
Axsen s.pl. CC91 ashes
Ay, ey s. C118,119,120,173,180,347,348, 356,616,682,697 etc egg
Ayen adv. C544 again
Ballokes s.pl. CC83 testicles
Bar(c)k-dust s. C360,547 pulverized tanbark
Barli-mele s. C35,244,347,555; CC98,166 barley-meal
Barlich-flour s. C63 barley-flour
Barwe(s)-smere, bar-smere, bor-smere s. C206,649; CC87 castrated boar's grease
Bayt v. CC167 to bathe
Be s. CC121 bee
Bene s. C371 bean
Bene-mele s. C348 bean meal, ground dried beans
Best s. 409,410 beast, animal
Bete s. **blake b.** C38,70 Beetroot

Bile, **byl(e**, **byil** s. C357,358,359,602; CC49,156,159,160,164 boil, ulcer
Blades s.pl. CC99 leaves of a plant
Bleyne s. C204 boil, pimple etc
Blinde Nettle s. R374 Dead Nettle
Bolnyng(ge s. C87,109,179,180,343,346, 498,525,526,534,636 swelling
Bolye s. C534,558 local swelling
Bonwrt s. C54 Comfrey, or a variety of plants used in knitting bones incl. Butcher's Broom, Daisy and Violet
Bor(is-gres s. 525; CC25 boar's grease
Bostes s.pl. CC54,132 boxes (for ointment)
Bounden a./p.p. C371 constipated
Brake s. C407 bracken, various ferns
Breid v. C371; CC65 to cook
Bretthelud a. CC129 see note
Brock s. C356,588; CC163 open sore, boil
Brock-lente s. C246 Water Lentil, or error for **brock-lemke** 'Brooklime' ?
Brosten p.p. CC71 burst, split
Broyt s. C408 broth
Bruse v. CC129 bruise
Brusure s. CC154 bruising
Bryn s. CC161 bran
Bul, **buyl** v. CC28,33,186 to boil
Bult v. CC133 to sift **bulted** p.p. C54 sifted
Burbul s. C54 bubble
Burre s. C360 'rounceval', Christ's-thorn (Paliurus aculeatus) ?
Burres s.pl. CC186 flowerhead of the Burdock
Bygmele s. CC83 barley meal
Byleue v. CC33 to remain (as residue)
Bynde s. C159,264 clinging plant, prob. woodbine / honeysuckle
Bytinge s. C535 bite
Cane(i)l, **canelle** s. C142; CC81,101 Cinnamon
Carloc-seid s. C3 seed of Charlock
Caste s. C370 vomiting (nausea)
Casten v. C372,401,410 to vomit
Castinge, **castyng** ger. C327,373 vomiting
Ceve s. C371 chive
Chanche v. C246 to staunch, cease flowing
Cha(u)ngel s. **red ch**. CC98 shingles, herpes zoster
Chaufed, achaufed p.p. CC75 inflamed
Chellez s.pl. C322 (egg)shells
Cheranse s. C400 see note
Cheriz s.pl. C480 cherries
Cheruing s. C375 cutting, griping sensation or pain
Chingles s. C161 shingles, herpes zoster
Cirope terceres s. CC175 a syrup used in treating tertian fever **c. rose** CC176 syrup of roses
Clawyn[g], **clawynge** s. C280; CC118 itching
Clise, **clyse**, **sclyse** s. C494; CC25,157 spatula, stirrer, slice
Cloutes s.pl. CC134 pieces of cloth, rags
Code s. C600 code, cobbler's wax
Colure s. CC16 collyrium, eye-salve
Confortatiue a. C371 invigorating, stimulating
Coporose s. C142 copperas, a metallic sulphate
Corwn p.p. CC151 cut, split (in two)
Costyf, **costiue** a. C406,465; CC34,63,167, 174 constipated
Cowesloppe s. C3; R599 Cowslip
Cowque s. CC51 cough
Cressen s. C570 Cress
Cristene malwe s. C559 Marshmallow ?
Crop s. R412 any part of a plant except the root
Cropen p.p. CC112 crept
Crous(c)ipe s. C547,578 error for 'crowsope', Soapwort (Saponaria officinalis) ?
Cruden s. C354 curds
Crum v. C121 to stuff, cram, fill to capacity
Culiz s. C371; CC137 strained, clear meat broth, cullis
Deliueren v. C371 to evacuate the bowels
Ditt v. C371 to prepare **dyth** p.p. C371 **ditz** imper. CC124
Docke s. C419; CC120 a plant of the genus Rumex
Douuue-muke s. CC98 dove dung
Dow s. CC139 dough
Draþth s. C399 draught
Drestes s.pl. C343,347,526,534 lees, dregs **wyn-d.**, **ale-d**. C675

Dropesie s. C466; CC183 **cold d.** C378 dropsy
Dryth s. C118 dirt
Duretyk a. C322 diuretic
Edere s. C409 serpent or snake
Eimeriez s.pl. C87,345 embers
Eindez s.pl. C105 extremities
Eirun, eyren s.pl. C108,322; CC130,144 eggs
Elen v. C612; CC134 to heal
El(l)erne s. CC66; R376 Elder
Elm s. R439 Elm
Enturspace s. C170 membrane separating nasal cavities
Erdene a. C618 earthen
Eth v. CC185 to eat
Euerfarn s. R455 Polypody, Oak Fern or Royal Fern
Ewerose s. CC170 rose-water
Eyerose, eierose s. C28,106 rose water ? see notes
Eyl s. CC10 eel
Eymerie s. C633 embers
Eyren s.pl. C108,547 eggs
Ey-s(ch)elle, hey-schelle, hye-schelle s. C227,228,256,516; CC72 eggshells
Facis, fases s.pl. CC9,147 the white rootlets of the leek
Fallynge evele, fallande e. s. CC121,123 epilepsy
Fane s. C578 a white-flowered Iris
Fantem s. CC31 delirium
Farn s. R163 Fern
Fencresse s. R412 Watercress
Fenkele s. C106,108,322,378,466,494,495, 547; CC174 fennel
Festrus s.pl. C359 fistulas
Feuere s. **f. cotidien** CC171 quotidian fever **f. quarteyn** CC173,179 quartan fever **f. tercine** CC172 **terciun f.** (tercine) CC175 tertian fever
Ffiches s.pl. R188 fig-worms
Filago s. C108 Cudweed or Mouse-Ear Hawkweed
Filles s. (pl.) CC1 see note
Flawn s. C160 'cake', growth
Flete s. CC181 to float
Flex s. C532,541,548,615; CC114,137,144 flesh
Fleys s. C54 flesh
Flour-ben s. C16 error for bean flour
Flynt s. C469; CC185 flint
Fole-fo(i)t s. C298,588 Coltsfoot or Purslane
Fom s. C676 foam, scum
Forbrent p.p. C371 burnt up
Fordo v. CC45 to dispel, relieve (pain)
Forþi adv. CC163 accordingly, therefore
Fox s. C478 fox
Fran(e)si, frenesi s. CC168,170 frenzy
Freckenez s.pl. C204 freckles, blotches on skin
Freind a. CC56 friendly, familiar
Freit s. C453 gnawing pain, gripes
Galle s. C215,438; gall bladder; C29,458; CC65 gall
Galt-smere s. C63 boar's grease
Gander s. C627 gander
Garle(c)k, garlec s. C305,475,484,485, 602,613; CC135,179 Garlic
Geet s. CC184 jet
Gendringe ger. C544 mating
Ginnen, gynnen v. C611; CC133 to commence, start
Gladene s. R380 Flag
Glaundre, glandren s. C161 swollen lymph nodes in neck as result of throat infection
Gluskynge s. C134 squinting, strabismus (leading to amblyopia)
God-mylk s. CC28 goat's milk
Golde s. CC12 Marigold
Gotes-terdle s. C244,545 goat's dropping
Gotuse a. C322 inducing gout
Goundi a. CC13 rheumy, bleary
Go(u)tefestre s. C237,571,572,609,613, 616,633,634,637,657,672; C131 fistulous sore, gouty swelling
Goutes s.pl. C646 guts, intestine
Grauel s. C509 pebbles; CC186 small stones formed in the urinary tract
Gres s. (a) C116,550,663; CC157 grease (b) v. C162,203,550,674 to grease, smear (c) C559,610; CC114,132,147,173,177 herb
Grete s. C170 thickness, breadth

Groip v. C170 to feel, touch with the fingers
Gro[t]s s. CC166 see **grotes**
Grotes s.pl. C326,371,378,46 hulled or crushed grain, oatmeal
G[r]u[e]l s. C322 gruel
Grund-ivi s. R202 Ground Ivy
Gute s. C654 gout **lous g.** C663 erratic gout
Gyltez-smere s. C206 sow's grease
Ʒesken v. CC47 to hiccup
Ʒeskyng(ge ger. C369,CC47 hiccuping
Hache s. C54,55,517,624,648 Smallage
Hamus s.pl. C170 back of the knees
Hasse s. C105 Ash
Hat a. C613; CC135,159,160 hot
Hauere-mel(e s. C466,664; CC37 oat flour
Hawe s. C91 fruit of the Hawthorn
Hayriue s. R374 Cleavers
Hechel v. CC14 to comb or dress flax
Heihoue, heyhowe, hayhoue s. C1,26,31, 327,401,546; R599 Ground Ivy
Heild v. C147 to pour
Helden v. CC15 to keep
Hele s. C85 eel
Hellerne s. C42 Elder
Herbe s. CC178 unidentified medical condition ?
Herberd, horberd s. CC78,81 a kind of fever
Herche s. C554 unidentified plant, error for merche ?
Herde, herþe s. C555; CC129 earth
Herdene a. CC56 earthen
Herdes/z s.pl. C466; CC143,147 hards, the coarse part of flax
Hert s. C35 hart
Herneles s.pl. R412 unidentified plant
Her[t]wrt s. C40,119 Viola or Selfheal
Heryth s. C672 hearth
Heschulschines s. C226 see note
Heuere-uern s. CC165 Polypody, Oak Fern or Royal Fern
Hewn p.p. C544 cut
Hil(len v. C54,371,612; CC88,101,124,134 cover
Hineray s. C611 an error ? see note
Hock-appel(us s.pl. C346,352 oak apple(s
Hoes a. CC49 hoarse
Hoesed s. CC48 hoarseness
Hoȝ s. CC66 hog (see note)
Hoik s. C408 oak
Hol(en v. C532,611; CC145 to heal; holed p.p. C547
Holle a. CC180 hollow
Holwort, hulwort s. C1,327,329,337 Pennyroyal or Wild Thyme
Holy-ake s. CC163 Marshmallow
Holy docke s. C602 error for 'Holy-hocke' ?
Holy malwe s. C179 Vervain Mallow ?
Honi-pere tre s. R374 'Honey-pear' tree
Horberd s. CC81 see **herberd**
Horshelin, horshelle, horshelme s. C203,277; CC51,56,118 ['scabbewrt'] Elecampane, Horseheal
Hors-mynte, hormynte s. C54,81 a variety of wild Mint
Horune, horhune, horoune s. C411; R202,483 Horehound
Hoste s. CC51 cough
Houndestonge s. R483 Hound's Tongue
Hound-fenkelle s. C356 Stinking Camomile
House s. C697 cover, protection
Hove s. R412 Ground Ivy
Howe s. C107,126 'haw' or excrescence in eye
Hulwort see **holwort**
Hulyn-barck s. C372 bark of the holly-tree
Hum(e)lock s. C44,186,266; CC102 hemlock
Huni-appul tre s. C558 a quince on to which an apple has been grafted ? Cf. R374 **huni-pere tre**
Hus(e v. C494,495 to use
Husleck, husseleck s. C554,578 Houseleek
Hwit mustard-sed s. R388 White Rocket, White Charlock
Ifulled p.p. C250 baptised
Ivi s. C39,299 ivy
Jaunes s. CC105 jaundice
Kattis-smere s. CC126 cat's grease

Kelen, akelen v. C359,540,599,649; CC163, 185 to cool down
Kerf v. CC144 to cut
Keruinge ger. CC147 cutting or griping pain
Knaue-child, k. schyld s. C54,109; CC143 male child
Kyl s. C348,356,649 boil, ulcer, sore
Laumpe-oyle s. C66 lamp oil
Leme s. C554,590 limb
Lemke s. R409 Brooklime
Lendes s.pl. C256,515,516,522; CC73 loins
Lente a. **l. fevere** CC165 a slow fever, a sort of ague
Lese v. CC151 to loosen, free, release
Letargie s. CC169 lethargy, a condition of morbid drowsiness, forgetfulness or even unconsciousness attributed to a phlegmatic aposteme in the fourth ventricle of the hindbrain
Lette v. CC53 to prevent
Letuarie s. C371; CC46,49 electuary
Leuck, leuke, leweck a. C373,599; CC33, 38,43,44 tepid, lukewarm
Leye s. C65,548; CC91 lye
Littli adv. CC161 gradually, little by little
Lokechestre s. C84,97 woodlouse
Loken p.p. CC150 (of wound) closed up on the surface
Lome s. C106,121 vessel
Loytwrt s. C524,559 plant identified with 'centaury'
Lyme s. C524,534 limb; C555 lime
Lyn s. C498 piece of linen
Lyth s. CC169 light
Maithe s. R194,234 Stinking Camomile
Mallow, malue, malwe s. C267 etc Mallow, Hollyhock ?
Mangewe s. CC119 mange, scabby skin condition at first applied to animals
Mariegolde s. C588 Pot Marigold
Marw(e s. C107,674 marrow
Maser s. C54 mazer wood
Mayde-schild s. CC143 female child
Maydeil s. C401 an error ? see note
Menysoun s. C397,398,399,412; CC68,183 diarrhoea **blodi m.** C398 discharge from the bowels containing blood
Merchaunt s. CC132 error for 'merche ant' ?
Mesel s. C209 a leper
Meseyl a. C208 afflicted with skin disease resembling leprosy
Metyng ger. CC31 vision, dream
Mis(e v. C526,534 to cut into small pieces
Molde s. C33 crown of the head
Moleward s. CC128 mole
Mond, mound s. CC15,78 month
Morsus diaboli s. C378 Devil's-Bit Scabious, or Autumnal Hawkbit
Mouble a. C682 movable
M(o)(u)gwed(e s. C63,397,511; CC95 Mugwort ?
Moules s.pl. C527 sore, chilblain
Muscelus s.pl. C371 morsels, small portions of food
My v. C317,465 to crumble
Mylte s. CC49,179 spleen
Narw s. C322 congestion, constriction
Nature s. C494 reproductive capacity ?
Neddere s. CC108 adder, snake
Nese-thirles s.pl. C25,147,170,177; CC168, 180 nostrils
Netus-fen s. C581 cow dung
Neysse, neisse, nessche a. C684; CC63, 64,118,144,163 soft
Nizteschode s. R442 Deadly Nightshade
Noted p.p. CC141 used
Notisoda-berien s.pl. C446 berries of the Deadly Nightshade
Nouele s. C361,496; CC65 navel
Nowre adv. CC121 in no way
Ock s. CC122 oak
Ole v. 545 to heal
Oncomus s.pl. C359 sore, eruption on the skin
Open v. CC171 to expect, believe
Oþerquile adv. C116 sometimes
Oversclaked p.p. CC157,158 abated, quenched
Overtaken v. C534 to extend over, cover
Owele s. CC124 owl
Oynde s. CC35 breath
Oyl a. C327 healthy, cured

Oyli rosetk s. C4 oil of roses (rose petals and olive oil)
Oyt(h), **hoyt** a. CC61,62,70,174 hot
Paper s. C218 eyelid (not recorded; cf. OF *paupiere*)
Parche v. C375 to roast, dry cook
Partyngale s. C322 unidentified plant (cf. persingale)
Pe de lyun s. C65 Lady's Mantle
Pekelede a./p.p. C205 spotty, speckled (of face)
Pellestre s. C50 Pellitory of the Wall
Peni-weythe, **peni-witthe** s. C399,466, 494; CC68 pennyweight
Perok s. C322 an error ? see note
Peyrit v. C371 impair; **p. þe syth** 'impairs your faculties, threatens your life'
Pick s. C66,593,600; CC158,164 pitch
Pigil, **pigle**, **pygel** s. C53,540,559; CC163 Stitchwort, Great Starwort
Pilgrym salue s. C585 a type of ointment or salve
Pleyen v. C466,526; CC143 to boil
Poket s. C493 pouch
Possot s. C635 hot milk curds used as a poultice
Potel s. C322,378; CC186 liquid measure corresponding to half of whatever gallon measure is used
Poyn(e (a) v. C69,119,403,408,485,590,602 to pound, crush with a pestle (b) s. C244 a handful
Puliol(e real, **pulial r.** s. C49,54 Pennyroyal
Puyne v. C69 to pound, crush with a pestle
Pyn s. C128 pin-like growth in the eye
Pyntul s. C496,498,500,505; CC85 penis
Quelp s. CC168 whelp
Quenteliche, **quentely** adv. C54,599 carefully, skilfully
Queston s. CC11 whetstone
Quike a. C613 live, burning
Quile s. CC169 quill
Quit(o)ur s. C119,548,613; CC135 pus, matter
Quyt, **quith**, **quyth** a. C374; CC145,185 white
Rancle s. C546,558 festering sore
Rancleinge, **rankeling** ger. C542,635 festering
Rasure s. CC144 razor
Ratounne s. CC126 rat
Ravenesfot s. R47 Polypody
Recheles s.pl. C173,180,359,549,612; CC2, 8,36,40,77,122,134,157, 158,163,164 incense ; **fre r.** C180 frankincense
Red hertistunge s. C636 possibly Chervil
Reed s. C628 reed
Reid wrte s. C53,56 a medicinal herb, variously identified as Tormentil, Madder, Red Cabbage
Remue v. C54,CC147 to change, replace, remove; C42 to relieve
Renne v. C374 to run
Res s. C143 stem, stalk
Ribbe s. C54 medicinal plant, probably Ribwort
Rib(be)wrt s. C563; CC22,163 Ribwort, or Hound's Tongue
Rie-dowe s. C143 rye-dough
Rime (of brains) s. C54 cerebral meninx
Rinde s. epidermal layer of plant or root **overeste r.** CC87 outer layer **mydeleste r.** CC87 middle layer
Rist v. 2nd sing. pres. C106 to rise
Roke-ay s. C526 rook's egg
Ropande pres. p. C494 viscous
Rosel s. C592 reed, rush
Rote v. CC39,156 to rot
Rounceval s. C360 Christ's-thorn (Paliurus aculeatus) ?; used from 1573 to designate a large variety of garden or field pea
Runiouse a. / s. C266 scabby
Rutelyng s. CC49 rattling sound in the throat
Sair s. C505; CC95 sore
Saltel v. C322 to settle
Sape s. CC163 soap
Sard s. CC126 see **scherdes**
Sarp a. CC180 sharp
Satlen v. CC15 to settle
Sausefleme a. & s. C203,206 (afflicted with) 'salt phlegm', facial spots attributed to salty humours
Saym, **seym** s. C73,99,359; CC67,143 animal grease
Scalt p.p. C682 scalded

Scabbe s. C265,284; CC118,119,120 itching skin condition, scabies
Schaf v. CC152,169 to shave
Schaue v. (i) C279 to save, cure; (ii) CC167 to rub
Schep(us-talwe s. C175,493,534,543,610, 664,675; CC88,89,90,132, 159,163,164 sheep's grease
Scher, scer v. C498; CC88,174 to cut
Scherd(es s(pl. CC99,153 earthenware pot or pieces of pot
Schire s./a. CC157,158 clarified (fat)
Schiuere s. CC143 flax straw
Schlaw a. CC143 slow
Schor v. C641 to cut, pare
Schou v. C50 to chew
Scle v. CC114 to destroy **sclawen** p.p. CC143 destroyed
Sclyse, sclyce s. CC157,163 spatula, stirrer
Score s. C480 ?
Scum v. C359 to skim
Selfhele s. R373 Selfheal
Sench(oun (of huse) s. C85,358,493 Common Groundsel
Sen(e)grene s. C105; CC10,89,166,183 Houseleek
Senevey s. C488 White or Black Mustard
Senewis s.pl. CC95 tendons
Senigle, sen(i)gel s. C53,554,559 Sanicle
Serchen v. C53,54 to explore, investigate, examine
Seym s. C406,498; CC158 animal fat
Seyrie s. CC59 see note
Shaif v. C67 to shave
Simnel s. C412 bread of light flour
Siþen adv. C317,371,381,408,494,682 later, subsequently
Slat s. C117 slate
Slayen p.p. C359 destroyed, eradicated
Slo, sclo v. C547,558,611; CC36,133 to destroy
Slo s. R140 Sloe, Wild Damson
Sloþorn-barck s. C534 bark of the Blackthorn
Smalache s. C378,582,588 Smallage, Wild Celery
Snacus s.pl. C374 snakes
Soer, soir, soyr s. C175,505,637,672; CC96,163 sore s.pl. **sorews** C527
Sope s. R256 soap
Sopuus s. C326 sops
Sounne s. CC169 sun
Souþistele s. C44; R226,382 various thistles esp. Sonchus oleraceus
Sowande a. CC15 painful, sore
Speccus s.pl. C67 shoe patches
Specun v. C147 to speak
Spelke s. C530 wooden splint
Sperewort s. R315 Spearwort (genus Ranunculus) ?
Spick s. CC175 Valerian
Spinuale webbe [error for 'spinnande' ?] s. C54 spider' web
Spurge s. (a) s. C166 Spurge, plant of genus Euphorbia
Spurgen v. C50; CC5,44,57,154 to cleanse, purify
Squannes-briddes s. CC20 cygnets
Squelle s. CC86 morbid swelling
Squere s. CC31 neck
Sque(e)t (i) s. C374; CC104 sweat; (ii) a. C558 sweet
Squete v. C374; CC56,101,103 to sweat
Squinacie, quinacie s. C170; CC183 quinsy, inflammation or swelling of part(s) of the throat
Squalws-nest s. C247 swallow's nest
Squot s. C444 soot
Stale v. C484 to urinate
Stele s. C611; CC133 stalk, stem
Step v. C372 to steep
Ster, styr v. CC157,158,163 to stir
Stichewort s. R606 Greater Stitchwort
Stoncrop s. R315 Stonecrop
Stopped a./p.p. C318 obstructed, congested, constricted
Stor v. C494 to stir
Stra(u)nge a. CC24,56 strong
Strencle v. C375 to sprinkle
Strik v. CC23 to rub or smear (into the eye)
Strou, strow(e, strue, strew v. C143,615; CC137,143,148 to strew, scatter
Sucre rosette s. CC75 a preparation combining sugar with a distillation of roses
Sucus s.pl. 378 juices
Suines-tord s. C223 swine's dropping

Suþernewode s. C27,31,650 Southernwood
Suur a. C465 sour
Swelt s. C116 swelling
Syth s. C371 see **peyrit**
Tame v. C54 to pierce, damage
Tate(s s.pl. C345,347,349 teat(s, nipple(s
Teis s. CC68 some sort of measure
Teit s. pl. CC36,40 teeth
Tent(e, teynte s. C556,611,612; CC133, 134,137,147 tent, pledget, seton
Tetus s.pl. C343 teats, nipples
Teye s. C54 membrane
Theus s.pl. CC91 thighs
Toyt-ache, toit-ake s. C173,180 toothache
Tunhoue s. C142,440,578 Ground Ivy
Tysan s. C323,371 tisane
Tysike s. C322 phthisis, pulmonary tuberculosis
Tyt, as tyt adv. CC27,32 immediately, promptly
þein adv. CC56 thence
þey conj. CC56 although
þius s.pl. C520 thighs
þole v. CC66,160 to suffer, endure
þrist s. CC45 thirst
þumbe-honde s. C540 right hand ?
Unhil v. C54 to uncover, bare
Unement s. CC124,130,178 ointment, unguent
Unslecked p.p. C555 unslaked
Urtyng s. CC151 source of pain
Verre s. CC1,16 glass
Vertegres, vertegrese, vertegrece s. C600,613,615,634,637; CC135,137,143 substance formed from action of dilute acetic acid on copper
Walm s. CC3 boiling, time taken to come to the boil
Walleres-eirde s. C229 mortar ?
Walnote-leves s.pl. C3 Walnut leaves
Walwe, a-walwe v. C611 to immerse
Walwrt s. 278,C578,597,599,610; CC7,8, 72,84,87,132; R409 Dwarf or Ground Elder
Wappe v. CC168 to deposit; wrap ?
Was(se, wass v. CC17,105,132,136,143,150 to wash p.p. CC173 washed
Wastel s. C412 bread of the finest flour
Weit v. C611 to moisten
Wenne s. R414 morbid lump, sebaceous cyst
Wer(c)k, werc(h) s. C663,CC1,4,6,7 etc pain, ache
Wered p.p. C54 worn
Werk v. C371; CC149 to ache, to hurt
Werkyng s. C256,515,516,525,558 aching
Wermele s. CC40 'worm-meal' (created by worms in the wood of Ash)
Wertes s.pl. C263 warts
Weybrode s. R374 etc. Greater Plantain
Weye s. C559 weight
Weyke a. CC180 weak, flabby
Wicke a. CC113 evil
Wilde Clote s. R601 Burdock
Wilde fuyr s. C684; CC98,99 erysipelas
Wilde sauge s. C665 Wood Sage
Wilde sethewale s. C653 Zedoary
Wilde Tasel s. R606 Wild Teasel
Wilw s. C267 Willow
Wilwe-leuus, wilwe-leue s. C66; CC56 Willow-leave(s)
Winballez s. C2 Mistletoe ?
Wirm, werm s. C73 etc. worm
Wis adv. C250 certainly
Wiþi-tre s. C71 Willow
Wod(e a. C535; CC115 rabid
Wodebinde s. CC183; R299 Honeysuckle
Woke s. CC1 week
Wombe s. C371,375,402,403,406,453; CC60,78,123,180,183 stomach; C413 womb
Wone a. CC180,182 accustomed
Wormod s. R202 Wormwood
Wort s. R189,376 wort, barley malt
Wose s. C610 juice
Wowe s. CC180 wall
Wrang (MS **wrarg**) adv. C545 imperfectly, improperly
Wrottus s.pl. C259 warts
Wrti s. R155 a plant
Wry v. CC173 to cover (for warmth)
Wynballez s.pl. C682 Mistletoe (see **winballez** above) ?
Wytston s. C532 whetstone
Yolke s. C587 egg-yolk

INDEX OF MEDICAL CONDITIONS TREATED

Topical conditions

Sores, ulcers, tumours

Skin Conditions

Non-localized Conditions

Gynaecology

Prognostics

Preparations

Medicaments

Unidentified or Non-Specific Medical Conditions

SELECT BIBLIOGRAPHY[1]

J. Alford, "Medicine in the Middle Ages: The Theory of a Profession", *Centennial Review* 23 (1979), 377–96

d'Aronco, Maria Amalia, "The Botanical Lexicon of the Old English *Herbarium*", *Anglo-Saxon England* 17 (1988), 15–33

D.C. Bain, "A Note on an English Manuscript Receipt Book", *Bulletin of the History of Medicine* 8 (1940), 1246–8

F. Barlow, "The King's Evil", *English Historical Review* 95 (1980), 3–27

G. Beaujean, "Fautes et obscurités dans les traductions médicales du moyen age", *Revue de synthèse* 89 (1968), 145–52

A. Bell, "A Thirteenth-Century MS Fragment at Peterborough", *M.H.R.A. (Bulletin of the Modern Humanities Research Association)* III,vii (June, 1929), 132–40

H.S. Bennett, "Science and Information in English Writings of the Fifteenth Century", *Modern Language Review* 39 (1944), 1–8

M. Benskin, "For Wound in the Head: A Late Mediaeval View of the Brain", *Neuphilologische Mitteilungen* 86 (1985), 199–215

____, & M. Laing, "Translations and *Mischsprachen* in Middle English Manuscripts", in M. Benskin & M.I. Samuels (eds.) (Edinburgh, 1981), pp.55–106

P. Bierbaumer, *Der botanische Wortschatz des Altenglischen* 1–3 (Bern, 1975–79)

W. Bonser, *The Medical Background of Anglo-Saxon England: A Study in History, Psychology, Folklore* (London, 1963)

W.L. Braekman, *Studies on Alchemy, Diet, Medicine and Prognostication in Middle English*, Scripta 22 (Brussels, 1988)

L. Braswell, "Utilitarian and Scientific Prose" in A.S.G. Edwards (ed.), *Middle English Prose: A Critical Guide to Major Authors and Genres* (New Brunswick, 1984), pp.337–87

G. Brodin (ed.), *Agnus Castus. A Middle English Herbal* (Uppsala, 1950)

C.F. Bühler, "A Middle English Medical Manuscript from Norwich" in his *Early Books and Manuscripts: Forty Years of Research by Curt F. Bühler* (New York, 1973), pp.544–54

M.L. Cameron, *Anglo-Saxon Medicine*, Studies in Anglo-Saxon England 2 (Cambridge, 1993)

M. Carlin, "Medieval English Hospitals" in L. Granshaw & R. Porter (eds.), *The Hospital in History* (London, 1989), pp.21–39

[1] For herbals and plants see bibliographies in T. Hunt, *Plant Names of Medieval England* (Cambridge, 1989) and W.F. Daems, *Nomina simplicium medicinarum ex synonymariis medii aevi collecta*, Studies in Ancient Medicine 6 (Leiden, 1993).

H.P. Cholmeley, *John of Gaddesden and the 'Rosa Medicinae'* (Oxford, 1912)

R.M. Clay, *The Medieval Hospitals of England* 2nd. ed. (London, 1966)

J.B. Colton (transl.), *John of Mirfield (d.1407), Surgery: A Translation of his Breviarium Bartholomei, Part IX* (New York, 1969)

M.P. Cosman, "Medieval Medical Malpractice and Chaucer's Physician", *New York State Journal of Medicine* 72 (1972), 2439–44

W.C. Crossgrove, "The Forms of Medieval Technical Literature: Some Suggestions for further Work", *Jahrbuch für Internationale Germanistik* 3 (1971), 13–21

W.R. Dawson, *A Leechbook or Collection of Medical Recipes of the Fifteenth Century* (London, 1934)

M. Deegan & D.G. Scragg (eds.), *Medicine in Early Medieval England. Four Papers*, University of Manchester, Centre for Anglo-Saxon Studies (Manchester, 1987; corr. reissue 1989)

L. Demaitre, "Scholasticism in Compendia of Practical Medicine, 1250–1450", *Manuscripta* 20 (1976), 81–95

W. Eamon (ed.), *Studies on Medieval Fachliteratur*, Scripta 6 (Brussels, 1982)

———, "Books of Secrets in Medieval and Early Modern Science", *Sudhoffs Archiv* 69 (1985), 26–49

A. Eccles, "The Reading Public, the Medical Profession, and the Use of English for Medical Books in the 16th and 17th Centuries", *Neuphilologische Mitteilungen* 75 (1974), 143–56

M. Faribault, "La Chirurgie par rimes: problèmes de compilation de recettes médicales en français", *Fifteenth-Century Studies* 5 (1982), 47–59

A. Fonahn, *Arabic and Latin Anatomical Terminology chiefly from the Middle Ages*, Videnskapsselskapets Skrifter. II. Hist.-Filos. Klasse. 1921. No. 7 (Kristiania, 1922)

P. Fordyn (ed.), *The 'Experimentes of Cophon, the Leche of Salerne': Middle English Medical Recipes (MS Add.34111, f.218r–230v)*, Scripta 10 (Brussel, 1983)

E.F. Frey, "Saints in Medical History", *Clio Medica* 14 (1979), 35–70

G. Frisk (ed.), *A Middle Englsh Translation of Macer De Viribus Herbarum* (Uppsala, 1949)

R.M. Garrett, "Middle English Rimed Medical Treatise", *Anglia* 34 (1911), 163–93

F.M. Getz, "Gilbertus Anglicus Anglicized", *Medical History* 26 (1982), 436–42

———, "John Mirfield and the *Breviarium Bartholomei*: The Medical writings of a Clerk at St. Bartholomew's Hospital in the Later Fourteenth Century", *Society for the Social History of Medicine, Bulletin* 37 (1985), 24–26

———, "Archives and Sources: Medical Practitioners in Medieval England", *Social History of Medicine* 3 (1990), 245–83

———, "Charity, Translation and the Language of Medical Learning in Medieval England", *Bulletin of the History of Medicine* 64 (1990), 1–17

———, "The *Method of Healing* in Middle English" in F. Kudlien & R.J. Durling (eds.), *Galen's Method of Healing: Proceedings of the 1982 Galen Symposium*, Studies in Ancient Medicine 1 (Leiden, 1991), pp.147–56

———, *Healing and Society in Medieval England: A Middle English Translation of the Pharmaceutical Writings of Gilbertus Anglicus*, Wisconsin Publications in the History of Science and Medicine 8 (Madison, 1991)

———, *Medicine in the English Middle Ages* (Princeton, 1998)

J.R. Gilleland, "Eight Anglo-Norman Cosmetic Recipes. MS Cambridge, Trinity College 1044", *Romania* 109 (1988), 50–67

R.S. Gottfried, *Doctors and Medicine in Medieval England 1340–1530* (Princeton, 1986)

M. Görlach, "Text-types and Language History: The Cookery Recipe" in M. Rissanen *et al.*,

History of Englishes: New Methods and Interpretations in Historical Linguistics (Berlin / New York, 1992), pp.736–61

P. Grymonprez (ed.), *'Here Men May See the Vertues off Herbes': A Middle English Herbal (MS Bodley 483, fols.57r–67v)*, Scripta 3 (Brussels, 1981)

M.-R. Hallaert, *The 'Sekenesse of wymmen'. A Middle English Treatise on Diseases in Women*, Scripta 8 (Brussels, 1982)

E.A. Hammond, "Incomes of Medieval English Doctors", *Journal of the History of Medicine and Allied Sciences* 15 (1960), 154–69

H.E. Handerson, *Gilbertus Anglicus: Medicine of the Thirteenth Century* (Cleveland, Ohio, 1918)

H. Hargreaves, "Some Problems in Indexing Middle English Recipes" in A.S.G. Edwards & D. Pearsall (eds.), *Middle English Prose. Essays on Bibliographical Problems* (New York, 1981), pp.91–113

———, "*De Spermate Hominis*: A Middle English Poem on Human Embryology", *Mediaeval Studies* 39 (1977), 506–10

M.P. Harley, "The Middle English Contents of a Fifteenth-Century Medical Handbook", *Mediaevalia* 8 (1982), 171–88

P.H.-S. Hartley & H.R. Aldridge, *Johannes de Mirfield of St Bartholomew's, Smithfield: His Life and Works* (Cambridge, 1936)

B. Harvey, *Living and Dying in England 1100–1540* (Oxford, 1993)

C.F. Heffernan (ed.), "The Wyse Boke of Maystyr Peers of Salerne. Edition and Study of a Fourteenth-Century Treatise on Popular Medicine", *Manuscripta* 37 (1993)

F. Heinrich, *Ein mittelenglisches Medizinbuch* (Halle a.S., 1896)

G. Henslow, *Medical Works of the Fourteenth Century together with a List of Plants recorded in Contemporary Writings, with their Identifications* (London, 1899)

C.B. Hieatt & R.F. Jones (eds.), *La Novele Cirurgerie*, ANTS 46 (London, 1990)

B.H. Hill, "The Grain and the Spirit in Mediaeval Anatomy", *Speculum* 40 (1965), 63–73

F. Holthausen, "Medicinische Gedichte aus einer Stockholmer Handschrift", *Anglia* 18 (1896), 293–331

———, "Zu den mittelenglischen medizinischen Gedichten", *Anglia* 44 (1920), 357–72

T. Hunt, "Recettes médicales en vers français d'après le manuscrit 0.8.27 de Trinity College, Cambridge", *Romania* 106 (1985), 57–83

———, "The Botanical Glossaries in MS London, B.L. Add.15236", *Pluteus* 4–5 (1986–7), 101–50

———, "The Medical Recipes in MS Royal 5 E VI", *Notes and Queries* 231 (1986), 6–9

———, "The 'Novele Cirurgerie' in MS London, British Library, Harley 2558", *Zeitschrift für romanische Philologie* 103 (1987), 271–99

———, "Horses and Courses", *French Studies Bulletin* 22 (1987), 1–4

———, "Early Anglo-Norman Recipes in MS London, B.L. Royal 12 C XIX", *Zeitschrift für französische Sprache und Literatur* 97 (1987), 245–54

———, "Materia Medica in MS London, B.L. Add. 10289", *Medioevo Romanzo* 13 (1988), 25–37

———, "The Trilingual Glossary in MS London, B.L. Sloane 146 f.69v–72r", *English Studies* 70 (1989), 289–310

———, *Plant Names of Medieval England* (Cambridge, 1989)

———, *Popular Medicine in Thirteenth-Century England* (Cambridge, 1990)

———, "An Anglo-Norman Medical Treatise" in G. Runnalls & P.E. Bennett (eds.), *The Editor and the Text* (Edinburgh, 1991), pp.145–64

———, *The Medieval Surgery* (Woodbridge, 1992)

———, "Anglo-Norman Medical Receipts" in I. Short (ed.), *Anglo-Norman Anniversary Essays*, ANTS Occasional Publications Series 2 (London, 1993), pp.179–233

———, *Anglo-Norman Medicine* 1 & 2 (Cambridge, 1994–97)

J. Jasin, "The Compiler's Awareness of Audience in Medieval Medical Prose: the example of Wellcome MS 225", *Journal of English and Germanic Philology* 92 (1993), 509–22

———, "The Transmission of Learned Medical Literature in the Middle English *Liber Uricrisiarum*", *Medical History* 37 (1993), 313–29

S. Jenks, "Medizinische Fachkräfte in England zur Zeit Heinrichs VI (1428/9–1460/61)", *Sudhoffs Archiv* 69 (1985), 214–27

I.B. Jones, "Popular Medical Knowledge in Fourteenth-Century English Literature", *Bulletin of the History of Medicine* 5 (1937), 405–51, 489–88

———, "Halford 16: A Mediaeval Welsh Medical Treatise", *Etudes celtiques* 7 (1955), 270–399

P. Murray Jones, "Four Middle English Translations of John of Arderne" in A.J. Minnis (ed.), *Latin and Vernacular: Studies in Late Medieval Texts and Manuscripts* (London, 1989), pp.61–89

———, "British Library MS Sloane 76; a translator's holograph" in L. Brownrigg & M. Gullick (eds.), *Medieval Book Production: Assessing the Evidence* (Cambridge, 1990), pp.21–39

———, "Medical Books before the Invention of Printing" in A. Besson (ed.) *Thornton's Medical Books, Libraries and Collectors: A Study of Bibliography and the Book Trade in relation to the Medical Sciences* (Aldershot, 1990), pp.1–29

———, "Information and Science" in R. Horrox (ed.), *Fifteenth-Century Attitudes. Perceptions of Society in Late Medieval England* (Cambridge, 1994), pp.97–111

———, "John of Arderne and the Mediterranean Tradition of Scholastic Surgery" in L. Garcia Ballester *et al.* (eds.), *Practical Medicine from Salerno to the Black Death* (Cambridge, 1994), pp.289–321

———, "Harley MS 2558: A Fifteenth-Century Medical Commonplace Book" in Schleissner (q.v.), pp.35–54

E.J. Kealey, *Medieval Medicus. A Social History of Anglo-Norman Medicine* (Baltimore / London, 1981)

———, "England's earliest Women Doctors", *Journal of the History of Medicine* 40 (1985), 473–77

G. Keil, "Magister Giselbertus de villa parisiensi. Beobachtungen zu den Kranewittbeeren und Gilberts pharmakologischem Renommé", *Sudhoffs Archiv* 78 (1994), 59–79.

G.R. Keiser, "Epilepsy: the falling evil" in L.M. Matheson (ed.), *Popular and Practical Science*, pp.219–44

———, "Reconstructing Robert Thornton's Herbal", *Medium Aevum* 65 (1966), 35–53

———, "Editing Scientific and Practical Writings" in V.P. McCarren & D. Moffat (eds.), *A Guide to Editing Middle English* (Ann Arbor, 1998), pp.109–22

C. Kren, *Medieval Science and Technology: A Selected, Anotated Bibliography*, Garland, Bibliographies of the History of Science and Technology 11 (New York / London, 1985)

M. Kurdzialek, "Gilbertus Anglicus und die psychologischen Erörterungen in seinem *Compendium Medicinae*", *Sudhoffs Archiv* 47 (1963), 106–26

M. Laing, "Dialectal Analysis and Linguistically Composite Texts in Middle English" in A. McIntosh *et al.* (eds.), *Middle English Dialectology. Essays on Some Principles and Problems* (Aberdeen, 1989), pp.150–69

S.J. Lang, "John Bradmore and His Book Philomena", *Social History of Medicine* 5 (1992), 121–30

M. Löweneck (ed.), *Peri Didaxeon. Eine Sammlung von Rezepten in englischer Sprache aus dem 11./12. Jahrhundert*, Erlanger Beiträge zur englischen Philologie 12 (Erlangen, 1896)

R.W. McConchie, "'It Hurteth Memorie and Hindreth Learning': Attitudes to the Use of the Vernacular in Sixteenth-Century English Medical Writings", *Studia Anglica Posnaniensia* 21 (1988), 53–67

———, *Lexicography and Physicke. The Record of Sixteenth-Century English Medical Terminology* (Oxford, 1997)

L.M. Matheson (ed.), *Popular and Practical Science of Medieval England* (Woodbridge / East Lansing, 1994)

C.F. Mayer, "A Medieval English Leechbook and its 14th Century Poem on Bloodletting", *Bulletin of the History of Medicine* 7 (1939), 381–91

P. Meyer, "Les manuscrits français de Cambridge", *Romania* 32 (1903), 18–120

———, "Notice du ms. Bodley 761 de la Bibliothèque Bodléienne", *Romania* 37 (1908), 509–28

———, "Manuscrits médiévaux en français", *Romania* 44 (1915), 161–214

D. de Moulin, " Historical-Phenomenological Study of Bodily Pain in Western Man", *Bulletin of the History of Medicine* 48 (1974), 540–70

G. Müller, *Aus mittelenglischen Medizintexten. Die Prosarezepte des Stockholmer Miszellankodex X.90*, Kölner Anglistische Arbeiten 10 (Leipzig, 1929)

J.K. Mustain, "A Rural Medical Practitioner in Fifteenth-Century England", *Bulletin of the History of Medicine* 46 (1972), 469–76

J. Norri, "Notes on the Study of English Medical Vocabulary from the Historical Point of View", *Mémoires de la Société Néophilologique de Helsinki* 45: *Neophilologica Fennica*, 335–50

———, Compound Plant-Names in Fifteenth-Century English, Publications of the Department of English, University of Turku 8 (1988)

———, "Notes on Some Corrupt Passages in Fifteenth-Century Medical Manuscripts", *Neuphilologische Mitteilungen* 89 (1988), 320–3

———, "Notes on Anatomical Vocabulary in Fifteenth-Century English" in K. Battarbee & R. Hiltunen, *Alarums & Excursions. Working Papers in English*, Publications of the Department of English, University of Turku 9 (1990), pp. 69–90

———, *Names of Sicknesses in English, 1400–1550: An Exploration of the Lexical Field* Annales Academiae Scientiarum Fennicae, Dissertationes Humanorum Litterarum 63 (Helsinki, 1992)

———, "On the Origins of Plant Names in Fifteenth-Century English" in J. Fisiak (ed.), *Middle English Miscellany. From Vocabulary to Linguistic Variation* (Poznan, 1996), pp.159–81

———, *Names of Body Parts in English, 1400–1550* Annales Academiae Scientiarum Fennicae, Sarja-ser. Humaniora nide-tom. 291 (Helsinki, 1998)

B. Odenstedt, *The Book of Marchalsi: A 15th C. Treatise on Horse-Breeding and Veterinary Medicine edited from MS Harley 6398* ... (Stockholm, 1973)

M.S. Ogden (ed.), *The 'Liber de diversis medicinis'*, EETS OS 207 (London, 1938; reprint with revisions, 1969)

P. Pahta (ed.), *Medieval Embryology in the Vernacular. The Case of 'De spermate'*, Mémoires de la Société Néophilologique de Helsinki LIII (Helsinki, 1998)

L.B. Pinto, "The Folk Practice of Gynecology and Obstetrics in the Middle Ages", *Bulletin of the History of Medicine* 47 (1973), 513–23

M. Pouchelle, *The Body and Surgery in the Middle Ages* transl. R. Morris (Oxford, 1990)

K. Rand Schmidt, "*The Index of Middle English Prose* and Late Medieval English Recipes", *English Studies* 75 (1994), 423–9

C. Rawcliffe, "The Profits of Practice: The Wealth and Status of Medical Men in Later Medieval England", *Social History of Medicine* 1 (1988), 61–78

———, "Consultants, Careerists and Conspirators: Royal Doctors in the Time of Richard III", *The Ricardian* 8 (1989), 250–58

———, *Medicine and Society in Later Medieval England* (Stroud, 1995)

O. Riha, "Gilbertus Anglicus und sein *Compendium Medicinae*. Arbeitstechnik und Wissensorganisation", *Sudhoffs Archiv* 78 (1994),59–79

R.H. Robbins, "Medical Manuscripts in Middle English", *Speculum* 45 (1970), 393–415

———, "Signs of Death in Middle English", *Mediaeval Studies* 32 (1970), 282–98

W. Rothwell, "Medical and Botanical Terminology from Anglo-Norman Sources", *Zeitschrift für französische Sprache und Literatur* 86 (1976), 221–60

S. Rubin, *Medieval English Medicine* (London, 1974)

M.R. Schleissner (ed.), *Manuscript Sources of Medieval Medicine: A Book of Essays*, Garland Medieval Casebooks (New York / London, 1995)

H. Schöffler, "Gedruckte mittelenglisch-medizinische Texte", *Archiv für Geschichte der Medizin* 11 (1918), 107–9

———, *Beiträge zur mittelenglischen Medizinliteratur* (Halle a.S., 1919)

G. Sigurs, "Le vocabulaire médical français aux XIVe–XVe siècles. Sa formation et son développement", *Revue des langues romanes* 76 (1964), 63–74

———, "La langue médicale française. Nouvelles datations", *Le Français Moderne* 33 (1965), 199–218

N.G. Siraisi, *Medieval and Renaissance Medicine. An Introduction to Knowledge and Practice* (Chicago / London, 1990)

O. Södergård, "Recettes pour les femmes", in K.B. Flemested *et al.* (eds.), *Mélanges d'études médiévales offerts à Helge Nordahl à l'occasion de son soixantième anniversaire* (Oslo, 1988), pp.187–96

A.C. Svinhufvud, *A Late Middle English Treatise on Horses edited from British Library MS Sloane 2584 ff.102–117b* (Stockholm, 1978)

I. Taavitsainen & P. Pahta, "Vernacularisation of Medical Writing in English: A Corpus-Based Study of Scholasticism", *Early Science and Medicine* 3 (1998), 157–85

———, "The Corpus of Early English Medical Writing", *ICAME Journal* 21 (1997), 71–8

———, "Authorities in Medieval Medical treatises", *The New Courant* (Publications of the Department of English, University of Helsinki) 3 (1995), 97–107

———, "The Corpus of Early English Medical Writing: Linguistic Variation and Prescriptive Collocations in Scholastic Style" in T. Nevalainen & L. Kahlas-Tarkka (eds.), *To Explain the Present. Studies in the Changing English Language in Honour of Matti Rissanen*, Mémoires de la Société Néophilologique de Helsinki LII (Helsinki, 1997), 209–25

E.W. Talbert, "The Notebook of a Fifteenth-Century Practising Physician", *Texas Studies in English* 21 (1942), 5–30

C.H. Talbot, "A Mediaeval Physician's Vade Mecum", *Journal of the History of Medicine and Allied Sciences* 16 (1961), 213–33

———, *Medicine in Medieval England* (London, 1967)

———, & E.A. Hammond, *The Medical Practitioners in Medieval England: A Biographical Register* (London, 1965)

L. Thorndike, "Notes on Medical Texts in Manuscripts at London and Oxford", *Janus* 48 (1959), 141–202

G.E. Trease & J.H. Hodson, "The Inventory of John of Hexham, a Fifteenth-Century Apothecary", *Medical History* 9 (1965), 76–81

H.E. Ussery, *Chaucer's Physician. Medicine and Literature in Fourteenth-Century England* (New Orleans, 1971)

L.E. Voigts, "Editing Middle English Medical Texts: Needs and Issues" in T.H. Levere (ed.), *Editing Texts in the History of Science and Medicine* (New York / London, 1982), pp.39–68

———, "Medical Prose" in A.S.G. Edwards (ed.), *Middle English Prose: A Critical Guide to Major Authors and Genres* (New Brunswick, 1984), pp.315–335

———, "Scientific and Medical Books" in J. Griffiths & D. Pearsall (eds.), *Book Production and Publishing in Britain 1375–1475* (Cambridge, 1989), pp.345–402

———, "The 'Sloane Group': Related Scientific and Medical Manuscripts from the Fifteenth Century in the Sloane Collection", *The British Library Journal* 16 (1990), 26–57

———, "'A drynke þat men callen dwale to make a man to slepe whyle men kerven him': A Surgical Anaesthetic from Late Medieval England" in S. Campbell *et al.* (eds.), *Health, Disease and Healing in Medieval Culture* (New York, 1992), pp.34–56

———, "Multitudes of Middle English Medical Manuscripts, or the Englishing of Science and Medicine" in Schleissner (q.v.), pp.183–95

———, "What's the Word ? Bilingualism in Late Medieval England", *Speculum* 71 (1996), 813–26

B. Wallner, "A Note on some Middle English Medical Terms", *English Studies* 50 (1969), 499–503

———, "Plant Names in the Middle English *Guy de Chauliac*", *Studia Neophilologica* 64 (1992), 35–44

www.ingramcontent.com/pod-product-compliance
Ingram Content Group UK Ltd.
Pitfield, Milton Keynes, MK11 3LW, UK
UKHW042007190726
13854UKWH00005B/2202

9 780907 570141